Doing Social Life

DOING SOCIAL LIFE

≺≺≺≺≺≺≺≺≺≺≺

THE QUALITATIVE STUDY
OF HUMAN INTERACTION
IN NATURAL SETTINGS

John Lofland
University of California, Davis

A WILEY-INTERSCIENCE PUBLICATION

JOHN WILEY & SONS, New York • Chichester • Brisbane • Toronto

Library of Congress Cataloging in Publication Data

Lofland, John.
  Doing social life.

  "A Wiley-Interscience publication."
  Includes bibliographical references and index.
    1. Interpersonal relations.   2. Social interaction.
3. Social role.   4. Social psychology—Experiments—
History.   5. Participant observation.
I. Title.

HM132.L63   301.11   76-25077
ISBN 0-471-01563-6

Printed in the United States of America

10 9 8 7 6 5 4

To
Juanita Jobe King
and
Keller Hoch

Preface

For several decades, social scientists have been using qualitative techniques of field observation to decipher the tactics, ploys, and ruses that people employ in the social interactions of their everyday lives. Inspired in part by such genius exemplars as Erving Goffman, dozens of observer-analysts have created a rich body of studies describing subtle strategies of interaction played out in a wide variety of important human situations.

Unfortunately, the personal individualism of these scholars and the inherent individualism of their methods have retarded collation and codification of their achievements. I try here to remedy this deficiency, first, by explicating the logic of how naturalistic studies of interaction strategies have been and are performed and second, by organizing and reviewing in detail more than a hundred reports of interaction strategies in everyday life. In addition, four incisive and lively studies of interaction strategies are presented in their entirety, to "ground" the more abstract aspects discussed.

The logic of qualitative studies of interaction strategies is developed in terms of the four concepts that orient observers as they engage in scrutiny of people interacting in real settings: the necessity to acquire personal, direct, and firsthand *intimate familiarity;* the need to delineate generic features of the *situation* in which action is being developed; the requirements of deciphering the *strategies* participants are constructing in dealing with the situation; and the desirability of developing and interrelating emergent concepts and accumulating data in a *disciplined* and grounded fashion. Part I devotes a chapter to each of these concepts. An additional chapter shows how they specifically structure research reports.

The qualitative studies of interaction strategies reviewed in Part II are organized in terms of the *scale* of their strategic and situational complexity—the amount of time, space, people, and equipment involved. *Encounters* are the smallest-scale strategic situations, typically involving only two people in face-to-face contact for a short time.

Strategies of the immediate management of superiors, stranger avoidance in public places, and unspoken tension in interaction are treated, among many such situations. Focusing on the individual performer, and extending the time span, *role-scale* strategies of interaction emerge, including tactics of entering, avoiding, terminating, and exiting roles. Observers of how people manage ongoing roles have documented strategies of gaining ascendance, defending against attack, and coping with stigma, among a wide variety of other situations discussed in the chapter on roles, which is especially detailed because qualitative analysts have concentrated on this level. A small number of people informally acting in concert over a reasonably extended period of time play out *group-scale* interaction strategies; studies of these have investigated the means groups choose to cope with demeaning and monotonous jobs and to mount protective cliques in situations of strife, among other topics. Large numbers of people formally pursuing goals generate *organizational-scale* strategies of interaction, focusing on such matters as attracting, selecting, socializing, and controlling members on the one hand, and acting on the environment on the other. Among the latter, studies of issue-raising tactics, program promotion ploys, reputational enhancement devices, and dissent management are reviewed.

The studies reprinted in Part III document interaction strategies in four inherently fascinating situations: the tensions of workers constantly exposed to the pain and death of others in an intensive care unit; the questings of young people for religious self-transformation; the boredom of industrial workers in monotonous jobs; the ritual of staving off but eventually dismissing junior college students doomed to academic failure. The observers of these situations expose the devices that make life at least bearable and even livable, the various scales of interactional gambits that make social life possible. Equally important, these rich, closely examined microscopic situations and their strategies show principles of *general* relevance and provide concrete illustration of the more abstract ideas addressed in Parts I and II.

It is often alleged that the family of social science perspectives informing this volume (symbolic interactionism, dramaturgic sociology, reality constructionism, etc.) is deficient because their respective stances are difficult or impossible to translate into—to bridge to—working programs of concrete and distinctive empirical inquiries. Like most claims, this one is true only in part. The translation or bridging problem is there, yes; but ongoing research that is implementing of and distinctive to those perspectives has not been as scarce as many commentators have at the same time claimed. There is a great deal more to bridge *to* than has commonly been recognized. If this is so, the task at hand is the spanning of a manageable river rather than the building of an endless pier into a limitless ocean. Believing the former to be the case, I have sought to construct a bridge of principles between abstract perspectives on the one shore and implementing, specific inquiries on the other.

In thus building a bridge, I have debts to residents of both sides of the river. On the perspective shore, my foremost debts are to Herbert Blumer, Erving Goffman, and Fred Davis. Beyond perspective, I am highly appreciative of the interest, kindness, and support they have extended me over many years. On the inquiry shore, I am indebted to each of the researchers whose reports are reviewed. Had they not been there, I would still be fabricating an endless pier. In a way, Barney Glaser and Anselm Strauss have tried previously to build a bridge, and I have learned from their efforts.

Over the years of its emergence and through good times and bad, Lyn H. Lofland reviewed, discussed, and believed in this book. She very much helped to make it possible and I am extremely grateful to her.

Rudy Haapanen, Juanita Wood, Fred Davis, several anonymous reviewers for publishers, and many students at Davis scrutinized all or part of the manuscript and provided a great deal of useful advice on revisions and extensions. The enthusiasm and insight of Eric Valentine, formerly of Wiley, always boosted my day. Karyn Principe heroically rescued my spelling while admirably typing the text.

Last, because it is different, I am thankful for the milieu of the University of California, Davis, and its Department of Sociology, which has provided the scarce resources of freedom, time and sundry support. The leadership of Leon H. Mayhew in that milieu has been particularly appreciated.

JOHN LOFLAND

Davis, California
July 1976

Contents

Figures

Doing Social
Life

CHAPTER ONE

Introduction

Lurking within the sprawling and conflict-ridden world of social science there is a genre of work that seeks to answer the question, "How do people do things?" The question, note, is "*How* do people do things," not "*Why* do people do things?" Whatever it is that people feel they want, need, are striving for, are coping with, *how* do they do it?

Compared to the overriding and eternal quest for "whys," concerted social scientific attention to "hows" is somewhat minor and in relative disarray. It is this body of material and its questions that I want to analyze, codify, extend, and support.

I speak too loosely in phrasing the question as "How do people do things?" It should be expressed, "How do people do *social* things?" The interest is not, for example, in the mechanical procedures by which astronauts fly space vehicles, but in how astronauts socially and psychologically handle the situation of flying space vehicles. The interest is not in the technicalities of food preparation and clean-up among communialists, but in how communards individually and collectively, socially and psychologically, manage the necessity to prepare food and to clean up after meals.

There is a particular kind of analytic stance requisite to asking how people do social things. It is the stance of the *radically naive* person. How do people get across the street? How do people wait for a bus? How do people find their way around? How do people show they are of one or another race or sex? How do people manage to acquire resources? How do adult-people cope with child-people, and vice versa? How do some people get other people happily to do their bidding? How do people rebel?[1]

The radically naive stance is only in part an analytic stance—a mental

1

operation by means of which the obvious is made problematic. The diversity and complexity of human life renders everyone radically naive relative to some things, most people radically naive relative to many things, and a few people radically naive relative to all things. And the abundance of naiveté creates ground for the growth of, and the need for, concerted efforts to analyze how people do social things.

It is naive and blocked practical action that answers the questions "Why should we care about how people do social things?" "Of what interest or relevance is it to us?" The "it" and "us" of course vary enormously, but three classes of "us" are readily visible. First, there is a directly practical "us," people concerned to act in or toward a particular and concrete situation or social type of people. For them, how a particular set of people do things has a direct bearing on their personal action, be the situation a classroom, a store, a lynching, an executive suite, or the main lair of the power elite.[2] Second, there is an indirectly practical "us" who are not concerned with a given concrete situation or group but have a practical interest in the *kind* of situation and social action displayed by the concrete situation or group. Thus the social psychological management strategies of astronauts can be of interest to anyone connected in a practical way with any situation of high risk. The juggling, frittering, and coping of students can be of interest to anyone connected in a practical way with any open-ended and ambiguous situation. For the indirectly practical "us," the question is, "What is there about that situation over *there* that may be useful in dealing with my situation over *here*?" For both types of practical interest, knowledge of how people do social things *opens up new lines of action.* Such newly learned lines of action may be imitated or shunned, lauded or condemned; but knowledge nonetheless permits new action. Third, there is a theoretical and generalizing "us" who have these two types of practical interest but in addition have an interest in such broad topics as the construction and dynamics of social action and social life *per se.* Generalized and theoretical interest has a practical import, too, although it is not so narrowly immediate or apparent and works, rather, at the level of conducing sensitivities and structuring how situations are conceived.

The analysis of how people do social things has a logic and displays a process of its own. I seek to explicate this logic and process, focusing on what appear to be the four main phases, aspects, or principles of developing the particular sociological discernment of how people do social things. These phases or aspects embody a particular approach to how people do social things, a qualitative methodology approach that interpenetrates and structures the concern with how people do social things and is elucidated throughout.

For introductory purposes, these four may be thought of as crucial phases or aspects of studying and analyzing a particular, concrete natural setting someplace in the real world. So viewed, studying how people do social things requires the following:

1. Getting close-up to people actually acting someplace in the real world and developing *intimate familiarity*.
2. Focusing on and delineating the prime or basic *situation* the scrutinized people are dealing with or confronting.
3. Focusing on and delineating the interactional *strategies*, tactics, and so on, by means of which the scrutinized people are dealing with the situation confronted.
4. Assembling and analyzing an abundance of qualitative *episodes* into *disciplined abstractions* about the situation and strategies delineated.

These four aspects are dealt with in Chapters 2, 3, 4, and 5, respectively. Two additional but somewhat different aspects are taken up in Chapters 6 and 7:

1. The results of any single inquiry into situations and strategies is best reported in a concrete *form* that is amenable to practical use and theoretical consolidation with other studies. Such a form is set out in Chapter 6.
2. The accumulation of separate, probing inquiries must be combined with other studies to be most fruitful. Though seldom attended to at this time, the problem of *consolidation* of studies must be posed, and lines along which it might occur need to be thought out. This is discussed in Chapter 7.

These six matters comprise Part I, "Principles of the Qualitative Study of Interaction Strategies." Even though they can be thought of as "steps of a study," they can also be considered in other ways, some of which should be mentioned. One, they are *descriptive* and analytic of sociological practice in the sense that I take as data the activities of a tradition in social science oriented to analyzing how people do social things. In an important sense, I am offering a codification of how a developing tradition operates. Since this tradition lacks any special referent label, I am forced, for expository reasons, to name it. For better or worse, I often call it "qualitative strategy analysis." Two, codification has implications. What exists points to what might be. The analysis of materials signals additional conceptualizations and conceptual points. Where I have seen such points, I have added them, particularly in discussing the concepts of situation and strategy. Three, my exposition is also somewhat exhortatory, endorsing "good guys" and condemning "bad guys." I, after all, stand someplace, and since I stand with the qualitative strategy people, I am also arguing against "misguided" social science as we go along. Finally, these aspects or phases may be thought of as principles of qualitative situation and strategy analysis in the sense of "prime directives" or most important elements.

Part II reviews and gently organizes some one hundred reports that more or less exemplify the perspective set forth in Part I. Situations and strategies are viewed as occurring on increasing scales of "size" involving ever larger amounts of space and equipment, periods of time, and numbers of people. These are labeled, respectively, encounters, roles, groups, and organizations. Studies at each level are discussed in Chapters 8, 9, 10, and 11. Although reviews are important in forming an estimate of what we have accomplished, they are equally valuable in beginning to show where we might go. Part II is therefore a "preview" as well as a "review."

The fundamental importance of inextricably intertwining qualitative data and abstract concepts is a major proposition of this treatise. It would be crucially incomplete without providing ample, specific illustration of this proposition. Part III does this by presenting four lively qualitative studies of situations and their strategies.

Finally, several more permeating features of what follows bear mention at the outset, the better to prepare the reader and to protect him or her from disappointment.

First, readers who are unfamiliar with the style of research explicated in this volume will find it helpful to begin by reading the four inquiries reprinted in Part III, "Selected Qualitative Studies of Interaction Strategies." Part I exposes the principles underlying these four (and many other) studies, and Part II places each one in a larger and more formal context. Indeed, it is most profitable to read this book by cycling back and forth between the concrete and full empirical instances provided in Part III and the principles that give them (and their kind) context and meaning, as explained in Parts I and II.

Second, this is a partisan and "unbalanced" treatise in that it explains and promotes a single kind of work, a special "package" of elements, and a particular perspective on and program for doing social inquiry.

It does not neutrally delineate the comparative advantages and disadvantages of various approaches such as "qualitative versus quantitative observations," "activist versus passivist" images of humans (distinctions explained in Chapter 5), or any other polarities. I recognize that a sophisticated and accommodative interpenetration of these and other contrasts might eventually be possible, but I do not believe that a synthesis or balanced assessment is feasible now or even desirable. This is a step that cannot solidly be completed until "opposing" approaches have themselves been fully articulated and elaborated to their respective limits. All principles carried to their logical conclusions are, of course, absurd. But to know the absurd limits, we must actually work out the principles, and indeed, certain other lines of social science inquiry are coming close to this state. The lines dealt with here have not been nearly so well elaborated. If I make it more possible for others to perceive and move toward such limits, and make it more possible for yet others to perform synthesizing integrations, one of my aims will have been achieved. But again, this itself requires the interim and "imbalanced" kind of partisanship shown in what follows. Furthermore, the "quantitative" and "passivist" approaches I take to task have in fact dominated the resources and thinking of current social science. Its practitioners have tended to exclude and patronize other approaches in much the same manner that white males have excluded and patronized sexual and ethnic minorities. As a member of a disadvantaged social science minority, I have preferred a degree of militance over accommodationist assimilation—at this time.[3]

Third, beyond partisanship, my treatment is incomplete. I have not addressed such topics as criteria for knowing when a situation and its strategies have been accurately observed, implications of the loss of detail and context as one abstracts "upward" into generic and social organizational categories, import of the larger structures and institutions in which social interaction is set, or causes of electing one rather than another strategy in a situation. Important as these topics obviously are, others in my view are even more significant and take logical precedence over them; it is to the logically prior matters that I have elected to attend.

<<<<<<<<

With this overview and these caveats, let us turn to considering principles of the qualitative study of interaction strategies.

NOTES TO CHAPTER ONE

1. Cf. the contrasting (and sexist) question posed by Ted Robert Gurr, *Why Men Rebel* (Princeton, N.J.: Princeton University Press, 1970).

2. Cf. the admonitions of Che Guevara: "Our task at the moment is to find the basic principles of this kind of fighting and the rules to follow by peoples seeking liberation; to develop theory from facts; to generalize and give structure to our experience for the profit of others." Guevara, *Guerrilla Warfare* (New York: Vintage, 1969, copyright 1961), p. 3.

3. For a general discussion of the minority situation and strategies of coping, see Chapter 9, Section IV.C, "Role Strategies Among Subordinates."

PART ONE

PRINCIPLES OF THE QUALITATIVE STUDY OF INTERACTION STRATEGIES

CHAPTER TWO

Developing Intimate Familiarity

I. INTIMATE FAMILIARITY

A. Nature. To be intimately familiar with a sector of social life is to have easy, detailed, dense acquaintanceship with it based on free-flowing and prolonged immersion. This immersion, first and ideally, may take the form of direct, bodily presence in the physical scenes of the social life under scrutiny, either in an indigenous role or in the role of someone known to be studying that world. This relation is known technically to social scientists as "participant-observation." Three of the four studies presented in Part III were performed by one or another variety of participant-observation and provide detailed illustration of immersion.[1] Though not ideal, a practical degree of intimate familiarity can often be attained by a second means—namely, long, diverse, open-ended, semistructured conversations with people who are participants in a situation or social world. Since some kinds of situations are not readily amenable to direct physical participation by analysts of them, selected participants must be induced to sit down for many hours, to discuss a wide range of concrete matters they confront and to talk about how they act toward them. Unlike more conventional "interviewing," which is oriented importantly to attitudes, "intensive interviewing" is oriented to collecting instances and episodes of action and instances and episodes of problems and how they are dealt with. A goal of intensive or "qualitative" interviewing is to construct records of action-in-process from a variety of people who have likely performed these actions time and time again. Key features of such "conversations" are their length and diversity. Unhurried, free-flowing talk encourages the emergence of a wide range and many levels of topics, prompting intimate familiarity. The study of "Changing Oneself" by Roger Straus (Part III, Chapter 13) illustrates use of this technique, as do many of the studies capsulized in Part II.[2] Third and marginal, but still possibly useful and valid, is immersion in a rich and varied *written* body of materials. Again, "diversity" and "richness" are key features productive of qualitative, intimate familiarity. The materials at hand must have depth sufficient to permit immersion; they must have variety sufficient to permit a playfulness of mind and a turning, searching, crevice-finding scrutiny. Direct participation in a natural setting most allows and fosters this, but some bodies of written materials sometimes permit a usable approximation. Two forms of written materials may be distinguished.

1.   Some kinds of things that people do are so noteworthy in the eyes of publishers and the public that they are written up, often autobiographically, in books and articles. A variety of these writings on a single topic or social category sometimes forms a reasonably useful cache of direct observation reports. I have in mind, in particular, the memoirs of personages such as military leaders, wives of presidents, professional athletes, adventurers, physically handicapped people, and members of disadvantaged ethnic and sexual minorities. Taken collectively and studied intensively, the writings by members of any single such category can sometimes provide intimate familiarity to their readers. Erving Goffman's *Stigma: Notes on the Management of Spoiled Identity* comes close to being constructed on such a basis.[3]

2.   Literate social groups often leave residues of writings in which they are trying to accomplish given ends. Such bodies of writings, especially when they are propagandizing, can sometimes be analyzed for the strategies and tactics employed. The model here is the development by Alfred Lee and Elizabeth Lee of the seven classic "tricks of the trade" of the propagandist, an analysis that evolved out of the authors' scrutiny of the printed speeches broadcast in the thirties by Rev. Charles E. Coughlin.[4]

B.   Need.   Why are this kind of "intimate familiarity" and its resultant close, telling data important? Why should we at all care to obtain such data? First, if social science is the study of what people actually do—if it is indeed the study of social action and interaction—then an empirical science must directly observe that which it proposes to study! To propose to study something is to commit oneself actually to look at it; to stand close to it and to scrutinize it; to go where one finds it and to watch it. Direct, empirical observation is *by definition* the basis of social, or any, science. How utterly simple, yet not done! Second, the consequence of *not* doing direct, empirical observation of what one proposes to study is to risk the likelihood of developing abstract *characterizations*, summarizations, and typifications of phenomena that are simply *wrong*—empirically untrue. And, the investigator is likely to develop *explanations* or theories of phenomena that are untrue—simply made-up and imposed notions that are foreign to the phenomena themselves. In an area of my own reasonable acquaintance, perhaps the most widely believed, longest lived, and slowest dying impositions on a phenomenon have been the numerous "strain" theories of juvenile delinquency. Unconstrained by direct knowledge of people involved in delinquency, proponents of strain theories sustained their substitutes for familiarity more than thirty years—successfully catering to a generation of social scientists, generations of middle-class innocents in college classrooms, and such innocents grown older and called government, business, and community leaders. One of these theorists once said to me humorously and as if it were of no consequence, "If I have ever seen a delinquent in the field, I don't know it." Happily, a decade of direct observation and the virtual death of his theory make that individual more circumspect these days.

Third, in the absence of "firsthand acquaintance, the research scholar will unwittingly form some kind of picture of the area of life he proposes to study. He will bring into play the beliefs and images he already has to fashion a more or less intelligible view of the area of life."[5] Often these are no more than current stereotypes; often his images are derived from a preformed social science doctrine. Untempered and untaught by the *discipline* of intimate familiarity, the social scientist simply plays out and elaborates his preformed, lay stereotype or more esoteric social science doctrine. Motives, meanings, actions, consequences are *imputed* rather than observed, discovered, and articulated. This happens because the more *ambiguous* an object—the further one is from a thing and the less one knows about it—the greater is the *freedom* of the observer and the *need* of the observer to supply features to the object, to construct greater definition in the optical sense of that term. Without the discipline of close-up observation—of intimate familiarity—even the wildest of the observer's fantasies may come to the fore and dominate the portrayal.

Fourth, concepts and analyses developed in the absence of intimate familiarity are not only prone to be wrong, and an elaborate preformed stereotype, they are prone to be ethereal and empty. Vast portions of current social science speak generally of social life or even of some particular social life in terms that have a highly indefinite relation to any actual, ongoing, empirical world.

> The preponderant majority of our concepts are conspicuously vague and imprecise in their empirical connotation, yet we use them right and left in our analyses, without concern about elaborating, refining, or testing their empirical connotation....The reader is invited to try to pin down the empirical meaning of the following representative array of commonly used social science concepts: mores, integration, social role, alienation, socialization, attitude, value, anomie, and deviance. Empirical meaning is not given by a definition that merely serves the purpose of discourse; it exists instead in a specification that allows one to go to the empirical world and to say securely in the case of any empirical thing that this is an instance of the concept and that is not. Let the reader try his hand at doing this with the above concepts in observing what happens around him.[6]

It is exactly their empty and malleable character that allows such concepts to survive in endless exegetical debate and speculation about empirical referents. But such are the activities of metaphysics, not science. An empirical science is constructed, rather, out of the interplay of data and perplexed perception that *gives rise to* concepts yet contains and *constrains* them by a context of concrete empirical materials.

> Most of the improper use of the concept in science comes when the concept is set apart from the world of experience, when it is divorced from the perception from which it has arisen and into which it ordinarily ties. Detached from the experience which brought it into existence, it is almost certain to become indefinite and metaphysical. I have always admired a famous statement of Kant which really defines the character of the concept and indicates its limitations. Kant said brilliantly, "Perception without conception is blind; conception without perception is empty."[7]

C. Scarcity and Substitutes. We come now to an irony. Despite the fundamental need for intimate familiarity in the senses I have indicated, this quality is seldom achieved and is very scarce in the practice of social science. It is rare for a social scientist to have much qualitative intimate familiarity and acquaintance with the kind of social life he is considered to be an expert about, much less familiarity with social life more broad and diverse than the academic or other bureaucratic setting of his employment. The social science establishment is populated with "experts" on medical institutions who have spent virtually no time in medical settings, experts on crime and law enforcement who are similarly unfamiliar with criminal or law enforcement settings, experts on religion who have had very little association with religionists and their organizations, experts on families who have had almost no contact with families, and so on through other areas of social life. That is, a variety of statistical enumerations of trends in social science methods and research show a massive drift toward research based only on highly remote devices such as quicky questionnaires, fast interviews, and experimental contrivances.[8]

How can it be that social science is dominated by practitioners who lack intimate familiarity? How is it possible? At the most proximate and simple level of work practices, it is possible because of the ready availability of data-generating devices that do not require intimate familiarity with actual social life. Four standard and well-known types of these substitutes for data on ongoing social life-as-it-is-lived may be mentioned. (a) Little rooms are built and people are paid to interact in them (often for a few points on an introductory course grade).[9] (b) Quick checklists are presented to people at their front doors, in their living rooms, or in their mailboxes, asking for no more than an hour or so of a person's time. (c) Census and other government records are endlessly cross-tabulated and correlated, by people scrutinizing the distributional residues of social life. (d) The writings of social worlds that generate written items are read, and the reports of other scholars and journalists are consumed for their respective intimate familiarity.

Taken together, these devices and the "output" they furnish make it possible to speak at great length on a given part of social life, to fill up long books, to offer courses, and to address bureaucrats and publics. Such substitutes gloss over any question of intimate familiarity. Intimate familiarity is, rather, *assumed*.

II. THE SITUATION OF STRATEGIC SUBSTITUTES

But the mere availability and popularity of substitutes only specifies a possibility and locates the proximate vehicles of its accomplishment. We need to go on to determine the features of the larger and more enduring situation of social scientists, and people who might be studied by social scientists, that provide a context in which these substitutes become so attractive and so tenaciously pursued. The substitutes for intimate familiarity are themselves a strategy of situational coping. What *is* the situation in which they cope? Features of that situation relate to social scientists and their proximate audiences on the one side and to people in social life itself on the other.

A. The Situation of Social Scientists. Regarding social scientists, we need to examine their personal proclivities, their occupational situation, the nature of the task of intimate familiarity in those contexts, and the audiences addressed.

1. Proclivities. First, it is inaccurate to think of social scientists as a *peculiarly* asocial, abrasive, retiring lot, since a large portion of all humans seem also to manifest such propensities. But peculiar to social scientists or not, many of those who populate the social science disciplines are temperamentaly unsuited for the less than traumatic mucking around in the real world outside the academy. Many seem, indeed, to have the greatest difficulty making their way in the academy itself: examples of alienation, abrasiveness, social ineptitude, and naiveté are legion. Again, although such qualities are not uncommon in the world at large, they appear to me to be unequally distributed to social scientists. The traditional bookish role of the academician and the reclusive nature of scholarship seem likely to exert a tendency toward selective recruitment of those who lack certain social graces; and the solitude characteristic of important portions of academic work does nothing to increase opportunities to learn to deal easily with situations involving unfamiliar people. Add to that the special nature of social sciences themselves, their attraction for persons experiencing social difficulties and seeing in such fields possibilities for dealing with their personal problems, and one has the making of an atypical bunch.

Let me add immediately that the social sciences are by no means bereft of individuals who can make their way smoothly and are able to penetrate larger social worlds—the population of these fields is enormously varied. Yet among sociologists, the group I know best, there seem to be relatively few people who can readily negotiate passage among diverse and conflictual elements, in carrying out, for example, the administrative functions of the academy. Those who are discovered to be suave, diplomatic, emotionally calm, and administra-

tively responsive are greatly sought after and handsomely rewarded—
often more sought after and more rewarded than most scholars.
However scarce is talent for scholarship, talent for interaction is even
more scarce and is rewarded because of its scarcity.

Once substitutes for intimate familiarity achieve hegemony over the
social sciences, as they appear to have done in our era, coming to
determine how social scientists are trained, both the process of selective
recruitment and *formally* trained incapacity for attaining intimate
familiarity are further exacerbated. Graduate curricula seem virtually
designed to ensure ineptitude among those who become professionals.
As put by one observer regarding sociology:

> At the end of their training most sociologists are prepared *only* to
> view the social world in the pure environment of lab settings or
> through the screens of mail-order questionnaires. They often have
> neither the personal values, temperament nor arts of sociability
> needed to gain the trust of ...[ordinary people] and take part effec-
> tively in their natural activities.[10]

Second, the process of attaining intimate familiarity in some realm of
life or social setting is a *humbling* experience. One must admit to mere
laymen that one is ignorant; one must live with that admission day after
day, week after week, month after month. If there is one lesson that a
professional learns (professional social scientists in this instance), it is
that he or she is an *expert*, a person with a leg up on mere lay people.
Indeed, lay people expect the expert to have a leg up. "What is with
this Ph.D. who is so dumb?" the layman witnessing the learning, therefore bumbling, social scientists can well say. It is inevitably painful and
anxiety provoking to leave the role of Ph.D., Professor, Expert,
Teacher, and become a mere student in need of instruction. The
various substitutes are far more attractive, and seem to be especially
attractive to social scientists who are particularly "professorial" in style
and to those who are older and male—persons with such features carry
a heavy load of the demand for dignity and authority. Indeed, perhaps
another word for dignity is more appropriate: arrogance.

Most social scientists who *do* attain intimate familiarity are
young—typically still in graduate training or very early in their professional careers. They tend overwhelmingly to cease attaining intimate
familiarity as they grow older. Among the many reasons they do is
likely the growing difficulty of regaining humility—a stance well known

to graduate students and young, unrecognized Ph.Ds, but more and more foreign as the investigators are treated with too much respect by too many people over too many years.

Third, attaining intimate familiarity requires more physical stamina and endurance than do its substitutes. The person needs to leave his office—be it at home, on a campus, or in a research organization. The substitutes have the common feature of locational proximity, thereby reducing the amount of energy that need be expended to do one's job in a given day. Energy tends to decline with age, neatly paralleling the declining frequency with which social scientists who do attain intimate familiarity go on doing it as the years go by.

2. *Job Constraints.*   Social science is itself an economically precarious and rather marginal enterprise. It is a creature of the academy and has its economic base there. Overwhelmingly, social scientists are employees of colleges and universities. They are teachers, in fact, and research social scientists *per se* either incidentally, partially, or half-way. Only a small minority work at being practicing social scientists full time (and the size of that small group is crucially a function of the funding activities of the United States government at any given time). In a significant sense, their first duty is to the educational institution that employs them. One of the reasons the institution becomes a "first duty" is that it is massively and overwhelmingly *there*, whereas one's field is a much more abstract, nonlocalized entity. The institution has buildings, lawns, phones, mail rooms, students, classes, committees, memos, and so on; the discipline has almost none of these in any proximate and concrete sense. The institution's brute existence gives it the leg up on how the social scientist's day is organized: its functionaries call on the phone to arrange meetings, students want to consult, the bookstore wants book-order lists, the classes meet Monday, Wednesday, and Friday at 10 and 2, office hours are Tuesday and Thursday from 2 to 4, the faculty meeting is the first Wednesday of the month at 4, the Kiwanis Club wants a lecture on recent whatnot, the campus committee on doodads has an emergency meeting tonight. These are the concrete components of the institution's edge over the practice of social science *per se*. Moreover, the institution can reward and punish acts toward it in a more proximate way. To ignore institutional "needs" is to provoke inquiries—phone calls, hallway questions, yearly appraisals—whereas the discipline will not "phone"—not immediately anyway—if one ignores its "needs."

Ask about this social location and occupational situation: What sort of social science *fits into*—is most congruent with—such irregular and chopped-up days? Answer: the various kinds of substitutes indicated (survey data, census data, little labs, library materials). Each has the auspicious feature of waiting on the convenience of the social scientist, or it is easily molded to fit the days of the social scientist. Inanimate objects and student subjects adjust themselves to the researcher rather than vice versa. To work at attaining intimate familiarity with the real, operating world is to engender difficulties of scheduling and competing obligations, to miss crucial occasions either in the educational institution or in the setting of one's attempted familiarity. "Why hassle it?" one can well say. Rewards come directly from the institution; perfectly legitimate substitutes for intimate familiarity are easily available and, moreover, these fit the quantitative, technician mentality of our time, a prime feature of the substitutes' clarity and congruence. Put differently, emphasis on quantification, control, and factoring serves the occupational situation of the academic. It is on campus and in campus laboratories and research centers that quantifying, controlling, and factoring are best accomplished. It is on the campus that the social scientist has the most control. He buys this control, though, at the expense of intimate acquaintance with social life.

3. Task Clarity and Congruence. The substitutes not only fit well into the day of the academician, they fit well *(a)* into the anxiety the social scientist is likely to have about doing original research of any kind and *(b)* into the dominant ethos about what constitutes proper social science.

(a) The processes of attaining intimate familiarity and, more important, of making good social science out of what one finds, are hazardous. Procedures for "doing" library, survey, demographic, and laboratory social science are fairly well codified and reduced more or less to "cookbook" routines of collecting and analyzing data. Indeed, these substitutes have reached the point that even undergraduate college students can now almost literally crank out professionally acceptable (if not lauded) products. This is not true for the process of collecting and analyzing materials from direct intimate familiarity in natural settings. For whatever reasons, little is known about the process of getting from the buzzing confusion and blur of the real ongoing world and one's intimate familiarity with it to coherent social science analysis. Many a rational social scientist has avoided living with such

darkness and has elected the much clearer routines of the substitutes. The substitutes virtually guarantee some kind of result for one's effort, whereas intimate familiarity may mean merely years of stewing about what exactly it is one knows in some social scientific sense, as distinct from direct, unanalyzed knowledge of some social world. Practical people who want pay raises and other rewards of accomplished scholarship quite reasonably avoid that which less than certainly provides these.

(b)   Moreover, when actually deciding on what sort of social science to do, it is prudent to take account of the fact that the major agencies funding and performing research are wedded to quantitative substitutes for intimate familiarity—questionnaires, censuses, and laboratory experimentations—as opposed to qualitative library investigations and fieldwork. Funding has its obvious attractions—higher salaries, paid summers, administrative and research assistance, lower teaching loads, empire building, and the like. Organizations that buy research (mostly some federal agencies and a few large foundations), of course, want to buy something that is *demonstrably deliverable.* Quantitative research is demonstrably deliverable by even the statisticians and clerical employees; and very often indeed they, rather than prestigious "principal investigators," actually deliver it in the form of many vaguely suggestive tables. But better a hundred pointless tables than the endless and meaningless field and interview notes that equivalent field workers are, on their part, likely to bring forth. On the whole and sadly, organizations that fund and buy research have probably acted reasonably in preferring to fund drone quantitativism rather than drone qualitativism, for, as indicated, one at least gets something out of the cranked machine of quantitativism, but qualitativism has had no machine that is easy to crank.

In addition, quantitative modes of doing social science fit into a broader ethos of quantification in the modern world. The procedures and quantification of physical science and administration have been so successful that it is not unreasonable to try out such procedures in the social science realm. The last fifty years or so have been such a "try out" of quantitative procedures. They have formed, indeed, *a* mainline, if not *the* mainline of social science development. If one wants to be "with it," support of them is prudent.[11]

4.   *Audiences.* Audiences for social science reports are structured in ways that are protective of substitutes for intimate familiarity. First, a large part of published social science dies at birth because it is ignored. For better or worse, there are enough social scientists and libraries with incomes sufficient to support a range of journal outlets that accomplishes the magic act of publication, although hardly anyone reads the material and takes it seriously. It is a curious kind of death in life. Second, lay people who are exposed to much social science are so cowed by the social prestige of the authors who have titles such as "Professor," that they question their own perceptions rather than those of the social scientists. This is particularly the case with the social scientists' largest audience: undergraduate college students. Third, most members of any lay or professional audience for a piece of social science lack any intimate familiarity with the given sector of social life or topic under analysis. They bother to listen to the social scientist precisely because they want to reduce their ignorance. Thus they more easily believe someone who is an expert and who claims to have performed a study. Last, reports are themselves structured in a manner arcane enough to discourage many potentially critical audiences from too close scrutiny.

B.   The Situation of Other People.   The proclivities, job constraints, methods, and audiences of social scientists deal with only half the story. The other half resides with people in ongoing social situations with whom social scientists might wish to establish intimate familiarity. People in settings have their own proclivities, constraints, methods, and audiences. And, in general, the social scientist seems most frequently an extraneous, bothersome intrusion into the real, practical affairs of the world.

In the range of instances of the social scientist presenting himself openly to be an "observer" and questioner, there are certain prime and proper questions: "What's in it for me or us?" "Why should we give you our time and make you privy to our lives?" "What do *we* get?" Often the observer offers to the leadership of the group to be observed information that will help with their own problems. More often, of course, the typical social scientist avoids such questions altogether by hurriedly giving out questionnaires that demand little time and departing quickly, or, more prominently, by making observational requests of *public* bureaucracies that are obligated to be open to investigation of various sorts, and by being or becoming a "passing," unknown observer so that the question of "what do we get?" does not come up.

Astonishingly, for example, current social scientists do not ask high officials in corporate or government posts to be allowed openly to watch important people as they go about their daily activities. Sycophant intellectuals (or those thought to be) are sometimes allowed a position approaching this, but it seldom seems to be allowed (or asked for, for that matter) by and for the social scientists *per se*. High officials are sometimes amenable to allowing observations of underlings—lower white and blue-gray collar workers—but overlings are a different breed of cat. (Observation of underlings promises, of course, to increase productivity.)

In all instances of attaining intimate familiarity, people in settings who know of, or become aware of, the presence of the social scientist are likely to ask themselves: "Will he sell us out?" "Will he tell openly the things we do around here that we would prefer not to have known publicly?" "Will he say false things about us?" "What if he publishes our secrets for our competitors to read, or for our enemies to read and use against us?" If these eventualities seem remote, the reader should seriously ask whether he wants someone watching how he goes about his life and how he does his life in various situations? The likely answer, and the reasons for the "no," are the reasons that lead other people to reject observation: it is inconvenient, inexpedient, possibly embarrassing; it is a potential source of information flow to audiences that would receive the information unsympathetically; and it is likely to be discrediting in other ways. The fear of disclosure has, moreover, some profoundly disturbing dimensions involving the interplay of the observer and the observed's loyalties. Actually to analyze the *strategies and tactics* of a social show is to give away that show, some analysts believe. Truly acute analysis of strategy and tactics is an act of disloyalty in a world of oppressive social divisions where oppressed categories must covertly manipulate those above them in order physically or psychically to survive. For example, now and again in conversation with me a superbly acute woman sociologist openly plays through and verbally analyzes in highly articulate fashion some of the micro gambits that go into the social performance—the social construct—"American woman on the make." Most frequently this is done in the context of "decoding"—analyzing—spates of behavior we have both just witnessed. I have often urged this sociologist to collect data and to explicate on paper her extraordinarily incisive strategic perceptions about the interaction tactics of women. She steadfastly refuses on the grounds that even though she cannot herself morally support the manipulative interaction tactics of American women, she also cannot sell out her own kind. So long as women are oppressed, they need these tactics and it is better that men not understand them very well, which they would be more able to do if she wrote them up. Men would thereupon be less manipulable by women and the oppressed would be worse off. We have, then, a most delicate problem: social scientists get a great deal of mileage out of telling other people's secrets in articulate form; and loyalty to whatever persons are under actual scrutiny inhibits searching scrutiny, or at least the public telling of the results.

It is for the concatenated variety of reasons relating to both social scientists and people in natural settings that the intimate access in fact developed by social scientists is remarkably skewed toward underling and leisure settings of American society, such as poor people, motorcyclists, religious extremists, social workers (and lower public workers of many kinds), patients in mental hospitals, police patrolmen, and assembly-line workers. These are the sorts of people who (a) do not have the power to say no, (b) are so discredited they no longer care who knows what, (c) are participants in an open, leisure setting from which no one is excluded anyway, or (d) are energetically proselytizing and put up with a variety of characters in the course of this quest. Moreover, the sorts of people who are attracted to social science, and particularly to "fieldwork," tend more strongly to identify with underlings and to be drawn toward them as "objects of study." Settings of power and consequence have none of these features, are anathema to many social scientists, hence are not much studied.[12] Unfortunately for the acute analysis of actual, ongoing social life, these most studied kinds of marginal settings are likely not to be all that important for a very wide range of matters with which we as social scientists and citizens concern ourselves.

In a profound sense, then, social scientists are not the only people who fear intimate familiarity. People in real settings do not really want social scientists to know—at least not to know about *them,* although they might well delight that *other people* are known about in an intimate way. It is only partly in jest that I suggest an inchoate "conspiracy" of sorts between social scientists and the people they seek to analyze: do not get too close, do not look too carefully, and we will give you money (jobs, research grants) as substitutes and compensations for not getting too close. We will fill out your innocuous questionnaires and supply college students for your laboratories. Social scientists' reply: done.

C. An Eerie Equilibrium. There is an eerie equilibrium between what social scientists find, how they find it (the four substitutes), and smooth relations with the host society. As a category, social scientists are reasonaly regarded by social groups that know about their existence. Social scientists tend not to go around upsetting apple carts—at least they do not disturb them much or very often. This is so, I am suggesting, because social scientists mostly ask to perform safe substitutes for intimate familiarity: they learn little that is very interesting about social life, and they stay physically out of the way.

Imagine the consequences of acting otherwise, of pushing forward on a main front of thousands and thousands of social scientists striving to establish intimate familiarity with a wide variety of social settings by means of direct and prolonged observation. Social scientists would doubtless come to be seen as an unacceptably nosy bunch of bothersome and unnecessary troublemakers. If their interests were diverse, they would not merely poke about among the lowlings, the leisured, and the deviant, but among "men of substance" (and I do mean "men," not humans in general). Business and professional types "can't be bothered" with such unimportant activities—meaning more accurately "believe they should not be bothered" and "have the power not to be bothered."

Such a main frontal effort would create a large public relations problem and a large issue of control over the practice of social science: who can be certified to practice it, under what circumstances, for what purposes? "What are we getting out of this?" is the question that likely would become central to lay people, particularly those who have to put up with their own investigation. Confidentiality of findings would be an exceedingly delicate matter. Since most of the research reports would be very discrediting of the groups studied (as all full disclosures inevitably are),[13] social scientists would become the targets of much popular suspicion—and there would be a demand for regulation and containment.

My conclusion, then, is that social science could be too acute for the society that hosts it. Current societies, anyway, would not tolerate large-scale close, telling, intimate familiarity. Indeed, involved social groups are in positions of power that make it easy for them not to have to tolerate very much scrutiny. Unlike free-lance journalists, reporters and other writers, social scientists by and large are employed by educational institutions that can easily be manipulated into keeping their social scientists out of the streets and markets, as it were, and on the campus. Federal requirements for protecting the rights of research "subjects" have already laid the foundations of such control. Campus committees on "Social and Behavioral Surveys of Human Subjects" are the direct instruments of that control.[14] This contrasts with the dis-

persed, lone, entrepreneurial situation of more journalistic observers of
social life, such as embodied in "the new journalism." Being often in
business for themselves, these writers are now in fact the forward edge
of observation and intimate familiarity, even though they are innocent
of social science sensitivities.[15]

III. A MARGINAL BUT VITAL ENTERPRISE

For all the foregoing situational reasons, I have no belief that social
science practice is going to change very much in the foreseeable future
from what it is now. Rather, uninteresting and dull substitutes will
reign. But, also, social science based on close-up observation and
intimate familiarity will continue as the marginal but vital enterprise
that it is now.

In expanding and enriching that enterprise however slightly, we
want to keep live the possibility that all relevant and professional social
science does not have to be done by people who make a living as social
scientists or have any such career in mind. The roamings of reflective
people possessing intimate familiarity with interesting situations and
worlds often bring them into contact with social science ideas and
modes of conceiving experience. I would hope that social science might
be greatly enriched through the temporary sojourn of such people in
the social science "frame" and by their casting and recasting of personal
experiences in broader, social scientific terms. Therefore, though
pessimistic about social scientists "going out," I would like to be
optimistic about variously experienced people "dropping in," "dropping by," or "stopping through," and leaving for others social scientifically articulated reports of their knowledge. Indeed, it is to such
people that this volume is in important part addressed. I hope to make
their task easier, and even fun.[16]

≺≺≺≺≺≺≺≺

By whatever means, technique, or strategy of access, the first step,
aspect, or principle of deciphering how people do social things is to get
close to the social life that is happening someplace, to make records of
people actually doing social things, and to develop intimate familiarity
with those things.

Intimate familiarity, however, is only necessary to acute social
inquiry; it is far from sufficient. Were it sufficient, we would have an

abundance of acute social science, which we do not. We begin with intimate familiarity and add to it *(a)* social science sensitivity and distance—one form of which I elucidate in Chapters 3 and 4; and *(b)* the discipline of actually recording—setting down on paper—the data one is collecting, then analyzing and reporting it—matters dealt with in Chapters 5 and 6. Many people develop intimate familiarity with some kind of social life, but only a few acquire social science sensitivity, and still fewer submit themselves to the discipline of recording, analyzing, and reporting.

NOTES TO CHAPTER TWO

1. For brevity's sake, I do not discuss the social or physical details of participant observation or other techniques of acquiring intimate familiarity. Details, however, are available in several manuals, including Robert Bogdan and Steven J. Taylor, *Introduction to Qualitative Research Methods* (New York: Wiley, 1975); John Lofland, *Analyzing Social Settings* (Belmond, Calif.: Wadsworth, 1971); Leonard Schatzman, *Field Research* (Englewood Cliffs, N.J.: Prentice-Hall, 1973), and the literature cited in these sources.

2. Detailed discussion of qualitative interviewing is available in Bogdan and Taylor, *op. cit;* Lofland, *op. cit.*, Ch. 4; Schatzman, *op. cit.*

3. E. Goffman, *Stigma* (Englewood Cliffs, N.J.: Prentice-Hall, 1963). See also Travis Hirschi, "The Professional Prostitute," *Berkeley Journal of Sociology,* 7:33–49 (Spring 1962).

4. Alfred McClung Lee and E. B. Lee, eds., *The Fine Art of Propagands,* (New York: Harcourt, Brace, Jovanovich, 1939). Their study is capsulized in Chapter 8, Section III.D, "Exhortatory Encounters."

5. Herbert Blumer, *Symbolic Interactionism* (Englewood Cliffs, N.J.: Prentice-Hall, 1969), p. 36.

6. *Ibid.*, p. 45.

7. *Ibid.*, p. 168.

8. Derek L. Phillips, *Knowledge from What?* (Skokie, Ill.: Rand McNally, 1971), especially pp. 6–10; James L. McCartney, "On Being Scientific: Changing Styles of Presentation of Social Research," *The American Sociologist,* 5:30–35 (February 1970); William E. Snizek, "The Relationship Between Theory and Research: A Study in the Sociology of Sociology," *The Sociological Quarterly,* 16:415–428 (Summer 1975).

9. For instances of overly cautious but encouraging efforts to enter natural settings, see L. Bickman and T. Hency, eds., *Beyond the Laboratory: Field Research in Social Psychology,* (New York: McGraw-Hill, 1972) or P. G. Swingle, ed., *Social Psychology in Natural Settings: A Reader in Field Experimentation* (Chicago: Aldine, 1973).

10. Jack D. Douglas, "Existential Sociology," in Jack D. Douglas and John M. Johnson, eds., *Existential Sociology,* (New York: Cambridge University Press, 1976) p. 50. See also C. Wright Mills, *The Sociological Imagination* (New York: Oxford University Press, 1959), especially Ch. 3.

11. See Mills, *Ibid.*, Blumer, *op. cit.*

12. Commenting on lack of talent and training for mixing with ordinary people, Jack Douglas observes that "traditional sociologists are immensely more able to study 'deviant' and lower class groups than to study the massive, dominant and 'successful' groups in our society. It is little wonder that traditional sociologists have done hundreds of studies of delinquency, gangs, homosexuals, and lower class groups of various kinds, but have almost never studied banks, real estate, and so on." Jack Douglas, *op. cit.*, p. 50.

    Since they are so often about the relatively powerless, actually performed studies of how people do social things tend to be typified by what radical social scientists (correctly) characterize as "triviality." Unfortunately, radicals tend to ascribe this triviality to the closeness of the method rather than to its proper source, the protective mechanism of social groups. They would advance their cause better by attacking the topics studied rather than the method or perspective used. I suspect that high quality and acute strategy analyses of members of the American elite would be the most "significant," politically meaningful, and potent pieces of social science it is possible by any means to produce. Ironically, the misascription of triviality to close and direct observation serves, in sequence, (a) to mislead social scientists who do not think the matter through, (b) to deter them from trying to get close-up material on elites, (c) to inhibit our knowledge, and (d) in the end to support the status quo by virtue of limiting the range of actions we can envision. Put bluntly, the radical social scientist's critique of close-up field observation serves the interest of conservative elites. More generally, the marked exhortatory propensity of radical social scientists and their reluctance to perform empirical research serves to discredit radical social science and thereby functions to support the American power elite. By and large, the conceptual and empirical sterility of social scientists who claim to be radicals renders them *functional* reactionaries. For some beautifully pointed commentary on this matter, see Andrew Hacker's review of G. W. Domhoff's book on the Democratic Party, *Contemporary Sociology*, **2**:421–422 (July 1973).

13. No group or category of persons wants its full, actual activities known publicly because all engage in, or have engaged in, matters they feel are embarrassing to themselves or others, and/or are otherwise discrediting or illegal. Unfortunately, no social scientist has a cloak of anonymity that fully covers those involved when the results are published. Participants and other locals can figure out and communicate true locations and personal identities—and one can never predict to whom they might tell these identities; or for what reasons.

14. A foundational document here is *The Institutional Guide to DHEW Policy on Protection of Human Subjects*, Department of Health, Education, and Welfare Publication No. (NIH) 72-102 (Washington, D.C.: Government Printing Office, 1971).

15. For a review and assessment, see Tom Wolfe, "Why They Aren't Writing the Great American Novel Anymore: A Treatise on the Varieties of Realistic Experience," *Esquire*, December 1972, pp. 152–159, 272–280.

16. Short of this pattern, social science is enormously enriched by means of the two career phenomena wherein a person enters social science after having pursued some other career for several years, studies social science, then goes back to the situations of his former career to do social science. The intertwining of the old familiarity, the

new social science perspective, and the new intimate familiarity often gives rise to some of the most acute social science work. I have in mind, for example, the career of John Irwin and his penetrating work in criminology, particularly his book *The Felon* (Englewood Cliffs, N.J.: Prentice-Hall, 1970). Graduate social science programs ought to encourage this kind of career movement far more often than they do.

CHAPTER THREE

Focusing on
Situations

Intimate familiarity requires focus. One type of focus is on the situations confronted by participants.[1] This chapter provides guides to *(a)* specifying the nature and "scales" of situations people face, *(b)* going from topical to generic conceptualizations of situations, and *(c)* appreciating the ubiquitously ambiguous character of modern situations.

I. NATURE, DIMENSIONS, AND SCALES OF SITUATIONS

A. The Concept of Situation. A situation is the wholistic array of people, physical objects, spaces, and time periods that an acting unit takes into account in constructing its action or that constrains action, regardless of whether the acting unit consciously takes a given aspect into account. A situation is the combination of real and defined conditions of action existing at a given time. A situation is the social and physical place in which people act; it is the context of their action. Like all highly abstract concepts and their definitions, this one serves only to get us started. We need immediately to refine and concretize it.

B. Dimensions of Situations. One prime line of concretization is in terms of the scale or "size" of situations. By scale or size I mean the amount or number of people, physical objects or equipment, space, and time involved.

First, situations in which people must act vary in terms of the size of the *human population* toward which action must be formulated. At one extreme, the population of proximate, physical "others" may be zero. There would seem to be no theoretical upper limit on the population size of a situation, although there are surely practical limits. As the population of a situation increases, persons tend to simplify it by means of categorization; thus a situation may have hundreds of separate others, but only two or three *social types* of others. Such simplification, however, does not gainsay the fundamental import of sheer numbers. In addition, the symbolic capacities of human beings make it possible to have a very live and active *phantom* population in a situation where the person is the only physical human present. Persons interact with "mental others" and "generalized others," as reiterated by fans of G. H. Mead.[2] To the degree that there are phantom others, and they enter into matters that the person takes into account in formulating action, such others must also be enumerated in the population, separately noted of course. Second, situations vary in the amount and kinds of *equipment* they contain and can therefore be utilized by persons in formulating and executing actions. Third, situations quite obviously occupy *space* and vary enormously in the *size* of the space occupied, using measures such as, say, cubic yardage or cubic miles. As the space occupied by a situation grows larger, there arise issues of subspaces and subspaces within subspaces and other elaborate physical and mental partitionings. Fourth, situations occupy *time,* ranging from a few seconds up to any period over which a person is willing to orient himself in formulating his action. (For the acronymically inclined, the initials of these situational variables spell "pest.")

C. Situational Scale. The four dimensions of situations regularly cluster in a few broad forms among the infinite number possible. Or, at least, we as pattern-imposing creatures tend to assimilate the infinitely occurring combinations to a relatively small number of types. For present purposes, we need identify only seven such "clusterings" of population, equipment, space, and time, of which only four occupy our attention. Defined broadly here, features of the "smallest" four are discussed more elaborately in the initial sections of each chapter in Part II of this book, for they provide the organizing principle of Part II.

1. Encounters. The "smallest-tightest" of situations typically involves only a few people using a modest amount of space over a brief period of time. Following Erving Goffman's terminology and analysis, we may refer to this most micro situation as the "encounter."[3]

Encounters usually last only a few seconds, minutes, or hours and involve face-to-face copresence (allowing, however, for single person "self-encounters"). The brevity of encounter situations tends to inhibit the amount and kind of population, space, and equipment employed, but the best organized of humans sometimes manage to work up quite complex population, space, and equipment arrangements for "mass encounters." Drugstore purchases, hallway conversations, job interviews, baseball batting, radio and TV broadcasts, doorstep sales pitches, public place entrances, waiting in public places, single meetings of college classes or laboratories, sports events, Nazi rallies, and evenings out all illustrate encounter-scale situations and some population, equipment, and space variations in them.

2. Roles. Role-scale situations last varying periods of time but seemingly a minimum of some weeks, a period sufficient for a person and his others to discover and act toward more enduring and broader variations in space, equipment, and one another as persons. Role-scale situations vary in scale. Smaller ones are illustrated by situations such as college courses, hospitalizations, summer camps, temporary jobs, and court trials. Larger and longer role-scale situations include those of being a given age, ethnicity, or gender, and being in an occupational career, a marriage, or a friendship.

The emphasis in role-scale situations is on the point of view of the single class of actor as he or she looks out on the world and acts on it.

3. Groups. Group-scale situations differ from role-scale situations in shifting from the point of view of a single class of "role occupant" to that of the point of view of multiple, interdependent persons. Thus three interconnected people play different roles relative to one another, and each deals with his own role-scale situation; but the three taken as a unit—as a group—must deal with a group-scale situation that is above and beyond the respective roles involved. Informal work groups, cliques, and families are prime illustrations of group-scale situations.

4. Organizations. Organizational-scale situations are the same as group-scale situations in the sense of employing the point of view of the acting unit *per se*. They differ in typically existing for longer periods of time, having larger populations, and employing a wider range of equipment. They are also more formally organized and have clearer, often written goals, and procedures. The situations of political parties, business corporations, and educational institutions illustrate organizational-scale situations.

For a variety of reasons, the analysis in this volume is confined to the four scales of situations just enumerated. They are dealt with at length in Part II, "Review of Qualitative Studies of Interaction Strategies." They do not, however, exhaust the scale of possible situations, and for the sake of adequate context I want to mention the major, larger ones.

5. *Worlds.* Complexly interrelated sets of encounters, roles, groups, and organizations seen by the participants as forming a larger whole are often and properly thought of as "worlds," as in the phrases "the business world," "the academic world," "the sports world." There is no central authority as with organizations, but participants take account of one another and view one another as engaged in related endeavors.

6. *Settlements.* Complexly interrelated sets of encounters, roles, groups, organizations, and worlds sharing territory, performing an important range of life-sustaining functions, and having to take one another into account form settlements, common types of which are villages, towns, ghettos, neighborhoods, and cities.[4] As is evident, "settlement-scale situations" operate on relatively large scales of population, time, space, and equipment.

7. *Societies.* Complexly interrelated sets of encounters, roles, groups, organizations, worlds, and settlements sharing territory, performing a wide range of life-sustaining functions, and in which one organization effectively claims ultimate life and death sovereignty over the participants, form a society. Basic types of "societal-scale situations" and types of society are formed by variations in degree of urbanization, type of rule, and mode of economic production.

As mentioned, the four dimensions of space, population, time, and equipment combine in infinite ways. Their variations serve, therefore, as *guides* in thinking about various scales of situations rather than as specific, defining features. Thus many modern, formal organizations are larger on all four of these dimensions than some settlements, but the tendency remains for organizations to be smaller than settlements. The same point applies to the other dimensions.

II. TOPICAL VERSUS GENERIC CONCEPTUALIZATIONS
OF SITUATIONS

A.   Topical.   Participants in social life tend to think about situations in a *topical,* or substantive fashion. By "topical" I mean the words and the terms used directly to speak about the ongoing organization of everyday life. Thus people in social life say:

> "The boss is coming in at three o'clock to look things over."
> "I couldn't believe what happened at the rally last night."
> "Our committee meets this afternoon, as usual."
> "We're living over in that huge apartment complex and is that something else again, the kinds of things that go on there!"
> "I am a teacher in a Headstart program."
> "I clerk in a clothing store."
> "I live in a commune."

Each statement makes a topical reference to a situation: the presence of the boss, a rally, a committee meeting, an apartment complex, a teacher in a classroom, a clerk in a clothing store, a commune. Referring to our definition of a situation, each one is a wholistic array of people, physical objects, space, and time periods that a person takes into account in constructing his action or that constrains action. Note that the *words* used to orient thought and action are the shared vocabulary of ordinary discourse and commonsensical units of organization, as in "rally," "committee," "clothing store," and "commune." Such terms constitute a *topical* conception of situations, an everyday, phenomenological conceiving of situations. It is library index reality.

For the purpose of doing the work of one's world, such topical conceptions are proper and instrumental. And even for the purposes of a proximately applied study of social life with the goal of instructing unknowledgeable others how to act in a given kind of social life, such a topical orientation is fine. It serves reasonably well the purposes of the directly practical people mentioned in Chapter 1.[5]

However it serves indirectly practical and theoretically oriented audiences less well. Since these two audiences may not be very interested in or concerned about, say, a particular committee or apartment complex or clothing store or commune, a depiction of a situation conceived in a merely topical fashion necessarily has a highly limited application and, by definition, the social circle for whom it holds any fascination is likewise limited. The plain fact is that only relatives, friends, and enemies care much about any given concrete set of persons, their situations, and their actions. Most concrete categories of people have few relatives, friends, and enemies; hence anything written at the merely topical level is of interest to virtually no one. It is only in terms of what *I* (the viewer) more generally get out of reading about various weirdos, yahoos, or whatnots that most people are interesting to most other people when kinship, friendship, or enmity are not involved. And, note that potential action payoff governs *all* forms of interest.

It is for the purpose of extending the range of application and relevance, then, that students of how people do social things strive to go beyond the topical content of situations and seek, in addition, generic aspects or features or themes of situations.

B. Generic. To conceive a situation generically is to discriminate and bring forward social aspects that possess more generalized, more common, more universal relevance. A given situation is scrutinized in terms of the *kinds* of general human concerns that are being coped with and acted toward. The analyst attempts to answer the question: "Of what abstract, sociologically conceived *class* of situation is this particular situation an instance?" Or, "What are the abstract features of this kind of situation?" Or, "What kind of situation is this?" To answer questions such as these is to offer a generic conception of a situation.

To scrutinize a situation generically is to seek out its abstract, transcendent, formal, analytic aspects.[6] It is by such an operation that the specific becomes general, the esoteric becomes exoteric, the obscure and irrelevant become clear and relevant. The following instances concretize this point:

1. The topical situation of student may be viewed as an instance of the generic situation of the *open-ended and never-ending task.*[7]
2. The topical situation of machine operator may be viewed as an instance of the generic situation of *monotony.*[8]
3. The topical situation of milkman may be viewed as an instance of the generic situation of *power asymmetry.*[9]
4. The topical situations of baseball fielding and batting may be viewed as instances of the generic situations of *certainty* and *uncertainty.*[10]
5. The topical situation of face-to-face contact between the physically

handicapped and the physically normal may be viewed as an instance of the generic situation of *threatened sociability interaction.*[11]

6. The topical situation of waiting in public places may be viewed as an instance of the generic situation of *socially unsupportive exposure to strangers.*[12]

7. The topical situation of traditional Chinese households may be viewed as an instance of the generic situation of *crowding.*[13]

8. The topical situation of taxicab driving may be viewed as an instance of the generic situation of the *fleeting relationship* "...fleeting, one-time contact with a heterogeneous aggregate of clients, unknown to one another...."[14]

It can be assumed that any topical situation possesses potential for conception in a vast multitude of generic ways. The number of generic ways in which any topical situation can be abstracted is limited only by the knowledgeability, inventiveness, and imagination of the person who is looking at the situation. Therefore, the issue for anyone close-up to a topical situation and seeking generic abstraction is not that of which is the "right" way generically to conceive the situation. A very wide variety of ways can be "right" in the sense that many generic depictions offered can be shown to reside in the actual, empirical materials gathered on the situation.

However scholars of social life who study "how people do social things" employ a practical and working guide for deciding which among a large number of possibilities they ought to single out and develop. This practical working guide is a question for which one must offer an answer: "What generic features of this situation are most *clear, exaggerated* and *sharp*?" "Of what is this the best example that one could conceivably find?" Everett Hughes, who inspired a generation of sociologists with it, calls this the "'more-so' principle."

> While any society [or other situation] at any time is of interest, any one at a given time may show some features of special interest. It may be, because of a combination of circumstances, the ideal laboratory in which to observe certain processes which will give us new knowledge of general interest.[15]

The notion is logically similar to the psychologist's proclivity to study highly unusual ("abnormal") persons in search of the principles of "normal" psychic functioning. One student of social life wanted his work "to exploit this special relevance to [the specific generic topic]...by tracing certain social processes as they operate in [the particular] more sharply focused setting. From such a study we can perhaps gain insight into the operation of the same but less sharply defined processes operating in a variety of contexts." Or, as phrased by a commentator, the scrutinized situation is treated as a microcosmic model of a larger class, on the assumption that the smaller "entity will operate according to the same general principles as hold for the larger system, but that the unusual starkness with which these principles are displayed...will aid in identification and analysis."[16]

Even when constrained by the "more-so principle," any situation can be developed generically in an infinite number of ways. Which ones, then, ought to be developed? Answer: those we humans care about, based on our actual experience and our desire for action. There is no immutable, unchanging, and finite set of generic situations to be analyzed. As people's interests and desires shift, the list of what are considered central and important situations shift. The prime generic situations of social science concern in 1960 need not be those in 1970 or 1980 or any other year. To search for an eternal set of generic situations is to pursue a chimera, a mirage. The concrete and topical content of social science inquiry is, rather, properly contextualized, relative, and conditioned by larger social forces. What remains the same is, instead, the commitment to be faithful to experience, to articulate it accurately, to abstract from it in generally useful ways, and so on through the principles explicated in these chapters of Part I.

III. VARIATION IN DEGREE OF DEFINITION

Among the multitude of topical and generic ways in which situations can vary, one requires special note and treatment. It is a variation, indeed, that creates the social and psychological need for situation and strategy analyses of social interaction.

Situations in modern society tend markedly to be unstructured and undefined, or at least to be subject to *competing* definitions that themselves give rise to doubt and hesitation in how a situation ought to be defined. I dare say that it is seldom easy for participant and analyst alike to answer the questions, "What *is* the situation?" "What *are* the things that need most importantly to be taken into account in this situation?" "What *are* the consequences of the varying courses of action

I or we have undertaken?" "What *will be* the consequences of various strategies of action I or we envision?" "What are the objective facilitants of our envisioned courses of action?" "Who or what is likely to support each possibility?"

Many situations of modern society admit of only imperfect and partial information and competing versions of what the basic information might be. Situations of modern society tend to elicit in their participants questions of identifying the applicable moral values and the priorities with which they are to be applied. In short, situations vary in the degree to which participants view them as clear, structured, known, and unambiguous on the one hand, versus unclear, unstructured, unknown, and ambiguous on the other.

What basic structural variations in situations might seem to affect the degree to which participants are able to form a clear definition of them (and, as a consequence, routine strategies for coping)? Using population, equipment, space, and time variations as an organizing principle, the following kinds of elements seem to be involved.

1. The larger, the more heterogeneous, and the more hierarchical the *population* of a situation, the more difficult it is to form a stable and clear definition of it.

(a) As the number of people involved in a situation grows, so does the number of actions that have reasonably to be known about in defining what is happening. There is an increase in the sheer amount of information that needs processing to permit definition of the situation. As the amount of information increases, the possibility for error increases, as does the number of ways in which the information can be organized and interpreted.

(b) The greater the social heterogeneity of the population of a situation, the greater the number of competing definitions of the situation that must be taken into account in forming one's own definition of the situation. Socially homogeneous populations—populations that are similar or identical in race, age, sex, social class, nationality, and so on—are populations likely to propose a more restricted range of definitions of situations. Conversely, the greater the diversity with respect to age, sex, race, class, and nationality, the greater the number of competing conceptions of what the situation is.

(c) Under modern conditions of change, the greater the degree to which the members of population of a situation are hierarchically arranged and otherwise segregated from easy and intimate familiarity with one another, the greater will be the ambiguity of the situation. People not well known are people whose definitions and likely actions are ambiguous, creating ambiguity regarding one's own situation. People who interact only with familiar others on a peer basis tend also to have clear and unproblematic definitions of whatever the situation. Thus in comparing four levels of management in an industrial plant, Norman Martin found that the lowest two levels (shift and department foremen) "are completely immersed in the realm of the familiar and the local. People they see and talk to from day to day and from month to month make up their social contacts. Correct anticipation of the reactions of others in many instances becomes almost second nature. At the division level the social world expands and extends; at the works manager level, over one-fourth of relationships are with people outside the plant."[17] As a consequence, the lower levels have

> status systems, behavior patterns, norms, etc. [that] are well formed within the in-group. Individuals come to know what is expected of them; they can correctly anticipate one another's reactions. Uncertainty in this respect is at a minimum. As an executive moves up, uncertainty increases.[18]

*   *   *

> The social world of the works manager is one characterized by a multiplicity of superordinate and subordinate relationships, which are to a considerable degree indirect in nature and extending to members of out-groups. Here there is a greater probability of uncertainty in anticipating how others will act.[19]

The key feature here is *competing definitions* of the situation: more people, more varied, and less known means diversity of definition. Diversity of definition implies hesitation and extra work in forming one's own definition of the situation.

2.   Hypothetically, the larger the amount, range, and complexity of *equipment* available and used in a situation, the larger the range of novel turns of events, breakdowns, repairs, and deployments that become possible. When a larger number of things *can* happen, this imposes a greater burden of calculating things that *might* happen, thus exacerbat-

ing the formation of a definition of the situation.

3. The larger the size and number of *spaces* in which and over which the situation has an existence, the greater the complexity of other peoples' possible lines of action, and the greater the number of possibilities that the definition-former need take into account. As space increases in size and complexity, the more difficult it is to *acquire* information on the present and likely actions of others. This problem, which is central to analysis of military operations, often is coped with by spy deployments.

As complex space combines with sophisticated equipment such as telephones and mail systems, even the nature of available information may change qualitatively: the richness of face-to-face dealing may be replaced by the uncertainties of electronically conveyed voices and typed memos. Martin says of the highest-level managers he studied:

> Considerable volume of correspondence crosses the desk of the works manager; many of his contacts are via telephone. While communication of a kind is conveyed by such means, it may be assumed that it is not so reliable as face-to-face relationships. Subtleties and nuances cannot be readily perceived. Anticipation may fail to be realized.[20]

4. As the "*time* frame" toward which action is oriented extends, the range of possible (therefore likely) actions of others increases, as do the possibilities for one's own range of actions. As the range of possibilities broadens, the ambiguity of the consequences of any one of them is likely to increase.

As the time over which action takes place increases, the consequences of temporally longer lines of action become more difficult to know. Feedback is attenuated. Referring again to Norman Martin's comparisons of the four levels of managers:

> The shift foreman is almost completely concerned with day-to-day production decisions. In this sense, he operates in the immediate present, with only slight extension into the present and future....At the works manager level, in sharp contrast, 50 percent of the decision situations observed were over a year's duration—of a distant or remote focus. Because the true meaning of an event cannot be ascertained until it is actualized, one of the consequences of being involved in situations of a distant time perspective is that the execu-

tive is in a difficult position to judge correctly the value and meaning of intervening events....When one has to project ahead, risks and uncertainty increase; the situation may change completely; new features intervene.[21]

Imagine, now, situations that are reasonably maximal along all these dimensions. The situations of nations at war, politicians, and corporation heads come to mind as important topical examples. In the light of the foregoing, it is not so surprising that so many of us think that so many important leaders do very poor jobs. It seems, rather, a feature inherent in "large" situations and in the stance we as an audience are bound to take toward those with responsibility for them. But imagine, too, situations considerably short of the highly unstructured, undefined one just portrayed. The typical situations of modern life abound in these elements of uncertainty, if only to lesser degrees. It is one important task of the social analyst as faithfully as possible to render choate events the participants, as harried actors, are likely to be experiencing as even more inchoate than a reflective, careful analyst would be able to decipher.

Moreover, appreciating that defining the situation can be a highly problematic act, one becomes more able to appreciate that *hard work* may be going into even seemingly more obvious kinds of highly structured situations.

≺≺≺≺≺≺≺≺

These matters of scale, generic construction, and degree of definition allow us to work with the concept of "the situation." Scale variations provide an orientation to the contexts in which people act. The notion of aiming for the generic broadens one's perceptions. Variations in degree of definition point up the need for both participants and analysts to work at knowing what *is* the situation in a given sector of social life.

Situations are what people act *toward*, they are what must be *dealt with*. Both participants and analysts must ask: What *is* the situation? What are the features of the objects toward which thought and action must be oriented? Situations are the "places," so to speak, where people act. In them people must actually *act*. Thought and action must be constructed to deal with the situation. It is to these matters of *strategy* that we now proceed.

NOTES TO CHAPTER THREE

1. Other types of focus of a qualitative kind are on structures (or types) and processes. For discussion, see Chapter 4, Section III, "Qualitative Strategy Analysis and the Larger Study of Social Organization."

2. See, for example, Gregory P. Stone and Harvey A. Farberman, eds., *Social Psychology Through Symbolic Interaction*, (Waltham, Mass.: Ginn-Blaisdell, 1970), Part Six.

3. Erving Goffman, *Encounters* (Indianapolis: Bobbs-Merrill, 1961), pp. 17–81.

4. Cf. the appropriate picture drawn by Norton Long, "The Community as an Ecology of Games," *American Journal of Sociology,* **60**:251–261 (April 1958).

5. One of the best of these by social scientists is Morris S. Schwartz and Emmy Lanning Shockley, with the assistance of Charlotte Green Schwartz, *The Nurse and the Mental Patient: A Study in Interpersonal Relations* (New York: Russell Sage Foundation, 1956).

6. These adjectives are meant to be suggestive rather than precise, for the present point is not quite, in particular, a contrast between substantive and formal in the sense of Barney Glaser and Anselm Strauss (*Discovery of Grounded Theory*, Chicago: Aldine, 1967, Ch. 4) or between concrete and analytic in the sense of Talcott Parsons (*The Structure of Social Action*, New York: McGraw-Hill, 1937, pp. 27–41). The fundamental statement, I lament, remains that of Georg Simmel, "The Problem of Sociology," available in Kurt H. Wolff, ed., *Georg Simmel: 1858–1918* (Columbus: Ohio State University Press, 1959), pp. 310–336. See also Herbert Blumer, *Symbolic Interactionism* (Englewood Cliffs, N.J.: Prentice-Hall, 1969), pp. 127–132.

7. Stan Bernstein, "Getting It Done: Notes on Student Fritters," *Urban Life and Culture*, **1**:275–292 (October, 1972), capsulized in Section V.A.2 of Chapter 8.

8. Donald F. Roy, "Banana Time: Job Satisfaction and Informal Interaction," *Human Organization*, **18**:158–168 (Winter, 1959–60), reprinted here in Chapter 13.

9. Odis E. Bigus, "The Milkman and His Customers: A Cultivated Relationship," *Urban Life and Culture*, **1**:*131*–165 (July 1972), summarized in Chapter 8, Section III.C.

10. George Gmelch, "Baseball Magic," *Trans-Action*, June 1971, pp. 39–41 and p. 54, summarized in Chapter 8, Section V.B.

11. Fred Davis, *Illness, Interaction and the Self* (Belmont, Calif.: Wadsworth, 1972), Ch. 8, summarized in Chapter 9, Section IV.C.3.

12. Lyn H. Lofland, "Self Management in Public Settings: Parts I and II," *Urban Life and Culture,* **1**:93–108, 217–231 (April and July, 1972), summarized in Chapter 8, Section II.A. (See also her *A World of Strangers: Order and Action in Urban Public Space*, New York: Basic Books, 1973).

13. E. N. Anderson, Jr. "Some Chinese Methods of Dealing with Crowding." *Urban Anthropology*, **1**:141–150 (Fall 1972), summarized in Chapter 10, Section III.B.3.

14. Fred Davis, "The Cabdriver and His Fare: Facets of a Fleeting Relationship," *American Journal of Sociology*, **65**:158–165 (September 1959), summarized in part in Chapter 8, Section III.C.

15. Everett C. Hughes, *The Sociological Eye* (Chicago: Aldine-Atherton, 1971), p. 140. When Julius Roth was a patient and sociological observer in a TB hospital, Hughes advised him that the relation of uncertainty, magic, and ritual "is one of the general problems to keep in mind, a problem that makes your observations of much wider

application. You are only quite incidentally studying life in a hospital" (letter from Everett Hughes to Julius Roth, *TB Patient's Journal* [Chicago: Committee on Human Development, University of Chicago, n.d., p. 152]). See also, Raymond Gold's account of Hughes' response to Gold's study of janitors, including Hughes' comments that "a fundamental matter of method in social science...[may be] that of finding the best possible laboratory for study of a given set of mechanisms." Raymond Gold, "In the Basement—The Apartment House Janitor," in Peter Berger, ed., *The Human Shape of Work* (New York: Macmillan, 1964) p. 49.

The genealogically attuned will see here the direct line of descent from Georg _immel to Robert Park to Hughes to Roth's generation and beyond. In *The Sociological Eye,* Hughes reports of Park: "If he was ever tempted to become an 'expert' on some particular human problem, he was held back by his conviction that every event had a place somewhere in the universal human process, that no situation can be understood until one finds in it those universal qualities which allow one to compare it to other situations—however distant in time, place and appearance" (p. 548). Park "was interested in current goings on, but never content until he could put a news story into some universal theme of human interaction. Thus came the apparent anomaly, that the man who wanted to make sociology deal with the news was also the one who based his scheme on the work of the most abstract of all sociologists, Georg Simmel. He had no desire to form a system, yet he was primarily a systematic sociologist" (p. 549).

16. Robert C. Carson, "Life Is *Not* a Game?" *Contemporary Psychology,* **15:**722 (December 1970). See, further, the remarks of Philip Selznick on the identification of "functioning institutional systems": "We view the structure we are studying as an instance of a class of objects whose general features are to be explored. The class may have only one member, but it is the *kind* of thing we are dealing with that interests us. We ask: What kind of social system is the Communist Party? We answer by developing a model of the 'combat party,' including its strategies." *The Organizational Weapon: A Study of Bolshevik Strategy and Tactics* (New York: Free Press, 1916), p. xiv.

17. Norman Martin, "Differential Decisions in the Management of an Industrial Plant," *Journal of Business,* **29:**258 (October 1956).

18. *Ibid.*

19. *Ibid.,* p. 259.

20. *Ibid.* And one may note that national leaders prefer in the end to meet one another face to face, to conduct what they define as their most important kind of business.

21. *Ibid.,* pp. 251–252.

CHAPTER FOUR

Focusing on
Strategies

I. NATURE, DIMENSIONS, AND SCALES OF STRATEGIES

A. Nature. People devise gauge, juggle, and *construct* their actions in
situations. Human action in situations does not just happen; it is pieced
together and built, thought about and tried out, formulated and
reformulated. People, in their aspects of interest here, *work* at acting in
the sense that attention is directed to the process of deciding whether
action is needed, what action is needed, how action is to be executed,
the execution of action, and the termination of action.

Human action, moreover, is directed to dealing with whatever is
identified as problematic, as requiring that action be taken in one kind
of situation or another. Situations are often situations *because* they
present themselves as requiring some kind of preventive, remedial,
reparative, corrective, or other circumstance-altering effort.

To grasp adequately these two *constructed-action-to-deal-with-problem-
atic-matters* features of human action, one must imbue oneself with an
activist imagery of the human being, an imagery that stands in stark
contrast to the passivist imagery that forms the basis of the overwhelming majority of contemporary social science. The activist imagery is
expressed succinctly in the thrusting kind of verbs its proponents are
happy to employ in their accounts of human action—contrasted to the
studied absence of muscular verbs in analyses built on a passivist imagery. I have in mind activist verbs of the following sorts, used in their
present progressive form:

adapting
aggressing
campaigning
confronting
coping
dealing
designing
dodging
fearing
fiddling
juggling
handling
managing
maneuvering
playing
scheming
striving
struggling
trying

Scholars of social life who employ an activist image of humans constructing their action and who are concerned with analyzing "how people do social things" focus, therefore, on depicting and articulating lines of action that people in fact develop in situations. Concretely, they are sensitized to observe and to use in analysis a range of nouns that designate *classes of action* that humans use to do things. Here is a list of such "humans doing things" nouns and phrases:

adaptational techniques
arrangements
artifices
contrivances
coping strategies
devices
dodges
feints
gambits
lines of action
maneuvers

mechanisms
methods
moves
plays
ploys
practices
procedures
programs
schemes
stratagems
strategies
tacks
techniques
tactics
tricks

Some of these terms appear more frequently than others in actual studies of how people do social things. The terms "mechanisms," "methods," "strategies," "techniques," and "tactics" are much more frequently used than the others, although all of course embody the same basic idea. Since the term "strategy" is the most commonly employed and understandable, I use it here as the general designation for lines of action in situations.

B.   Dimensions and Scales of Strategies.   Strategies vary in much the same way as do situations with regard to amounts and kinds of population, equipment, space, and time. At one polar extreme, the "simplest-shortest" strategies involve *(a)* a person acting alone, *(b)* employing no equipment, in *(c)* a single, simple space, over *(d)* a time span of a few seconds. At the other polar extreme, the "most complex–longest" strategy involves *(a)* millions of coordinated persons *(b)* employing a vast array of complex, diverse, and abundant equipment, in *(c)* multiple, diverse, complexly interrelated and vast spaces, over *(d)* a time span of generations. These are, of course, only ideal-typical extremes, rarely if ever embodied in empirical instances. They represent the end-point possibilities between which more typically occurring strategies may be located.[1] Among the array of more typically occurring "sizes" of strategies, four seem to be most important. As can be seen, these are the same as scales of situations, seen now in strategic perspective.

1. Encounter-scale strategies require a few seconds, minutes, or, at most, a few hours for their execution. The term "play" is useful here in suggesting briefness, as in "the action between two downs in football," in "the action in which cards are played after bidding in a card game," and in all ball games using the expression "in play." The terms "act," "ploy," "gambit," "method" (among others) are likewise suggestive of brief, situationally directed, and relatively simple lines of action. The term "act" is perhaps the most commonly employed everyday designation, as in "acts of homicide," "hostile act," "friendly act," and the like. The terms "procedure" and "activity" (plural as well as singular) are also sometimes used to indicate human lines of action of this duration. Examples of encounter-scale strategies include the fritters of student work avoidance, the rituals, taboos, and fetishes of baseball players, the styles of protective self-management of people waiting in public places, and the accounts offered by people whose conduct is questioned, to mention a few of those discussed in Chapter 8.

2. Role-scale strategies require varying periods of time from weeks to years, and varying populations, equipment, and space. Role-scale strategies include informal, argot roles and social types, methods of acquiring, defending, and maintaining power in roles, and mechanisms of managing a psychic relation to a role, among others discussed in Chapter 9. Concepts such as "life style," "personal style," "career," and "personality" capture (in part) the role scale of strategizing.

3. Group-scale strategies involve conjoint, coordinated, collective action lasting for weeks or more, as in the boredom-relieving devices of workers in monotonous machine shop jobs, the tactics intimates employ to rejuvenate their relationship, the games of stealing time practiced among metropolitan bus drivers, and the group-based esteem-protection mechanisms of low-status workers, among others reported in Chapter 10.

4. Organizational-scale strategies likely require months or years to execute, involving perhaps hundreds or thousands of people in a formally coordinated manner, as in, for example, the cooling-out processes employed by junior colleges in terminating students, the cooptation practices of organizations in defusing opposition, the pene-

tration strategies of combat parties in politics, and the service strategies of marginal education enterprises, among others detailed in Chapter 11. In everyday life the terms "program," "plan," and "campaign" often designate strategic efforts of this scale.

As was the case with situations, there are three larger scales of strategy—worlds, settlements, and societies—but for practical reasons we do not deal with them in this book.

In all these scales of strategies, *time* is perhaps the key dimension. How long does it take to *do* it? The longer it takes, the more people, equipment, and space are likely to become involved. Hence, by definition, the scale of social organization is likely to escalate as time increases. The first dimension to examine, then, in determining the strategic scales of action employed in a situation, is time and the amount of it involved.

II. SCALES OF SITUATIONS AND STRATEGIES: A SIMPLIFICATION

Encounters, roles, groups, and organizations can be and are both *contexts* of action—situations—and *units* of action—strategies (the latter being Herbert Blumer's apt but unappreciated "acting unit").[2] Considered conjointly as in Figure 1, it is also clear that any given scale of situation can be approached at various scales of strategy. Thus an organizational-scale situation (e.g., a university on the edge of bankruptcy) might be approached on the encounter scale of one or more conversations, the role scale of creating a position to deal with the matter, the group scale of a clique deciding to cope with the crisis, or the organizational scale involving the entire institution. That is, every scale of situation is likely to involve a complex array of strategic scales of coping. It is also likely to be useful carefully to distinguish scales in actual research and discussion.

These points form a prelude to indicating that although these variations of scale are evident in the materials reviewed in Part II of this volume, I have chosen to deemphasize them. I have largely acted as though encounter-scale situations are dealt with only, or at least mainly, with encounter-scale strategies, and so on, for the cells labeled 1 through 4 in Figure 1. I recognize that this may even be an unacceptable oversimplification of the studies treated, but without it the task of

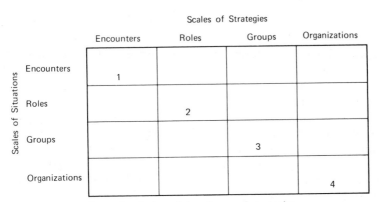

Figure 1. Scales of situations and strategies.

analysis becomes excessively arcane and intricate. That is, it is possible to be more accurate but at the sacrifice of interest and readability.[3]

III. QUALITATIVE STRATEGY ANALYSIS AND THE LARGER STUDY OF SOCIAL ORGANIZATION

The perspective expounded and the materials codified in this treatise form only one class of appropriate effort within a larger set of tasks involved in analyzing social organization. For the sake of clarity, I want to sketch these other and larger tasks and to indicate the place of the present work in that bigger picture.

The "bigger picture" has four prime types of concern: *(a)* units of social organization, *(b)* qualitative forms of social organization, *(c)* quantitative linkages of social organizations, and *(d)* analyses that are generic and novel.

A. Units of Social Organization. The most fundamental and generic subject matter of social science is not situations/strategies but *social organization,* the patterned, transpersonal conduct of human beings, the patterned way humans are interrelated.

Patterned ways in which humans are interrelated display *scale,* as has been explicated in this and the previous chapter. It needs now to be seen that the seven units we have conceived as "situations" and "strategies" are not only or merely contexts and scales of action but also entities or systems in and of themselves. They are creatures having their own dynamics. These seven—encounters, roles, groups, organizations, worlds, settlements, societies—or some more refined successor to them, are the basic subject matter, the objects, of a generically attuned social science.

B. Qualitative Forms of Social Organization. One asks questions of the units of social organization. One class of question is *qualitative* in that it seeks to identify basic aspects of such units regardless of the frequency of the aspects and their causes and consequences. There are three basic kinds of qualitative questions.

1.   What type of *structural* unit of social organization is this? What are its defining and general features?[4] Moving close within all the basic units of social organization, the effort is to identify detailed types. For example:

Encounters: focused, unfocused.
Roles: formal, informal, argot; hero, villain, fool.
Groups: clique, cabal, intimate.
Organizations: combat, bureaucratic, symbolic.

2.   What *processes* are found in various kinds of social organizations? What typical stages, phases, sequences, or cycles do various types of social organizations go through? For example:

Encounters: greeting, entering, leave-taking.
Roles: socialization, conversion, defection.
Groups: instrumental-expressive cycles, expulsion processes.
Organizations: co-optation, formalization, differentiation, recruitment, growth-decline.

3.   How do people do things in units of social organization? What are their generic situations and *strategies*? It is to this third qualitative question, virtually alone, that this entire volume is addressed.

C. Quantitative Links. All the qualitative depictions just mentioned of structure, process, and strategies have their antecedent causes, as well as consequences or functions.

1.   Whatever the unit of social organization and the more detailed

qualitative structure, process, or strategy, what are its causes, the conditions under which it is present or absent or present or absent to some degree?

2. All such detailed units are themselves causes in the sense that they have effects on other units of social organization and their participants. What are such consequences or functions?[5]

All these classes of questions appear interrelated in Figure 2. Column 7 is the almost exclusive focus of the present work. Matters of structure and process *per se*, on the one hand, and causes and consequences, on the other, are decidedly background and enter only to the degree they bear on the qualitative, strategic thrust of immediate concern. And, as has been said, attention is additionally confined to more micro units of social organization; namely, the cells in column 7 labeled *a, b, c,* and *d.*

D. Novel, Generic Analysis. Expressed as a governing ideal, actual research in any of these areas (table "cells") is guided by a desire for the "generic," as that term has been defined in Chapter 3, and by a desire for the *novel.* By "novel" I mean that the expenditure of human effort in social science is in part justified by seeing and showing something not already known, at least to the audience viewing it. The guidelines set forth in Part I only provide sensitivities to basic organizational and formal aspects of social reality. They do not of themselves say anything about specific, substantive, "generic" matters. Those have to be invented by the observer-analyst. It is a fundamental, creative task that remains, happily, lodged with the probing human developing intimate familiarity.

The achievement of novelty is facilitated, however, by some prior and reasonable acquaintance with what social scientists have already reported on a given topical or generic matter, ensuring that one avoids "discovering" what others in the field already take as common sense and as obvious. Such reasonable acquaintance also facilitates the conception of new variations on what is already known and accepted. In "type" terms, (question class B.1 in Figure 2), for example, there are questions such as the following: There is socialization here?[6] What special, new kind of socialization is it? We have families here? What special, novel kinds of families are they? We have careers here? What new types of careers are they? We have negotiated order here? What kind of negotiated order is it? Do they use hand gestures? What new, abstract class of hand gestures are they? All "type" questions can also be

A. Units of social organization ↓ / B. Qualitative forms →	D. Novel, generic analyses								
	1. Structures			2. Processes			3. Strategies		
	Types (1)	C. Quantitative links		Types (4)	C. Quantitative links		Types (7)	C. Quantitative links	
		Causes (2)	Consequences (3)		Causes (5)	Consequences (6)		Causes (8)	Consequences (9)
Encounters							*a*		
Roles							*b*		
Groups							*c*		
Organizations							*d*		
Worlds									
Settlements									
Societies									

Figure 2. Basic topics in the analysis of social organization.

rendered in process terms (question class B.2 in Figure 2), as in "What are special, new stages or phases of socialization?" And, they have a strategy rendering (question B.3 of Figure 2), the focus of this book, as in "What are novel strategies of socialization or self-socialization?"[7]

IV. TOPICAL VERSUS GENERIC CONCEPTUALIZATIONS OF STRATEGIES

Although not commonly thought of as strategies of dealing with situations, the topically designated actions and activities of everyday life do constitute such strategies. A random assortment of terms like working, reading, greeting, asking, confessing, lying, smiling, grimacing, and toting, among thousands of ordinary words designating action, are topical designations of strategies in the same way that a range of other terms were previously discussed as topical designations of situations.

Any act or more complex activity is a strategy to the degree that it is enacted to deal with a situation. To the degree, too, that any act has some determinate impact on a defined situation of interest, intended or not, it may be considered, for analytic purposes, to be a strategy.[8] As such, *topical* variations in strategies are legion and infinite in the same way that topical variations in situations are legion and infinite.

And, as indicated about situations, for purposes of extending the range of application, thereby maximizing usefulness, it is wise to reach beyond topicality and toward generic delineations of strategies. The previous elucidation of the term "generic" is precisely applicable here, modifying only the reference. Modifying that elucidation, then, we say that to conceive a strategy generically is to discriminate and bring forward social aspects that possess more generalized, more common, more universal relevance. A concrete strategy is scrutinized in terms of the following kinds of questions: Of what abstract, sociologically conceived class of strategy is this particular strategy an instance? What are the abstract features of this kind of strategy? What kind of strategy is this? To answer such questions about a concrete strategy is to offer a generic portrayal of that strategy.

Eight illustrations of generically conceived *situations* were offered in discussing generic construals of situations in Chapter 3. We may now consider the "other half" of the *same* eight studies, indicating some of the prime generic strategies reported by these observer-analysts:

1. Aspects of the topical activities typically engaged in by students (e.g., reading, writing papers, going to the library, studying with friends) may be viewed as generic *fritter strategies,* including such generic tactics as "rest on your laurels," and "what's my rate?"[9]
2. Aspects of the topical activities of machine operators (e.g., operating a punch machine, taking a break) may be viewed as instances of the generic strategies of *the game of work* and *times,* among others.[10]
3. Aspects of the topical activities of milkmen (e.g., delivering milk, collecting bills) may be viewed as instances of the interpersonal, generic strategy of *cultivating,* including such generic tactics as "the sincerity act," "contrived disclosure," and "accentuated honesty."[11]
4. Aspects of the topical activities of baseball players (e.g. batting, pitching, and their attendant routines) may be conceived as generic and strategic *rituals, taboos, and fetishes.*[12]
5. Aspects of how physically handicapped people interact over time with physically normal people (e.g., joking allusions to the handicap, highly attentive and sympathetic stance toward the normal) may be conceived as a generic strategy of *deviance disavowal.*[13]
6. The mundane, topical activities people often engage in while waiting in a public place (e.g., reading, looking about at objects in the place, arranging and rearranging packages being carried) may be conceived of as generic strategies of *protective self-management,* including the styles of "the sweet young thing," "the nester," and "the investigator."[14]
7. Aspects of the mundane and topical routines of traditional Chinese households (e.g., sleeping, eating, talking) may be conceived as generic strategies for *making crowded conditions acceptable,* including such arrangements as sharp differentiation of function by room and loose and flexible time management.[15]
8. Aspects of cabdrivers' daily activities may be conceived as generic strategies of *uncertainty reduction and calculability enhancement,* including such arrangements as a cab culture typology of cab users and tactics and stratagems of fare management.[16]

Each of these studies strives to lay out *classes* and *types* descriptive of how people in the given (generically delineated) situation deal with that situation. Each of the italicized terms listed is a "line of action," "strategy," or whichever of those virtually interchangeable terms one prefers to use. Read in the context of its own complete report, each provides a picture of "how people do social things" in the situation each respectively specifies.

V. VARIATIONS IN DEGREE OF DEFINITION

As with situations, the degree to which strategies are clear, structured, known, and unambiguous varies greatly. Comparing four levels of management, Norman Martin observed the shift foremen

> to function almost completely in terms of alternatives which are ready-made and enduring—given in the form of rules. In the words of one division superintendent, "Once the foremen decide that something has to be done, the rest is pretty well a matter of course—what they do and how." Action is here almost "ministerial," in that the basic question is whether or not a specific situation warrants invoking a particular rule.
>
> At the other extreme, the works manager frequently encounters situations in which the alternatives must be constructed. To illustrate, the works manager had received instructions from his superior to reduce costs. While the general direction is clear, here was a situation in which the various possible alternatives were not given. They had to be constructed. Formulations of these alternatives were based upon cues provided by production and cost data. The "how," however, had to be developed and worked out.
>
> In between these two extremes, the division superintendent and department foremen levels were concerned with decision situations of a mixed form.[17]

The content of variations in degree of definition in this illustration is technical, but the principle is otherwise the same: the "social how" of the situations of everyday life in modern society is differentially given and is differentially known to participants. Those that are best known and most standardized we call, indeed, rituals, formalities, protocol, and matters of etiquette. Other situations—say, delivering bad news to someone—are much less well defined in the sense that people who happen to be involved in them often do not have a sure sense of how to act or even of the range of ways in which they might act. And it is precisely these least codified strategies that most deserve close empirical study in an effort to transform the inchoate into the choate.

VI. STRATEGIC CONSCIOUSNESS AND STRATEGIC SIGNIFICANCE

The terms strategy, tactics, ploys, and so on, imply human intention or "goal-directed" behavior. They imply persons who are *consciously* choosing and engaging in action in order to deal with matters of concern to them. This is as it should be. People *do* often consciously choose and engage in action in order to deal with matters of concern to them.

But according to the "passivist" students of social science (discussed in the next chapter), people are very often not acting in such a conscious, calculating, goal-directed manner. They are merely reacting or complying. Calculation, deliberation, and intention are absent from their consciousness. Scholars of social life who emphasize human consciousness and strategic orientation tend even to overimpute, to see strategic consciousness, intent, and savvy where little or none exists. To the degree that they overimpute, they misrepresent humans in the social life under scrutiny, critics say. Specifically, in the works of Erving Goffman, especially in *Presentation of Self in Everyday Life,* there is overimputation of strategic consciousness, intent, and savvy.

These allegations require comment at two levels. First, it seems to be definitely true that situation and strategy studies overimpute strategic intent, consciousness, and savvy to the people studied. Of course many of them carry brief disclaimers, on the order of

> The extent to which [the milkmen studied]...were cognizant of the fact that they were manipulating, persuading, and so forth was minimal. I mention this to avoid leaving the impression that they saw themselves as game players, consciously employing tactics and strategies.[18]

But such isolated, disclaiming passages are exactly that: isolated disclaimers. The actual studies rest centrally on a thoroughgoing, strategically conscious, and savvy actor. Or at least, a *collective actor* or type emerges who is much more sophisticated than any one or a few of the people studied are likely to have been. Indeed, it is the very pooling and compositing of the limited, partial, and intermittent strategic consciousness and savvy of a large number of people in a situation that gives rise to the collective, supersavvy, superstrategic, supercalculative social type conveyed in situation-strategy studies.

Second, I would defend this overimputation and the emergent collective superstrategist as a virtue rather than a vice, a strength rather than a weakness. Actions have strategic consequences in, upon, and on, a situation regardless of whether anyone in that situation consciously intends those consequences. "Unthinking," "mindless," "habitual," "routine" action does not necessarily lack strategic *significance* (consequence or import) simply because the person performing it does not consciously perceive or intend strategic significance. Situations and strategies have an objective existence, a makeup, and systemic interaction that is independent of what any particular participant might hold in consciousness. Therefore the limits of participant consciousness should not set limits on analyst discernment of strategic significance.[19]

The relation between a so-called paranoid person and his associates aptly elucidates this distinction between strategic consciousness and significance. When we say that thinking is "paranoid" we usually mean that a person imputes strategic consciousness *and* strategic significance to the acts of his associates. A distinction between consciousness and significance allows us to see that the paranoid person's associates may well be acting in a manner that can plausibly be imbued with strategic significance, though not consciousness. The associates may in fact be acting in ways that have systematic malevolent consequences for the person, even though the associates attach no such consciousness, intention, or conspiratorial meaning to their own actions. The paranoid may be making an accurate strategic analysis of the strategic significance of his associates' acts, although he is incorrectly construing their consciousness and their relations among themselves with regard to carrying on a conspiracy. If we now substitute "situation" for "paranoid person" we have a statement of the frame of mind assumed by situation and strategy analysts when scrutinizing social life in terms of its strategic construction.

Along different lines, there are humanistic or moral grounds for analysts to overintentionalize action. Passivist social science (my expository nemesis to be introduced shortly) seems to be dedicated to demonstrating that people are controlled and trapped—to the proposition that humans are, as Herbert Blumer puts it, media through which impersonal, objective, uncontrolled, and uncontrollable forces operate. Humans are puppets and pawns. Such an image is demonstrably true to a degree, but only to a degree. In contrast, activist social science is dedicated to demonstrating that humans can act back and perhaps to a degree sometimes "get free." To discern, to find strategic significance in action where perhaps *none* of the participants sees any, is to imbue that action with strategic relevance, thereby extending the range of strategic consciousness. When analysts point out, say, the strategic character of "a young American middle-class girl playing dumb for the benefit of her boyfriend," or more importantly that being the "young American middle-class girl" is itself a performance, even though the participants are not aware of it,[20] comprehenders of such an analysis *have extended the range of what now they can make choices about.* To extend the range and variety of strategic consciousness through overimputing strategic consciousness is to extend the range and variety of matters over which people in social life *can* exercise control and change their strategies, or their situations, if they so desire. Strategic consciousness, arising from rampant imputing of strategic significance, promotes freedom.

More broadly, overintentionalizing may be thought of as an appropriate corrective to the dominant practice of underintentionalizing. Passivist social science encourages humans in everyday life to de-emphasize a belief in their own intentionality, will, or ability to make choices. "My role demands that I do this, I therefore must do it." "My childhood socialization forces me to act in this despicable way." "I'm fat because my wife has too much food around the house." (Predating social science: "God led me to this.") These kinds of statements are bad faith declinations to assume responsibility for one's own actions—one's own intentions and one's own capacity to make decisions. Given the ubiquity of such statements, an intentional overcorrection of under-intentionality seems to be appropriate. To "overintentionalize" is, morally speaking, to insist on responsibility for one's actions, regardless of how the actor may at the moment conceive himself and his relation to his acts.

VII.   VARIATIONS IN STRATEGIC CONSCIOUSNESS

For better or worse, acute strategic consciousness seems to be the *consciousness of underdogs,* such as ethnic and sexual minorities and individuals seen as personally peculiar. Underdogs are those not in power; those dependent, those who can be deprived; those cast out and done violence to. Disadvantaged thus, they become sensitive to what "the man," "men" (or whatever) are doing, what the overdogs want, and what they might "really mean" by their actions. Disadvantaged thus, they become highly sensitive to the impression their actions are making on the overdog: "Do my actions elicit favor or punishment from the overdog?" In being sensitive to the powerful because the powerful can by definition reward or punish them, the underdogs' sense of self develops a dramaturgic quality, a consciousness of how they can and do manipulate others. Being less fearful of others, overdogs are not situationally induced to develop quite the same kind of wedge between their actions and their calculation of subtle, manipulative effects.[21]

VIII. THE DRAMATURGIC ASPECT OF STRATEGY: WHAT PEOPLE DO VERSUS THE WAY THEY DO IT

To appreciate more acutely the strategic character of human action, it is useful to distinguish *what* people do from the *way* in which they do it. By "what people do" I mean the bald behaviors in which they engage—the lowest level, the least interpreted portrayal of the motions they go through. "A said he disagreed with B." "A did not consult with B before doing X." The "what" of people doing is the nonevaluative, legalistic view of their verbal and physical action. In contrast, the "way" of people doing concerns the manner, style, and nuance "laid over," "on," or "around" the sheer what of their doing. A can disagree with B, but there are many manners and styles in which this can be accomplished. A can decline to consult with B, but there are a great many manners and styles of so declining.

Humans appear to be the kind of creatures for whom the *way* other people do things is virtually as important as *what* they do. It is a matter of familiar observation that two people can engage in virtually identical substantive actions, but one person hedges and embeds his "what" in a set of stylistic definitions and gestures that prompt participants and witnesses to perceive the one action and its actor as drastically different from the other actor and his action. Thus some observers of relations between the United States Senate and the President in 1973 claimed that Senate animosity toward Richard Nixon (over, e.g., impoundment, war powers, Watergate, executive privilege) had less to do with the

President's mere assertion that his office had extraordinary powers and privileges in these matters (the "what") than with the President's failure to give Senators individual courtesies and to abide by traditional etiquette of Senate-President relations (the "way"). In the words of Senator Hubert Humphrey:

> That's what got most of these fellows mad around here. Nixon robs you without any courtesy. Now, Johnson used to rob the Senate, but when he wanted to take something from you, he'd invite you to lunch. He'd put his arms around you and talk to you while he picked your pocket. You'd go away thinking you'd contributed something, and you'd at least feel consulted. But Nixon sticks you up in the night. You don't even see him. It's like rape without any personal contact. I mean, the Senators are used to being had, but not to being ignored. That drives them mad. Under Nixon, you find out about program cuts on cheap departmental press releases. You don't get advance notice from the President, and the Senators miss that White House stationery.[22]

How, more concretely, do the "ways" of people acting vary? Adopting the point of view of the person who must attend to his own "ways" of doing, one can point to four prime clusters of items typically subject to actor effort to control and modify in order to guide the way of doing. Such clusters are major dimensions along which strategies vary when seen "dramaturgically."

A. Manner. Most obvious and most overtly, "way" involves personal manner, style, or nuance. By tone of voice, facial gestures, body postures, content of verbal utterances, and the like, persons embed the sheer "what" of their actions, as we know from everyday observation. It is useful to think of personal manner in terms of the three phases during which it is problematic: *(a)* preparation for a strategy, *(b)* execution of a strategy, and *(c)* follow-up on a strategy. A strategic personal manner in one phase need not be the most effective and appropriate in another phase; a manner that can be sustained for one phase may not be sustainable in another.

Within each of these phases the task toward which the tactics of personal manner are directed may be *(a) preventive* (effort taken to forestall difficulties in furthering the strategy), *(b) constructive* (activity necessary directly to furthering the strategy), or *(c) reparative* (effort directed to shoring up an emerged difficulty that the participant is now striving to contain, encyst, encapsulate, cover up, or annihilate).

Relative to encounter-scale strategies, Eugene Weinstein has offered some suggestive thinking on the phasing of personal manner tactics in the situation of "insuring appropriate interpretation." Among his many observations, let me point up:

> When an act can have several meanings to another, which carry different evaluative implications regarding the actor, one way of trying to insure favorable evaluation is to offer an interpretation prior to action (preinterpretation or printerp). "Now, be sure not to take this the wrong way. I don't want you to think...."
>
> [After an act] the other person's responses may provide us with information that he has drawn inferences from our acts which are undesired. Posterps are used as corrective devices. "Oh, no, that's not what I meant..." followed by some statement taking the apparent evaluative sting out of some prior act is a ubiquitous postinterpretation.[23]

B. Identity. Ways of doing vary in terms of who the person claims to be. Psychological social psychologists have been assiduous in showing that *who* does a "what" is rather centrally important to the manner in which identical actions are perceived and received. Having known and appreciated this long before there were any psychological social psychologists, astute strategists have always given careful attention to how they might manipulate who they say they are, or have been, or will be, most auspiciously to control the reception afforded their projected, current, or past actions. A general principle in such manipulation is: the more extraordinary the action one wants others to define favorably, the more extraordinary a person one must claim to be. Thus extraordinary acts such as murder, rape, adultery, and military conquest often prompt their engagers to lay claim to identities such as God, Son of God, God's Right-Hand Man, Super Man, or some equivalently important identity that "weighs as much," as it were, and "balances the action."

C. Place. "Way" varies importantly but somewhat less obviously in terms of the place or places where the "what"—the bald strategy—is prepared, executed, and followed up. This has already been spoken about in terms of the physical variations of (*a*) population, (*b*) equipment (or props), and (*c*) space (or container). In addition to these extremely gross (but fundamentally important) elements, refined strategists take assiduous account of what David Bennett and Judith Bennett have analyzed as *(d)* "modifiers":

Light: sources, intensity, direction, color.
Sound: volume, pitch, intensity, duration, source, direction.
Color: hues, location, mixture, chromatic intensities.
Texture: location, mixture.
Odor: sources, mixture.
Relative temperature and humidity.[24]

Dramaturgic experts in social life practice "the principle of the extra-ordinary" with regard to places, too. Stated most generally, the more extraordinary the "what" a person wants to pull off, the more extraordinary the "way" in which the what is likely to be embedded. The more out of the ordinary and egregious the bald actions, the more out of the ordinary and egregious are embellishments of the act, a principle long central to the practice of mystics and politicos. Relative to places, we thus find, as reported by Bennett and Bennett, that "the physical building or space which forms the symbolic edifice of superhuman power, whether God, Hero, or State, seem to have [certain] universal characteristics":

1. Tremendous size in relation to other buildings, or, when diminutive in actual size, as in the case of some shrines in both Oriental and Occidental civilizations, a scale (i.e., a relation of the elements of the object to the whole), which suggests tremendous size.
2. An expression of great stability, durability, and immutability, often achieved by symmetry, and when not, by a highly stylized arrangement of objects or parts of the whole.
3. A carefully organized progression of spaces (be it the entrance to an ancient Egyptian royal tomb, the path through the Acropolis of Athens, the forecourt to a Shinto shrine, the road to Versailles, or the monumental steps up to almost any seat of judgment of any time or place in the Western world) arranged so that they are experienced as a linear sequence of events invested with awesome meaning. Similarly, other symbolic-physical arrangements seemingly have the same cross-cultural uniformity.[25]

D. Timing. The astute strategist consciously deliberates, last, the timing aspects of his act: *(a)* when, *(b)* for how long, and *(c)* with what type of progression is the act carried forth? First there is a question of *when* to perform an act, to avoid acting either too soon or too late, or in inappropriate juxtaposition with what might occur before or after the act. Second, there is a question of the *duration* of the act, the degree to which it can be drawn out with good effect, or needs to be shortened with good effect. Third, any given action contains a degree of internal flexibility posing decisions of *progression* of internal elements of the act.[26]

I have tried in this chapter to indicate the nature of and variations in interaction strategies, to set the qualitative study of situations and strategies in the larger context of analyzing social organization, to indicate the relation of strategic consciousness to strategic significance, and to explain the dramaturgic dimension of social action.

We return to methodological aspects in the next chapter, specifically, to the form in which data and concepts can most auspiciously be reported.

NOTES TO CHAPTER FOUR

1. Although this "most complex," "longest" strategy is intended as a logical rather than empirical possibility, it is eerily faithful in representing the "size" of the strategic thinking and acting of American rulers in the post-World War II period. See David Halberstam, *The Best and the Brightest* (New York: Random House, 1972).

2. Herbert Blumer, *Symbolic Interactionism* (Englewood Cliffs, N.J.: Prentice-Hall, 1969).

3. On how social science easily becomes more involved than anyone cares about, see Murray Davis, " 'That's Interesting!': Toward a Phenomenology, of Sociology and a Sociology of Phenomenology," *Philosophy of Science,* 1:309–344 (January 1971).

4. Cf. Max Weber, *The Methodology of the Social Sciences* (New York: Free Press, 1949), pp. 89–112; Joseph Lopreato and Letitia Alson, "Ideal Types and the Idealization Strategy," *American Sociological Review,* **35**:88–96 (February 1970); Julian Simon, *Basic Research Methods in Social Science* (New York: Random House, 1969), Ch. 4, "Types of Empirical Research."

5. For more detailed discussion of quantitative links among units of social organization, see John Lofland, *Analyzing Social Settings* (Belmont, Calif.: Wadsworth, 1971), Ch. 3, "Causes and Consequences."

6. I draw here and below from my "Styles of Reporting Qualitative Field Research," *The American Sociologist*, **9:**101–111 (August 1974).

7. One answer to this specific question is provided by Roger Straus, "Changing Oneself," in Chapter 13 of this book. On organizational-scale strategies of socialization, see below, Chapter 11, Section III.B, "Socializing." For further discussion of the problem of novelty, see the brilliant analysis of Murray Davis, "That's Interesting," *op. cit.* On the analysis of social organization more generally, Marvin Olsen's text, *The Process of Social Organization* (New York: Holt, Rinehart and Winston, 1968), especially Chapter 14, "Analysis of Social Organization," is quite helpful.

8. The relation of strategy to human consciousness and intention is discussed in a moment.

9. Stan Bernstein, "Getting It Done: Notes on Student Fritters," *Urban Life and Culture*, **1:**275–292 (October 1972), capsulized in Section V.A.2 of Chapter 8 in this book.

10. Donald F. Roy, "Banana Time: Job Satisfaction and Informal Interaction," *Human Organization*, **18:**158–168 (Winter, 1959–60), reprinted in Chapter 13.

11. Odis E. Bigus, "The Milkman and His Customers: A Cultivated Relationship," *Urban Life and Culture*, **1:**131–165 (July 1972), summarized in Section III.C of Chapter 8.

12. George Gmelch, "Baseball Magic," *Trans-Action*, June 1971, pp. 39–41, 54, summarized in Section V.B of Chapter 8.

13. Fred Davis, *Illness, Interaction, and the Self* (Belmont, Calif.: Wadsworth, 1972), Ch. 8, summarized in Section IV.C.3 of Chapter 9.

14. Lyn H. Lofland, "Self Management in Public Settings: Parts I and II," *Urban Life and Culture*, **1:**93–108, 217–231 (April and July, 1972), summarized in Section II.A of Chapter 8. See also her *A World of Strangers: Order and Action in Urban Public Space* (New York: Basic Books, 1973).

15. E. N. Anderson, "Some Chinese Methods of Dealing with Crowding," *Urban Anthropology*, **1:**141–150 (Fall 1972), summarized in Section III.B.3 of Chapter 10.

16. Fred Davis, "The Cabdriver and His Fare: Facets of a Fleeting Relationship," *American Journal of Sociology*, **65:**158–165 (September 1959), capsulized in part in Section III.C of Chapter 8.

17. Norman Martin, "Differential Decisions in the Management of an Industrial Plant," *Journal of Business*, **29:**255 (October 1956).

18. Bigus, "The Milkman," *op. cit.*, p. 141.

19. Cf. Sheldon L. Messinger, *et al.*, "Life as Theater," *Sociometry*, **25:**98–109 (March 1962).

20. The illustration is from Erving Goffman, *Presentation of Self in Everyday Life* (Garden City, N.Y.: Doubleday-Anchor, 1959), pp. 74–75.

21. For further discussion see Section III.C of Chapter 9, this book, and R. Stephen Warner, David T. Wellman, and Lenore J. Weitzman, "The Hero, The Sambo and The Operator: Three Characterizations of the Oppressed," *Urban Life and Culture*, **2:**53–84 (April 1973). More generally, however, a basic strategic consciousness in the sense of regularly envisioning and deliberating courses of action and their comparative consequences is at the very core of being both human and social. Indeed, deficiencies in the habits of "perceiving options" and "thinking of consequences" make trouble for participating in social life at all (but are correctable). See the

provocative research of Jerome Platt, George Spivack, and their associates, including: Jerome Platt and George Spivack, "Social Competence and Effective Problem-Solving Thinking in Psychiatric Patients," *Journal of Clinical Psychology,* **28:**3–5 (January 1972); Jerome Platt, William Scura, and James R. Hannon, "Problem-Solving Thinking of Youthful Incarcerated Heroin Addicts," *Journal of Community Psychology,* in press.

22. Hubert Humphrey, quoted in Taylor Branch, "Profiles in Caution: The Senate's Bad Advice and Grudging Consent," *Harper's Magazine,* July 1973, p. 72. Indeed, Richard Nixon seems to have fallen less because of what he did, than because of the inept dramaturgic manner in which he managed what he did.

23. Eugene A. Weinstein, "Towards a Theory of Interpersonal Tactics," in Carl Backman and Paul Second, eds., *Problems in Social Psychology* (New York: McGraw-Hill, 1966), p. 395. See also John Hewitt and Randall Stokes, "Disclaimers," *American Sociological Review,* **40:**1–11 (February 1975).

24. David J. Bennett and Judith D. Bennett, "Making the Scene," in Gregory P. Stone and Harvey A. Farberman, eds., *Social Psychology Through Symbolic Interaction* (Waltham, Mass.: Ginn-Blaisdell, 1970), p. 196. See further their complete paradigm of "the components and dimensions of scenes," focusing on *(a)* the setting, *(b)* modifiers, *(c)* duration, and *(d)* progression.

25. *Ibid.*

26. More detailed materials on the dramaturgics of social action are capsulized in the various chapters of Part II. Dennis Brissett and Charles Edgley, eds., *Life as Theater: A Dramaturgical Sourcebook* (Chicago: Aldine, 1975) strives to depict the general perspective. The anthology just cited appeared as this work was completed and I could not take account of its contributions or incorporate them into this treatise.

CHAPTER FIVE

Developing Disciplined Abstractions

The notions of "situation" and "strategy" discussed in Chapters 3 and 4 provide a perspective on thinking about human action. Chapter 2 on "intimate familiarity" and the present chapter differ from those on situations and strategies in that they propound a view of a requirement for (i.e., intimate familiarity) and a characteristic of (i.e., disciplined abstractions) one kind of important human knowledge.

Most simply stated, the view advanced in this chapter is that the human mind using a situation-strategy perspective and intimate familiarity with a sector of social life can, does, and should produce a valuable form of analysis made up of "disciplined abstractions." By "disciplined abstractions" I mean generic and generalized types and aspects of situations and strategies that emerge from personal immersion in concrete, qualitative data and remain adequately grounded in such data in written reports.

The first part of this chapter sets forth characteristics of disciplined abstractions and indicates how they are developed. The second part contrasts this form of social science analysis and reporting with four other forms.

I. DISCIPLINED ABSTRACTIONS

The label "disciplined abstractions" is composed of two concepts that are inextricably interdependent but I must nonetheless and for a moment separate them for purposes of explication.

A. Abstractions. Abstractions are words "disassociated from any specific instances," to quote a dictionary. It is one of the marvels of the human creature that we have the capacity for (and sometimes, sadly, the propensity to indulge in) what is rightly called "abstract thinking," which is thought "disassociated from any specific instances." Despite pitfalls, abstraction is fundamentally necessary to summarize and order what otherwise is incoherent, un-understandable, therefore unaction-able, raw reality. Through the process of articulate abstracting—literal-ly naming—we humans *create* the world through linguistic calling at-tention to aspects of it. Through labeling, it becomes possible to "see" what was there all along but was otherwise invisible. In Sherlock Holmes' famous phrase, "You see but you do not observe."[1] It is through the magic of labeling that matters formerly obscure even become obvious, as one commentator has said of genius labeler Erving Goffman: "Like the hidden face in the picture, it's not hard to see, once it's pointed out; Goffman not only sees it, but makes the rest of us see it too."[2]

The studies capsulized in Part II of this volume have been reduced for reporting purposes to their essential abstractions. The array of them illustrate abundantly the notion of the ordering, informing char-acter of abstractions *per se*.

B. Disciplined. Abstractions alone, however, are an abomination upon the land, a fact the materials as reported by me in Part II also illustrates. The human mind has the capacity for virtually pure abstract thought—"thought disassociated from any specific instances." Like other capacities, people are prone to exercise it for the sheer joy of the act in and of itself, as with running, talking, or sexing. However much fun and/or fruitful the sheer exercise of abstracting may be for many purposes, it is, in my view, debilitating in social matters. It is in the nature of social matters that abstractions become highly indefinite and misleading unless they are constantly constrained and disciplined by continual reference to and interplay with concrete, qualitative data. Herbert Blumer's characterization of the problem, quoted in Chapter 2, is so apt that I repeat it here:

> Most of the improper use of the concept in science comes when the concept is set apart from the world of experience, when it is di-vorced from the perception from which it has arisen and into which it ordinarily ties. Detached from the experience which brought it

into existence, it is almost certain to become indefinite and meta-physical. I have always admired a famous statement of Kant which really defines the character of the concept and indicates its limitations. Kant said brilliantly, "perception without conception is blind; conception without perception is empty."[3]

The question, then, is how to have abstractions—concepts—that do not become empty.

C. Disciplined Abstractions.   Abstractions seems most likely to be disciplined when they, first, *develop* out of an observer's own intense, good-faith, intimate familiarity with a sector of social life. Guided by a general perspective (such as situation-strategy), the observer tunes himself into the flowing, yet tangible life presented him either directly in participant observation, less directly in intensive interviewing, or in some more indirect but reasonable manner.[4] He immerses himself in qualitative data, by which I mean immersion in that we typically describe as

episodes
incidents
events
exchanges
remarks
happenings
conversations
actions

He strives to accumulate a *raw record* that is eventful in the sense of a set of things that strike him as "noteworthy occurrences." Data are collected, that is, by means of attending to and recording the running episodes of everyday life. Procedurally, the analyst is a compulsive looker, reader, and notetaker (and/or intensive interviewer and tape recording transcriber), building up perhaps hundreds or thousands of pages of episodes. Either during the observation/interviewing/reading period or after, the episodes are sorted and classified, re-sorted, and reclassified until a faithful and detailed analysis is achieved. (Since the minute procedural and technical details of these processes of "participant observation," "intensive interviewing," and other techniques of qualitative analysis are reasonably straightforward and are amply described in standard manuals, I will not dwell on technical aspects.)[5]

Second, because of the intimate interplay between perspective (situation-strategy notions in the present context), the accumulating qualitative data, and the emergent abstractions, written reports have an interpenetrated character; that is, the abstractions and qualitative data coexist as one whole.[6] Each depends on the other for enlightenment and meaning. Taken separately, the abstractions and data may have slight interest or merit. The abstractions are likely to be dull because the reader has an inadequate conception of the concrete, empirical reality to which they might refer. The qualitative data alone are dull because the reader has little notion of generic patterns involved, save those he might himself be imposing. But interpenetration through minute and continual alternation between abstraction and episodes makes the whole more than the parts. This discussion will itself be less abstract and more disciplined (!) if the reader scrutinizes in this context the four studies appearing in Part III of this volume. I have felt it imperative, indeed, to provide several studies to make it possible easily and concretely to see this point *in vivo*. The capsules of studies that compose Part II commit, in contrast, the sin of excessive abstraction. I have tried to redeem that sin with the examples of disciplined abstraction offered in Part III, where the example studies continually alternate between *(a)* abstract categories of situational features and types of generic strategies and *(b)* description of concrete things that people are doing that embody these abstract categories. Abstractions are continually "touched down" by concrete instances, because in developing analysis, concrete instances have "touched off" abstractions. In this sense, the concrete and the abstract coexist.

Independent of such interpenetration, there is a question of the portion of a report that ought to be abstractions and concepts, as opposed to concrete, qualitative episodes. There are no set rules about this, and there likely should not be. Actual reports vary considerably, but it is my impression that the more credible and lauded of reports are some 30 to 40 percent abstractions and some 60 to 70 percent qualitative events. That is, reporters and readers alike seem to feel best informed when more than half a report is events, anecdotes, episodes, and the like, and a strong minority of the work is conceptual discussion. Inspection of the four studies in Part III reveals considerable variation, but a tendency to this kind of a "balance."

It is, then, out of the interplay between abstract sensitivities and hundreds of episodes that the emergent generic delineation of the situation and its strategies has the character of being grounded in the concrete reality of the empirical world. The analyst

1. Begins with an abstract sense of what a generic situation is and what generic strategies are.
2. Immerses himself in the concrete items of the actual social life under study.
3. Develops and constructs a generically framed analysis of situations and strategies from the organic intertwining of items 1 and 2.

Qualitative strategy analysts are simultaneously deductive (Chapters 3 and 4 on situations and strategies are "principles") and inductive (episodes are the unanalyzed data), a straddling that Barney Glaser and Anselm Strauss have aptly termed a "grounded" approach.[7]

And these procedures and forms are founded on the epistemological conviction that effective human thought and action are best facilitated by disciplined alternation between the abstract and the concrete. To deal only at the level of the concrete is to be a prisoner of minutiae—to not see the forest for the trees. To deal only at the level of the abstract is to be limited to empirically empty concepts—to deal in floating, airy, mental entities divorced from empirical reality. Each direction alone is sterile. It is through the intimate interplay of the concrete and the abstract that knowledge, understanding, and action are most effectively developed.

II. CONTRASTING FORMS

This "qualitative-analytic-descriptive" form of data collection, analysis, and reporting stands in sharp contrast to several other types of efforts to describe and analyze situations and strategies in particular and social life in general. To clarify them all, let us briefly outline these forms and make comparisons.

A. Undisciplined Abstractions. Strategies and situations are of course the signal concern of what is commonly called "game theory," a tradition of thought heavily relying on mathematical and statistical images, notations, and operations, often in conjunction with laboratory

experimentation or "simulation." This tradition seems to be most outstanding in the degree to which it disattends empirical materials on
actual people engaged in action in real situations. The enterprise of
game theory is impressively hypothetical, giving rise to extremely
complex and esoteric models that are divorced from empirical reality in
the sense that the real-world situations and strategies "modeled" appear to be much more straightforward and commonsensically intelli-
gent than game theory constructions construe them to be. Game theory
representations of relations among nations are especially striking in this
respect, displaying a remarkable tendency to depict an international
world that is complex and involuted far beyond the cognitive operations (and capacities) of actual rulers. One suspects that the rulers of
the real nations of the world would not perform at all well in the
make-believe international relations worlds of game theory. But of
course the real actions of real nations are far from being the empirical
data to which game theory addresses itself, and game theory therefore
is little inconvenienced by features of empirical reality. In short, there
is a situation and strategy genre that is abstracted, nonempirical, and
formalistic, a toy of a particular set of intellectuals.

Less complicated than game theory and more rampant is what might
be called "abstracted conceptualism," a practice parallel to what C.
Wright Mills termed "abstracted empiricism."[8] In abstracted
conceptualism, the analyst becomes so involved in the dynamics of his
analysis *per se* (categories, variations, types, properties, etc.) that he
ceases to care about the empirical materials he is trying to understand.
Mills labeled the armchair and macroscopic version "Grand Theory,"
but a broader term is needed adequately to characterize it among
researchers who supposedly have collected data and are microscopically
focused. (None of this applies to Grand Theorists.) In one fieldwork
variant, the researcher makes some brief forays into a natural setting or
performs a few fast interviews, then sits down to spin out all the
features, properties, and categories he can imagine about rapidly chosen conceptions of the situation and its strategies. The analysis is only
tenuously suggested by or developed out of the few materials at the
observer's command, however. The report may contain elaborate
claims about fieldwork, grounded theory, and the like, but it is more
representative of reporter imagination and than of events from the real
world. The report consists of virtually pure exercises in abstracted
conceptualism in the form of ungrounded, arid essays on interaction
strategies (and many other matters) that do not even pretend to an

intimately familiar, disciplined empirical component. However laudable his work might be otherwise, a significant portion of Erving Goffman's essays move in such a direction.[9]

B. Narrativism. At the other extreme, there are reporters, commentators, and scholars of ongoing public events who deal constantly with materials that lend themselves to situation and strategy analysis. Historians, political scientists, the more thorough journalists (such as David Halberstam[10]), especially, deal in the stuff of current events, the ongoing flow of social life. They often report with great acuteness, and they habitually refer to intentions, goals, strategies, and so forth. Unlike game theorists, they are in possession of real data on real people in real situations. But they do not use an articulate situation and strategy or any other generically attuned framework. They are more oriented to a simple rendering of events, largely unanalyzed, or not very thoroughly analyzed—at least not analyzed in a situation and strategy perspective.

The work of many qualitatively oriented *social scientists* is sometimes difficult to distinguish from that of lay narrativists, but several salient forms are nonetheless identifiable. In the most "narrativistic," the *protocol style,* the report starts with a paragraph or two saying that the area studied represents an important kind of social life or social problem and provides a set of interview or observation transcripts. In some cases the author has written four or five of the document's thirty to sixty pages. The assumption seems to be either that the significance of the raw materials is so obvious that no further work on the author's part is required, or that the material is interesting enough to render superfluous any analysis by the author.

Somewhat less narrativistic is the *Then They Do This* style. Direct observation of a setting makes evident that participants do many kinds of things over and over, hour to hour, day to day, week to week, and the organization of a report can be based on this fact. If the social life observed is exotic, descriptions so organized are fascinating. Indeed, a significant portion of what qualitative field researchers define as good or excellent fieldwork is in the style of "Then They Do This, Then They Do That." Its interest arises from being about social life that is exotic to readers. Reader approval is a response to "cute," "interesting," "startling," or "erotic" descriptive content. Field workers not wanting to suffer through analysis are best advised, indeed, to pick exotic field settings. Yet the "Then They Do This, Then They Do That" style is not to be disparaged *per se*. An account of repetitive activities is absolutely fundamental and indispensable. But such an account is not yet an analysis.

There are two main variations on "Then They Do This." One provides a composite picture of events, the kind of common-sense typification encountered in the Sunday supplement and slick magazine articles describing settings and occupations. People are quoted and field notes are extracted in an artful way. Seldom found in print, the other variation is mostly circulated in manuscript form. It relies heavily on multiple-page quotes from unedited field notes. Raw field notes tend to be ungrammatical, rambling, and free-flowing. A variety of observations on different topics are interspersed with longer descriptions of events. Authors who quote field notes at length in their reports appear to believe that their chaotic scribblings are precious. Four and five page extracts, inflicted unedited on readers, are used to illustrate simple points. (Unlike the protocol style, these reporters write a few, double-spaced pages between their long, single-spaced extracts.)

When the reporter *does* have a conceptual sensitivity to situations and strategies (or some other kind of basic question), difficulties sometimes arise in the form of *hypereventfulness*. The conceptual components are strong (perhaps even novel), but grounded to the teeth. The recital of incidents, histories, episodes, and so forth, goes on seemingly without end and becomes a bore and frustration.

The 60–70/30–40 balance guideline applied to a report as a whole must also and especially be applied to a report's micro units, to the rendering of events themselves, particularly events and quotations set single space. Perhaps merely for reasons of eye strain, well-received presentations of quotations, episodes, and events appear rarely to run over a half-page single-spaced, and often much less. In addition, even though the analyst may have, say, 200 concrete instances of some aspect of a structure, process, or strategy, the presentation of more than three or four tends to be repetitive, excessive, and boring. It is the exceeding of such informal, micro level rules that prompts labels such as "hypereventful."

Last and least narrativistic, but still partaking of this style, is *analytic interruptus*,[11] the practice of starting to perform a certain task but not following through to the implied or logical conclusion. An initially implied climax does not occur. Many studies imply an analysis of mechanisms, devices, strategies, and the like, but they do not actually do it. Presentations remain unsystematic, elusive, and simply suggestive of what given sets of such mechanisms might be as they have evolved in some social situation. By actually following through, I mean more specifically that the investigator goes to the time and trouble to deal with the following tasks.

1. To assemble self-consciously all his materials on how a given problematic topic is dealt with by the persons under study.
2. To tease out the variations among his assembled range of instances of strategies.
3. To classify them into an articulate set of what appear to him to be generic types of strategies.
4. To present them to the reader in some orderly, preferably named and numbered, manner.

The result of such careful work is a set of mini concepts relating to the construction of social life and social order. These efforts are articulate depictions of little rivulets of constancy in the flux of social life.

In sum, game theory and related forms of undisciplined abstraction have an appropriate sensitivity but they disregard data; narrativism in its various forms has a regard for data but does not employ a thorough strategy sensitivity and discipline. The "qualitative-analytic-descriptive" approach described at the beginning of this chapter moves between these two extremes of nonempirical abstractionism and non-abstraction-empiricism. This "down the middle" approach respects the urge to abstract, to articulate, and to find generic social phenomena, but insists that such abstraction must be disciplined, harnessed, and geared into the real, empirical world as it in fact exists. And this middling approach respects narrativism's appreciation of the ongoing, concrete events of social life, though insisting that greater leverage can be got on social life through searching out generic features of situations and strategies (among other perspectives).

It is the divorce of efforts such as game theory from empirical reality and of narrativism from abstract summation that flaws them as fully useful ways to understand social life, to gain "morals" about social life, and to learn principles ("strategies") that can be applied in social life. Abstract discriminations simultaneously and abundantly developed from and grounded in empirical instances seem best to point out possibilities for new lines of action. *Grounded and disciplined abstractions* in qualitative situation and strategy studies broadens and extends the range of action possibilities.

C. Passivist Quantitativism and Activist Qualitativism. Qualitative situation and strategy studies can be contrasted to a third genre, *passivist-quantitative* social science, in the terms relating to passivism and activism already mentioned, and some others.

1. Existential-Perceptual Aspects. In many of its phases, passivist-quantitativism is oriented to "bulk thinking." It is the aim of a great many statistical operations to specify the "typical," as in the various routines of sampling and forms of averaging and standardizing. "Descriptive statistics," in their very nature, seek to specify the more frequent versus the less frequent, the more typical versus the less typical. As actually consumed, interest centers on the things found to be "most frequent" and "most typical." And inferential statistics attempt to determine things most strongly covarying, to find "the most of those that are the most of that." Both these sponsor a main tendency, a bulk tendency image of social life. They lust for things most frequent and things most strongly correlated, giving the impression of delight in finding the largest frequency and the strongest causes in human situations. Bulk quantitativism seems, indeed, to be a microcosmic expression of the American macrocosmic doctrine "bigger, larger, and stronger are better." Bigger, larger, and stronger statistical statements embody an appropriate imagery of domination, of overwhelming existence, and of an iron fatefulness in how social variations are hooked together. American manifest destiny lives, even in the fourfold table. Put differently, it fosters imagery of jail cells and chains, as in statements such as "the larger the family, the lower the average intelligence of the offspring," and thousands of like generalizations. We of course "know" that no statistical statement of actual research is ever very "big," "large," or "strong."[12] I speak not of scientific reality, however, but of how statistical operations get reported, summarized, consumed, understood, fondled, and acted on. Passivist bulk quantitativism as *social product* sponsors a world of victims and a world of puppets on social strings.[13] Its advocates are quite plain on the point, asserting their *central* and *defining* task to be that of showing, in the words of one, "why people behave as they do, by studying the influences of their group memberships."[14]

Thus bulk quantitativism functions to narrow the range of matters over which people believe they can or might exercise control. In contrast, qualitative strategy analysis seeks to increase ranges of *action options* engaged in by people in situations regardless of their frequency or correlation. Indeed, in searching out the fullest range of what people actually do in situations, it is the empirically least frequent strategies that are likely to be the most inventive, novel, and important to readers of reports on how people deal with given generic situations. Rather than extending for readers the list of the range in ways they can feel trapped, qualitative strategy analysts extend the range of ways in which they may act differently—ways they may not have conceived. In a sense, qualitative strategy analysis is the empirical codification of social action wisdom. If, as mentioned in the last chapter, people under study emerge as superstrategists and supersophisticated, this is fitting. For an appropriately empirical social science is a usable putting-together of the scattered, partial, and private wisdom of persons in social life. Indeed, when such codifications of action are read, understood, and taken into account when people act, they seem likely to give rise to additional and new levels of strategies and kinds of situations, requiring ever-new scrutiny and codification. This feeds back, and the cycle begins anew.

The difference between bulk, quantitative passivism and qualitative activism is both so fundamental and so simple that it is on these accounts difficult to grasp. We are (properly) accustomed to many things being extremely complicated and involuted. A simple, even though fundamental, distinction can therefore be the most difficult to comprehend. Figure 3 displays graphically the simple yet profound contrast in the two root images. In one, forces converge on the person in social life and the person is in one or another way a resultant of these convergent forces. In the other, the person is the source of actions and strategies toward social life. The activist-passivist contrast is

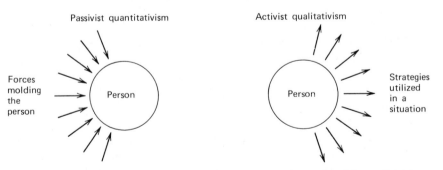

Figure 3.   Contrasting root images of passivist quantitativism and activist qualitativism.

so psychologically difficult that a second graphic depiction is useful, an analogy provided by the classic figure-ground picture found so often in introductory psychology texts. One of these is given in Figure 4. Looked at "one way," the figure "is" a vase. Looked at "another way," the figure "is" a pair of face-to-face profiles of two human heads. The point, of course, is that both are "there" and both are "true." What one "sees" is a matter of one's "set" toward the drawing. The activism-passivism contrast is also of that character. Both are true of human beings; both are there; it is a matter, rather, of how one chooses to attend.

For better or worse, a few people are able to see Figure 4 in only one way. Such a problem of perception is, unhappily, much more frequent with regard to the activist-passivist contrast, and it gives rise to con-

Figure 4. A perceptual analogy to the activist-passivist contrast.

siderable acrimony in social science, especially defensive acrimony, such as I display here, against the powerful forces of passive-quantitativism. For as mentioned in Chapters 1 and 2, the ruling circles and funding sources of social science are dominated by the passive-quantitative mentality. The minority with the active-qualitative view develop—unsurprisingly—a minority defensive mentality.[15]

The passivism-activism contrast is psychologically and existentially *isomorphic* with the contrast between qualitative and quantitative data. Qualitative data (reports of conversations, episodes, events, etc.) point to the concrete, real world of action possibilities, most especially when presented to illustrate strategies in situations. *Analyzed concrete instances* is the form of how people learn to do anything. Qualitative data are activist data. In contrast, sets of abstract frequencies and correlations contain almost no information on how action is in fact carried on. They consist of passivist data. It is amusingly ironic to note that manuals of instruction in passivist-quantitative research are themselves organized very importantly in qualitative situation and strategy terms. If passivist-quantitative research has the enormous virtues its promoters claim, one wonders why the manuals of doing it are not simply sets of frequencies and correlations, path diagrams, and the like, rather than codified sets of instances of generic research situations and "formula" strategies that researchers can employ in dealing with them.

2. *Practical Aspects.* Passive-quantitativists argue along another dimension: "The actions of your active actors have causes, and their actions have effects." "Properly to know both these linkages, you must engage in statistical operations." One can agree with these statements in principle. The only final way to determine *causal* connection is by means of quantitative operations. Even when this is done, however, statistical operations cannot validly substitute for qualitative grounding wherein the range of action options is highlighted and the concrete nature of action is maintained in consciousness. Equally important, though, is the practical role of quantification in social studies. Quantification done properly is a final arbiter of causal disputes, but it seems clear that quantification is unnecessary—a redundant and expensive waste of time and effort—for a large range of matters. Many things analyzed in a strategy perspective using qualitative data are so repetitive and so well and clearly linked that elaborate quantitative operations are superfluous. I refer in particular to "smaller," encounter-scale situations and strategies. Highly repetitive situations and strategies involving a few people over short periods of time in essence run through

thousands and thousands of contrasted and correlated cases in a fashion so obvious that no one bothers to count them. Thus: in situations of problematic sales, milkmen sometimes use the tactics of the sincerity act, contrived disclosure, and accentuated honesty.[16] One could perform elaborate quantitative enumerations of such a statement, pushing on to show exactly when various tactics are used, and so forth. For practical purposes of knowing situations and strategies, hardly anyone cares to have greater rigor.[17]

In practical terms, choices have to be made about the manner in which to expend finite resources. One could abide the most minute of trivial quantifications in a perfect world of infinite resources (not least of which would be infinite time, a resource I experience as highly limited, since one life is not very long). But that is not the real world. In the real world, the enormous range of things about which generic situations and strategies can usefully be figured out, codified, and presented (and subjected to other types of qualitative studies) lends credence to the idea that very few things are worth the time and expense of quantification.

Some things *are* definitely worth quantification. As situations and strategies get "larger, looser, and longer," as for example in organizational-scale matters, the causal, strategic significance of actions becomes more problematic. The causal chains "stretch out" through time and become, seemingly, attenuated and more difficult to trace because of the sheer amount of time needed for a sequence to play through and consequent reduction in the number of cases that can easily be scrutinized, among other reasons. We enter here the standard field of what is nowadays called "evaluation research"—research addressed to deciphering the effects of such grand strategies as "rehabilitation programs," "Wars on Poverty," and economic regulations.[18] Where frequency or causal statements at issue have a signal theoretical significance, or importantly affect public policy, the expense of quantification is justified. Most frequently, and especially when the strategies are short term, statistical frequencies and correlations are superfluous.

Social science is a social-practical enterprise in a complex, industrial society. It *is* possible to trace out extremely elaborate quantitative webs. It *is* possible to give excruciatingly detailed, quantified accounts of teeny, tiny, controlled variations. Social scientists in fact do it, and their numbers are increasing. But who cares to have such precision about minutiae when an enormous, diverse, and kaleidoscopic world demands careful deciphering of its most fundamental structures, processes, and strategies? One is reminded of the report that even as

Allied tanks rumbled in the streets of Berlin and the Third Reich was disintegrating, German civil servants were estimating next year's paper clip requirements.

All this is partly a matter of one's view of what, social scientifically, is important, what social scientists already know, and what can be known. To be caught up in passivist-quantitativism, one must necessarily assume that basic social structures, processes, and strategies, their dynamics, their contexts, and their functional import, have already been sufficiently sketched out. It remains only to provide *precise* depiction of an already known world. The focus of passive, bulk quantitativism on tiny and precisely determined variations assumes, therefore sponsors, a smug, institutional, in-drawn, comfortable, and orderly world.[19] The alternative imagery is obvious. Basic social structures, processes, and strategies, their dynamics and functions, are not known. The social world is *terra incognita* in any significant analytic sense. Social scientists need to be, instead, humble, exploratory, restless, outward-pushing, wrestlers with disorder—and uncomfortable.

Quantitativism is not, then, the only issue. There is, rather, an issue of the *appropriateness* of such a narrow vision in a rapidly changing world that requires much more flexible, mobile, and thrusting modes of inquiry if some minimal comprehension is to be attained. Put differently, one issue is the degree to which one believes the age of revelation is over, or is continuing. Passive, bulk quantitativists act as if the age of social science revelation has ended. It remains only to fill in the gaps and work out the implications, the proper task of theologians. Active qualitativists feel that the age of revelation is continuing—that there is no "age" *per se*. Revelation goes on all the time. Every social scientist is in that sense his own messiah and prophet.

D. The "How To" Genre. The concept of "disciplined abstractions" has required contrasts with the three traditions of undisciplined abstraction, narrativism (nonabstract empiricism), and passivist-quantitativism. Let me now mention a fourth contrasting and more "popular" (as distinct from scientific-scholarly) tradition. I speak of the well-known "how to" genre, which perhaps ought to be called "how should" because of its concern for "best," "most effective," "proper," or "successful" actions. Niccolò Machiavelli (author of *The Prince*)[20] and Dale Carnegie (author of *How to Win Friends and Influence People*)[21] are likely the two best known, serious (a qualification that excludes Stephen Potter)[22] practitioners of the social "how-to/should" tradition.

The social (as distinct from mechanical or technical, as in "How to Fix Your Car" manuals) how-to/should tradition is lush and abounding, shouting from book club enticements, publishers' advertisements, magazine articles, and community college curricula. The following current examples are concretely indicative.

"Managing a Sales Territory"

"How to Go to Work When Your Husband Is Against It, Your Children Aren't Old Enough, and There's Nothing You Can Do Anyhow"

"How Successful Executives Handle People"

"Housing Management"

"How to Read a Book"

"How a Prince Must Act in Order to Gain Reputation" ("How Flatterers Must be Shunned")

"Supermanship, or How to Continue to Stay on Top Without Actually Falling Apart"

"Secrets of Successful Selling"

"Managing the Major Sale"

"More than 100 Ways to Sabotage a Project"

"Rules for Radicals" ("Whenever Possible, Go Outside the Experience of the Enemy")

"How to Win Friends and Influence People" ("Six Ways to Make People Like You," "Twelve Ways to Win People to Your Way of Thinking")

"How to Make Out in Graduate Sociology"

"How Not to Get Drunk"

"What to Do with Your Bad Car: An Action Manual for Lemon Owners"

Even though these works are situation and strategy oriented and are often useful, how-to/should writings frequently display one or more of four features that disqualify them as serious, informed, grounded, fully useful, and scientific studies of social life. First, it frequently happens that the authors have not thoroughly, assiduously, and systematically searched out a range and depth of episodes on which analysis can be performed properly. Their "data collection" is highly limited, partial, and haphazard. Sometimes these works seem to be based on only a handful of accidentally happened-on relevant instances. Second, the thinness of the empirical base combines with a marked concreteness of mind among how-to/should authors. They write and organize at low and mundane levels of abstraction, focusing on low-level particulars, rarely if ever rising to the "generic" level, discussed in Chapter 3. The very nature of their practicality means, certainly, that abstraction and generality are not among their goals. To fault them for not doing something they do not set out to do may seem ungenerous, but it is nonetheless the case that how-to/should books and articles are limited in this respect.

Third, the authors are consumed with an interest in how *should* rather than how *do,* a perspective that imposes a crucial set of blinders. In being centrally attuned to "best," "most successful," "most effective," and so forth, they become inattentive to the vast range of human actions in any situation that have less than spectacular effects or outcomes, and, curiously, they are inattentive even to startlingly clear actions that are "failures." It is patent that any lovingly empirical and social scientific study of human action must be mindful of full ranges of actions in circumstances, not simply selected parts, no matter how those parts are selected.

Last, the moral and technical perspective these authors impose on the reporting of human action is incompatible with social science *per se.* Social science *qua* social science is mute on questions of what people should, in a moral sense, do. Not so with how-to/should writers. Their explications of narrow, technical efficacy, even, are also injunctions to morally superior action. A root, organizing principle of their presentations is moral-technical preference. Given the thinness of their work, I am tempted to guess that this characteristic is attributable to overly strong moral concern itself. In not taking pains fully to understand the construction of social action in situations *per se,* and in being narrowly concerned with moral "how to," they are prepared to forego standards of rigor, depth, fullness, abstraction, and generalization. A strong proclivity to moral "how to" might, indeed, be incompatible with rigorous analysis in an additional sense. It may be incompatible in a sheer *empirical/psychological* sense: The greater the propensity to "moral how-to," the less the personal capacity to execute full and rigorous analysis.

The concepts of "intimate familiarity" and "disciplined abstractions" form a perspective on the nature of *knowledge and method.* On the other hand, the concepts of "situation" and "strategy" are one way to con-

ceive human action, a *theoretical perspective.* The two sets of concepts are different in this sense, yet they are complementary, highly congruent, and similar in other senses. The activist view of human action that suffuses the concepts of situation and strategy fits together with an insistence on observing action by means of intimate familiarity and reporting it by means of disciplined abstractions. Intimacy *reveals* struggle and activism to the *observer,* and disciplined abstractions *report* struggle and activism to the *reader.* In a manner of speaking, they form a friendly family of notions, all different but each supporting the other. Or, as stated more conventionally by social scientists: every theory implies a method; every method implies a theory.

Having explained these four rather general aspects of qualitative strategy analysis, I move in the next chapter to a very specific description of the structuring of actual reports embodying these principles.

NOTES TO CHAPTER FIVE

1. A. Conan Doyle, "A Scandal in Bohemia," in *The Complete Sherlock Holmes* (Garden City, N.Y.: Doubleday, 1930), pp. 162–163.

2. T. C. Schelling quoted in R. L. Birdwhistell, *Kinesics and Context* (Philadelphia, University of Pennsylvania Press, 1970), p. 340.

3. Herbert Blumer, *Symbolic Interactionism* (Englewood Cliffs, N.J.: Prentice-Hall, 1969), p. 168. See further the too-neglected views of Charles Horton Cooley, "The Roots of Social Knowledge," *American Journal of Sociology,* **32:**59–70 (July 1926). See also John Lofland, *Analyzing Social Settings* (Belmont, Calif.: Wadsworth, 1971), pp. 1–7.

4. See discussion, Section I, Ch. 2.

5. The technical sources are cited in Note 1 of Chapter 2.

6. I draw here and below from concepts and language appearing in my "Styles of Reporting Qualitative Field Research," *The American Sociologist,* **9:**101–111 (August 1974).

7. Barney Glaser and Anselm Strauss, *The Discovery of Grounded Theory* (Chicago: Aldine, 1967).

8. C. Wright Mills, *The Sociological Imagination* (New York: Oxford University Press, 1959).

9. See, for example, Erving Goffman, *Interaction Ritual* (Garden City, N.Y.: Doubleday-Anchor, 1967), Chs. 1 and 4, in particular, and *Strategic Interaction* (Philadelphia: University of Pennsylvania Press, 1969). It is ironic that scholars who call for the "grounding" of "theory" and have been caustic toward people who do not ground their work engage in the same practice (when not doing "narrativism," which is discussed next). Thus the remarks of Barney Glaser and Anselm Strauss on Peter Blau [*Exchange and Power in Social Life* (New York: Wiley, 1964] can be directed to their own *Status Passage: A Formal Theory* (Chicago: Aldine, 1971): "an example of formal theory that sounds 'nice' and 'neat' but appears 'useless' to us—because its

relevance as an explanation of anything or its dubious fit to the real world has not been demonstrated [sic] but simply assumed out-of-hand" (Glaser and Strauss, *Discovery*, p. 91). As they assert, the problem springs from a lack of intimate familiarity on which disciplined abstractions can be built and meaningful consolidations (see Ch. 7, this book) effected: "Speculative or ungrounded theory derives from any combination of several sources: whimsy and wisdoms of usually deceased great men, conjecture and assumptions about the 'oughts' of life, and other extant speculative theory. The usual method of developing theory is to deduct logically from these sources. The weaving in of some grounded theory usually helps, but does not save or even compete well with the theorist's emphasis on speculative sources" (Glaser and Strauss, *Status Passage*, p. 177). Pseudoempirical abstracted conceptualism is, nonetheless, better than social science *scholasticism*, a legacy of Europe that is deceptive because of its claim to empiricism, to "phenomenological fidelity," and to activist purity (in the guise of "reality constructionism"). Among more recent works, see the papers in George Psathas, ed., *Phenomenological Sociology* (New York: Wiley, 1973). Curiously, Psathas' personal research is mostly in the solid tradition of intimate familiarity and disciplined abstractions.

For a summary of the game theory approach mentioned, see Clifford H. Swensen, Jr., *Introduction to Interpersonal Relations* (Glenview, Ill.: Scott, Foresman, 1973), Ch. 11, "Conflict and Game Theory."

10. See, for example, David Halberstam, *The Best and the Brightest* (New York: Random House, 1972). See also such run-of-the-mill and typical works of political science as Donald Hadwiger and Ross Talbot, *Pressures and Protests: The Kennedy Farm Program and the Wheat Referendum of 1963* (San Francisco: Chandler, 1965).

11. I draw in the following from my "Interactionist Imagery and Analytic Interrupts," in Tomatsu Shibutani, ed., *Human Nature and Collective Behavior: Papers in Honor of Herbert Blumer* (Englewood Cliffs, N.J.: Prentice-Hall, 1970), p. 39.

12. See the material summarized in Derek L. Phillips, *Knowledge From What?* (Skokie, Ill.: Rand-McNally, 1971), pp. 6–10.

13. Peter Berger, *Invitation to Sociology* (Garden City, N.Y.: Doubleday-Anchor, 1963), Chs. 4 and 5.

14. Melvin Tuman, *Patterns of Society* (Boston: Little, Brown, 1973), p. 11.

15. On the situations and strategies of minorities and other stigmatized categories, see the materials capsulized in Section IV, "Role Strategies Among Subordinates," of Chapter 9.

There is, of course, a huge literature revolving around the contrasts between passivism-activism and qualitativism-quantitativism or both. For varying reasons, I have found the following most useful: Herbert Blumer, *Symbolic Interactionism;* Norton Long, "The Political Act as an Act of Will," *American Journal of Sociology*, **69:**1–6 (July 1963); William Gamson, *The Strategy of Social Protest* (Homewood, Ill.: Dorsey, 1975), Ch. 9; James S. Coleman, *The Mathematics of Collective Action* (Chicago: Aldine, 1973), pp. vi–5.

It needs further to be indicated that the Rooseveltian, robust, rough-rider imagery (advocated and *embodied* by activists such as Herbert Blumer) is apropos but neglectful of the quieter and more gentle side of the activist perspective. Reflecting on the diverse people he has studied over the years, Fred Davis voices this gentler side in stating the image of the person that pervades his work: "Regardless of whether the actor is a student nurse, the parent of a polio child, or a paraplegic confined to a wheelchair, the underlying existential stance remains the same—a perplexed, somewhat anguished, yet essentially well-intentioned character groping his way among alternatives, most of which are given him by the world and some more nearly of his own making. He sees none of the alternatives as ideal, although he reasons that one *must* after all be better than all the rest. The object of his quest is to decide on that alternative. Since life can offer no certainty that he has indeed chosen best, what else to do but fashion with the help of others a small 'master plot' of language, thought, and action which in its playing out convinces him, most of the time, that he has chosen wisely." Fred Davis, *Illness, Interaction and the Self* (Belmont, Calif.: Wadsworth, 1972), pp. ix–x.

Future and extended treatments of the activist-passivist and associated contrasts will need also to deal with some ironic and contradictory coincidences of tendencies. For example, despite a passivist image of humans, passivist-quantitativists are highly "agentic" as that term is used by David Bakan and discussed by Rae Carlson and Jessie Bernard. Conversely, activist-qualitativists tend to "communion," Bakan's contrast to agency. See David Bakan, "Psychology Can Now Kick the Science Habit," *Psychology Today*, **5**:26, 28, 86–88 (March 1972); Rae Carlson, "Sex Differences in Ego Functioning: Exploratory Studies of Agency and Communion," *Journal of Consulting and Clinical Psychology*, **37**:267–277 (April 1971); Jessie Bernard, "My Four Revolutions: An Autobiographical History of the ASA," *American Journal of Sociology*, **78**:783–788 (January 1973).

16. Odis Bigus, "The Milkman and His Customer: A Cultivated Relationship," *Urban Life and Culture*, **1**:131–165 (July 1972).

17. Cf. Barney Glaser and Anselm Strauss, *Discovery of Grounded Theory, op. cit.*, Ch. IX.

18. See, for example, Peter H. Rossi and Walter Williams, eds., *Evaluating Social Programs: Theory, Practice and Politics* (New York: Seminar Press, 1973); George Fairweather, *Social Change: The Challenge to Survival* (Morristown, N.J.: General Learning Press, 1972); Elmer Struening and Marcia Guttentag, eds., *Handbook of Evaluation Research*, two volumes (Beverly Hills: Sage, 1975).

19. It is appropriate that the necessarily wealthy purchasers of social science work prefer to buy passive-quantitativism. Each supports the other's preferred conception of social reality.

20. Niccolò Machiavelli, *The Prince* (New York: New American Library, 1962, and numerous other editions).

21. Dale Carnegie, *How To Win Friends and Influence People* (New York: Simon & Schuster, 1936).

22. Stephen Potter, *The Complete Upmanship Including Gamemanship, Lifemanship, One-upmanship, Supermanship* (New York: Holt, Rinehart & Winston, 1971, and numerous other editions).

CHAPTER SIX

Reporting an Inquiry

I have pointed out the necessity to achieve intimate familiarity with people actually acting (Chapter 2), elucidated focusing on situations (Chapter 3) and strategies (Chapter 4), and argued the need to assemble, analyze, and report a rich array of concrete episodes in the context of close-up focus on situations and strategies (Chapter 5). We come now to matters of concretely reporting analyses with all these features.

As in other research genres, qualitative strategy analysts employ certain reportorial conventions, the better to facilitate understanding both the social life under study and the report of it by the analyst. Without descending to the level of the style manuals or rules on the form of scientific papers, it can be said that qualitative strategy reports typically contain four main and utterly unsurprising sections. Although named inventively and diversely, these sections boil down to:

1. Introduction.
2. The situation.
3. Strategies.
4. Summary and implications.

I. THE INTRODUCTION SECTION

1. For the generically attuned analyst, the report begins with a discussion of the transcending aspect or aspects of the situation and

strategies under scrutiny. Even though the analyst has been close-up to some people, his report of them "jumps off," so to speak, with the generic constructions he has evolved that lift those concrete people out of the realm of the particular, unique, and irrelevant and into the realm of the general, the commonplace, and the relevant. Thus having been a milkman and having interviewed many who did the same work, Odis Bigus begins his report about them by discussing the generic situation and strategy that organize his analysis:

America is a service society—so much so that essentially non-service institutions, such as stores, take on service-like characteristics. This emphasis on service has given rise to a preponderance of a particular kind of social activity, which I will refer to as "cultivating," and an associated kind of social relationship, which I will refer to as the "cultivated relationship." "Cultivating" as it is used here refers to the courting and wooing activities engaged in by servicers in relations with those whom they service. Cultivating techniques are employed with the intent of either directly or indirectly gaining a reward (usually monetary). "Cultivated relationships" are relationships which are carried out with the primary intent of gaining such a reward. They include but are not limited to service relationships. They are usually asymmetrical, with the less powerful party utilizing cultivating tactics to bring the relationship closer to a state of symmetry.[1]

2. It is only after the main contours of the general situation and/or strategies have been introduced that the particular, empirical vehicle is then brought into the text. Continuing with Bigus' report:

One such relationship—that between milkmen and their customers—will be discussed in this paper. The structure of the milkman-customer relationship, for reasons to be discussed below—is one of extreme asymmetry, with the milkman initially exercising very little control. However, by employing cultivating techniques, milkmen are able to transform this initially asymmetrical relationship into one which more closely approximates symmetry.[2]

3. The descriptive introduction to the particular group or category of people and empirical materials at hand is followed by a section on how the materials themselves were collected (by interviewing, observa-

tion, library documents), over what period of time, and the like.[3]

4.   Sometimes a paragraph or so is devoted sheerly to reporting on demography and social location. Such matters include the number of participants, their ages, sexes, ethnicities, occupations, other aspects of personal background, and relevant features of the physical circumstances.

5.   Finally, the introduction section often ends with a capsule overview of how the report to follow is organized, providing the reader with a set of "sign posts" that he can use to find his way through the analytic details.

II.   THE SITUATION SECTION

Qualitative strategy analysts treat the "situation" section of their reports in a more diverse manner than other sections. Some even say relatively little about the nature of the situation, assuming that the reader already possesses an adequate commonsensical notion. Following from what has been said about situations in Chapter 3, though, certain minimal suggestions may be made.

1.   Ideally, a set of generic and abstract features has been developed from the qualitative materials so that analytic description of the situation can be organized and presented in terms of such features. Thus in addressing the situation of encounters between the visibly handicapped and normals, Fred Davis analyzes that circumstance as having four prime features, a fourfold "threat posed by the handicap to sociability:... its tendency to become an exclusive focal point for the interaction; its potential for inundating expressive boundaries; its discordance with other attributes of the person...and its ambiguity as a predicator of joint activity."[4] Elucidation of these four features runs four pages in hiis polished report, given the elegant captions: A Focal Point of Interaction, Inundating Potential, Contradiction of Attributes, Ambiguous Predicator.

2.   To report a striving toward generic depiction is not to say that actual reports always so strive for or attain the generic. It is a tendency, as in the foregoing example from Fred Davis, that moves toward the generic but does not fully attain it. At minimum, however, the depiction should be *analytic* in the sense of summing up the situation in terms of salient features, as in the Davis example. And even when not

analytic, reports, empirically, provide description of the situation in sheer physical terms.

3.   Regardless of the degree to which the report emphasizes the generic, the analytic, the physical, or all these, the depiction is made more meaningful if it is structured to point up a *contrast* of the studied situation with one or more other empirical or hypothetical possibilities. The situation at hand is etched more sharply if it is "played off" against a markedly different situation or situations. Thus a paper by Stan Bernstein on student fritters of time opens by setting up this contrast of situations:

> Social roles vary in the degree to which their constituent tasks are "closed" or "open" in character. At one extreme are roles such as assembly-line worker where precise definitions communicate when the task starts, one's progress in it, and when it ends. At the other extreme are roles such as student, where the tasks are highly open or never-ending. The role of student, in particular, involves learning to think and learning the "facts" of various fields. The infinite expand-ability of these tasks places no practically determined restrictions on the amount of time occupants can dedicate to the role. Like politi-cians, housewives, and other entrepreneurs, students' work is never done. Indeed, students are counselled that people only stop learning when they die. Death is not, students lament, in sight, but learning demands are.[5]

For purposes of such etching, the contrast need not be one that can be pointed to in the real, empirical world. It can be merely a logical or hypothetical possibility. Its contrast with the reality at hand serves to make more bold, perceivable, and problematic the features of the real situation at hand.

4.   Moreover, devoting a modest amount of space to the *historical* development or antecedents of the situation at hand lends a certain depth, texture, and context to the report. The embroidery of history contributes measurably to an ambience of nuance and anchoring.

III.   THE STRATEGIES SECTION

Again, to indicate the kinds of things that many situation and strategy analysts typically report (and perform) is not to commit any given analyst to a rigid format of necessary items; most certainly it is not to promote a given *order* of dealing with items in sections of reports. Even though there are clearly some general and agreed-upon lines of endeavor, within that framework, flexibility, inventiveness, and innovation are keynotes.

1.   Perhaps even more than with situations, the emphasis is on the generic in depicting discovered or documented strategies. As *action-options,* generically articulated strategies have a transferable and applicable quality that situations do not possess. Phenomenologically, situations present themselves, but strategies are sought out, invented, adopted, and constructed. The latter are more planned than the former. Hence the tendency for analysts both to be more assiduously generic when analyzing strategies and to devote more space to them when writing reports.

2.   Most typically, qualitative strategy analysts simply present a list of types of strategies found employed in the studied situation, or merely depict one or a very few major strategies observed. Even though the strategies have an inherent time dimension, this dimension is frequently slighted. As a consequence, even the most "activist" of those who study the construction of action often end by presenting very static, structural portrayals of people fabricating action. As useful and valid as these are, lists of techniques, practices, and the like lack the dynamic of life-as-lived.

In observing, analyzing, and reporting, it seems more fruitful and faithful, instead, to push toward analysis of phases, stages, sequences, and cycles within and between strategies. These *processual* aspects are always "there," of course, though hidden in lists of static strategies. They so typically remain "hidden" and unexplicated, I suspect, simply because we operate with a cognitive apparatus—a mental set—that emphasizes static categories. But in recognizing such a mental disposition to statics and structures, it becomes possible (if not easy) to transcend it.

Grounded processual renderings are so rare that it is particularly important to call attention to notable exceptions, among which is Burton Clark's work on "cooling out" in higher education (reprinted in Chapter 15). Analyzing the situation of disjunction between educational aspiration and talent among junior college students, Clark asks: How do junior colleges manage the situation of dealing with large numbers of students whose academic aspirations for a B.A. exceed the individuals' talent and performance? Noting the "hard" dismissal strategy of some four-year schools, he found that the junior college he studied had evolved a contrasting and complex "soft" strategy for coping with disjunctions between student aspiration and performance. He calls this "the reorienting process" or the "cooling-out process" and explicates its five main steps:

    a. Intensive preentrance testing and assignment to remedial work, the facts of which are recorded in a counseling folder.

    b. A counseling interview at the beginning of each semester in which the student's record of failure is brought to his attention with increasing force.

    c. Entrance into an "Orientation to College" course designed to reveal occupational ambitions and appraise them in light of performance.

    d. If B.A. ambitions remain unsurrendered, "need for improvement" and "request for conference" notices are issued by counselors who "delicately...but persistently" confront the overambitious student.

    e. Finally, the student may be put on a drawn-out probation, in a "slow killing-off of the lingering hopes of the most stubborn...[failing]students."[6]

    3. Communication and application of documented strategies (and situations) are facilitated when they are *named* or otherwise clearly signaled for the reader. Summarizing captions, and simple, easily remembered labels, *crystallize* and *articulate* recurrences in the ongoing flow of social life, facilitating one's ordered appreciation of what is otherwise a blur. Reality is in a most significant sense created through apt naming, through striking signals of existence. As Scott Greer has put it:

> Much of our individual experience is symbolized in vague and unstandardized ways. There is, as we say, no word for it. One of the great contributions of creative scientists and artists is to make communicable what was previously moot, to sense new meanings possible in the emerging nature of human experience, giving them a form which makes communication possible. The phrase-maker is not to be despised, he may be creating the grounds for new social reality.[7]

Greer nonetheless demurs in also noting that a labeler may "merely be repacking an old product," not articulating what previously was inchoate. I would want to go further and claim merit for "mere" repacking of old products. All symbol constructs seem destined to sink into the slough of our "common-sense reality," to become habitual and unthinking, to lose their freshness and charm, to be drained of their meaning—the possibilities for action they once presented. If that is the misfortune to which all symbols, all labels and thoughts, are heir, there is a need to "make them fresh again," to revive them. For it is often not the idea or the practice *per se* that loses its usefulness, but, rather, our capacity to apprehend it while clothed in the tired old verbal garments. Our labels and habitual modes of thinking interfere with our apprehension of the idea. Repackaging gives the old a new life. It makes possible a new appreciation. It is perhaps the deadening tendency of all habitual use in social science that in good part explains its lack of codified and cumulative language. Everyone needs to find and express that special quality of freshness for him- or herself and is prone to invent new terms and new definitions of old terms to embody and signal that sense of freshness. Let us, then, not lament relabeling; let us have ever more of it: each is a reaching for new and renewed understanding.[8]

4. Since emphasis is on explicating and documenting the full range and types of strategies in the studied social situation, strategies merit reporting and analyzing regardless of the frequency with which they occur. Indeed, strategies that are infrequently employed but have a dramatic effect (both successful and unsuccessful) can do much to reveal the otherwise hidden possibilities for action in a situation and/or the extant but veiled limits of action in a situation. Humans seem to be endlessly inventive of devices concocted to deal with the problematic, and sheer folk-strokes of genius can regularly be discovered by attentive observer-analysts. Through analysis, these strokes of genius (and, of course, also stupidity) become available to those who are less inventive.

IV. THE SUMMARY AND IMPLICATIONS SECTION

If the introductory section is an appetizer or entrée and the situation and strategy sections the main course, the summary and implications section is the dessert. As such, it embodies the sweet-fruit of one's previous endeavors. This may take a number of forms, although not necessarily in the order presented here, nor need all these be covered.

1. Not untypically, a paragraph or two summary of the situation and its strategies is provided.

2. As befits a discipline that aims, with varying degrees of success, at being generalizing and cumulative, lines along which the particular analysis might be generalized may be elucidated. In his analysis of cooling out in a junior college, after he presents a process-strategy (just summarized), Burton Clark goes on to suggest the more abstract "features which are likely to be found in other settings where failure or denial is the effect of a structured discrepancy between ends and means...."[9] The five such generalized strategic avenues involve:

a. Providing achievement alternatives that do not appear to be very different from the one denied.
b. Performing the denial gradually.
c. Documenting assiduously and abundantly the reasons for denial, forcing blame on the aspirant rather than on the organization.
d. Providing numerous and patient counselors who themselves believe in the alternatives offered to the failed aspirant and promote their acceptance.
e. Promoting a conception of diverse kinds of abilities, each valuable in its proper place.[10]

By such a more generalized formulation that uses signaling labels such as Alternative Achievement, Gradual Disengagement, Objective Denial, Agents of Consolation, and Avoidance of Standards that are themselves based on the one situation studied, it becomes more possible for others to perceive how the "lessons" of this situation might apply to other situations of this kind. Such efforts, moreover, aid in consolidating qualitative studies of situations and strategies (see Chapter 7).

3. While belonging to a different realm of discourse, it is not uncommon (nor especially inappropriate) for the analyst to point up the policy or practitioner implications of what he has reported. If in situation X we find the range of strategies a, b, and c, then morally speaking, perhaps, something ought or ought not to be done to alter the situation or strategies. What might be done, or not done, can be spelled out.

The sequence of activity for a single inquiry is now complete. Intimate familiarity focused by means of an emergent analysis of a situation and its strategies is presented in a qualitative, grounded, and disciplined manner, using the straightforward format described in this chapter. The reader might find it useful again at this point to inspect the four full studies appearing in Part III. Each exemplifies most if not all of these principles and guidelines.

The accumulation of such studies poses questions of how they themselves "fit together," a matter to which we now turn.

NOTES TO CHAPTER SIX

1. Odis Bigus, "The Milkman and His Customer: A Cultivated Relationship," *Urban Life and Culture*, **1**:131 (July 1972).

2. *Ibid.*, p. 132.

3. For detailed discussion of the content of such methodological sections, see John Lofland, *Analyzing Social Settings* (Belmont, Calif.: Wadsworth, 1971), pp. 130–133. In book-length reports, a brief discussion in the introduction is ofttimes amplified in a longer appendix on methods.

4. Fred Davis, *Illness, Interaction and the Self* (Belmont, Calif.: Wadsworth, 1972), pp. 134–138, and capsulized in Section IV.C.3 of Chapter 9.

5. Stan Bernstein, "Getting It Done: Notes on Student Fritters," *Urban Life and Culture*, **1**:275–292 (October 1972), capsulized in Section V.A.2 of Chapter 8.

6. Burton R. Clark, "'The Cooling-Out' Function in Higher Education," *American Journal of Sociology*, **65**:569–576 (May 1960), reprinted in Chapter 15.

7. Scott Greer, *The Logic of Social Inquiry* (Chicago: Aldine, 1969), p. 46.

8. There are of course variations in the skill with which people do new labeling and relabeling. Some perform with elegance; others are atrocious; most of us are in between. As the years go on, I blush over many of my youthful labeling ventures that saw print: what once seemed to be elegant can later appear preposterous.

9. Clark, "Cooling Out," *op. cit.*, p. 574.

10. *Ibid.*, pp. 574–575.

CHAPTER SEVEN

Consolidating Inquiries

Qualitative strategy analysts have published relatively little to indicate concern with how their inquiries might cumulate or be consolidated into larger wholes. Each of their studies tends to be, rather, an individual cameo, a pretty thing standing more or less alone. Each is, of course, informed by a shared perspective (the kind of perspective explained in Chapters 2 through 5) but not by any strict sense of programmed, specific contribution to an existing and clearly articulated "theory." This is in marked contrast to more conventional social science in which inquiries are designed and geared from the outset to test hypotheses that are part of received theory.

The tendency of qualitative strategy analysts to ignore questions of cumulation and consolidation has several bases; prime among these is the feeling that solid and humanly meaningful social science knowledge will likely emerge from diverse, discovery-oriented inquiries that are subsequently collated, rather than from brittle exercises in disproving preformed assertions. This, however, is only an article of faith. It has not been translated into working procedure. Indeed, perhaps it is only in recent years that we have accumulated enough relevant inquiries to make it possible sensibly to consider the question; and it may be premature to raise it even now. Let me nonetheless try provisionally to indicate one consolidating direction in which qualitative strategy analyses might move.

I. GOALS

The problem of cumulation raises at the outset a question of what such efforts should "look like," what features they should have. In the case of qualitative situation and strategy studies, the following may be reasonable features of (and procedures for doing) successful consolidations.

1. An array of inquiries is assembled, displaying the features outlined in Chapters 2 through 5 and addressed to the same generic situation.
2. Each study is disassembled into its situation and strategy components.

   a. A composite, variegated analysis of the generic situation and ways in which the situation itself varies is constructed from the separate accounts.
   b. The documented strategies in the separate accounts are reviewed for their similarities and differences and a composite, master set of strategies is drawn up.

3. The emergent and integrating new statement brings forth—retains—an ample amount of the qualitative data appearing in each of the individual reports. That is, the consolidating statement takes care to keep its abstractions disciplined.
4. Since not all strategies are likely to be found in all varieties of the generic situation, new generalizations are offered about the contexts and limits of given strategies. Thus in the case of the generic situation of delivering bad news, materials presently available suggest that the role-scale strategy of "nice-guy impersonality" is most attractive when the bearer and recipient of bad news do not know each other.[1]

II. PROBLEMATICS

To my knowledge, no one has yet completed a consolidating effort with the features just enumerated. Among proximate and practical reasons is lack of sufficient studies on any given situation. Happily, that deficiency is on the edge of remedy for at least a few generic situations.

When consolidations of the foregoing character are undertaken, at least two problems will have to be worked out. One, how many studies addressed to a given generic situation are necessary in order properly to effect a consolidation? The answer depends in part on the quality and detail available in inquiries at hand. Conceivably, a hundred sparse reports might be too few and a dozen rich reports might be ample. The answer depends, too, on the scale of the consolidating effort. Book-length efforts presumably require much more material than do articles. Two, practical and financial difficulties are posed by the organic relation between abstraction on the one hand and on the other, the context and detail that is at the heart of the qualitative approach. Presentation of qualitative grounding requires a great deal of direct quotation from published reports. New forms of acceptable presentation of already published material will need to be devised, since summaries and standard, brief quotation probably will not suffice. Extended quotation for these specific purposes will need to be legitimated. Moreover, the course-reader explosion of the boom sixties in America prompted social science journals to charge high reprint fees ($10, $15 or more a page) in a quest to share in the income of textbook editors. Since the consolidations envisaged here require large numbers of quoted pages and are unlikely to achieve a compensating text-scale market, some new understandings will clearly be necessary.

III. SHORT–CIRCUITS AND WAY–STATIONS

The absence of adequate data bases has not, of course, stopped qualitative-strategy scholars from proceeding directly to general statements that have at least the superficial appearance of being consolidations in the sense just outlined. Indeed, in the absence of adequate data, it has been necessary to "short-circuit" to be able to produce more general statements at all—and such orienting statements have certainly been necessary. The most prominent short-circuitings are the products of Erving Goffman. His three most famous works on situations and strategies have dealt with the situations of failure,[2] strangers,[3] and stigma.[4] Not having had solid bodies of studies and their entailed data and concepts on which to build—to consolidate—Goffman and others have had to improvise in ways that "ungrounded" their analyses and imparted an unfortunate quality of abstraction.[5]

Short-circuiting is not, however, the only way of dealing with a desire to consolidate insufficient studies of a given generic situation. A more modest approach is to assemble relevant studies into an edited collection that one acknowledges to be incomplete and loosely organized. Such a collection is then a useful way-station and sourcebook on the path to full consolidation. One hopes that it can stimulate further relevant inquiries and subsequent consolidations. Though only partly oriented to strategies, Barney Glaser's edited way-station on *Organizational Careers*[6] is an important model.

IV.   THE PROXIMATE TASK

Consolidations of the kind indicated are the goal, but as mentioned, few if any solid ones, or even good way-stations, are yet possible. Indeed, it appears to be necessary to complete a task even before establishing way-stations, to make consolidations and way-stations more possible. This task is the assembly and enumeration of what qualitative strategy analysts *have* accomplished, to make more clear what might *then* be accomplished. This is the basic (and somewhat primitive) task of Part II, "Review of Qualitative Studies of Interaction Strategies." The effort is to create archives or a data bank, at least in miniature, that can be drawn on in doing specific inquiries, way-stations, and full consolidations.

Because of limitations of space, the inquiries catalogued have had to be stripped of their qualitative data. This, sadly, produces the kind of lifelessness and abstract quality that I have said must be avoided. Read from start to finish, one is likely to develop a sense of climbing through an endless lattice of types of situations and strategies. Therefore, and also because Part II is a sourcebook, this material should be consulted and sampled in a variety of ways, rather than being read from start to finish in the usual fashion. The originals of seemingly interesting inquiries should themselves be read, and the catalogued materials as a whole should be viewed as *points of departure* for a specific study, an edited way-station, a consolidation, or even (heaven forbid!) a short-circuited general statement.

NOTES TO CHAPTER SEVEN

1. See Lachlan McClenahen and John Lofland, "Bearing Bad News: Tactics of the Deputy U.S. Marshal," *Sociology of Work and Occupations*, in press, capsulized in Section III.F of Chapter 8.

2. Erving Goffman, "On Cooling the Mark Out," *Psychiatry*, **15**:451–463 (November 1952), capsulized in Section IV.C.6 of Chapter 9.

3. Erving Goffman, *Presentation of Self in Everyday Life* (Garden City, N.Y.: Doubleday-Anchor, 1959), capsulized in Section III.A of Chapter 8.

4. Erving Goffman, *Stigma: Notes on the Management of Spoiled Identity* (Englewood Cliffs, N.J.: Prentice-Hall, 1963), capsulized in Section IV.C.1 of Chapter 9.

5. See, for example, William J. Goode, "A Theory of Role Strain," *American Sociological Review*, **25**:483–496 (August 1960); Robert Merton, "The Role-Set," *British Journal of Sociology*, **8**:106–120 (June 1957); Murray Davis, *Intimate Relations* (New York: Free Press, 1973), capsulized in part in Section II.B of Chapter 10. Furthermore, I fear that some qualitative strategy analysts have made a virtue out of the interim necessity to short-circuit. Thus after propounding and practicing a laudable "grounded theory" approach in the middle sixties, Barney Glaser and Anselm Strauss moved, in the next decade, toward an explicit stress on theory at the expense of grounding. In their *Status Passage* (Chicago: Aldine, 1971), for example, the data base is avowedly (p. 187) and actually quite narrow and thin. See also Strauss' forerunner statement on "Discovering New Theory from Previous Theory," in Tamotsu Shibutani, ed., *Human Nature and Collective Behavior* (Englewood Cliffs, N.J.: Prentice-Hall, 1970), pp. 46–53.

6. Chicago: Aldine, 1968.

PART TWO

REVIEW OF QUALITATIVE STUDIES OF INTERACTION STRATEGIES

The four chapters of Part II organize and capsulize more than a hundred studies and essays that reasonably exemplify and/or advance the qualitative situation/strategy analysis of social interaction in natural settings.

1.   My rendering is the provisional one of establishing a commonality of interest and focus, of concretely starting to codify many heretofore scattered efforts. As such, my reliance on others is ruthless and shameless. I note this because many practitioners in this broad wing of social science publicly ignore the work of others, although they privately build on it and out of it. As Part II reveals, I feel we need to act quite otherwise. Without the type of loving appreciation and regard for the work of others that I aim to practice, there can be no cumulation of knowledge; and specifically, there can be no future for a direct, intimate, qualitative social science. It was rightly said that we must hang together or we will surely hang separately.

2.   The capsulized materials are, in the first instance, organized in terms of social organization scale of situations and strategies: encounters, roles, groups, and organizations. Of each report/essay I asked: What is the *prime* focus, the prime acting unit or the prime scale of action? Most reports, of course, involve several scales of both situations and strategies, and a few were difficult to classify. But for the most

part, reports have a rather clear *relative stress* on encounters, roles, groups, or organizations. When a single, generic situation is dealt with at various scales of strategy, I have often reported them all at a single place, noting the mix of scales involved.

3. These materials could have been organized in other ways. As explained in Chapter 7, the best would be in terms of the generic situations to which they are addressed. As desirable as this is, it is not feasible because there are too few materials on given situations. Another principle is the one used as the prime way internally to organize chapters: beginning, maintaining, and ending aspects. Each of these taken separately, especially the first and third, is actually quite thin, however; thus that possibility seemed unwise. Rather, at the present stage in the development of this kind of social science, it seems best to highlight generic units of social organization, especially since these fit well into the larger and wider tradition of analysis elucidated in Section III of Chapter 4, "Qualitative Strategy Analysis and the Larger Study of Social Organization."

4. Adequately to convey the detailed character of qualitative strategy analysis, I have had to relax criteria for including studies. I would have preferred to capsulize only empirical inquiries that strongly display all four of the features explained in Chapters 2 through 5: *(a)* founded on intimate familiarity, *(b)* focused on a generic situation, *(c)* articulated rendering of strategies, *(d)* presented in a disciplined fashion. Well less than half the materials recounted here strongly display all four of these features. I have sacrificed purity to comprehensiveness. This has been especially necessary because some of the most seminal works in the genre are ungrounded essays from which the more empirically minded do (can, and should) take guidance. Erving Goffman's efforts are notable in this respect. Virtually none of Goffman's works are exemplary on any of the four criteria, but they have been so important on the additional criterion of novelty (a criterion discussed in Section III of Chapter 4) that I have included them anyway.

5. In studying the strategy materials within each of the major scales of social organization, I have experienced them as falling "naturally" into three basic topics: questions of starting, doing, and ending.

    a. Starting questions focus at the level of *getting into* (or avoiding) an existing unit (discovering, choosing, preparing, etc.) or at the level of *forming* a unit (an encounter, role, group, or organization).

    b. Doing questions focus on the ways and processes of dealing with or managing an existing unit.

c. Ending questions focus at the level of the person getting out of a unit or at the level of dissolving/terminating the unit itself.

Although phrased in a variety of ways from chapter to chapter, these are the major divisions within each. Additional distinctions and concerns are explained as we proceed.

6.   As mentioned in Chapter 7, the interim and archival character of Part II and the deletion of data that has been necessary make for an unfortunate but unavoidable lifelessness and abstract quality when the material is read in the usual uninterrupted fashion. To avoid this lifelessness, I suggest approaching these chapters as one would approach any other archives: as a storehouse to be drawn from rather than as reading merely to be mastered. These materials and the manner of their organization are more important for the directions in which they point than for where they now reside. And as also indicated in Chapter 7, such directions involve specific inquiries, way-station editings, and full consolidations of studies on generic situations and strategies.

CHAPTER EIGHT

Encounter–Scale Situations and Strategies

I. NATURE OF ENCOUNTERS AND VARIATIONS

A. Nature. The "encounter" is the smallest scale unit of social organization. For purposes of initial definition it may be thought of as the system formed during any single occasion of two or more people in one another's immediate presence. An encounter exists only over the span of a single occasion of people being together.

1. Time. Given the limits of human biology, the life span of encounters as "creatures" is quite short. The upper limit is imposed by how long people can endure a single coming together. Most typically, encounters seem to last from a few seconds to a few hours, although some hardy souls (mostly encounter group enthusiasts) have been observed to endure fifteen or so hours!

2. Equipment. The amount of equipment employed is variable, but most typically there is little save for adornments of the body and some fixtures of the place.

3. Space. The short life span of an encounter tends also to limit the amount and complexity of space utilized even for "mobile" encounters.

4. Population. Encounters typically involve only two or a handful of people; but such convergences as ball games, rallies, and riots are also, strictly speaking, encounters.

B. Variations

1. Section I.A. defines the encounter in the form that is the easiest to see. Let me now complicate the picture by adding the possibility of the "self-encounter." All encounters involve people in immediate inter-action, but not all interactants need be in separate bodies. By means of memory, consciousness, and symbolization, humans summon particular past humans (more accurately, a residue composite of one) and com-posite categories of persons ("them," "my family," "the government," etc.) into the forefront of consciousness, taking account of what are projected to be their belief and action when dealing with a situation. No other person need physically be present for there to be social interaction in this sense. It is *social* interaction in that the individual is taking other people into account when constructing his own action. Moreover, people interact sheerly with themselves, or, rather, different aspects or dispositions of themselves. To the degree that people engage in internal dialogues with themselves, we may speak of self-encounters, or in the context of situation and strategy analysis, *self-management encounters.* Conversely, when other people are physically present, we may speak of *other-management encounters.*

Cast in strategy terms, we may ask: Who is the most proximate audience of an action in an encounter, self or other? Is the person conducting his strategy primarily to deal with his own thought and action, or primarily to deal with the imputed thought and action of other people?

2. Activity in encounters is usefully distinguished in terms of whether it consists of words or action. Both are almost always involved, of course, but not always, as Section V of this chapter, "Self-Manage-ment Encounters," demonstrates.

Methodologically, these two sets of distinctions can be seen as a kind of checklist in specific empirical inquiry, allowing the investigator to ask himself: Am I overlooking major forms of strategies utilized here? Thus, for example, in only observing people, not interviewing them, one is likely to document only strategic *actions* directed to *others,* shown as cell 1 of Figure 5. Those silent *words* called thoughts directed to *self* are particularly prone to neglect (cell 2), an "error" to which those who study public places are prone.[1] And, words directed to others (cell 3) and action directed toward self (cell 4) are always salient.

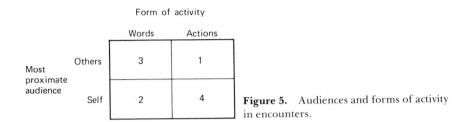

Figure 5. Audiences and forms of activity in encounters.

3. Not all encounters are face to face. Writing, printing, electric signals (as transmitted over telephones), and electronic signals (as in television) make *mediated* encounters possible. These are perhaps as important as the face-to-face variety, although not yet as fully attended to as encounters *per se.*

4. Encounters may, of course, by typed and distinguished in countless ways: self-other, word-action, and direct-mediated are only three basic and formal distinctions. Beyond such basic variations, the cutting edge of dividing them up resides in becoming sociologically substantive. Distinguishing first between self- and other encounters, and putting self-encounters aside for the time being, we may examine three major aspects of other-management encounters: *(a)* starting/avoiding, *(b)* managing, and *(c)* terminating/exiting.

II. OTHER–MANAGEMENT ENCOUNTERS, 1: STRATEGIES OF STARTING/AVOIDING

As ubiquitous, small entities abounding on the social landscape, encounters must be grappled with, first, in terms of either getting into or avoiding them. Two structural variations in this general class of situation must immediately be recognized. One, does the person want to start/join an encounter or not? Two, are the people toward whom the individual is acting personally known to him or not?[2] The dichotomized cross-classification of these two variations allows us to consider four basic starting/avoiding situations:

1. Stranger avoidance.
2. Stranger seeking.
3. Acquaintance avoidance.
4. Acquaintance seeking.

A. Stranger Avoidance. Topically, the situation of stranger avoidance consists of being alone in concrete, public places; and as actually studied so far, the concrete situation of waiting in public places such as bus depots. Scholars of this topical situation, such as Lyn H. Lofland, have asserted it to be a generic situation of socially unsupportive exposure to strangers. The normal protections and supports of personal knowledge of others are absent. The situation is therefore threatening to a degree, and it requires devices that serve to decrease the likelihood of contact with these threatening strangers.[3]

In Lyn Lofland's formulation, as here recast, these strategies of management work at two levels: wholistic body styles and micro body tactics. There are three prime, wholistic body styles:

1. *The Sweet Young Thing* [generally a female]. Once having taken a position, usually a seated one, she rarely leaves it. Her posture is straight; there is no potentially revealing or suggestive "slouching."
2. *The Nester.* Having once established a position, such persons busy themselves with arranging and rearranging their props, much in the manner of a bird building a nest.
3. *The Investigator.* Having first reached a position, the investigator surveys his surroundings with some care. Subsequently he leaves his position to begin a minute investigation of every inanimate object in sight.[4]

Such gestalt body styles are composed of innumerable, micro body tactics, and some main ones as follows:

1. Minimized expressivity, the maintenance of an impassive face.
2. Minimized body contact.
3. Carefully looking before sitting, to maximize distance from others.
4. Minimizing eye contact, perhaps with the use of the "middle distance stare."
5. Fleeing when in doubt about interaction starting.
6. Carefully disattending when in doubt.[5]

B. Stranger Seeking. The abstractions offered by Murray Davis are not "disciplined" in the sense explained in Chapter 5, but he has nonetheless provided some acute clues to strategies and tactics in the situation of a person attempting to begin interaction with a stranger, more specifically, the situation of the "pickup." Recasting from his formulation based on "tasks," Davis points up tactics of

1. Finding qualifiers that make interaction worthwhile.
2. Determining whether the other is free for the encounter.
3. Finding an opener for interaction.
4. Discovering an integrating topic.
5. Projecting a come-on self.
6. Scheduling a second encounter.[6]

C. Acquaintance Avoidance. I am not aware of any study of how people avoid others they know. A college class on social interaction makes, however, these orienting suggestions:

1. Scowling.
2. Rapt attention "elsewhere" in pretend "not seeing" because of another focus such as the landscape, books or papers.
3. Literal and figurative "crossing the street."
4. Honest telling of a desire not to have any more encounters.[7]

Tactics of this kind are, of course, conditioned by such additional variations in the situation as *(a)* how often the acquaintances have to see each other, and *(b)* avoidance altogether versus having the encounter but striving to minimize its temporal duration and psychic involvement.

D. Acquaintance Seeking. Likewise, tactics of acquaintance-seeking encounters have not to my knowledge been investigated. In advance of actual study, a seemingly important variation might be mentioned. The concepts of "known," "unknown," and "acquaintance" require more specification. Two varieties of "known" others are particularly important. One, the name and face of the other can be known to the person without the two having interacted. Second, the person and the other may know each other's names and faces and may have interacted a great deal. The former is the case of introduction seeking, whereas the latter is reencounter seeking.[8]

III. OTHER–MANAGEMENT ENCOUNTERS, 2: STRATEGIES OF MANAGING

Once involved in an encounter—wanting it or not—action must be forged. Action forged, of course, is a function of what the situation is.

And there are a multitude of possible kinds of situations. Proceeding in terms of what the accumulating literature provides, I want to point up eight situations that have most concerned naturalistic investigators or have been speculated about in a systematic fashion: (a) polite stranger, (b) manipulating subordinates, (c) manipulating superordinates, (d) exhortatory, (e) morally questioned conduct, (f) bad news, (g) situated self-constriction, and (h) management in unfocused gatherings. These are largely "bad vibes" situations, as they said in the sixties. Sociologists quite rightly study and theorize about what bothers them, about what engages their anxieties. But it needs also to be stressed that because this is true, the list is not immutable. Its items reflect the problems and preoccupations of the times and locations that produced them. Therefore we should expect any listing of particular situations studied to shift as problems and preoccupations change.

A.   Polite Stranger Encounters.   Unhappily, the champion study of encounters among strangers is not a study in the strict sense—the sense elucidated in Part I. It is, rather a wide-ranging, somewhat disorganized essay. Its detailed insights and suggestions are unsurpassed, however, and it must be dealt with here. I speak of Erving Goffman's *Presentation of Self in Everyday Life*[9] and his related statements.

In Goffman's view, the topical situation of two or more strangers engaged in polite interaction is a *generic situation* with these features:

1.   By definition, each interactant knows very little about the other person. Each knows mostly only what is available there and then in that encounter.

2.   Therefore, what is known and is becoming known in the encounter is crucial in forming judgments of one another. Such judgments typically relate to matters of honesty, propriety, self-control, and deception. What is known and being seen is taken as symptomatic, as indicative of what is not known, of what lies outside the encounter. The prototypical empirical examples are service and sales relationships in modern society, and Goffman uses such instances in profusion: furniture salesmen, doctors, watch repairmen, auto dealers, and the like. They epitomize the "polite stranger" encounters of more recent urban order.

3.   Insofar as the interactants are at some level aware of inferences about the unknown being made from the immediately known, to that

degree they orient their behavior toward controlling and guiding the impression they are making. (Intention aside, behavior can have impression management [strategic] significance even if it lacks consciousness, as pointed out in Chapter 4).

4. But sadly, social life is inherently such that events unfavorable to the impression fostered are constantly occurring. Sometimes these are major inconsistencies, but often they are minor:

> Even the best run interactions throw up events that are expressively somewhat inconsistent with effective claims regarding self. Men trip, forget names, wear slightly inappropriate clothes, attempt to buy a too-small amount of some commodity, fail to score well in a game, arrive a few minutes late for an appointment, become a trifle overheated in an argument, fail to finish a task quite on time. In all these cases, a momentary discrepancy arises between what the individual anticipated being and what events imply he is.[10]

In either event, these are interactionally serious, ongoing discreditings of impressions fostered. Goffman categorizes these discreditings loosely and haphazardly throughout *Presentation of Self*. To the degree they are organized, they fall into four general classes of discrediting events and information: individual, team, role, and region:

(a) The *individual* performer is a source of many types of (1) "performance disruptions," including those of muscular control, showing over- or underconcern in the interaction, doing unmeant gestures, making inopportune intrusions.[11] (2) The front presented may contain inconsistencies among its parts (p. 25).[12] Motivation may fail in the forms of role cynicism (pp. 20–21), derisive collusion (pp. 186–189), communication out of character, (pp. 169–170) or self-distantiation (p. 81).

(b) Individuals cooperating in giving a social performance—a *team*—must keep many kinds of strategic, inside, dark, and other kinds of secrets that may be "sold out" (pp. 141–143).

(c) Various discrepant *roles* emerge to damage the show, most especially the *"informer"* (p. 145), but many others have discrediting potential, as with the colleague, the go-between, and the confidant (Ch. IV).

(d) Social performances frequently have front and back *regions*. Discrediting information openly inhabits the back region. Members of the audience must therefore be kept out, but this is always problematic.

If these are features of the *situation* of polite stranger encounters, what are *strategies* employed to foster, protect, and sustain a positive, consistent impression?

1.   The *individual performer* is seen often to employ strategies of:

(a)   *Role sincerity*—an inner belief in the part he is playing (pp. 20–21).

(b)   *Mystification*—a tendency to shroud performances in an ambience of mystery, the sense that the performer is not fully knowable and has very special knowledge and powers (even though most knowledge and power are on the order of those exercised by the Wizard of Oz—and mystified for that reason) (pp. 67–70).

(c)   *Make-work*—efforts to appear at work when it may not be fully necessary to work (pp. 109–111).

(d) · *Idealization*—efforts to endow the performance with the appearance of more skill, difficulty, and accomplishment than are in fact possessed or required (pp. 34–51).

(e)   *Guarded disclosure*—ambiguous, tentative, and small revelations of self from which the performer can easily retreat if the disclosure is not supportively received (pp. 192–193).

2. (a)   *Teams* need, by definition, to control members, and this often requires a "dramaturgic director" who selects performers, allocates parts, and sanctions conduct (p. 99). Dramaturgic discipline, dramaturgical loyalty, and team morale must be built and maintained; that is, there are a variety of *member control strategies* (pp. 214–217, 175).

(b)   Familiarity among teammates and demeaning treatment of the absent audience are activities having the strategic significance of promoting *team solidarity* (pp. 82–83, 133–134, 170–174).

(c)   Teams as coordinated performers give rise to a new level of strategic activity. A variety of *staging tactics* become possible and necessary, including patterns of staging cues (pp. 177–186), staging talk (pp. 175–176), team collusion (pp. 176–177), double talk (pp. 194–195), and the use of shills (pp. 146–147).

3. (a)   The backstage *regions* of the performance arenas provide opportunities for "backstage fraternization" (p. 196) and "audience derogation" (pp. 171–175) that contribute to team discipline and loyalty.

(b)   Audience segregation, the precaution of confining differing performances to different, appropriate audiences, however, may constitute the major regional strategy of promoting and protecting the impression fostered (pp. 49, 137).

4. Last, but far from least, fostered impressions are strategically protected by *audience tact,* a tactful overlooking of and disattention to occurring discordances (pp. 229–233). Reciprocally, the performers are likely to act tactfully regarding audience tact, thereby facilitating the performance (p. 234).

Two other efforts to analyze polite stranger interaction command our attention. The first is, happily, an empirical inquiry. Laurel Walum focused on the topical situation of the door-opening ceremony between the sexes, suggesting that it was a generic situation of domination generally and sex domination specifically. Occasions of men opening doors for women express men as creatures of authority, activity, and independence, and women as creatures of subordination, passivity, and dependence. This, at any rate, was the traditional situation. The coming of women's liberation in the American seventies spawned challenge and confusion and increasing instances of "deference confrontations," at least on the Ohio State University campus in the early years of the decade, the time and place of Walum's observations.

"What stances do people take to make sense out of their changed ceremonial world?"[13] Walum found people displaying strategic stances of the following kinds:

1. The confused—males bumbling ahead despite all.
2. The tester—males inquiring into the woman's disposition.
3. The humanitarian—males attempting equalitarianism.
4. The defender—males persisting righteously in the traditional ceremony.
5. The rebel—women who aggressively confront in the situation.

The second effort, by Eugene Weinstein, is but an insightful essay sketching out the situated problem of not giving offense to another in polite stranger (and other) situations. Among other tactics, Weinstein points to the following:

1. The *preinterpretation* that staves off offended reception; for example, "Now, be sure not to take this the wrong way."

2. The *postinterpretation* that corrects possibly offended receptions; for example, "Oh, no, that's not what I meant...."

3. The *preapology* that begs others not to be too hard on what one is about to say; for example, "I'm not too sure of this, but...."[14]

B. Manipulating Subordinate Encounters. Given that the social world is massively divided in a hierarchical fashion and thoroughly divided into superordinates and subordinates, attention turns reasonably to how encounters are handled between subs and supers. (Role-scale strategies between them are discussed in Chapter 9.) The best single study—in the formal sense promoted here, and even though not perfect—is provided by Carol Dixon on the topical situation of how preschool teachers manage preschool children in the classroom. Generically, this is a situation of particularly recalcitrant subordinates who have several proclivities that define the situation for the superordinates in that the former:

1. Ignore the directives of their superiors.
2. Force the situation.
3. Engage in passive resistance.
4. Engage in active resistance.
5. Smother the superordinates with affection.[15]

Considered collectively, the micro strategies of coping with this situation form what Dixon calls "the guided options management strategy," a strategy of control falling midway between permissivism and authoritarianism. Its major components relate to managing disruptive behavior on the one hand and anticipating it on the other.

1. Six major tactics are employed in *managing* disruptive behavior:

   a. Ignore the child, if possible.
   b. Demand a response from it.
   c. Introduce a diversion.
   d. Leave the matter up in the air.
   e. Wear it down with explanations.
   f. Seclude the offender if all else fails.

2. A number of tactics function to *forestall* disruptive difficulties, including the following practices

   a. Keeping demands simple and short.
   b. Introducing new activities often.

c. Employing preemptive praise.

d. Making promises.

3. The better to mollify the recalcitrants, benign motives are ascribed to them. By always attributing their disruptive behavior to "accidents" and "forgetting," alone, more abrasive and conflictful constructions of conduct are avoided.

It is important specifically to comment on the paucity of material available on strategies superordinates employ in managing subordinates. One would think that observers of the business, government, and educational worlds, especially, would have long ago evolved a rich literature on how people in those worlds actually do their superordination. Unhappily, my study of their productions suggests they have done little, although there is an enormous literature on how people *ought* to manage. As with so much of life, reality is sacrificed to desire.

Continuing with what we have, the classic but essayistic statements of Willard Waller on how teachers manage school children remain unsurpassed (although, one hopes, they soon will be supplanted by close observation). In Waller's view, teaching is a situation of mixed rapport and discipline in which five main techniques are employed:

1. Sheer command.

2. Formal punishment.

3. Manipulation of the student's relation to his peers.

4. Displays of temper.

5. Appeals.[16]

Superordinates witness a variety of negatively sanctionable activities among their subordinates. For a variety of reasons they prefer not to sanction the guilty underlings, not to "make anything of" what they have seen. More specifically, some types of superordinates witness rather severe psychic impairments among those they could incarcerate or otherwise deal with but which they prefer to avoid. Such is often the case for police in encountering citizens. As reported by Egon Bittner, the police encounter citizens who are easily construed by others as well as by them as being mentally ill, but practical and ideological factors prompt the police to avoid the use of custody. The question for them then is: How is custody to be avoided? Two main strategies are employed:

1. *Restitution of Control.* An effort is made to locate persons the

"potential patient" may know and to leave the individual in their custody.

2. *Psychiatric First Aid.* On encountering the distraught-disturbed person, an effort is made to remove him from the immediate scene and to humor him. His seemingly bizarre claims are not challenged. Thus in a case of "continuing care":

> [A] young man approached an officer voicing an almost textbook-type paranoid complaint. From the statements and the officer's responses it could be gathered that this was a part of a sequence of conversations. The two proceeded to walk away from an area of high traffic density to quieter parts of the neighborhood. In the ensuing stroll the officer inspected various premises, greeted passers-by, and generally showed a low level of attentiveness. After about twenty-five minutes the man bade the officer good-bye and indicated that he would be going home now. The officer stated that he runs into this same man quite often and usually on the same spot. He always tried to lead the man away from the place that apparently excites his paranoid suspicions. The expressions of inattentiveness are calculated to impress the person that there is nothing to worry about, while, at the same time, the efforts the man must make to hold the officer's interest absorb his energies. This method presumably makes the thing talked about a casual matter and mere small-talk. Thus, the practices employed in sustained contacts involve, like the practices of "psychiatric first aid," the tendencies to confine, to disregard pathological material, and to reduce matters to their mundane aspects.[17]

The most successful of superordinates are sometimes alleged to develop "a look of success," a "slick, sealy look," "a special pride" that exudes their behavior. As often presented, this allegation becomes virtually mystical[18] but is in fact a most important topic in interaction strategy analysis. I agree that many highly successful people do "look" different; the question is, how is that look *performed*?[19]

C. Manipulating Superordinate Encounters. For every overling, there are underlings. They too have their day, or at least their way. Although not brought to a fully generic level, Odis Bigus' analysis of milkmen provides us with solid starting material on the situation of the kind of subordinate who is highly and precariously dependent on making sales to a public. The *topical* situation is one in which processes of suburbanization, the growth of supermarkets, price regulation, and certain other factors have made it increasingly difficult for milkmen to make a living in the home delivery of dairy products. Generically, it is a situation of extreme dependence on reluctant "superordinates," or as Bigus calls it, a situation of "power asymmetry."

Milkmen cope with their tight and declining situation through strategies of *customer cultivation.*

1. In acquiring new customers they employ soliciting tactics of "personalizing" and "dealing."
2. Once acquired, a variety of tactics are employed to promote customer trust, including the "sincerity act," "contrived disclosure," and "accentuated honesty."
3. In carrying out their tasks, they nurture pseudofriendship and promote a customer's sense of obligation to themselves.[20]

Among other service-subordinates, attention should be drawn to the generic situation of the cabdriver, which as analyzed by Fred Davis consists of "fleeting, one-time contact with a heterogeneous aggregate of clients, unknown to one another...."[21] This reduces control the cabbie has over the clients and increases his risk. "Propriety, deference, and 'face' are, in the nature of the case, weaker than in most other service relationships."[22] At the level of encounters, certain "tip strategies" arise in an effort to cope with this weakness:

1. Fumbling in the making of change.
2. Giving the passenger a hard-luck story.
3. Making fictitious charges for service.
4. Providing a concerted show of fast, fancy driving.[23]
5. Displaying extraordinary courtesy.[24]

Clients of state bureaucracies are profoundly subordinate in the structural and objective senses, democratic and socialist ideologies to the contrary notwithstanding. Citizen clients must strategize approaches to the bureaucrats. *Appeals* must often be made. As conceived in the insightful work of Brenda Danet and her associates, there is a range of typical situations involving appeals: *(a)* necessary and legitimate action by the bureaucracy must often be *activated, (b)* the *discretionary power* of officials must often be influenced, *(c) refusals* may require countering.[25]

Studying letters to customs officials in Israel (letters I take to be crude but inexpensive substitutes for observation of encounters), Danet and others have delineated three master types of motives ascribed as appropriate for the superordinate to use in, hopefully, granting the appeal.

1. *Appeals to Impersonal Norms.* For example, explicit rational-legal norm ("I am a new immigrant"); appeal for a show of deference ("I have a high level job in the Ministry of Education"); appeal for support of family obligation ("I have a wife and five children to support").
2. *Appeals to the Norm of Reciprocity.* For example, customs-specific compliance ("I filled out all the required forms on time"); appeal to the norm of reciprocity as a fellow Jew ("I sacrificed a great deal...to come and live in the Jewish state").
3. *Appeals to Altruism.* For example, appeal to official's altruism ("If you don't grant this request, you will deprive me of my rights"); deprivation ("I am a sick man!"); appeal for a favor ("Granting my request will help me a great deal").[26]

The most recognizable and standard of subordinates are, of course, neither service personnel or petitioners of bureaucracies. They are, rather, employees of organizations with relationships to a traditional "boss," captives of organizations with relations to custodians, and those oppressed because of class, race, or sex subordinations to oppressors. We meet many examples in discussing role-scale strategies in the next chapter. For now, we may examine the special situation of subordinates who dislike their proximate, short-term setting but do not want overtly to rebel. They face the problem of how most auspiciously to "get through" the situation with the least effort and inconvenience. Specifically, how are orders avoided, once received? Mark Krain has examined this in the concrete-topical situation of army reservists on weekend duty during the years when military service was required in America. As he reports it, the Compleat Decliner of Assignments went about his warrior weekend equipped with these devices for deflecting:

1. *The Prior Assignment.* The enlisted man claims he already has a task, making it impossible to start a new one.
2. *Urgent Situation.* A long-standing foul-up, examples of which are plentiful in the Army, is related to the superior as an urgent situation that must be attended to now.

3. *Incapacity*. The assignment cannot be accepted for reasons of sickness (a relatively rare excuse), permanent medical restrictions, lack of technical knowledge, or lack of legal right (as in driving a vehicle or operating a projector).

4. *Shunning*. The assignment is laughed off as "not serious" and the decliner withdraws. "The aim...may be to convince the NCO that the EM is really too nice a guy (because he is 'funny' and 'hip') to be assigned such a task. It may also be a kind of smokescreen. The enlisted man confuses the superior by the use of humor and withdraws in a cloud of guffaws from the superior's visual field with the final responsibility for completing the task not firmly placed."[27]

Seen more generically, this is a situation of onerous assignments, phenomena in which the world abounds. So framed, it is easy to see how strategies such as Krain reports are not unique but are also employed by children in relation to their parents, workers in relation to foremen, and so on throughout a wide range of topical, subordinate situations.[28]

D. Exhortatory Encounters. Super- and subordination are certainly the fundamental modes of human association; but there is a marginal and rarely achieved additional possibility: equalitarian relations. Relations of equality (or something approaching them) are themselves of many varieties, involving many sorts of generic situations. Although not exclusively confined to equalitarian relations, one of these can be thought of as the *exhortatory* encounter, an encounter of relative fervor in which one party encourages and strives to incite the other party into a view or line of action different from that previously espoused or enacted. Exhortation is more likely to occur among equals, or at least in the fictive equality of talk between strangers or other roles of public life. Exhortatory encounters must be thought of as occurring in two basic forms, face to face versus mediated (with print or audio signals). Although this distinction is irrelevant for many lines of strategic analysis, it is important here because it seems that the most acute work so far has been on mediated exhortations—those printed or radio broadcast. This condition may well arise merely as an artifact of data availability. Printed pages and transcripts of radio broadcasts are already frozen in print or can easily be frozen in print, facilitating their study.

Among analysis of such mediated, exhortatory encounters, the most classic and outstanding effort is that of Alfred McClung Lee and Elizabeth Bryant Lee on techniques employed by radio priest of the thirties, Rev. Charles Coughlin. Seven marvelously generic devices are articulated:

1. *Name Calling.* Omnibus, negative names for the party or parties opposed are employed (e.g., "sissy," "moron").
2. *Glittering Generality.* The proponent-supported ideas and programs are characterized with words that "everyone" supports (e.g., "civilization," "motherhood").
3. *Transfer.* The authority, sanction, and prestige of a widely respected figure is invoked as supporting or rejecting the beliefs advocated or opposed.
4. *Testimonial.* The direct words of an authority are employed for support. Testimonial differs from transfer in the directness of the support lent.
5. *Plain Folks.* The proponent and his proposals are good because they are "of the people"—plain, simple, basic, honest.
6. *Card Stacking.* Facts are selectively marshaled, ordered, and omitted, to make the strongest case.
7. *Bandwagon.* Everyone is coming along and climbing aboard, therefore you should.[29]

Egregiously underattended, Pearlin and Rosenberg's "Propaganda Techniques in Institutional Advertising" is an important analysis of corporation efforts to exhort the American public at the encounter level. Scrutinizing a selection of radio commercials promoted by U.S. Steel, Standard Oil of California, and the Association of American Railroads, the authors ask: What are the techniques by means of which large, "institutional" corporations carry on their efforts to win "good will" from a potentially hostile public? Six devices are elucidated:

1. Elaboration of latent consequences.
2. Humanization.
3. Denial and conversion.
4. Creation of ego-involvement.
5. Status contagion.
6. Omission of profane or divisive subjects.[30]

Although not grounded and disciplined, *Administrative Strategy*, by H. C. T. Hardwick and B. F. Landuyt offers evocative sensitizations for investigation into the encounter exhortations of administrative infight-

ing. Among other suggestions on the situation of overcoming precedent, they note the following strategems:

1. Crediting the new idea as much as possible to those who support
   precedent.
2. Making the new *sound* as much as possible like the old.
3. Asserting that competitors are already doing it or are likely to do
   it.[31]

E. Encounters of Morally Questioned Conduct. Irrespective of
sub-, super-, or other ordination, humans sometimes find their conduct
morally questioned. Others assert or imply that a person's past, present, or projected action is untoward; that is, it strays from the other's
conception of the proper. Action is thus blocked or stalled. The key
feature is *moral* questioning that requires moral management. This is to
be distinguished from merely questioning in neutral terms that requires more neutral, cognitive management.[32]

Such blocking or stalling of action is a situation requiring verbal
response to the newly raised moral question. The person is required to
offer the *motives* of his action. As C. Wright Mills put it: "Motives are
imputed or avowed answers to questions interrupting acts or programs."[33] Motives so seen are not springs of or spurs to action but
trans-acted words believed or denied to be "adequate grounds
for...conduct."[34] That is, seen social situationally, "motives are strategies of action."[35] As such, they are strategized. Unhappily, this fundamentally important activity of motive-offering *to others* (as distinct from
oneself, to which we come in Section V.A.1 of this chapter) has not yet
received adequate empirical treatment. We are still forced to rely on
the abstract and brief but insightful overview provided by Marvin Scott
and Stanford Lyman, who refer aptly to this social production of
motives as "accounting" and "accounts." There are four main aspects of
strategizing accounts.

First, sometimes the questioned person knows in advance that his
action will be subject to moral questioning, and this affords him the
opportunity to consult with others about what his account will be.
These account-forming sessions have yet to be investigated, but impres-
sionistically salient themes include assessment of what the questioner
believes to be plausible and moral in general, the better to gauge the
specific case; guesses relating to what facts the questioner knows; and
enumerations of a range of alternative accounts, which are subjected to

tests of morality and practicality in the eyes of the projected questioner.[36]

Second, such sessions may involve strategizing of *avoiding accounts* altogether. Regardless of whether any account-forming session occurs, one important strategic option in the actual encounter is that of declining to account. This, suggest Scott and Lyman, is likely to take one or more of three forms.

1. *Mystification.* The questioner admits that an accounting is relevant but claims dire, unrevealable facts prohibit accounting.
2. *Referral.* An account is admitted to be relevant, but the questioned person is not the one to give it.
3. *Identity Switching.* The questioned person is not the one the questioner implies, therefore the question is improper or unnecessary.[37]

Third, if an account cannot be avoided, it must be cast in some strategy of delivery, some body-language dramaturgic style. There are numerous dimensions of this. Scott and Lyman are struck with delivery variations in *formality*, ranging from extremely intimate and informal to very distant and stiff. In their terms, these are:

1. Intimate.
2. Casual.
3. Consultative.
4. Formal.
5. Frozen.[38]

Fourth and last, since accounts have content, there must be strategies of content. Scott and Lyman divide accounts into two basic types: *excuses,* wherein the questioned person says he is wrong "but denies full responsibility," and *justifications,* wherein the questioned person denies he was wrong and claims positive value for the action.

Excuses are further analyzed into the following:

1. Claiming an accident.
2. Claiming defeasibility.
3. Reference to biological drives.

Justifications, following Sykes and Matza[39] are further specified as follows:

1. Denial of injury to anyone.
2. Denial of the victim's morality.
3. Condemnation of the questioner's morality.
4. Appealing to higher loyalties.[40]

F. Bad News Encounters. Also irrespective of sub-, super-, or other ordination, existence is subject to bad news. "People die, become crippled, maimed, and chronically ill; they lose their fortunes, souls, self-esteem, spouses, offspring, and friends to death or other humans. Bad news and potentials for its occurrence are woven tightly into the fabric of social life."[41] Modern society is mediated such that the objects of bad news do not always witness the event directly, or are not always able easily to interpret the occurrence as bad news even if it is witnessed. There arises the necessity for someone, a "bearer of bad news," to deliver/interpret the information. Two extreme varieties of bad news bearers may be distinguished: amateur (who do it infrequently) and occupational (who do it routinely as part of making their living).

Lachlan McClenahen and I have tried to analyze one such occupational bearer of bad news, the Deputy U.S. Marshal, a functionary who regularly takes accused persons into custody, delivers convicted people to federal prisons, and serves subpoenae. The *generic* situation of routinely and occupationally delivering bad news is one of deputy concern to:

1. Avoid the moral taint of delivering bad news.
2. Keep the recipient under emotional control.
3. Keep his own emotions under control in the presence of the recipient.

These problematic aspects of the situation are managed at three stages: preparing, delivering, and shoring-up after delivery.

1. Preparing tactics and strategically functional arrangements include: *(a)* distancing by means of anonymity, differences in race/class/education identities, and distinctive equipment and settings; and *(b)* presaging the message.

2. Delivering tactics center on treating the news as "it's just routine."
3. Shoring tactics include *(a)* manipulating the news by (1) scaling down the badness ("it's not as bad as you think," "it could have been worse"), (2) playing up the positive; *(b)* mitigating the stress by displays of being constrained by impersonal roles, use of quips, and tactful disattention.[42]

G. Situated Self. The foregoing situations happen only routinely, occasionally, or sporadically. None is a constant, abiding feature of human existence. Bad news is likely to come only on occasion. Polite stranger contacts are frequent but not continuous, and so on. Let us now consider, by means of the genius of Erving Goffman, a constant and inescapable situation and the ubiquitous strategy people employ to deal with it.

Recasting Goffman into our format of situations and strategies, therefore exercising some license, we may conceive the fundamental and abiding situation of the "situated self" as a situation constructed of three salient aspects or assertions. First, humans play multiple roles that have corresponding social selves and concrete, specific situations in which they are played out. Humans tend to conceive themselves as having many social selves, and as a rule they give allegiance to each. Second, it is in the nature of things that a person can actually *do* only one of these selves at a time. Life is lived in concrete, particular circumstances, in "situated activity systems," as Goffman calls the tiny, immediate task-scenes of everyday life.[43] Every situated activity system offers its participants only the situated role and situated self appropriate to, germane to, a task-scene that is underway. "Doing is being," as Goffman likes to quote Sartre as saying. Third, situated selves are constricting, for while the person can be only that given role and situated self of the moment, he is in fact many roles and situated selves. What he "is" is many things, and the momentary situated self does not of itself allow this to be adequately expressed. Put more broadly, the range of felt demands of the moment may not be adequately provided for by means of the situated self then occupied. Goffman suggests three forms of such inadequacy and consequent constriction. *(a)* Events of the moment may suggest a discrepancy between the more abstract, idealized concept of the role embraced by the person and what the person must now do, as when, perhaps, teachers have to wash their own chalkboards.[44] *(b)* An officially irrelevent role-self, such as a friendship with a coparticipant, may be felt necessary to express. Or, using Goffman's illustration, an adult riding a merry-go-round may feel compelled to express being an adult and not merely and only a rider of merry-go-rounds, the situated self he is then occupying.[45] *(c)* The continued smooth functioning of the situated activity system itself may require expressions beyond those provided for or relevant to the situated self. Other participants may need masked and gentle sanctioning, emotional arousals may require "easing down," and the person's own self control may require bolstering.[46]

How, then, are such discrepancies between momentary being—the situated self—and these other realities handled? As in many of his other works, Goffman is much more careful in delineating and developing analysis of situations than of strategies, first-rate core ideas not withstanding. A single strategy is propounded, the strategy of *role distance.* Role distance is a label for the myriad of concrete behaviors by means of which the person expresses himself to be something more than and something different from what the momentary, situated self defines him as being. No detailed, orderly analysis of acts of role distance is offered by Goffman. Only examples are tossed off, including

joking
sullenness
muttering
irony
sarcasm
being away—being in a "brown study"
playing a jester role
guying
teasing
satirization

Such pointed expressions of incomplete acceptance of the moment serve subtly to inject other realities in a contained manner. The "contained" aspect is crucial. The person is not totally rejecting the role or rebelling. He is simply "holding a role off a little, inserting a small wedge between" himself "and his role."[47] The person is saying "I am more than what is now said by my situated role." Seen close, Goffman notes nicely, people become a blur, "a simultaneous multiplicity of selves."[48]

H. Management in Unfocused Gatherings. We now add another distinction to our initial list of ways in which encounters vary (given in Section I.B of this chapter). "Encounter" is actually shorthand for the more precise term "focused gathering." A focused gathering/encounter involves, following Goffman's usage, two or more face-to-face people maintaining "a single focus of attention, typically by taking turns at talking."[49] The most common of everyday conversations between two acquaintances is a focused gathering/encounter. Except for Lyn Lofland's materials on strategies of avoiding strangers (Section II.A of this chapter), all the situations of other-management thus far reviewed involve focused gatherings. Indeed, the circumstance analyzed by Lyn Lofland involving people in one another's immediate presence but not speaking to one another—not maintaining "a single focus of attention"—defines an *unfocused gathering.*

Avoiding strangers is only one kind of other-management work people do in unfocused gatherings. As suggested earlier (Section II.A), unfocused gatherings and public places lack conventional supports of and protection for the individual's sense of secure identity and dignity. "Making a fool of oneself" by body mismanagement is a potent possibility, even though all those present may be perfect strangers. The lurking potency of body-foolness makes for care and guardedness in how people control their bodies in the wide range of small, "topical" situations that make up the obstacle course structure of public places. Among these is the situation of moving from one public place to another, from being "outside" and "in the street" to being "inside" and "in the place." Such an accomplishment might seem the easiest of actions requiring no strategies at all. But looked at closely, as did Lyn Lofland, one begins to see a startling array of strategic maneuvers that seem to function (at least) to ensure a smooth, unfoolish, protected route through entrances. The act of entrance has three phases, and each one displays some distinctive tactics.

First, "checking for readiness" involves numerous variations on ways in which the individual "checks out and, if necessary, rearranges his body presentation to make certain nothing in his appearance will jar the image he wishes to convey."

Second, there are four major tactics of the "taking a reading" phase, the phase of quickly familiarizing oneself with the situation:

1. Tunneling, or taking a quick look around and proceeding in as though wearing blinders.
2. Blasé pausing at the entrance and taking in the scene.
3. Partial reading, or concentration on some small part of the setting.
4. Avoiding a reading, by for example, walking into the setting backward.

Third, tactics of "securing a stopping place" in the setting are determined by tactics used in the previous stages, producing multiple sequences, such as:

1. The beeline tactic, a further prosecution of the tunneling stance of the second stage.
2. The object concentration tactic, a further prosecution of the partial reading behavior of the second stage.[50]

IV. OTHER–MANAGEMENT ENCOUNTERS, 3: STRATEGIES OF TERMINATING/EXITING

Unlike other units of social organization, encounters are quite short-lived, lasting a day or so at the outside and perhaps modally more on the order of a few minutes. Such a brief life span means that encounters are "dying" around us all the time. And even when not moribund, they are constantly losing personnel before death. In encounters of more than two people, any exit is a small presence of death.

How are such exits and deaths managed? For whatever reason, this area has been virtually unattended, much less treated from a qualitative situation and strategy perspective. The one most salient, existing effort, by David Knapp and his associates, is of an extremely quantitative bent and is less than auspiciously informative. Some trends observed by the Knapp group, however, include preparting increases in agreement words (e.g., yeah, uh-huh), breaking eye contact, shifting the feet and legs, and exaggerated movement such as slamming the feet on the floor or slapping the hands on the desk.[51]

In the study of termination/exiting, it would be of particular interest to scrutinize people who do not seem to know how to break from or terminate encounters. Such people would talk on forever if others did not break away from them, thus how others *do* break from them provides a strategic locus of observation.

V.   STRATEGIES OF SELF-MANAGEMENT ENCOUNTERS

I previously distinguished among encounters in terms of whether the most proximate audience consists of others or oneself. Thus far others have been the most proximate audience. We turn now to encounters characterized by action directed most proximately to managing one's own internal self, one's own states. Other people may or may not be present—that is not relevant here. What counts is the primacy of the person's taking himself—his internal feelings—as his prime object of management.

This class of "encounter" is itself usefully divided into whether the mode of acting is primarily *words* or *action*. Concrete, empirical cases are, of course, always a mixture. But the analytic distinction remains and, important here, studies differ in this *focus*, if not in exclusive emphasis. I deal first with studies of word-oriented self-management.

A.   Word-Oriented Self-Management.   Studies or important theoretical statements emphasizing word-oriented self-management on the micro, encounter scale have dealt with six kinds of internal, situational states: morality management, anxiety of the endless task, rejection by others, maintaining emotional detachment, managing guilt, and dealing with self-tension over interaction.

1.   Morality Management.   The situation of the individual whose conduct is subjected to questioning by others has already been described (Section III.E). The next logical possibility is the individual questioning himself in the same terms and having to provide an account of his morality that is acceptable to himself. What kinds of devices do people employ to find their conduct morally acceptable? Unfortunately, there are no close, disciplined studies of this matter, only a suggestively general essay on juvenile delinquency by Gresham Sykes and David Matza, who tried to identify the definitions that are "favorable to the violation of law." What definitions make delinquent acts seem to be less than delinquent acts, even seem to be moral? Calling these definitions "techniques of neutralization," they point to five strategies.

   a. The denial of one's personal responsibility for the act.
   b. The denial of anyone's being injured by the act.
   c. The denial of the victim's right to protection, because he is a disreputable person.
   d. The denial of the condemners' rights to condemn the perpetrator, because they are hypocrites and the like.
   e. The claim that loyalties to one's friends or other groups supersede loyalty to rules set down in law.[52]

2. *The Endless Task.*   Task situations vary in the degree to which the work required is finite versus infinitely expandable and endless. Many work roles, such as assembly-line worker, are quite precisely finite. The work possibilities of other roles, such as housewife, politician and student, can be expanded without restriction. If infinite expansion is one potent type of human situation, how do people in that spot cope with it? Reflecting on his own experience as a student and interviewing other students, Stan Bernstein asked himself this question and answered it by means of developing the conception of the fritter—"a justification a student gives to himself for not doing student work in response to felt pressures to work."[53] There are four main classes of fritters:

   a. Person-based, including "biological necessity" and "rest on your laurels."
   b. Social-relations based, including group discussion and group work fritters.
   c. Valuative-based, including fritters of "the Higher Good," "experience broadens," and "existential moods."
   d. Task-based, including work scheduling (e.g., "time symmetry" and "great divide" fritters), preparation and creativity fritters (e.g., "the first step is the hardest").[54]

3. *Managing Rejection.*   Life is filled with small and large social rejections, snubs, dismissals, condescending politeness, and questionings of one's moral and intellectual integrity. The individual must decide between accepting such treatment as valid and rejecting it and defining it in a self-protective way. For easily understood reasons of psychic economy, people tend to reject rejections. *How* do they do so? Focusing only at the micro, encounter level, I once investigated how a group of religious radicals dealt with rejection. The group had the sociologically strategic feature of experiencing rejection a great deal, since they aggressively promoted a new messiah who convinced hardly anyone (at the time I studied them, at least). Experiencing a great deal of rejection, they did a great deal of defining. The strategic definitions they employed are phrased rather topically, but the generic implications are evident:

    a. Suffering and rejection were viewed as necessary to one's spiritual growth for the coming new kingdom.

    b. The individuals' personal suffering was placed in the context of the rejection received by Jesus and their own Christ, in comparison to which their experiences were minor, therefore bearable.

    c. People who treated them badly would be punished in the present world when they used up "the good that was in them" and also when put on trial after the new kingdom was established.

    d. Any merit the rejecting person had in the sight of God accrued to the member who was rejected, making him better off.

    e. In failing to recognize the member as an emissary of God, the rejector was therefore rejected by God.[55]

4. *Maintaining Emotional Detachment.* Some environments subject their participants to the continued presence of death, suffering, and emotional upset. Participants experience fatigue, frustration, and a hectic succession of events. Despite such emotionally arousing and trying events, the participants are expected to—and do—remain emotionally cool, controlled, and detached.

Experiences of these kinds occur in the topical situation of intensive care units of hospitals, like the one studied by Robert Coombs and Lawrence J. Goldman. Given these stresses, they want to identify the "coping mechanisms used by...persons as they confront emotionally trying situations."[56] What are the psychosocial techniques employed "to maintain the necessary emotional detachment while caring for critically ill and dying patients?"[57]

The overall strategy, available in full detail in Chapter 12, is one of emotional disassociation and rather aloof coldness; but this is accomplished through the following specific practices:

    a. Humor, which releases tension.

    b. Escape into work, which deflects attention.

c. Language alternation (a proclivity for highly technical labels for illness and injury), which obscures the reality.

d. Rationalization (defining death as the best thing), which redefines tragedy.[58]

5. *Managing Guilt.* Humans sometimes define themselves as having a morally tainted responsibility for what they conceive as morally tainted situations or events. Imagining that they have played a negative role in an untoward episode or arrangement, they may engage in morbid self-reproach, perhaps manifesting "marked preoccupation with the moral correctness of...[their] behavior." They engage, that is, in the self-accusation we commonly label *guilt.*[59] Given the unpleasantness of this feeling, people also desire release from it. How do they accomplish this?

James Henslin has usefully asked himself this question for the special guilt situation of the intimate survivors of people who have committed suicide. He found such guilt following suicide to be constituted of three main concerns:

a. Often not having been aware of the intimate's suicidal intent.

b. Feeling that they should have been able to prevent the suicide.

c. Feeling that perhaps they had done something to cause the suicide.

What are "ways in which...[they] handle or attempt to handle their guilt feelings: their techniques of quilt reduction and neutralization?"[60] Thirteen "guilt neutralization techniques" are explicated.

a. Defining others as being responsible for the suicide.

b. Viewing impersonal factors as "suicidogenic."

c. Denying the suicide.

d. Emphasizing the inevitability of the act.

e. Emphasizing the uncertainty of purposive human acts.

f. Emphasizing the irrevocability of the past.

g. Minimizing the suicide.

h. Conceptualizing the act as good.

i. Defining altruism as the suicide's motive.

j. Atoning for wrongdoing.

k. Using thought transference.

l. Conceptualizing the deceased negatively.

m. Using "guilt neutralizers."[61]

6. *Managing Interaction Tension.* An encounter *qua* encounter is it-self a situation about which the individual must manage his internal states (and external behavior). Perhaps the signal social psychological feature of focused encounters is the shared expectation of *spontaneous, conjoint involvement,* as Erving Goffman puts it. Two or more persons are face-to-face agreeing and striving to maintain a "continuous en-grossment in the official focus of activity."[62] Spontaneous involvement is mandatorily crucial and central, Goffman has theorized, because it does three things.

a. [It] Tells others what...[the person] is and what his intentions are, adding to the security of others in his presence....

b. [It] brings the sharers into some kind of exclusive solidarity and permits them to express relatedness, psychic closeness, and mu-tual respect; failure to participate with good heart can...express rejection of those present or of the setting....

c. [It] confirms the reality of the world prescribed by the [official focus] and the irreality of other potential worlds....[It] is upon these confirmations that the stability of the immediate definition of the situation depends.[63]

But sadly, spontaneous, conjoint involvement in the official focus of an encounter seems to be a precarious, unsteady state, difficult to achieve and to maintain.[64] Interaction euphoria is rare. There is often, instead, a *discrepancy* between what acknowledged overtly and formally the spoken part of the encounter is to be about and where people's actual consciousness lies. Dysphoria rather than euphoria reigns.[65] Some *forms* of this discrepancy between official and actual focus, as Goffman has analyzed (but not studied) them, are as follows:

a. External preoccupation with something unconnected to the topic of that moment, as when a person is performing a currently irrele-vant physical task.

b. Self-consciousness in which the individual becomes preoccupied with how he is doing as an interactant. Sweating, stuttering, and embarrassment are some signals of self-consciousness.

c. Interaction consciousness in which the person has bracketed the flow of words itself as his actual focus, disattending the content of the official focus. This is a malady of hosts and hostesses. "Painful silences" due to lack of "safe supplies" for small talk may evoke interaction consciousness.

d. *Other-consciousness* in which the person focuses on another person in the encounter *qua* person rather than on their officially relevant talk and action. This may arise from the person's striking personal manner (as in being haughty) or appearance (as in being very beautiful or ugly).[66]

Signals of this tension, this discrepancy between official and actual focus, are legion and include, in Goffman's terminology, flooding out incidents, and leaky words,[67] as well as more ordinary embarrassment, loss of words, sweating, and the like.

Goffman's analysis of this situation resembles other works of his, as noted, in being much stronger and better developed than his analysis of strategies that people employ to deal with the situation. Indeed, the first, basic observational work still lies ahead. Gleaning out, however, what little Goffman has suggested about strategies in this situation, we find items relating to preventing, reducing, and recovering.

a. Preventive strategies center on efforts to control the sorts of people one has encounters with in the first place. People productive of discrepancy between official and actual focus—of dysphoria—are avoided. In "Fun in Games" Goffman suggests the ideal interaction partner to be a person rather like oneself in the standard social ways of age, culture, race, and the like, but not *too* similar, because that is productive of boredom.[68] In addition, the official focus of the encounter needs to be, substantively, something that is neither too serious nor too trivial, something that relates in a masterable and challenging but not overwhelming manner to the external, larger social world.[69]

b. Once having occurred, though, reducing or masking strategies brought into play include

(1) Attempting to "ground" the tension through mentioning it openly and attempting an integration.
(2) Shifting the topic.
(3) Performing rituals of apologies, excuses, or disclaimers.
(4) Engaging in furtive byplay with a member of the encounter.
(5) Straining to affect a look of spontaneous involvement.[70]

c. After the encounter, the residue of continuing tension over and concern about the discrepancy is sometimes released in postencounter encounters in which the tense subset of members from the first encounter "flood out" and openly discuss the previous interaction tension.

B.   Act Oriented Self-Management.   These six word-oriented studies and theoretical statements are highly verbal, forming a womb of words, words, words in which people envelop themselves. But words are only one way in which people deal with their relationship to that phantom interaction partner they carry around inside. They deal also and obviously at the level of action (as can also be seen in any of the six studies just discussed).

George Gmelch's analysis of baseball players and their ploys provides perhaps a virtually pure instance of act-oriented self-management. Starting generically, Gmelch observes that tasks in life vary in the degree to which their completion is certain or uncertain, the degree to which there is risk of failure. Topically, the tasks of doing baseball differ in the degree to which performance outcomes are problematic. Thus getting a hit is a relatively problematic matter. Overall, players get hits about 25 percent of the time. Pitching is likewise uncertain. Success is dependent on a complex array of factors, many of them outside the pitcher's control. Loss is frequent. Fielding, in contrast, is rather certain. It is done successfully 97.5 percent of the time.

Important task events shrouded in uncertainty provoke anxiety. Anxiety becomes a state that must then itself be managed in relation to the uncertain situation. How? Gmelch, who was once a professional baseball player, reports that this situation of anxiety over uncertainty about task success is coped with (in part) among professional players by means of rituals, taboos, and fetishes, which are "superstitious," "compulsive," self-obligatory, and "magical" practices done in the belief that they aid performance.

   a. Routines of action called *rituals* include such activities as tapping the bat on home plate a precise number of times and taking a "lucky" automobile route to the ball park.
   b. Rituals prescribe positive action, whereas *taboos* forbid given actions in the belief their occurrence is unlucky. Never mentioning a no-hitter while one is potentially in progress is a taboo shared by all players. Personal taboos include avoiding a given "unlucky" food before a game.
   c. Objects too can be endowed with supernormal powers, can become *fetishes*. A pair of shoes, an old baseball cover, even a hairpin

may be used, kept, and cherished in the belief that it brings special luck.[71]

All these studies of self-management encounters, then, go to the question of dealing with oneself as the *most proximate* audience. Certainly all thought and action *also* have strategic relevance for managing others and not simply oneself. The point is one of primacy, not exclusivity. Gmelch's baseball players are not observing their rituals, taboos, and fetishes for others, they are aiding themselves.[72] Bernstein's students are balming themselves with fritters importantly to deal with felt internal pressure to work. Indeed, we might say more generally that people can be more than their own worst enemy, they can be their own worst interaction partner.

I have tried archivally to assemble, order, and explicate studies of and essays on encounter-scale situations and strategies. Available materials appear to vary significantly in terms of the most proximate audience of the encounter (self or other) and phase of the encounter (starting/avoiding, managing, terminating/exiting). Management of others seems unsurprisingly to be the most active area of work. Within it, attention has focused most prominently on situations and strategies among strangers, subordinates, and superordinates.

NOTES TO CHAPTER EIGHT

1. For detailed discussion of this problem, see Lyn H. Lofland, *A World of Strangers: Order and Action in Urban Public Space*, Ph.D. dissertation, Graduate Program in Sociology, University of California, San Francisco, 1971, pp. 298–310.

2. The question of senses in which people are "known" is complicated and important but need not detain us here. For an excellent analysis and clarification, see Lyn. H. Lofland, *A World of Strangers* (New York: Basic Books, 1973), pp. 13–20.

3. *Ibid.*, Chapter 1.

4. *Ibid.*, pp. 146–151.

5. *Ibid.*, pp. 151–157. See also Margaret R. Henderson, "Acquiring Privacy in Public," *Urban Life and Culture*, **4**:446–455 (January 1975). Howard S. Becker's treatment of dance musicians reports interesting material on use of physical barriers to avoid encounters with patrons. See his *Outsiders* (New York: Free Press, 1963), pp. 96–97.

6. Murray S. Davis, *Intimate Relations* (New York: Free Press, 1973), Ch. 1. On stranger seeking and gaming in public places, see also L. Lofland (*op. cit.* Ch. 8). For an undeveloped account of six ways of opening conversations, see Peter Farb, *Word Play* (New York: Knopf, 1974), pp. 96–97.

7. Selected suggestions from a classroom "analytic exercise" with Sociology 126, Social Interaction, University of California, Davis, Fall 1974.

8. In addition to collecting new data by means of interview and observation, there is much to be learned from the study of memoirs by champion introduction seekers such as Dick Cavett, a man who became a celebrity in part through engineering introductions and doing self-introductions to celebrities. His strategies, as reported in his book *Cavett,* with Christopher Porterfield (New York: Harcourt Brace Jovanovich, 1974), were exceedingly ingenious. Coming at the question of acquaintance seeking from the passivist paradigm (as explained in Chapters 4 and 5, above) there are, of course, some suggestive works on arrangements of settlements that encourage or inhibit acquaintance encounters. One of the most poignant and moving is Christopher Alexander, "The City as a Mechanism for Sustaining Human Contact," in William Ewald, ed., *Environment for Man* (Bloomington: Indiana University Press, 1967), pp. 6–102.

9. Garden City, N.Y.: Doubleday, 1959. I am indebted in what follows to a card index "conceptual inventory" extracted from *Presentation of Self* by Allan Moll, University of California, Davis, Spring 1974. His diligence has facilitated my sorting.

10. Erving Goffman, *Encounters* (Indianapolis: Bobbs-Merrill, 1961), p. 104.

11. Goffman, *Presentation of Self,* pp. 52 and 209.

12. When summary-analysis of a work produces a bead-string of footnote *"Ibids.,"* in the interest of clarity and economy I employ textual page references. When such analyses end, I return to footnote citation. This analytic summary of *Presentation of Self* is not intended to be a full accounting. It offers, rather, main or prime elements.

13. Laurel Richardson Walum, "The Changing Door Ceremony: Notes on the Operation of Sex Roles in Everyday Life," *Urban Life and Culture,* **2:**511 (January 1974).

14. Eugene A. Weinstein, "Toward a Theory of Interpersonal Tactics," in C. Backman and P. Secord, eds., *Problems in Social Psychology* (New York: McGraw-Hill, 1966) pp. 394–398. A tactic of Benjamin Franklin in this situation is worth retrieving: "I made it a rule to forbear all direct contradiction to the sentiments of others, and all positive assertion of my own. I even forbid myself the use of every word or expression in the language that imported a fixed opinion, such as *certainly, undoubtedly,* etc., and I adopted, instead of them, *I conceive, I apprehend,* or *I imagine* a thing to be so or so; or it *so appears to me at present.* When another asserted something that I thought an error, I deny'd myself the pleasure of contradicting him abruptly, and of showing immediately some absurdity in his proposition; and in answering I observed that in certain cases or circumstances his opinion would be right, but in the present case there *appear'd* or *seem'd* to me some difference, etc. I soon found the advantage in this change in my manner; the conversations I engag'd in went on more pleasantly. The modest way in which I propos'd my opinions procur'd them a readier reception and less contradiction; I had less mortification when I was found to be in the wrong, and I more easily prevail'd with others to give up their mistakes and join with me when I happened to be in the right." From B. Franklin, *Autobiography* (1791) (London: J. M. Dent & Sons, Ltd., Everyman's Library Edition,

1908), pp. 162–163, quoted in Robert W. White, *The Enterprise of Living* (New York: Holt, Rinehart & Winston, 1972), pp. 216–217.

15. Carol Dixon, "Guided Options as a Pattern of Control in a Headstart Program," *Urban Life and Culture,* **1:**203–216 (July 1972).

16. Willard Waller, *The Sociology of Teaching* (New York: Wiley, 1932), pp. 198–210. See also Waller's discursive but suggestive discussion of "buffer phrases" employed by teachers in maintaining social distance, a topic quite worthy of full investigation, in *ibid.,* Ch. 17, "Social Distance: Buffer Phrases."

17. Egon Bittner, "Police Discretion in Emergency Apprehension of Mentally Ill Persons," *Social Problems,* **14:**290 (Winter 1967).

18. See, for example, Charles McCabe, "The Look of Success," *San Francisco Chronicle,* November 13, 1974, p. 51.

19. One special superordinate, the WASP male in relation to his women, deserves concerted analysis of how he manages his superordination show. Some leads on encounter-scale ploys used to keep women at housework, for example, are available in Pat Mainardi, "The Politics of Housework," in Robin Morgan, ed., *Sisterhood Is Powerful* (New York: Random House, 1970), pp. 447–454.

20. Odis Bigus, "The Milkman and His Customer: A Cultivated Relationship," *Urban Life and Culture,* **1:**131–165 (July 1972). As with most actual studies, this one is not purely at the encounter scale but contains a heavy element of role-scale strategies.

21. Fred Davis, "The Cabdriver and His Fare: Facets of a Fleeting Relationship," *American Journal of Sociology,* **65:**158–165 (September 1959).

22. *Ibid.,* p. 159.

23. See further on "fancy driving," Anthony P. Cantiello, "Strategic Interaction Among Cabdrivers," M. A. thesis in sociology, City University of New York, 1974.

24. Davis, *op. cit.,* p. 163.

25. Brenda Danet, "The Language of Persuasion in Bureaucracy," *American Sociological Review,* **36:**847–859 (October 1971).

26. See also Elihu Katz, Michael Gurevitch, Brenda Danet, and Tsiyona Peled, "Petitions and Prayers: A Method for the Content Analysis of Persuasive Appeals," *Social Forces,* **47:**447–463 (June 1969). The work of this group is unfortunately marred by strong allegiance to quantitativism.

27. Mark Krain, "On Staying Loose in the Army Reserve," unpublished paper, University of Kansas, 1974, summarized and quoted by permission of the author.

28. One rather massive encounter strategy of subordinates requires separate mention. Analytically speaking, *riots* are encounters, albeit very well populated ones. Much interesting work can and should be done from the perspective of riot-creation strategies. A simple separation of strategic significance and consciousness (as done in Chapter 4, Section VI) allows the examination of "how they are done" despite the fact that agents provocateurs are most frequently not involved, contrary to the conservative's image.

29. Alfred McClung Lee and Elizabeth Bryant Lee, eds., *The Fine Art of Propaganda* (New York: Harcourt Brace Jovanovich, 1939).

30. L. Pearlin and Morris Rosenberg, "Propaganda Techniques in Institutional Advertising," *Public Opinion Quarterly,* **16:**5–26 (Spring 1952).

31. H. C. T. Hardwick and B. F. Landuyt, *Administrative Strategy* (New York: Simon-Boardman, 1961), pp. 202–205. See, further, their nice suggestions on appeals to subordinates and others, especially their discussion of a strategy of surprise (pp. 418–421). Another observation of Benjamin Franklin requires preservation in this context. Trying to start a public library, Franklin encountered resistance and developed this device: "The objections and reluctances I met with in soliciting the subscriptions made me soon feel the impropriety of presenting one's self as the proposer of any useful project that might be supposed to raise one's reputation in the smallest degree above that of one's neighbours, when one has need of their assistance to accomplish that project. I therefore put myself as much as I could out of sight and stated it as a scheme of a *number of friends,* who had requested me to go about and propose it to such as they thought lovers of reading. In this way my affair went on more smoothly, and I ever after practis'd it on such occasions." This extract appears in White's treatment of the autobiography (*op. cit.,* p. 216) quoted from Franklin (*op. cit.,* pp. 139–140).

32. Marvin B. Scott and Stanford M. Lyman, "Accounts," *American Sociological Review,* **33:**46 (February 1968).

33. C. Wright Mills, "Situated Actions and Vocabularies of Motive," *American Sociological Review,* **5:**905 (December 1940).

34. *Ibid.,* p. 906.

35. *Ibid.,* p. 907.

36. As is likely apparent, the "Watergate tapes" of Richard M. Nixon provide a rich source of raw material for analyzing strategies of account formation.

37. Scott and Lyman, "Accounts," *op. cit.,* pp. 57–58.

38. *Ibid.,* pp. 55–57.

39. Gresham M. Sykes and David Matza, "Techniques of Neutralization: A Theory of Delinquency," *American Sociological Review,* **22:**664–670 (December 1957).

40. Scott and Lyman, "Accounts," *op. cit.,* pp. 47–51. For further suggestions, see Erving Goffman, "Remedial Work," in his *Relations in Public* (New York: Basic Books, 1971), pp. 108–118; John Lofland, with the assistance of Lyn H. Lofland, *Deviance and Identity* (Englewood Cliffs, N.J.: Prentice-Hall, 1969), pp. 84–103, and the materials on self-management in Section V of this chapter. A fifth aspect of accounting might be mentioned in passing: postencounter recovery sessions. After occasions of accounting, like-minded accountees withdraw, not untypically to imbibe or smoke and to trot out the accounts they forgot at the previous scene, thus to discredit their questioners. These are among the primordial sessions of solidarity in social life and, as such, commend themselves to study.

41. Lachlan McClenahen and John Lofland, "Bearing Bad News: Tactics of the Deputy U.S. Marshal," *Sociology of Work and Occupations,* in press.

42. *Ibid.* For less developed but helpful thoughts, see Erving Goffman, "On Cooling the Mark Out," *Psychiatry,* **15:**451–463 (November 1952).

43. Erving Goffman, "Role Distance," in his *Encounters* (Indianapolis: Bobbs-Merrill, 1961), pp. 85–152.

44. *Ibid.,* p. 134.

45. *Ibid.,* p. 135.

46. *Ibid.,* pp. 122–126.

47. *Ibid.*, p. 108.

48. *Ibid.*, p. 132.

49. Erving Goffman, *Behavior in Public Places* (New York: Free Press, 1963) p. 24.

50. Lyn H. Lofland, *World of Strangers, op. cit.*, pp. 141–146. See also these useful, starting reports: Charles A. Sundholm, "The Pornographic Arcade: Ethnographic Notes on Moral Men in Immoral Places," *Urban Life and Culture*, **2**:85–104 (April 1973); Margaret R. Henderson, "Acquiring Privacy in Public," *op. cit.*; David A. Karp, "Hiding in Pornographic Bookstores: A Reconsideration of the Nature of Urban Anonymity," *Urban Life and Culture*, **1**:427–451 (January 1973).

51. Mark L. Knapp, Roderick P. Hart, Gustav W. Friedrich, and Gary Shulman, "The Rhetoric of Goodbye: Verbal and Nonverbal Correlates of Human Leave-taking," *Speech Monographs*, **40**:182–198 (August 1973).

52. Sykes and Matza, "Techniques of Neutralization," *op. cit.* See also my expansion and reformulation of these for the deviant act as a general class of acts, pointing to the basic devices of conventionalization and special justification (including the mechanisms of "deserving victims," "lack of personal control," and "transcending commitments") in Lofland with the assistance of Lofland, *Deviance and Identity, op. cit.*, pp. 84–101.

53. Stan Bernstein, "Getting It Done: Notes on Student Fritters," *Urban Life and Culture*, **1**:277 (October 1972).

54. This cryptic capsule of Bernstein's analysis does not, alas, convey that it is a work of genius in creative discernment, a brilliant example of "the gift" that I mention in Chapter 16.

55. John Lofland, *Doomsday Cult* (Englewood Cliffs, N.J.: Prentice-Hall, 1966), pp. 210–211.

56. Robert H. Coombs and Lawrence J. Goldman, "Maintenance and Discontinuity of Coping Mechanisms in an Intensive Care Unit," *Social Problems*, **20**:346 (Winter 1973), reprinted in Chapter 12.

57. *Ibid.*, p. 346.

58. *Ibid.*, pp. 343–349. See also Isabel E. P. Menzies, "A Case-Study in the Functioning of Social Systems as a Defense Against Anxiety: A Report on the Study of a Nursing Service of a General Hospital," *Human Relations*, **13**:95–121 (May 1960).

59. The quoted phrase is from *Webster's Third International Dictionary*, the entry on quilt.

60. James M. Henslin, "Guilt and Guilt Neutralization: Response and Adjustment to Suicide," in Jack D. Douglas, ed., *Deviance and Respectability* (New York: Basic Books, 1970), p. 204.

61. Henslin, *Ibid.*, pp. 203–205. See also James M. Henslin, "Suicide and Significant Others," in James M. Henslin, ed., *Down to Earth Sociology* (New York: Free Press, 1972), pp. 305–315.

62. Erving Goffman, *Encounters*, p. 11.

63. *Ibid.*, p. 40.

64. Erving Goffman, "Alienation from Interaction," in his *Interaction Ritual* (Garden City, N.Y.: Doubleday-Anchor, 1967), pp. 113–136.

65. Goffman, *Encounters*, pp. 17–81.

66. Goffman, "Alienation From Interaction," in *Interaction Ritual*, pp. 117–125.

67. Goffman, *Encounters*, pp. 55–58.
68. *Ibid.*
69. *Ibid.*
70. *Ibid.*, p. 61.
71. George Gmelch, "Baseball Magic," *Trans-Action,* June 1971, pp. 39–41, 54.
72. The response of others, however, might well transform a self-management action into an other-management strategy. Thus rituals and the like among baseball players might be such good public relations "color" that they are produced, often, especially for the fans!

CHAPTER NINE

Role-Scale Situations and Strategies

I. ROLES DEFINED

A. Nature. Humans often organize their conduct in terms of and on the basis of socially shared and abstract categories of types of persons. Jobs or occupations and positions in formal organizations are among the most obvious (to Americans) examples of "socially shared and abstract categories of types of persons." These biographically preexisting categories supply the individual with an enduring sense of his or her "place" and "self," a set of goals, and a set of relations with other "socially shared and abstract categories" with whom it is defined as appropriate and necessary that the individual interact. Such categories provide labels in terms of which people identify one another; they supply answers to the socially ubiquitous question "who is he/she?" We commonly call these categories *roles,* as well as other abstractions, including statuses, positions, locations.

1. Population. Encounters, small groups, and organizations[1] are, by definition, multiperson units of social organization. Relations among several people constitute the units of analysis. Temporal duration and scale of organization are what saliently differ among the three. A role is different in this regard. The focus is the single individual playing his role. This is *not,* however, to say that analysis of roles involves studying only one person. Adequate analysis almost always requires that many performers of a single, given, topical role be compared and contrasted appropriately to elucidate whatever aspect is of interest, be it structure, process, cause, function, or, in the present context, strategy. Role as the single individual is, rather, an analytic feature of role as a unit of social organization.

2. *Time*. As "abstract categories of types of persons that people often use to organize their conduct," roles require some reasonable time to develop and play out. It is difficult to think of a role of less than at least a few days duration, and perhaps weeks are required for their reasonable flowering. At the other extreme, though, some roles are literally "lifetime," as with sex and ethnicity. Some occupational and organizational roles are especially long-lived, making "careers" and "career strategies" possible.

3. *Equipment*. Enormous variation in the temporal duration of roles—therefore also, often, the elaboration of their development—renders some roles quite sparsely equipped and others quite lavishly outfitted.

4. *Space*. Likewise, the foregoing classes of variations are reflected in the physical size of the world occupied by a given role. Temporally brief, less well equipped roles may tend to occupy and range over small amounts of space, and vice versa.

As befits the passivist paradigm, the study of roles has largely been the study of socialization to them, expectations within them, and pressures for conformity to them.[2] Most role theory has aptly been characterized as a species of conformity theory.[3] We desire to strike a different pose, a pose well signaled in Erving Goffman's declaration that a role "is not a material thing to be possessed and then displayed; it is a pattern of appropriate conduct, coherent, embellished and well articulated. Performed with ease or clumsiness, awareness or ignorance, guile or good faith, it is nonetheless something that must be *enacted* and *portrayed*, something that must be *realized*."[4]

Strategies of doing roles cluster around three prime, previously employed, aspects:

a. Strategies of entering/avoiding (Section II of this chapter).
b. Strategies of doing and managing, requiring a distinction between "strategic roles" (Section III) and "role strategies" (Section IV).
c. Strategies of terminating/exiting (Section V).

All three involve "others" as the prime target of action. But as with encounters,[5] strategies can also be directed primarily to the actor's self, a matter treated in Section VI.

B. Distinctions

1. Role-scale strategies differ from encounter-scale (and other) strategies very importantly in terms of the temporal duration required for execution. Roles themselves involve weeks to decades of involvement. Role-scale strategies likewise temporally endure the same kinds of time periods. Encounter-scale strategies, in contrast, have the common feature of briefness, of requiring only moments or at most hours for execution. And role-scale strategies differ from group and larger-scale strategies in requiring for their execution only the single individual in his role. Group and other scale strategies require, in contrast, *coordinated* activity of a *plurality* of persons for their execution.

2. Roles differ in the degree of their formality and social articulation. At the most extreme of articulate formalization, abstractness, and impersonality, roles are embodied in codes of law specifying who can occupy the role, what the performance requirements are, and what constitutes grounds for removal. Many occupations—such as barbers, hairdressers, medical doctors, and bureaucrats—are of this sort. At the opposite extreme, many roles are inarticulate, concrete, and highly personal. Getting in or out of them and doing them is a study in vagueness. Examples of such roles are "tightwad," "philanderer," "good guy," and "asshole." The language is well populated with such "social types," as Orrin Klapp has beautifully and lovingly documented in many studies over several decades.[6] Social types are as much roles as are the more "formal" variety, and perhaps they deserve an even greater share of our attention.

II. STRATEGIES OF ENTERING/AVOIDING ROLES

The initial and most general of role-scale situations involves not having a role—not having, at least, a role that is desired—for all humans occupy roles, like them or not.

A. Discovering. Not having a desired role and strategizing for one requires a first distinction between situations where the role wanted is known and where it is not. That is, some persons develop uneasiness over present roles without having decided what other role or roles they might want. They merely possess a polymorphic propensity toward a new role. This is itself a situation involving a strategic role and strategies of its own, a role sometimes called "the seeker."[7] Seeking occurs in all institutional realms (the political, the familial, the educational, etc.), but it has been given the most attention in the religious. Usually and unhappily, seeking is treated in the passivist paradigm. Recently, though, Roger Straus has made a seminal contribution in beginning to elucidate strategies of seeking new religious roles. In work presented fully in Chapter 12 and only summarized here, he articulates the strategy of *creative bumbling*, whose first stage is *searching* in which the person acts and reacts to promote the discovery of potential transformations. This involves:

1. Making strategic use of situations as they occur or are made to occur.
2. A vague quest of "wanting change."
3. Exploitation of societal understandings about "friendliness"—a breaking down of social distance through "friendly" strategies which range from smiling at strangers to systematic ways of getting strangers to impart information on a friendly basis.
4. Search tactics designed to lead to discovery of agents and information about "trips"—new styles of life.

   a. Facilitating tactics include geographical moves, changing social hangouts or cliques, or the nature of work and recreational activities.

   b. Searching has temporal sequence:

   (1) Closet seeking by using objectified representations such as books and TV programs. Such use tends to bring seekers to *want* change and become covert seekers.
   (2) Covert seeking in prodding friends and contacts for information about changes, eventually becoming aware that they are seekers after *something* and they "come out" as overt seekers.
   (3) Overt seekers are willing to interact as seekers and able fully to develop search tactics.[8]

We can hope that this kind of discernment will soon be forthcoming from studies in other institutional realms. What strategies, for example, do disaffected women employ in discovering more "liberated" roles?

B. Choosing. For some few people, more than one role becomes possible and even attractive. At minimum, each new role encountered can be assessed for possible incumbence, regardless of whether it is objectively available for the possible aspirant. Strategies and tactics of assessment are necessary. Here again, the efforts of Roger Straus provide a lead with regard to seekers assessing "transformation trips" they discover. There are often:

1. Jiujitsu tactics: Getting agents to define one as a "good prospect" and reveal "inside" information about the trip, its promises and techniques of entry. These include the use of extended friendly tactics, "What can your trip offer me?"

2. Checking-out tactics: Recognized agents and trips are checked out at a more rational, cognitive level to make sure of accuracy of first impressions, that the trip really is "for me," and to discover how to exploit the trip to the seeker's advantage. These tactics include a conventional wisdom of "caveat emptor" with seekers wary of "being taken" and often occurs over a period of time, using friendly tactics and other information extraction devices, asking questions and comparing answers with one's sense of reality, testing means of change, and feeling out the "vibes."[9]

C. Inventing. Seekers after new roles can go in two basic directions: invent a new one, or gain entrance to an existing one. Most people, of course, take up existing roles. A few creative and hardy types, however, engage in *role enterprise* and create roles whole-cloth. Founders of religious and other organizations are the most conspicuous examples of this, as are various kinds of "eccentrics." Robert Simpson, an elderly man who for many years picketed the California State Capitol building outfitted in sandwich boards, well illustrates the latter.

By "invent" I do not mean that the role concocted is something new under the sun. Organizational and philosophical founders and eccentrics are the most ancient of human roles. The point, rather, is that such roles start out unvalidated and socially unsupported. They move against an indifferent or hostile world. This is in contrast to simply deciding as a result of seeking to enter college or to marry or to become a parent or to get a job. Roles such as student, spouse, parent, and employee are the most prosaic of socially recognized, accepted, and supported roles.

Since there are to my knowledge no (qualifying) studies of how people invent roles, there is much to be accomplished in this area. (Since, however, this topic also often involves group and organization formation along with role invention, it overlaps with discussions in the two chapters that follow.)

D. Gaining Acceptance.   For the less inventive and hardy—for most of us—there are existing roles. Having discovered one, a person encounters many problems of gaining access, of convincing the "gatekeepers" that he is a worthy aspirant. (Some social organizations are, of course, so understaffed that entrance is little problem, a circumstance reported once to have obtained among small midwestern high schools.[10]) The occupational and educations realms have been the most evidently problematic in recent America and have on that account spawned a rich literature advising people "how to" get the job or college "of their choice." It is sad that such literature is overwhelmingly advice rather than empirical inquiry.[11] In the religious realm, we may refer again to Roger Straus' work on seekership and the stage of *creative exploitation* of which *realizing transformation* is a central component and involves:

1. Verifying—getting the transformation made real to self and others. Various tactics are used, ranging from introspective assessment of feeling and perceptual/cognitive change, exploitation of institutionalized provisions for verification, and, most prized, "unsolicited" outside validation accomplished through manifesting one's changedness in action and behavior.
2. Immersing—the realizing tactic of "the way to be changed is to act changed." The verified transformee now seeks to immerse self in the day-to-day world of a citizen of the new cosmos. This involves (*a*) discovering how to act properly changed, (*b*) acting that way, and, (*c*) stabilizing these behaviors as unnoticed habit and routine. One accomplishes this by first acting as a *redhot,* exploiting the processes, mechanisms, and potentialities of commitment. This includes

   a. Practice of the technology, social and private.
   b. Participation in the formal scenes and activities of the trip.
   c. Acting in an idealized manner, complete with whatever appearances, languages, behaviors, and so on, are ascertained as signifying a committed Christian, Scientologists, etc.[12]

Straus has noted wryly that the best catalogs of acceptance strategies have likely been written by participant-observer sociologists who have long confronted problems of getting into and along with a wide variety of social settings.[13] The strategizing of courtships and affairs also seem to be important locales in which role acceptance efforts can more easily be "seen."

In the context of highly informal roles, Orrin Klapp has provided many helpful leads on what I read as strategies of becoming a hero, a villain, or a fool. Regarding heroes, Klapp asks himself how talented but undramatic figures conduct themselves to facilitate their audience's thinking of them as heroes. He sees four basic kinds of strategies:

1.   Aspirant heroes provide "color," which is the judicious use of eccentricity, the avoidance of total propriety and conventionality. This takes such concrete forms as *(a)* acceptably odd practices (e.g., Ronald Reagan eats jelly beans); *(b)* trademarks (e.g., General Patton's pearl-handled revolvers); *(c)* dramatic acts (e.g., Toscanini, on the spur of the moment, conducting *Aida* entirely from memory).
2.   They act alone. They avoid an overshadowing, too talented, and too ambitious staff. They credit others generously, but hog the main scenes carefully.
3.   They are aggressive, but carefully and guardedly so.
4.   They promote personal encounter in dramatic moments.[14]

Perhaps no one wants to achieve villainy, but for anyone who does, Klapp has discerned some strategies.

1.   Aspirant villains contrive to resemble established villain types in appearance, demeanor, and background.
2.   They allow themselves to become publicly a big and powerful party confronting a small and powerless party who is defeated; that is, they appear to "take advantage," to employ power too ruthlessly.
3.   They attack popular heroes.
4.   They allow themselves to seem too clever.[15]

And strategies promoting others to define one as a fool include the following:

1. Promoting a fiasco, a failed project that is not a tragedy or disaster, as in General Pershing's unsuccessful pursuit of Pancho Villa in Mexico.
2. Encountering comic frustration, a ludicrous display of ineffectuality, as also exemplified by Pershing and Villa.
3. Encountering belittling juxtapositions, as in the relation between campaign prankster Dick Tuck and Richard Nixon.[16]

E. Preparing. On occasion, a person is accepted into a role some weeks or months before actually assuming it, as when people are drafted by the military, accepted by a college, or engaged to be married. The interstitial period is then itself a situation with which to cope. It is a "limbo," waiting, and projecting situation. How is it managed? David Hamburg and his associates posed this question about fourteen highly competent and successfull college-bound high school seniors whom they interviewed eleven times from the spring of their senior year to the end of their first year of college. Strategies depicted are summarized by the investigators (quite abstractly) as a

> tendency to reach out for new experience, a tendency to be active in dealing with challenge and an enjoyment in the sense of mastery. This pleasure in effectance served to facilitate an active involvement and pleasure in coping with the new situation.
>
> In addition, more specific mechanisms were observed. Through a variety of ways, these students developed and maintained an *image of themselves as adequate* to the perceived requirements of the new situation. Students referred back to analogous situations in the past which had been adequately mastered, thus reassuring themselves about their ability to handle these situations in the future. They referred also to their present self-image as evolving gradually in desired directions, and through *anticipatory detachment* saw themselves as ready to establish new relationships at college. By *seeking out information* about the new situation, they reduced some of the ambiguity in it and, in so doing, felt better prepared to deal with it.
>
> By *role rehearsal* they prepared for the new situation by rehearsing in advance forms of behavior which they associated with college students. In addition, they rehearsed behaving more like adults before going off to college. Their summer job experience confirmed their self-image as people adequate to master tasks in the adult world.

* * *

Other mechanisms seemed understood best as ways in which distress was contained within manageable limits. Our students were not without anxiety about college, but derived considerable support from an awareness that others were experiencing anxiety as well. "We're all in the same boat" was the attitude that was most common in maintaining anxiety from becoming overwhelming. Experiencing anxiety did not in turn signal a feeling of uncomfortable distance from others, but rather as something that was shared.[17]

F. Avoiding. The situations of discovering, choosing, inventing, gaining acceptance, and preparing for roles all imply desire for a role either as a general propensity or as a concrete object. We know that some people are presented with roles they do not want to take up. This occurs with alleged frequency regarding military, marital, and parent roles. The concepts of "draft dodging" and "shotgun weddings" express such possibilities. People who are reluctant to assume roles that are proffered presumably have their ways, too. Perhaps someday we will learn about them.

III. STRATEGIC ROLES: ROLES FOR MANAGING SITUATIONS

Once having entered a role or larger scale situation, role-scale strategizing can begin. Role strategizing itself occurs on two levels of scale that can be captioned strategic roles versus role strategies. The term "strategic role" refers to the role itself taken *in toto* as a strategy. "Role strategy" refers to the smaller, internal strategic components that make up how the role is fabricated. This distinction in scale of view is schematized in Figure 6, where role strategies are represented as "internal" to the role taken as a strategy. Every role has an overall strategic significance and *also* micro role strategies by means of which the role is performed, which "add up to" global, strategic role significance. Roles *are* strategies as well as being constructed *of* strategies.

The distinction is one of distance and detail. Overall and general depictions of roles and their strategic relation to their containing situation provide merely a "strategic role" analysis. Closer, more detailed, internal analysis of micro gambits provide a "role strategy" analysis. I should be clear that this distinction arises out of studying how investigators have actually presented analyses of roles. Some important analyses have the more distant and global structure captioned strategic roles. Other analyses stand closer-up.

A. Strategic Formal Roles. The strategic view of roles is clearest with regard to highly formal and articulated roles. It is most especially evident in the context of newly established formal organizations and the roles of which they are composed. An organizational "head" or "coordinator" is typically established, and various internal partitionings

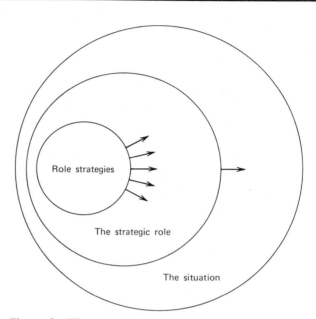

Figure 6. The strategic role versus the role strategy focus.

into divisions or committees are performed for the purpose of "getting things done." Roles are seen by participants as tools in the performance of functions. This case in which the strategic nature of roles is most obvious, then, should help us to see that any and all roles may be scrutinized for their strategic significance.

B. Strategic, Informal Roles in Occupations. It is but a short step to appreciating that formal roles in occupations and organizations develop informal, "underlife" supplements that are further forms of strategy in coping with role-scale situations. The older but still basic study is that of Ralph Turner on the *topical* situation of the Navy disbursing officer and his *generic* situation of being socially ground between the ideal of bureaucratic impersonality and the realities of bureaucratic life. Three such realities are that (*a*) regulations are often in conflict, providing no sure guide to action, (*b*) persons of higher rank than the disbursing officer can bring pressure on him, and (*c*) informal ties and groups can make strong "improper" claims. The generic situation of the disbursing officer is thus quite difficult and is coped with, at the strategic role level, along these global lines:

1. The *Regulation* type approximates the true bureaucrat in that he remains impervious to rank, informal structures, and the orders of his superiors....

2. Opposite is the [*Scoffer*]...who doubts the potency of the General Accounting Office and...will do anything for a friend or superior without debate....

3. On a different axis...is the *Sincere* type...[who] fails to recognize conflicts between regulations and orders from superiors and is unaware of the importance of informal systems....

4. The commonest type is the *Realist*. Regulations are seen as illogical concatenations of procedure...[which] often, when strictly applied, defeat...the purpose for which they were constructed....They [can] assume the regulation facade...but know how any payment may be made "legally" if the request comes from an important enough source.[18]

Sufficiently elaborated and carried out over decades, it becomes meaningful to speak of informal *career strategies* in occupations and organizations. One such study is provided by **Oswald Hall** for medical doctors, who exist in the role-scale situation of a need to "accumulate, retain, refer, and transmit patients; levy and collect fees; work out satisfactory relationships with colleagues; and find niches in the medical institutions of the community."[19] Hall discovers three basic types of strategic roles physicians employ in acting toward their shared situation:

The prominent features of a [*friendly* career] are loyalty to patients and solicitude toward the careers of a few colleagues who [are] defined as friends. [The *individualistic* career]...is characterized by open competition with other doctors for clientele and by an implicit acceptance of a medical career as a commercial venture. [The *colleague*]...career differs from both in its close identification with the medical institutions of the community....It involves meticulous etiquette as far as a group of similarly placed colleagues is concerned.[20]

C. Strategic Social Types. The myriad of ways in which people cope with role-scale situations are hardly confined to formal and informal occupational and organizational roles. Social life is highly fluid and changing and makes formal and informal strategic roles decidedly insufficient to allow people adequately to make their way about. Much more is needed to be able to construct one's own action and to decipher the actions of others. "Social types," as that concept has been developed by Orrin Klapp, are one important class of such supplementary devices. Social types may be thought of as "concepts of roles that have not been fully codified and rationalized...[that are] a chart to role-structures otherwise largely invisible and submerged."[21] They are constructs that fall, conceptually, somewhere between what we define as individual and idiosyncratic behavior on the one side and formal/informal role behavior on the other. "Between knowing a person's formal status only and knowing him intimately there is a kind of knowledge that 'fills in.'"[22] Social types make possible a "finer discrimination than the formal...structure recognizes."[23] From thousands of them, consider:

underdog
bigshot
smart operator
dude
good guy
bully
liar
cheat
two-timer
uncle Tom
dragon lady
sambo
crackpot
fanatic
simpleton
sissy
sad sack[24]

As we move further away from formality we, as participants in social life, have a stronger and stronger tendency to conceive the roles people play as being "really them," as being the outward manifestation of their inner being. If there is a central tenet of sociological dramaturgics, it is that such a tendency "ain't necessarily so." What we see people being is not especially what they inwardly are; it is merely what we see them being. Submission is not necessarily submissiveness, rebellion is not necessarily rebelliousness.[25] That is, social types such as those listed are auspiciously seen as *social roles,* not personal, deep being. As such, they can be assumed and cast off much like roles in stage plays, despite our propensity as viewers to collapse role and self in social life.

This point gains special meaning and significance in the context of social types that develop among subordinated and oppressed categories such as American blacks and women. Among both, there has been a relatively widespread "sambo" social type or role, a role having central traits of, in the case of blacks, incompetence, deference, and apathy, and passivity and nurturance in the case of women. Often both oppressor and oppressed believe that patterns of such conduct reveal "personality" and "deep character." A social type view, in contrast, sees the sambo (and other types, discussed in a moment) as strategies of dealing with a situation of domination and oppression.

> Rather than seeing subservience and emotionality as personality traits of women, we may view them as manipulative strategies to attain desired goals....[I]nstead of viewing deference and ignorance as characteristics of black personality, we open the possibility that they may be subtle techniques for attaining desired ends.[26]

"Character type" imputations of some sort are probably inescapable nonetheless. A view sponsoring a maximum interpretation of conduct as role behavior must itself sponsor *some* concept of deep character, a fact about which Stephen Warner, David Wellman, and Lenore Weitzman have been candid. They allow that the necessary character conception might best be thought of as the "operator" deep-character perspective. It is a perspective, however, that has less salient character implications than other perspectives, "...primarily the imputation that the oppressed [and presumably and other] individual retains the capacity to calculate."[27]

> In the case of both women and blacks, the Operator often exhibits a Sambo posture of deference, the appearance of ignorance, weakness and subservience. In both cases, one's real feelings are concealed in an attempt to outwit the dominant party....A shared characteristic of all Operators is an extreme sensitivity to the points at which the dominant group is susceptible to influence....This sensitivity is necessary because both women and blacks must skillfully employ informal power and manipulation if they are to succeed.
>
> The Operator perspective allows us to see the stupidity and ignorance attributed to women as a dramaturgical posture. "Through

long centuries, women have had to interest men somehow, if they were to achieve any economic security and social status at all, and so those who were not stupid and silly by nature had to carefully cultivate such stupidity and silliness until it came naturally!" Women often adopt a passive demeanor to assure men of their unchallenged superiority in the relationship. But behind the passive demeanor is an active role player.[28]

Surveying social types in black ghetto folklore and reality, Richard Millner notes the two persistent though variously named types of the gorilla or bad man and the trickster (e.g., cat, pimp). These seem to be two different role strategies of dealing with dominant white society: "the devious (trickster) and the open confrontation (bad man)."[29]

They are...in a very practical sense...strategies for survival. After all, when you are on the bottom of the social order, there are only two basic ways to beat the Man: you can fight him directly or you can trick him.[30]

Note the striking parallel with Thomas Hobbes, according to whom there are only two basic forms of social relations: force (the bad man) and fraud (the trickster). Social types such as these are the role elaboration of these two basic possibilities.

D. Strategic Personal Roles

1. If we can conceive a wedge between doing and being in the instances of formal and informal occupational and social type roles, we can perhaps then go on to conceive the possibility that what we consider most "internal," as most inherent—our "personality"—is itself a learned social role, built over time and taking account of given situations and known-about personality-role strategies. Said differently, perhaps even when we feel we are seeing people as most "themselves," as acting most "naturally," as playing out their highest or lowest impulses, we are again seeing another type of strategic role, one we label "personality." The same of course applies to our perception of ourselves as "being ourselves." Thoughtful personality theorists such as Robert White have long entertained such a possibility, although I fear empirical elaboration of the notion has not proceeded very far. White has himself suggested such personality styles as:

a. The derogatory style.
b. The humorous style.
c. The cool, intellectual style.
d. The impulsive style.[31]

Along these same lines, James Barber, a political scientist, has set about analyzing the strategic personal styles of United States Presidents in terms of activity versus passivity and happiness and optimism versus sadness and irritability.

a. The "active-positive" type tends to show confidence, flexibility, and a focus on producing results through rational mastery (e.g., Harry Truman).
b. The "active-negative" tends to emphasize ambitious striving, aggressiveness, and a focus on the struggle for power against a hostile environment (e.g., Lyndon Johnson, Richard Nixon).
c. "Passive-positive" types come through as receptive, compliant, other-directed persons whose superficial hopefulness masks much inner doubt (e.g., William Howard Taft).
d. The "passive-negative" character tends to withdraw from conflict and uncertainty, to think in terms of vague principles of duty and regular procedure (e.g., Dwight Eisenhower).[32]

2. One class of "personality" roles is especially intriguing from a strategic view—that class of role we dub "mental illness," "craziness," "madness," and the like. One of the most salient features of the crazy role is that like *all* roles, it is a shared, known about label of a type of person. All ordinary people carry stereotypes of craziness in their heads. They employ such labels in deciphering and coding other people's conduct.[33] It should not surprise us then to conceive of people electing to play such a known-about role in dealing with certain situations. As one commentator has phrased it:

That mental illness is a mode of life chosen, more consciously than unconsciously, by a person is not a popular view. A person chooses his neurosis, or even his psychosis, to save him from some fate far more terrible than the inconvenience of mental illness. Who of us has not met the person who, at the height of his powers, suddenly resigns from life, takes to his bed, or develops some symptoms which make it impossible for him to continue with the business of effective living? Threatened with the murder of his personality, and that is what all the threats come down to, a man will adopt any role which will lessen his conflict with life, itself, which is the threat. Dope, fear of heights, booze, compulsive washing, deviant sex, all the ticks of the psyche, in fact—these are not accidents, or punishments. They are choices.[34]

Study of people in mental hospitals "diagnosed" as "schizophrenic" has suggested, indeed, the accuracy of an "operator" model of their functioning. On the basis of a series of detailed studies of mental hospital living, the psychologist team of Benjamin Braginsky, Dorothea Braginsky, and Kenneth Ring declare:

What appeared most blatantly erroneous to us in the psychiatric conception of the schizophrenic was his portrayal as a weak, acquiescent and ineffectual individual. Everything that we saw pointed to exactly the opposite characterization: The schizophrenics we observed were, as a rule, manipulative and resourceful individuals whose behavior was calculated to serve their primary motivations, which they were able to satisfy with surprising frequency and ease.[35]

*   *   *

The [prototypical] patient emerges as an individual who...very often chooses, though not necessarily consciously, institutionalization as either an intermittent or enduring way of life. Once in the institution, the schizophrenic exploits his environment in a wholly effective and rational manner in order to extract from it personally satisfying outcomes.[36]

The mental hospital and its role of mental illness can be a strategic and perhaps even attractive alternative in many yet not clearly understood situations.

Institutional life...obviously has many advantages. First...one moves into a world that will provide some sense of temporal stability; it is as if one steps out of a maddening swirling river onto the comforting immobile shore. Second, it is a simpler world and one...over which it is possible to exercise a considerable amount of fate-determination. Third, leisure time activities, and in general, a hedonistic pursuit of them, are not only possible but are embedded into the very structure of hospital life itself. Such an environment, we submit, would be appealing to *anyone*, but especially to a person for whom the outer world is a source chiefly of melancholy and despair.[37]

Mental hospitals and the crazy role therein provide a "last resort"—as the subtitle of the psychologists' report suggests—in the ironic sense of a place of leisure for economically disadvantaged people. The wealthy have always had less stigmatized resorts to which they repair in the leisure role, obviating temptations to enter those government-sponsored havens known colloquially as nut houses.[38]

E. Strategic Captivity Roles. Having squeezed down the conventional notion of self and reclassified its content as role, we may pull back to two sets of materials more easily seen as role behavior. One set is a logical subset of subordinate roles as a general class, one of which (the sambo) has been mentioned in the discussion of social types. This is the "captivity role," a kind of role occupied and coped with by inmates of prisons, mental and other hospitals, and prisoner of war camps, among other total institutional locales. Perhaps because of ease of access, liberal government funding, and public fascination, captivity roles have (seemingly) been a much more popular object of study than virtually any other subordinate role. Among studies of prisons, John Irwin has identified three broad approaches to coping with that setting:

1. Jailing: modes of cutting oneself off from the outer world and making a permanent home in the world of the prison.
2. Doing time: modes of retaining outside commitments without undergoing any change of self in prison.
3. Gleaning: modes of seeking to change oneself in prison to prepare for a changed life outside of prison.[39]

Such broad strategic stances are operationalized in a wide variety of more specific "argot roles," as they are called in the sociology trade, some of the more colorful being the "wolf," "tough," and "ball buster."[40]

Hospitals, even the strictly medical kind, are total institutional settings in which the patient's day is planned and his possessions reduced and governed; personal information is gathered and recorded on him, and his spheres of life are collapsed.[41] What wholistic tacks do people strike toward such a situation? Observing a rehabilitation institution they call Farewell Hospital, Julius Roth and Elizabeth Eddy document the major strategic roles of

1. Escaping.
2. Attacking.
3. Colonizing.
4. Talking the party line.[42]

F. Strategic Superordinate Roles. Social scientists have been so ideologically disdainful of superordinates that they have apparently felt it unnecessary to develop clear pictures of their situations, much less their strategies, save in a few rare cases. Among them, Melvin Dalton's *Men Who Manage* shines for its recognition of the ambiguity of the environment in which many superordinates operate and the necessity to improvise moving sets of actions. The industrial managers scrutinized by Dalton operate in a situation he sums up (somewhat too topically) as having to

> (1) show that his relations with the union are good but not too good; (2) defeat the ambitions of those seeking his position; (3) meet the cost pressures of higher management, and (4) protect himself against the poaching and intrigues of other departments; (5) oppose stratagems of the union without offending superiors or revealing his techniques and pacts to other departments; (6) aid the advancement of clamoring subordinates, while considering the effect on his own position and the department as well as the organization if he allows able people to quit the firm; and weigh the ego-problems in his department when he sponsors a man; (7) avoid complications with staff groups; and finally, (8) to advance his own career.[43]

Dalton characterizes the most general strategy for dealing with this complexity as "learning to live with ambiguity," but the details of his model are unfortunately underdeveloped, too elusive and complex for further rendition here.[44]

On the strategy side, the more general literature on organizational superordinates documents again and again three basic styles of "leadership":

1. Work-oriented, including elements of directiveness, structuredness, authoritativeness, restrictiveness, and so on.
2. Person-oriented, including elements of democracy, permissiveness, participativeness, and so on.

3. Structured, a blend of work- and person-oriented styles.[45]

This instrumental-expressive, active-passive, order-freedom, contrast runs deep into all life and activity, emerging everywhere and time and again in myriad forms and blends. Among them, the special situation of women who play high-level political, bureaucratic, and business roles furnishes a special cast to the contrast. Occupying contradictory statuses, their strategic styles reflect the specialness of their situation, according to Naida West, who observed and interviewed the fourteen most powerful and prominent women of northern California. One of the main styles was basically person oriented but displayed the variant form of what West calls "playing Mama," a style with these features:

1. Developing people's potential as a means of increasing production.
2. Hiring by "chemistry," by feeling.
3. Use of tactics designed to increase informality (e.g., everyone goes by first name; addressing people as Dear, Sweety-pie, Poor Baby, Love, etc.); arriving early to chat with people, getting involved with their personal problems; assigning work by empathy rather than strictly formal job categories; hand clasping, hugging, patting, and walking arm-in-arm with people of all social ranks; extensive use of humor to "relax people" and ease tensions.
4. Use of special ways of relating to people who are prejudiced against her, designed to "win them over."
5. Tendency to develop a "following" among workers and former workers.
6. Shows emotion, both hot and cold.
7. Tendency to use flamboyant language and style.
8. Thinks of herself as more devoted to the organization or the "cause" than as filling an office.[46]

The contrasting style, what West calls "one of the boys," approximates the traditional work-oriented style:

1. The main goal is increasing production, by whatever means.
2. Comfortable with formality.
3. No special strategies for handling people other than what is formalized by the organization.
4. More likely to think of self as "doing the job the best way possible" than being devoted to a "cause."
5. Tendency to hide some emotions.

6. Uses perceived male standards of behavior when in doubt.
7. Little bodily contact.
8. Maintains social distance.
9. Does not typically discuss personal problems with co-workers.
10. More emphasis on work ethic.[47]

IV. ROLE STRATEGIES: STRATEGIES OF MANAGING ROLES

Looked at close-up, roles are composed of the array of microstrategies
here termed "role strategies." Studies of them are again usefully classified in terms of hierarchal location: superordinate, subordinate, and
equalitarian. This is not to imply, certainly, that a given strategy appears only or even mostly at one of these three levels. Many do so
appear, however, and it is appropriate to highlight such a tendency
despite the omnilocationality of some strategies.

A. Role Strategies Among Superordinates. Role-scale strategies
among superordinates have focused upon situations of ascending,
coaching, maintaining order, assessing subordinates, defending against
attack, and "cooling out" failed subordinates.

1. Ascending. An individual typically begins his superordination as a
"successor," as the replacement of a preceding leader. Often the prede-
cessor was well liked, and this leads to resentment from subordinates and
other difficulties with them. Liked or not, subordinates have worked
out some structure of accommodation that the successor is feared to
threaten. When the successor views himself, indeed, as a "change-
agent" rather than as a "caretaker,"[48] certain lines of strategy become
mandatory for his survival, much less power ascendance over subordinates. As analyzed by Alvin Gouldner, these include the following:

a. Pretended friendliness.
b. Close supervision.
c. Appeasement.
d. Strategic replacement.
e. Bureaucratization.[49]

2. Coaching. The "coach" is one special kind of generic superordinate. A coach is someone who "seeks to move someone else along a

series of steps."[50] The coach's situation is one of balancing "two poles: he must not pressure the student by his own impatience, yet he must force movement at those junctures when the follower appears ready but reluctant to move, is in fact really 'there,' but does not realize it."[51] *Timing* is therefore central to the situation. Generalized tactics of coaching, as depicted by Anselm Strauss, include the following:

a. The prescription: sets of exercises and lessons.
b. The schedule: conceptions of rates of proper progress.
c. The challenge: moments when the pupil is pushed forward into what he defines as the risky or dangerous.
d. The accusation: moments of calling attention to backsliding.[52]

3. Maintaining. Ascending and coaching entail efforts to establish or change situations. It is likely, however, that much superordination strives merely to maintain a *status quo.* Among policemen as superordinates, for example, a large portion of effort is directed to the reactive activity of "peace keeping" rather than to the proactive activity of "law enforcement," Egon Bittner reports.[53] This is the prime focus in skid row areas especially, where Bittner says that three broad strategies of peace keeping are employed. These involve:

a. Particularization of knowledge: officers aggressively develop and cultivate a detailed knowledge of persons and places in the skid row area.
b. Restricted use of culpability: arrest is employed as only one among many resources available for keeping the peace.
c. Ad hoc decision making: officer actions are geared to reducing the aggregate troubles of the moment rather than to evaluating who merits what.[54]

4. Assessing. As dispensers of resources, superordinates need to assess the comparative merits of candidates more numerous than resources available to support them. Since merely formal criteria are almost always inadequate, and excessively time-consuming to follow, *informal* and time-saving strategic guidelines typically evolve. Thus among managers of philanthropic foundations, grants of money are decided along the two main informal dimensions of "worthiness" and "dependence," Kenneth Larsen has found.

a. Worthiness as a strategic consideration is elaborated in terms of eliminating the i) whimsical, ii) enthusiast, and iii) heavy rivvie [sic] or foundation slick *candidates,* and i) consciousness raising; ii) social service, and iii) research *programs.*

b. Dependency as an informal classifying device eliminates candidates who are incorrigibly reluctant fund raisers and involves many "tests" of authenticity.[55]

Foundation managers, candidates, and grantees are, of course, simply one instance of a larger class of "candidates for, and grantees of, some higher or lower position in the status order of an institution or relationship. We are often subjects of information collection and classification by observers whose classifications of us advance or impede our advancement toward a status to which we aspire or, at times, toward a status we would like to avoid. We are, of course, also status information collectors and classifiers ourselves. To name a few examples: in banks there are candidates for loans, loan 'grantees,' and loan officers; in welfare, welfare applicants, welfare recipients, and eligibility workers; in graduate schools, degree candidates, degree holders, and faculty; in the criminal justice system, suspects, criminals, and judges."[56]

5. **Defending.** As holders of power, superordinates have, for whatever reasons, a tendency to corruption. Those who are corrupted become vulnerable to hostile forces gathering evidence and making accusations. Yet rather than plead guilty and take the punishment, the corrupt office holder chooses to erect defenses. Since he is guilty, the task is not an easy one and requires considerable finesse or at least audacity. In the case of corrupt politicians, extremely bold moves are necessary because the individuals frequently occupy the delicate situation of being both court defendant and candidate for office. As analyzed by James Boyd in his brilliant "The Ritual of Wiggle: From Ruin to Reelection," standard maneuvers at various phases are of these varieties:

a. Nothing is admitted until the worst is known. The accused hides and waits if the accusation gives promise of blowing over.

b. If speaking becomes necessary, the accused confesses what is known, evades what is unknown, and cries (e.g., Nixon's Checkers speech of 1952).

c. The accused gives the money back if possible—or to someone.

d. When partial confession and restitution fail, the accused becomes the "stranger in paradise." He cannot help it if he has such good fortune.

e. When things are at their worse, the accused announces for re-election.

f. The accused engineers a series of endorsements by prominent churchmen.

g. The accused picks a scapegoat.

h. The accused requests an official investigation.

i. The accused threatens a multimillion dollar libel suit which is either not filed or withdrawn before trial.

j. The accused claims constitutional immunity in the face of judicial proceedings.

k. During the proceedings, the accused (1) never appears in public without his entire family; (2) feigns illness and assumes a glazed mien; and (3) repeatedly tells the press he welcomes the chance to clear his name.[57]

6. Firing. When a subordinate fails to "measure up," and a decision is made to "let him go," there arises the reportedly delicate and anxiety-ridden situation of carrying out the actual dismissal. It is, as conceived by Erving Goffman, a situation of "cooling the mark out," in that "the mark," generically conceived, is a person who has presented himself as a type of person that others refuse to endorse him as being. The "cooler," the person in the classic confidence game assigned to keep the mark quiet, must devise containing strategies. As discerned by Goffman, these strategies move along the lines of:

a. Giving the task to the most auspicious cooler, who might be a very high status person, a friend or peer, or, in the society at large, a doctor or priest.

b. Softening the blow by offering the mark an alternative status or another chance to qualify.

c. Encouraging the mark to blow off steam in controlled circumstances.

d. Bribing the mark through agreeing to maintain the appearance the mark is leaving of his own accord if he will in fact leave.[58]

B. Role Strategies Among Equals. As mentioned in the preceding chapter, since equals are rare, studies of them appear infrequently.

Indeed, even relations that seem to be "equal" may be asserted "actually," and "underneath," not to be equal at all. Be that as it may, in a few circumstances the participants, even if no one else, view themselves as more or less equals or as having to pretend to act that way.

One such assiduously documented role relation is that of the purchasing agent for business organizations vis-à-vis the departments for which he purchases and the organizations from which he purchases. His situational obligation is to purchase at the best possible terms and to make sure supplies are delivered on time. But the typically ambitious agent desires also to be considered an expert on markets and new materials and to be given authority in supply decisions. These responsibilities and aspirations bring him into conflict with the engineering and production departments in manufacturing enterprises and give rise to a complex set of negotiating tactics over what to buy and when the material is delivered. These include, as delineated by George Strauss:

1. Rule-oriented tactics, involving appeal to higher authority, reference to rules, and insistence on written and reasoned requests.
2. Rule-evading tactics, involving appearing to comply without doing so and ignoring.
3. Personal-political tactics, involving exploitation of friendships, reliance on past favors, and use of alliances.[59]

C.   Role Strategies Among Subordinates.   Subordinate locations differ in terms of the degree to which they are stigmatizing, the degree to which the hierarchal difference displayed is defined as a *shameful* difference. Thus there is a large degree of difference in shame between being a corporation vice-president relative to the corporation president and being hair-lipped relative to normals. That is, the former carries a much lighter load of shame than the latter. Of course, what is shameful is always relative to some audience, posing the possibility that some corporation vice-presidents are much more shamed subordinates before the audiences to whom they play than many hair-lipped people are before the audiences to whom they play. Here, however, the assumed audience is "all of us" in our role as participants in the public, shared standards of common American identity culture. Subscribe to it or not, we are all forced to play off it, revel in it, and cower before it.

Let us first look at locations bearing the brunt of shameful subordination and tendencies to employ strategic cowering, then moving to the less shamefully subordinated and their more aggressive ways.

1. Stigma Strategizing. Erving Goffman's essay-book called *Stigma: Notes on the Management of Spoiled Identity*[60] is the seminal and most general work on the situation and strategies of shameful subordination, "...the situation of the individual who is disqualified from full social acceptance" (p. ii),[61] the individual who has an attribute that is "deeply discrediting" (p. 3). Such attributes include, most spectacularly, physical handicaps, mental disorders, criminal conviction, and socially devalued racial, national, or religious status. Shameful subordination is of course a matter of degree, and it is likely that everyone has matters over which he or she feels shame (p. 128). Therefore the world is divided not into the stigmatized and the normal, but, rather, in terms of how often any given person feels it necessary to manage something shameful. Shameful subordinations are locations rather than features of persons (p. 138).[62]

The *situation* of the stigmatized as a general category has several salient features, aspects that must perforce be managed. First, its central feature is the problem of acceptance, the problem of receiving less "respect and regard" than the person expects (pp. 8–9). Second, normals develop and use a theory of his stigma, a theory of the origins and course of his imperfection, and they interpret his conduct in its terms (pp. 5–6). Third, "professional" workers present to him a normal-serving code of how he ought to act, to protect normals and professionals from embarrassing interaction with him (pp. 106–111, 115–123). Fourth, these proffered forms of advice stimulate a hyperconsciousness of interaction in him, posing a problem of management. Fifth, other people bearing the same stigma assume that he is "naturally" one of them (pp. 112–113). Sixth, he is likely to suffer conflict and ambivalence over the competing pulls of those who are also stigmatized like him and normals (pp. 106–107). Seventh, his situation is likely to contain normals who are willing to overlook his stigma—called generically by Goffman "the wise"—but for whom there is always the possibility of reversion.

Within this common situation of the stigmatized, two subtypes differ in situational features and require distinguishing. On the one hand, there are the *discredited* whose defining feature is that their stigma is known to others and they must therefore *manage* encounter and role *tension* generated by this knowledge. Knowing the stigma, normals find contacts with such persons "shaky" (pp. 18–19). Knowing that normals know and feel shaky, the discredited is likely to feel "on," unsure, and exposed (pp. 13–16). On the other hand, there are the *discreditable* whose stigma is not at a given moment known to others but constitutes *information* the person must manage and hide. It is likely that some normals know and some do not, posing problems of "double-living" and various kinds of blackmail (pp. 33–34, 42–44, 75–79).

If this is the common and variant situation of the stigmatized, what are typical types of *strategies* of dealing? First, there are some strategies *common* to the discredited and the discreditable, including *(a)* "breaking with reality," *(b)* using the stigma as a hook on which to hang all one's failings, *(c)* conceiving the stigma as a blessing in disguise, *(d)* feeling that the stigma deepens one's knowledge of the limitations of normals (pp. 9–12), *(e)* avoiding normals and isolating oneself, and *(f)* "covering," to minimize the obtrusiveness of the stigma, visible or not (pp. 102–104).

Second, the *discredited* must manage encounter-scale and role-scale tension over relations to normals. At the encounter scale there are common tacks of *(a)* defensive cowering, *(b)* hostile bravado, *(c)* vacillation between cowering and bravado (pp. 17–18), *(d)* fool-making, put-downs, put-ons, and cold stares (pp. 135–137), *(e)* minstrelization or playing out the most egregious stereotype (p. 110), and *(f)* refraining, tactful cooperation. At the role scale one finds *(a)* disidentifiers or efforts pointedly to display attributes that contradict one's stigma-stereotype (pp. 44–45), *(b)* hyperaffiliation with one's "own" kind, facilitating circulation of sad tales, atrocity tales, trickster tales, and the like (pp. 19–24), *(c)* full-blown advocacy involving agitation for a softer label, publications, worked-up ideologies, exemplary moral tales of "our boys who made good," and so on (pp. 24–27, 113–114, 125).

Third, the *discreditable* must manage information available to normals. *(a)* The central process is passing, and its phases of learning the normal point of view, learning to cope with it, and learning to pass, sometimes involving, passing "for fun" and learning to trust oneself to secrecy (pp. 79–80, 101–102, 80–81). *(b)* Passing itself is constructed out of techniques of information control, and some important ones are (1) obliteration of signs, (2) disidentifiers in the sense just indicated, (3) passing the sign of one stigma off as the sign of another less discrediting one, (4) constructing a protective circle of wise (pp. 91–101). *(c)* Passing as a process has problems of breakdown and exposure including (1) in-deeperism or the forced elaboration of progressively thinner lies, (2) confrontation and showdown and the fear thereof, (3) debilitating supersensitivity to situations because of fears of showdown, and (4) "living on a leash," the necessity to limit one's travel to distances and periods affording return to one's disguise service and repair station (pp. 83–91).

As indicated, stigma is a variable. Likely everyone feels more or less stigmatized about something as a function of the historical period in which they live. During the McCarthy fifties, intellectuals in the United States appeared to have felt especially stigmatized, for example, and many even developed the standard array of defensive, role-scale devices to cope with the period's anti-intellectualism, emphasis on conformity, and their own isolation. Interviewing a sample in the middle fifties, Melvin Seeman found the following remarkably widespread role-scale strategies:

   a. Direct acceptance of majority stereotypes (e.g., intellectuals are soft, snobbish, radical, eccentric, asocial, unreliable, hopelessly academic.....
   b. Concern with in-group purification.
   c. Approval of conformity to the larger society.
   d. Denial of membership in one's own group.
   e. Fear of group solidarity.[63]

These are of course the elements of only one basic type of posture that members of a stigmatized category can strike. Overall, it might be labeled the *cowering* posture, an attitude also widespread among many sexual and ethnic categories of the fifties. As became clear in the sixties, many other strategic postures are possible.

2. *Stigma Strategizing: The Wise.* People in stigmatized locations often have close associates who come themselves to have "courtesy stigma," as Goffman labels it. They assist the stigmatized in defining and acting toward his situation, and they may undertake to represent the interests of the stigmatized. Kin of the stigmatized are especially prone to fill this wise or courtesy stigma role. One such situation devolves on the parents, especially the mother of children defined as mentally retarded. These wise define their task as importantly that of obtaining medical and other official assistance. But they experience a highly frustrating, impersonal, uncoordinated, bureaucratic maze.

   What parents of the mentally retarded expect and want from physicians is substantially the same as what other persons want, namely, information about the medical problem or disorder for which medical assistance is being sought (including a diagnosis), treatment, advice on how to deal with the problems relating to the illness or disorder, and emotional support when this seems indicated.[64]

But they do not get it. "How do they cope with this?" Charlotte Green Schwartz asked herself and twenty-three mothers so situated.

  a. Most prominantly, mothers employed a strategy of *passive acceptance* and tactics of (1) indirect messages, only alluding to what they wanted, (2) concerted attempt to project an image of "good client" that would win the approval of professionals, (3) opting out of medical care for brief periods, and (4) transfer to other medical settings.
  b. A minority employed a strategy of *active quest* involving tactics of confrontation, direct expression of disagreement, insistence on recognition of their competence, use of outside pressure, and search for compatible medical helpers.
  c. A few *withdrew* from the system and warded off contact by professionals.[65]

3. Disavowing Deviance.   People with visible, physical handicaps live in an encounter and larger scale situational world of dis-ease with "normals." As analyzed by Fred Davis, their visible handicap tends:

  a. To become a focal point of interaction in encounters with normals, a point of discomfort and stickiness.
  b. To inundate the expressive controls of the normals.
  c. To seem to normals a puzzling or unsettling contradiction of the "positive" attributes of the handicapped person.
  d. To be an "ambiguous predicator" of doing social activities with the handicapped.[66]

In this situation as felt and defined by the normals and perceived by the handicapped person, the latter cannot build a relation with a normal unless he disavows his deviance in the sense of devising ways to "keep it at bay, dissipate it, or lessen its impact upon the interaction."[67] Focusing at the role scale, Davis' interviews with handicapped people elicited three phases of the strategic process of disavowing deviance. First, the handicapped person plays along with the fictional acceptance the normal accords him but without being circumscribed by it. Second, as trust develops, the handicapped person and the normal begin to "break through."

  The handicapped person projects images, attitudes, and concepts of self which encourage the normal to...take his role...in terms other than those associated with imputations of deviance.... As the handicapped person expands the interactional nexus he simultaneously disavows the deviance latent in his status; concurrently, to the degree to which the normal is led reciprocally to assume the redefining...self-attitudes, he comes to...view as more like himself...those aspects of the other which at first connoted deviance for him.[68]

* * *

The ways in which the visibly handicapped person can go about disavowing deviance are...many and varied. These range from relatively straightforward conversational offerings in which he alludes in passing to his involvement in a normal round of activities, to such forms of indirection as interjecting taboo or privatized references by way of letting the normal know that he does not take offense at the latter's uneasiness or regard it as a fixed obstacle toward achieving rapport.[69]

Third, the handicapped person strives to *institutionalize* the subsequently "normalized definition in the face of the many small amendments and qualifications that must frequently be made to it."[70]

4.   Getting By.   Most subordinates are not, of course, deviant subordinates in the sense of laboring under an enormous load of shame, ambiguity, and social stickiness. Most are mere normal subordinates who labor under a modest load of shame, ambiguity, and social stickiness.

The role-scale stances of normal subordinates vary importantly in terms of the degree to which they are defensive and reactive or offensive and proactive. In the vernacular, subordinates at the extremes may be "getting by" or "making out." What are called "staff" or technical advisory personnel in relation to "line" authority in large formal organizations provide exemplary illustration of weakly situated, normal subordinates who orient themselves to getting by. Melvin Dalton's study of staff in two manufacturing plants found their situation to be studded with rivalries and conflicts over matters of authority, changes in production, staff rules of production (particularly safety rules), and abrasiveness arising from differences in age, education, and social class style between members of the two groups.

Staff coped with their marginality, lack of authority, and the actual or probable rejection of their ideas by line by quitting at a high rate and pushing for expansion of staff size and authority. More generically and at the role-scale, staff:

 a. Strengthened their ties with top line as much as possible.
 b. Adhered to the staff role, but "leaned over backward" to avoid trouble down the line that could reverberate to the top.
 c. Compromised with the line below top levels.[71]

5. Making Out. Getting by is importantly an orientation to cutting one's losses; making out is importantly an orientation to maximizing one's gains. Following into college the fourteen highly competent and successful high school students mentioned earlier in connection with preparing for roles (Section II.E), David Hamburg and his research team strove to explicate the proactive lines of action these students used to deal with their new situation, a situation of new subject matters, heavier workloads, increased requirements for iniative, and new demands for self-regulation. Though somewhat excessively focused on "self-action" strategies, these investigators delineate the following tacks:

 a. Projecting a clear self-image as an effective doer.
 b. Mobilizing new combinations of skill.
 c. Using assets to test new images of growth potential.
 d. Using upperclassmen as resource persons.
 e. Identifying with faculty-at-a-distance.[72]

Disappointments were handled by means of such short-run tactics as:

 a. Recentering one's efforts within a long-term purpose.
 b. Working out alternative sources of gratification, often extracurricular.
 c. Remodeling prefabricated images of a vocational role.
 d. Setting intermediate goals in working out long-term plans.
 e. Referring to the high academic standards by which they were selected.
 f. Using interpersonal supports.[73]

Making out can occur anywhere, among those in privileged as well as in marginal and disadvantaged locations, although the conventional wisdom holds it to issue most forcefully from marginal locations, as enshrined in the images of Sammy Glicks, hustlers, dragon ladies, and various theories of the relation between deprivation and rebellion. Furthermore a portion of making out activity often has a desperate, even pathetic quality. At least it often seems to have such a face even if it has other faces. Thus in the vast churning of the modern world, a variety of marginal and "status-insecure" occupations are thrown up, one notable instance being the engineering technician. Hierarchically bracketed between the "real engineer" above and the craftsman or skilled worker below, he partakes of both but is neither. His title, the nature of his work, education, and training, rate and method of compensation, and self and public image are marginal, generating discomfort, reports William Evan.[74] This marginality generates a range of role-scale coping tacks, many of which are of a sad, making-out variety and include:

a. Job-hopping in the hope of finding an employer who will take one as an engineer despite lack of an engineering degree.
b. Searching for a setting yielding intrinsic work satisfaction.
c. Searching for a setting where status differences between oneself and engineers are de-emphasized.
d. Joining in collective action—such as a technicians' union—to improve the lot of the occupation (an organizational-scale strategy).
e. Focusing ones values away from the occupational marginality and toward other work values, such as job security.
f. Working laboriously, through many years of part-time engineering courses, to obtain an engineering degree.[75]

Among other marginal occupations on the make, the role-scale efforts of photographers/artists to define their photography as art especially invite our attention. Art photographers view themselves as artists but their situation lacks the elements that provide other artists legitimacy. Their situation, rather, is one of (a) insufficient apparatus of critics, (b) a shortage of appropriate schools, (c) (c) a shortage of museums and galleries that show their work, and (d) a shortage of clients, Richard Christopherson relates.[76]

They strive to cope with this at the ideological–role-scale level through activities that have two functions.

a. To *disavow* the photographer's role, claiming that art, like what they do, is more than (1) technique, (2) product, or (3) snapshot.

b. To *identify* with the artist's role by claiming that art, like what they do, is (1) traditional, (b) intentional, and (3) a matter of talent.[77]

The assiduous making out efforts of people who strive to enact the role sometimes called "traditional woman" among the Americans provides what may be one of the most promising fronts for analysis of role-scale strategies among subordinates. The "traditional woman," like all roles, is "the end product of a methodical series of...[people's] talk and behavior."[78] Women (and men alike) "...are all continually achieving...[their] sexual status, indeed, every taken-for-granted aspect of the social world is continually being assembled by...[the participants'] methodical practices."[79] This assumes special interest in the case of traditional women because that construct requires simultaneous, synthesizing embodiment of many contradictory attitudes and their strategies, a synthesis sometimes called the "madonna-whore combination." At the level of stereotypes, "Miss America and *Playboy's* centerfold are sisters over the skin."[80] The ideal is to be "both sexy and wholesome, delicate but able to cope, demure yet titillatingly bitchy."[81] And this, again, ideally, must be (and *is* often) performed while not appearing to make effort, as written by one female to others:

> [Although] you are not passive, that must be the chief impression conveyed to the man so that he will think the conquest entirely his....You do not sit by, and through just BEING, lure him into your net, no, being a woman is an active thing, you MAKE yourself into a woman, you create the role and play it....To be a woman you must please and attract the man, and to do that a thousand little postures and tricks are required...and there are rewards reaped by any actress who plays her role superbly.[82]

The array of encounter- and role-scale strategies composing such performances are themselves supported by a *strategic ideology* widespread among many subordinates: "admiring the oppressor, glorifying the oppressor, wanting to be like the oppressor, wanting the oppressor to like them, mostly because the oppressor...[holds] all the power."[83]

The role- and encounter-scale analysis of roles such as traditional woman involve such subtleties and subterfuges that we have achieved virtually no systematic understanding of their construction; the remarks quoted here provide the slimmest of beginnings.[84]

6. Failure Coping.   Like everyone else, subordinates experience failure—that is, occasions when the self one presents to others is not supported by the facts known to those others. The self presented to others has, in a sense, died. This discrepancy between presentation and reality must be dealt with by the presenter. Some general lines of dealing, aside from mere acceptance, have been suggested by Erving Goffman in his treatment of "cooling the mark out," including:

a. Entering into sustained personal disorganization.
b. Registering a complaint with presumed-to-be-authoritative third parties.
c. Turning sour.
d. Going into business for oneself through forming one's own group.[85]

Failures themselves differ in their sharpness and corrigibility. Some are sudden and seen as correctable over foreseeable periods, as in being fired from a job. Others are slow and chronic and defined as not subject to correction in the foreseeable future. Such is the case for many "second-choice" and marginal occupations, where a sense of failure pervades and must be managed. Comedians at seedy burlesque shows are an example of this class, reports Marilyn Salutin, who studied their coping practices, including the devices of off-stage degradation of strippers and namedropping of celebrities they had met.[86]

Role-scale situations and strategies are not, assuredly, only matters of subordination, superordination, and equality. There are many "transcending" situations, as it were, situations that everyone faces regardless of his hierarchical location. Some of these have been studied at the encounter level, as the preceding chapter indicates.[87] Very few, however, have been performed at the role level, even though there are a handful of suggestive essays. These include William Goode's formulation of the universal situation of "role strain" (including the mechanisms of compartmentalization, delegation, and elimination),[88] Robert Merton's essay on role conflict,[89] and Hamburg, Adams, and Coelho's treatment of menopause.[90] The Hamburg group point, indeed, to "phases of the individual life cycle" as providing an auspicious set of generic situations.

a. The attainment of coordination between mother and infant.
b. The initial transition to an out-of-home facility (school, day-care center).
c. Puberty.
d. Major educational transitions.

e. The first serious occupational commitment.
f. Marriage.
g. The first pregnancy.
h. Geographic moves.
i. Children's milestones.
j. Economic setbacks.
k. Retirement.[91]

V. STRATEGIES OF TERMINATING/EXITING ROLES

There has been much more work on getting into roles (discovering, judging, selecting, etc., as discussed in Section II) than on getting out. Since one often involves the other, we encounter an omission of perspective rather than of opportunity; that is, to collect data on role seekings and entrances is to be in the neighborhood of data on role exiting. Because of a mental set toward role entrance, investigators have chosen simply not to attend to the exiting aspect. This omission is psychologically understandable, to be sure. We as participants in social life find locating and getting into roles much more problematic than getting out of them. Other people are felt to control entering, while we ourselves control exiting. Such an assumption, like all assumptions, is only sometimes valid. When the role occupied is a devalued one, when it provides scarce services to others, when replacements are scarce, when its relative rewards are very high, and when alternative roles are hard to enter, it may be very difficult to "get out." Conditions of these kinds, for example, probably characterize the role of the fool, and tactics for escape from this role have been sketchily suggested by Orrin Klapp.

1. Avoiding the fool imputation by "taking" a joke and "laughing it off."
2. Using counterjokes and repartee to "turn the tables."
3. Employing the fool role as a "ruse" and trap for turning the tables on pretentious opponents.
4. Showing "fight" against a larger opponent.
5. Revealing unexpected merit, à la the Cinderella pattern.
6. Encouraging others to "go too far" in mistreatment of one, which arouses the sympathy of witnesses.[92]

VI. ROLE–SCALE SELF–MANAGEMENT

In discussing encounters, a distinction was drawn between the condition of the most proximate audience being the person himself, or other people. The latter was termed "other management" and the former was labeled "self-management."[93] This chapter has dealt only with other-management, and we come now to circumstances and devices of self-management at the role-scale.

Also in discussing encounters, I distinguished between a strategy being primarily words versus deeds.[94] We again employ this distinction and first discuss word-oriented self-management.

A. Word-Oriented Self-Management. In the initial and most familiar instance, role-scale self-management primarily executed as words are the "defense mechanisms" of psychoanalytic fame. The list (with slight variations) is a standard one: denial of reality, fantasy, compensation, introjection, projection, rationalization, repression, reaction formation, emotional insulation, regression, sublimation.[95] Like all good insights, the idea of defense mechanisms has been run to the ground, or more accurately to the psyche, to its detriment. The excesses of psychoanalytic zealots ought not to prompt us, however, to throw out the baby with the bath. Specifically, in the classic cast the defense mechanisms are exactly that, defensive and negative practices, asserted to be deleterious to human functioning. This emphasis requires correction. A vast but inadequately documented range of "defense" mechanisms seems, rather, to have an active, expanding, coping significance rather than a rigidifying, constricting, retreating character, as Theodore Kroeber and others have so well indicated.[96]

Moreover, in many situations of extreme trauma, the positively strategic value of the more classic, denying defense mechanisms is evident. The research group around David Hamburg has examined in this light a set of people suffering severe burns. Such a physical trauma gives rise to concern over the capacity to be loved by others, dependence on others, resentment, feelings of inadequacy, and other fears. A range of the classic mechanisms is activated in the period immediately following the burn injury, a set of devices that the Hamburg group calls "emergency defense mechanisms." This array deals with the "emergency orientation," which might be verbalized as: "I must avoid too much recognition, thinking, or feeling about the situation I am in—if I let it get on my mind too much, it will get me down."[97] The prime emergency mechanisms and their verbal forms are:

1. *Delusion-Illusion-Hallucination Formation:* "I am not in this situation at all, but in a better one."
2. *Denial:* "Even though I may be in the hospital, I am not hurt at all"; "I am hurt, but it is only a minor injury."
3. *Repression:* "I know I was badly hurt, but I cannot remember it; I have no feelings about my illness."
4. *Constriction:* "I know how seriously hurt I am, and I remember how it happened, but I have no feelings about anything."
5. *Suppression:* "I am well aware of the whole situation, and how serious it is, but I will not let myself think about it (unless I have to)."[98]

Less traumatic situations perhaps require less drastic, but still positive, role-scale strategies of self-management. Being an inmate of a mental hospital might be a less drastic, yet threatening situation, involving, as it sometimes does,

> great pressures to accept the fact of illness and the therapeutic potential of the hospital. [But]...by becoming a patient, one's self-image is threatened insofar as [one]...recognizes the prevailing negative attitudes toward [mental] illness.
>
> If [mental patients] are to achieve maximum therapeutic benefit from their experience, they must resolve this conflict in a way that permits acceptance of the fact of their patienthood while minimizing the stress occasioned by the perceived disparagement of their status.[99]

Placed in this bind of a situation, many patients, as reported by Howard Kaplan and associates, evolve a number of strategic definitions of their situation that "apparently function to mitigate this stress." These involve the following devices:

1. Asserting the commonality of illness among the total patient population.
2. Favorably comparing their situation with those of less privileged patient groups.

3. Denying the superiority of the staff and extrainstitutional population.
4. Emphasizing any rewards that might attach to the position of "mental patient."
5. Confining their temporal orientation to the immediate present.[100]

B. Action-Oriented Self-Management. Many strategies of dealing with trauma and less dramatic situations are clearly motor in character. Studying the parents of children slowly dying from a malignant disease, the Hamburg research group found not only the more usual defenses of isolation of affect and denial, but a strong pattern of sheer *motor activity* as a way to deal with impending death. In addition to instrumentally directed acts,

> parents took long walks or became occupied in sewing or knitting in order to combat developing anxiety and to "forget about" their situation. There was also a good deal of simple restlessness, undoubtedly similarly motivated but less organized and more at random. Motor activity was [moreover] likely to be a consciously determined strategy, generally accompanied by a determined and deliberate suppression of negative feeling.[101]

Parents of dying children, the severely burned, mental patients, and those in other traumatized situations seem to differ in degree more than kind from the rest of us, participants in presumably less overwhelmingly stressful circumstances of everyday life. In a way, however, the very nature of being modern has certain seemingly traumatizing dimensions. As a host of observers have analyzed the modern world, it is pluralistic, a world of diversity, a world of conflicting definitions of "objects, events, and human nature."[102] Unlike the protective provincialism and ignorance of yesteryear, moderns live in the naked cosmopolitanism of known and competing basic conceptions of good and bad, right and wrong. Persons are objects of competing definitions of their merit. Anyone who is anyone at all lives with the knowledge that he or she has enemies, has others who question his or her basic competence, talent, achievements, integrity. Everyone is likely to have others who question, indeed, the worthwhileness of his entire existence. They may see no merit in one's occupation, how one does that occupation, one's interpersonal style, one's friends, family, personal tastes and preferences, as well as one's philosophies and creeds. The modern environment is in many ways socially hostile because it contains hostile information and persons who bear that information.

Let us assume that people do not take this "subtraumatic" situation lightly, that they perceive it and do not much like it. We can, at least, assume that some people are sensitive to these matters and can feel "hurt" and "threatened" by the presence of negative information. J. L. Simmons was once concerned with this situation and addressed himself to how it was dealt with in a small community he called "the espers," a collection of people espousing the existence of spirit-persons, vibratory levels, reincarnation, and the like. For them, as for the rest of us, the world was filled with negative opinions and information.

How is the self-doubt of negative information avoided? As analyzed by Simmons (and somewhat adapted here), five prime mechanisms are involved:

1. *Differential Association.* The omnibus strategy of dealing with situations generally, not just this one, is avoidance of people who disagree with one and active exposure to people who cognitively and affectively support one. By such a simple means, hostile input is reduced and loving input is enhanced.[103]
2. *Selective Attention.* If the negative is encountered nonetheless, attention can be directed toward "not seeing" what is incongruent and positively "seeing" what is supportive.
3. *Active Structuring.* Going beyond self-manipulation of consciousness, persons can act to produce situations that have supportive import. The process has this formal structure:

a. A thinks B is Y.
b. A treats B as Y.
c. B responds as Y.
d. A thinks B is Y.

For example, "A female may, by her behavior, her speech, her dress, and her grooming, create the impression that, while she is sexually attractive and broadminded, she is not a loose woman. Assuming that this impression coincides with aspects of her self and behavior that is effectively conveyed, it should evoke congruent behavior from men. They are not likely to treat her as if she were either promiscuous or prudish."[104]

4. *Exploiting Ambiguity.* A large range of experience does not seem to have any clearly hostile or supportive significance for a given person. Lacking sufficient information, many experiences are simply ambiguous. Being ambiguous, such experiences are easily interpreted as supportive.[105]

5. *Dogmatizing.* At the more complex levels of role-scale strategizing, people elaborate or adopt complex ideologies and they espouse them with fervor. Zealously and vociferously pontificated, complex doctrines serve to protect their espousers by providing them a sense of finality and superiority. The unambiguous understanding gained generates a protective arrogance which psychically barricades against hostile input.[106]

At the almost purely motor level of analysis, Anne Davis and Virginia Olesen became interested in Israeli *kibbutzim* as instances of the generic situation of extreme fusion of work and private roles. Assuming that people desire to maintain some separation among their various roles and from the group to which they belong, how was it achieved in such a totalistic setting? Focusing only at the level of action, they describe the following rather more topical than generic strategies:

1. Work maneuvers for social and physical distance:

a. Attaining a low-contact job.
b. Doing overtime work.
c. Negative emotional expression at work that put others off.

2. Distance-inducing strategies away from work:

a. Eating, showering, and so on, earlier or later than others.
b. Visiting and courting.[107]

Also at the extreme, behavioral level, in observing patients confined to a physical rehabilitation center, Kathy Calkins was impressed with their experience of themselves as having an overabundance of time. How was it to be filled? Calkins reports a lush range of time-using lines of self-management, summarized as:

1. Passing time.
2. Waiting.

3. Doing time.
4. Making time.
5. Filling time.
6. Killing time.[108]

≺≺≺≺≺≺≺≺

Roles are socially shared, abstract categories of "types of persons" that humans employ in organizing their dealings with one another and themselves. The role-scale level of situation and strategy analysis focuses on the single individual plying his role over the time span of at least weeks and perhaps decades. The strategizing of roles necessitates management of one's relations to one's *self* and to *others*. The role-scale management of *others* has three main aspects: *(a)* entering/avoiding, *(b)* using and managing, *(c)* terminating/exiting. *(a)* Strategies of entering/avoiding may involve processes of discovering, inventing, choosing, preparing for, gaining acceptance in or avoiding. *(b)* Strategies of managing require a distinction between strategic roles and role strategies, the former denoting the global strategic significance of a role and the latter denoting the microstrategies of a role. There are at least six important types of strategic roles: formal, informal occupational, social types, personal, captivity, and superordinate. Studies of role strategies revolve around who the person is acting toward: a subordinate, an equal, or a superordinate. Role strategies among superordinates have focused on ascending, coaching, and maintaining the status quo, assessing subordinates, defending against attack, and firing. There are few studies of role-scale strategies among equals. Role-scale strategies among subordinates have focused on how stigma is managed, how deviance is disavowed, how people get by, make out, and cope with failure. *(c)* Strategies of terminating/exiting roles have also been little studied. At the level of words and thoughts, the role-scale management of self involves various mechanisms of defense, especially as applied in their less traumatic versions in everyday life. At the level of action, self-management devices have emphasized means of avoidance.

NOTES TO CHAPTER NINE

1.   And other units of social organization; namely, worlds, settlements, and societies.
2.   See, for example, Bruce Biddle and Edwin Thomas, eds., *Role Theory* (New York: Wiley, 1966).

3. Ralph H. Turner, "Role-Taking: Process Versus Conformity," in Arnold Rose, ed., *Human Behavior and Social Processes* (Boston: Houghton Mifflin, 1962), pp. 20–40.

4. Erving Goffman, *Presentation of Self in Everyday Life* (Garden City, N.Y.: Doubleday Anchor, 1959), p. 75, emphasis added.

5. Chapter 8, Section V.

6. See below, Section III.C, on social types.

7. See, for example, discussion of the seeker role in John Lofland, *Doomsday Cult* (Englewood Cliffs, N.J.: Prentice-Hall, 1966), pp. 44–49, 166–174.

8. Roger Straus, "Changing Oneself: The Creative Transformation of Life Experience in Transcendental Quests," Chapter 12, this volume.

9. Straus, *ibid.*

10. Roger Barker and Paul Gump, *Big School, Small School* (Stanford, Calif.: Stanford University Press, 1964).

11. See Chapter 5, Section II.D on the difference between study of "how to" and "how do."

12. Straus, *op. cit.* This section of Straus' analysis bears on yet another important area: self-confirmation. Having chosen to play a role, the new incumbent sometimes needs to convince himself he has made the right choice, to sell his decision to himself.

13. *Ibid.*

14. Orrin Klapp, *Symbolic Leaders* (Chicago: Aldine, 1964), Chs. 3 and 8. See also W. Lloyd Warner, *The Living and the Dead* (New Haven, Conn.: Yale University Press, 1959), pp. 270–273, on how the wealthy, effete, and elitist Abraham Lincoln was artfully reconstructed into the hero, Honest Abe, rail splitter, the "rude man from the prairie." Is there nothing sacred?!

15. Klapp, *op. cit.*, Ch. 7.

16. Klapp, *ibid.*, especially pp. 165–169; 206–207.

17. Earle Silber *et al.*, "Adaptive Behavior in Competent Adolescents: Coping With the Anticipation of College," *Archives of General Psychiatry*, **5:** 354–355 (1961), italics supplied.

18. Ralph H. Turner, "The Navy Disbursing Officer as a Bureaucrat," *American Sociological Review*, **12:** 342–348 (June 1947). See also the spruce analysis of the situation of the academic offered by Alvin Gouldner in his articles, "Cosmopolitans and Locals: Toward an Analysis of Latent Social Roles—I and II," *Administrative Science Quarterly*, **2:** 281–306, 444–480 (December 1957, March 1958). Unfortunately, Gouldner is enamored of survey research and provides skimpy portraits of the strategic roles of locals and cosmopolitans and their subtypes. There are, moreover, numerous enumerations of informal occupational roles that are less than fully useful because they report roles but give little analysis of the situation in which such roles are presumably strategic. That is, there are many reports that offer carts without horses. Chapter 2 of John Lofland, *Analyzing Social Settings* (Belmont, Calif.: Wadsworth, 1971) summarizes many such studies.

19. Oswald Hall, "Types of Medical Careers," *American Journal of Sociology*, **55:** 246 (November 1949).

20. *Ibid.*

21. Orrin Klapp, "Social Types," *American Sociological Review,* **23:** 674 (December 1958).

22. *Ibid.*

23. *Ibid.*

24. This list is drawn in part from Orrin Klapp, "Heroes, Villains, and Fools as Agents of Social Control," in his *Social Types: Process, Structure, and Ethos* (San Diego: Aegis Publishing, 1971), p. 12. The appearings and disappearings of given social types are, of course, important indices of social change.

25. R. Stephen Warner, David T. Wellman, and Lenore J. Weitzman, "The Hero, The Sambo and The Operator: Three Characterizations of the Oppressed," *Urban Life and Culture,* **2:** 81 (April 1973).

26. *Ibid.,* p. 61.

27. *Ibid.,* p. 75.

28. *Ibid.,* pp. 60–61.

29. Richard B. Milner, "The Trickster, The Bad Nigga, and the New Urban Ethnography," *Urban Life and Culture,* **1:** 115 (April 1972).

30. *Ibid.,* p. 116. Milner, following Kluckhohn, conceives mythology as "a storehouse of supra-individual type solutions." "The problems faced by mythological heroes are...the problems of ordinary...[people] writ large. And the solutions used by heroes have been enshrined in oral tradition for the use of ordinary mortals who draw on that tradition." *Ibid.* Detailed descriptions of some black ghetto social types are available in Samuel Strong, "Negro-White Relations as Reflected in Social Types," *American Journal of Sociology,* **52:** 23–30 (July 1946); Ulf Hannerz, *Soulside* (New York: Columbia University Press, 1969), esp. Ch. 2; Harold Finestone, "Cats, Kicks and Color" *Social Problems,* **5:** 3–13 (July 1957), among other sources. On social types among ghetto males more generally, see Harvey Feldman, "Ideological Supports for Becoming and Remaining a Heroin Addict," *Journal of Health and Social Behavior,* **9:** 156–164 (June 1968). On social types in the cultural and religious realms, see Fred Davis with Laura Munoz, "Heads and Freaks: Patterns and Meanings of Drug Use Among Hippies," *Journal of Health and Social Behavior,* **9:** 156–164 (June 1968); John Lofland, *Doomsday Cult, op. cit.,* Ch. 8, "Prospect Alignments."

31. Robert H. White, *The Enterprise of Living: Growth and Organization in Personality* (New York: Holt, Rinehart & Winston, 1972) Ch. 15, "Strategies of Living."

32. James David Barber, "Passive-Positive to Active-Negative: The Style and Character of Presidents," in Charles Peters and Timothy J. Adams, eds., *Inside the System* (New York: Praeger, 1970), pp. 60–96. See also Barber's book on the same subject, *The Presidential Character: Predicting Performance in the White House* (Englewood Cliffs, N.J.: Prentice-Hall, 1972).

33. For elucidation, see, for example, Thomas J. Scheff, *Being Mentally Ill* (Chicago: Aldine, 1966), Ch. 3, "The Social Institution of Insanity."

34. Charles McCabe, "Cures," *San Francisco Chronicle,* May 4, 1972, p. 41, © Chronicle Publishing Co., 1972.

35. Benjamin M. Braginsky, Dorothea T. Braginsky, and Kenneth Ring, *Methods of Madness: The Mental Hospital as a Last Resort* (New York: Holt, Rinehart & Winston, 1969), p. 40.

36. *Ibid.*, p. 162.

37. *Ibid.*, p. 170.

38. In the same vein, physical illness can also have strategic functions, as documented by George Pickering, who argues that "Illness...may have...a protective function as in Charles Darwin and Florence Nightingale, whose illness [sic] relieved them of the dissipation of their time and energy which would have defeated their purpose." *Creative Malady* (New York: Oxford University Press, 1974), p. 283. Along these general lines, see further Dorothea Braginsky and Benjamin Braginsky, *Hansels and Gretels: Studies of Children in Institutions for the Mentally Retarded* (New York: Holt, Rinehart & Winston, 1971).

39. John Irwin, *The Felon* (Englewood Cliffs, N.J.: Prentice-Hall, 1970), pp. 68–79.

40. Rose Giallombardo, "Social Roles in a Prison for Women," *Social Problems,* **13:** 285 (Winter 1966). On the range of strategic roles in Korean prisoner of war camps, see Edgar H. Schein, "The Chinese Indoctrination Program for Prisoners of War: A Study of Attempted Brainwashing," *Psychiatry,* **19:** 149–172 (May 1956), which describes the "get alongers," the resisters (with four subtypes), and the cooperators (with six subtypes).

41. Julius Roth and Elizabeth Eddy, *Rehabilitation for the Unwanted* (New York: Atherton, 1967), Ch. 8.

42. *Ibid.* The authors acknowledge their large debt to Erving Goffman's brief but important prior formulation of "tacks" in *Asylums* (Garden City, N.Y.: Doubleday-Anchor, 1961), pp. 61–66.

43. Melvin Dalton, *Men Who Manage* (New York: Wiley, 1959), p. 249.

44. *Ibid.*, p. 252. See also William C. Mitchell, "Occupational Role Strains: The American Elective Public Official," *Administrative Science Quarterly,* **3:** 210–228 (September 1958) on the seven main features of the elective situation: "(1) insecurity of tenure: (2) conflict among public roles; (3) conflicts of public and private roles; (4) ambiguities in public situations; (5) diffused responsibility and limited control of situations; (6) time and pressure of demands; (7) and, status insecurity" (p. 212). Like Dalton, Mitchell delineates the situation but not strategies.

45. Ralph M. Stodgill, *Handbook of Leadership* (New York: Free Press, 1974). I draw from the characterization of William Bowen, "Almost Everything You Ever Wanted to Know About Leadership," *Fortune,* June 1974, pp. 241–242.

46. Naida S. West, *Leadership with a Feminine Cast* (San Francisco: R and E Associates, 1976), pp. 103–104.

47. *Ibid.* p. 104. A "blended," or "structured" style also appears among women West studied, and she labels it "Orphan Annie." For analysis of a similar situation of status contradiction, this time among wealthy and other elite Chinese Americans, see Dean Lan, *Prestige with Limitations: Paradoxes of the Chinese American Elite* (San Francisco: R and E Associates, forthcoming).

48. The terms are Alvin Gouldner's in "Taking Over," *Trans-Action,* March 1964, pp. 28–34.

49. *Ibid.*

50. Anselm Strauss, *Mirrors and Masks* (Mill Valley, Calif.: Sociology Press, 1969), p. 110.

51. *Ibid.*, p. 113.

52. *Ibid.*, pp. 113–114. See also Michael Harrison's description of how people are coached into speaking in tongues: "Preparation for Life in the Spirit: The Process of Initial Commitment to a Religious Movement," *Urban Life and Culture,* **2:** 390–401 (January 1974).

53. Egon Bittner, "The Police on Skid Row: A Study of Peace Keeping," *American Sociological Review,* **32:** 669–715 (October 1967).

54. *Ibid.*

55. Kenneth Larsen, "Foundation Managers, Candidates and Grantees: A Study of Classification and Control," *Urban Life and Culture,* **3:** 396–441 (January 1975).

56. *Ibid.*, pp. 437–438.

57. Restated and condensed from James Boyd, "The Ritual of Wiggle: From Ruin to Reelection," *The Washington Monthly,* **2(7):** 28–43 (September 1970). See further the acute but essayistic observations of Marge Piercy on how (sixties) Movement *machers* defended themselves against their large contingent of Movement women by "jiggling the sexual balance" of groups and other defenses that keep the women in line in the first place. "The Grand Coolie Damn," in Robin Morgan, ed., *Sisterhood Is Powerful* (New York: Random House, 1970), pp. 412–438.

58. Erving Goffman, "On Cooling the Mark Out: Some Aspects of Adaptation to Failure," *Psychiatry,* **15:** 451–463 (November 1952). The situation of firing is so difficult for executives in large companies that an organization called THinc does a brisk business in firing executives *for* companies and finding them new jobs (at 15 percent of the mark's annual salary). See "The Fine Art of Firing," *San Francisco Chronicle,* June 18, 1973, p. 14.

59. George Strauss, "Tactics of Lateral Relationship: The Purchasing Agent," *Administrative Science Quarterly,* **7:** 161–186 (September 1962). See also the interesting work of James D. Barber, "Leadership Strategies for Legislative Party Cohesion," *Journal of Politics,* **28:** 347–367 (May 1966).

60. Englewood Cliffs, N.J.: Prentice-Hall, 1963.

61. As previously, rather than employ a string of *ibids.* I temporarily revert to textual citation.

62. Furthermore, the normal and stigmatized social locations exhibit some remarkable, structural similarities, Goffman notes, *ibid.*, pp. 130–136, esp. pp. 133–134.

63. Melvin Seeman, "The Intellectual and the Language of Minorities," *American Journal of Sociology,* **64:** 25–35 (July 1958). Also valuable on the stigma of oldness and strategies of coping with it is Sara Matthews, "The Vernacular of Oldness: Maintaining a Precarious Self Identity," manuscript, University of California, Davis, 1974.

64. Charlotte Green Schwartz, "Strategies and Tactics of Mothers of Mentally Retarded Children for Dealing with the Medical Care System," in Norman Bernstein, ed., *Diminished People: Problems and Care of the Mentally Retarded* (Boston: Little, Brown, 1970), p. 84.

65. *Ibid.*, pp. 85–95. See also on the wise relation to the stigmatized, Travis Hirschi, "The Professional Prostitute," *Berkeley Journal of Sociology,* **7:** 40–41 (Spring 1962).

66. Fred Davis, "Deviance Disavowal: The Management of Strained Interaction by the Visibly Handicapped," in his *Illness, Interaction and the Self* (Belmont, Calif.: Wadsworth, 1972), pp. 133–138.

67. *Ibid.*, p. 138.

68. *Ibid.*, pp. 141–142.

69. *Ibid.*, pp. 142–143.

70. *Ibid.*, p. 145.

71. Dalton, *Men Who Manage, op. cit.*, Ch. Four. On getting by, see also David Mechanic's analysis of devices employed by graduate students in preparing for their Ph.D. preliminary examinations *(Students Under Stress* [New York: Free Press, 1962], especially Chapter 7 on the defensive devices of favorable comparison, joking and humor, seeking comforting cues, feeling like a member of a select group, magical practices, and hostility. Other somewhat useful efforts are Julius Roth and Elizabeth Eddy, *Rehabilitation..., op. cit.*, Ch. 8, "Living in the Cracks," on how hospital patients do their small daily rounds, especially by means of the strategy of "making do"; *Newsweek,* November 16, 1970, p. 113, on "The Artful Dodgers," techniques of avoiding creditors; Nels Anderson on "'Getting By' in Hobohemia," Chapter 4 of his *The Hobo* (Chicago: University of Chicago Press, 1923), especially the tactic of "carrying the banner." On a theoretical level, W. Peter Archibald, "Face to Face: The Alienating Effects of Class, Status and Power Divisions," manuscript, University of Western Ontario, London, 1975, is quite good.

72. George Coelho, David Hamburg, and Elizabeth Murphey, "Coping Strategies in a New Learning Environment," *Archives of General Psychiatry,* **9:** 422 (November 1963).

73. *Ibid.*,

74. William Evan, "On the Margin—The Engineering Technician," in Peter L. Berger, ed., *The Human Shape of Work* (New York: Macmillan, 1964), pp. 83–112.

75. *Ibid.*

76. Richard W. Christopherson, "Making Art With Machines: Photography's Institutional Inadequacies," *Urban Life and Culture,* **3:** 3–34 (April 1974).

77. Richard W. Christopherson, "From Folk Art to Fine Art: A Transformation in the Meaning of Photographic Work," *Urban Life and Culture,* **3:** 123–157 (July 1974). See further, on janitor techniques of making out, Raymond L. Gold, "In the Basement—The Apartment House Janitor," in Peter L. Berger, ed., *Human Shape of Work, op. cit.* Ch. 1. For a "how to" treatment (not a "how do" one, which would be more appropriate as discussed in Ch. 5, above) of making out in graduate sociology, see John Lofland, "How to Make Out in Graduate Sociology," *Kansas Journal of Sociology,* **7:** 102–115 (Fall and Winter, 1971).

78. Marvin Israel, "Comment on James Coleman's Review of Harold Garfinkel's Studies in Ethnomethodology," *The American Sociologist,* **4:** 335 (November 1969).

79. *Ibid.*

80. Anonymous, "No More Miss America," in Robin Morgan, ed., *Sisterhood Is Powerful* (New York: Random House, 1970), p. 523.

81. *Ibid.*

82. O. Densmore, 'Sex and the Single Girl," *Journal of Female Liberation,* **1:** 74 (1969), quoted in Warner, Wellman, and Weitzman, "Three Characterizations of the Oppressed." *op. cit.*, pp. 60–61.

83. Pat Mainardi, "The Politics of Housework," in Robin Morgan, ed., *Sisterhood Is Powerful, op. cit.*, p. 452.

84. Organizations tutoring the role of traditional woman (or any other role) are

strategic sites for collecting data that decompose the construct. Among such sites, Helen B. Andelin's Santa Barbara-based Andelin Foundation for Family Living is especially bold and systematic. See Dave Smith, "Fascinating Woman and the Big Old Meanie," *Los Angeles Times*, Part IV, pp. 1, 4, December 5, 1975; Betty Liddick, "An Affirmation of Homemakers' Values," *Los Angeles Times*, Part IV, pp. 1, 5, December 5, 1975. Some quantitative efforts are reviewed in Barrie Thorne and Nancy Henley, "Difference and Dominance: An Overview of Language, Gender, and Society," in B. Thorne and N. Henley, eds., *Language and Sex* (New York: Newbury House, 1975) pp. 5–42. Perhaps the most intriguing and even most important decompositional effort is a by-product of behavior therapist efforts to change the behavior of "transsexual" boys. To make such boys "male," exact analysis of offending "feminine-gesture mannerisms" and voice inflection have been attempted by O. Ivar Lovaas and his associates (and applied in "treatment" with considerable success, but that is another matter). See George Rekers, O. Ivar Lovaas, and Benson Low, "The Behavioral Treatment of a 'Transsexual' Preadolescent Boy," *Journal of Abnormal Child Psychology*, **2**: 99–116 (June 1974); George Rekers and O. Ivar Lovaas, "Behavioral Treatment of Deviant Sex-Role Behaviors in a Male Child," *Journal of Applied Behavior Analysis*, **7**: 173–190 (Summer 1974).

Regarding subordination more generally, see also Gresham Sykes' discussion of strategies of friendship, reciprocity, and defaulting used by prisoners on prison guards in "The Corruption of Authority and Rehabilitation," *Social Forces*, **34**: 257–262, (March 1956).

85. Erving Goffman, "On Cooling the Mark Out," *Psychiatry*, **15**: 451–463 (November 1952).

86. Marilyn Salutin, "The Impression Management Techniques of the Burlesque Comedian," *Sociological Inquiry*, **43**: 159–168 (July 1973).

87. See, for example, the various studies in Section III of Chapter 8.

88. William J. Goode, "A Theory of Role Strain," *American Sociological Review*, **25**: 483–496 (August 1960).

89. Robert Merton, "The Role-Set," *British Journal of Sociology*, **8**: 106–120 (June 1957). See also the less than informative quantitative work of Rivka Bar-Yosef and E. O. Schild, "Pressures and Defenses in Bureaucratic Roles," *American Journal of Sociology*, **75**: 665–673 (October 1966).

90. David Hamburg, George Coelho, and John Adams, "Coping and Adaptation: Steps Toward a Synthesis of Biological and Social Perspectives," in George Coelho, David Hamburg, and John Adams, eds. *Coping and Adaptation* (New York: Basic Books, 1974), pp. 419–424.

91. *Ibid.*, p. 424. See also Rudolf Moos, ed., *Human Adaptation: Coping with Life Crises* (Lexington, Mass: Heath, 1976).

92. Klapp, *Social Types, op. cit.*, p. 9.

93. Ch. 8, Sections I.B.1 and V.

94. Ch. 8, Section V.

95. The classic composite is Anna Freud, *The Ego and the Mechanisms of Defense* (New York: International Universities Press, 1946).

96. Theodore C. Kroeber, "The Coping Functions of the Ego Mechanisms," in Robert W. White, *The Study of Lives* (New York: Atherton, 1963), pp. 179–189; Mechanic,

Students Under Stress, op. cit., A. R. Lindesmith and A. Strauss, *Social Psychology,* 3rd ed. (New York: Holt, Rinehart & Winston, 1968), "Coping Mechanisms," pp. 327–343.

97. David Hamburg, Beatrix Hamburg, and Sydney DeGoza, "Adaptive Problems and Mechanisms in Severely Burned Patients," *Psychiatry,* **16:** 19 (February 1953).

98. *Ibid.* See also H. Visotsky, David Hamburg, Mary Goss, and Binyamin Lebovitz, "Coping Behavior Under Extreme Stress: Observations of Patients with Severe Poliomyelitis," *Archives of General Psychiatry,* **5:** 27–52 (November, 1961).

99. Howard Kaplan, Ina Boyd, and Samuel E. Bloom, "Patient Culture and the Evaluation of Self," *Psychiatry,* **27:** 120 (May 1964).

100. *Ibid.,* pp. 116–26.

101. Paul Chodoff, Stanford Friedman, and David Hamburg, "Stress, Defenses and Coping Behavior: Observations in Parents of Children with Malignant Disease," *American Journal of Psychiatry,* **120:** 746 (February 1964).

102. Tomatsu Shibutani, "Reference Groups as Perspectives," *American Journal of Sociology,* **60:** 564 (May 1955).

103. See further, Howard Becker's discussion of self-segregation among dance musicians in *Outsiders* (New York: Free Press, 1963), Ch. 5.

104. Paul Secord and Carl Backman, *Social Psychology* (New York: McGraw-Hill, 1964), p. 587.

105. J. L. Simmons, "On Maintaining Deviant Belief Systems," *Social Problems,* **11:** 250–256 (Winter 1964).

106. John Lofland, *Doomsday Cult, op. cit.,* Part III.

107. Anne Davis and Virginia Olesen, "Communal Work and Living: Notes on the Dynamics of Social Distance and Social Space," *Sociology and Social Research,* **55:**191–202 (January 1971).

108. Kathy Calkins, "Time: Perspectives, Marking and Styles of Usage," *Social Problems,* **17:** 487–501 (Spring 1970).

CHAPTER TEN

Group-Scale Situations and Strategies

I. GROUPS DEFINED

A. Nature. Groups as entities represent a fundamental shift in scale of social organization and they share several properties with formal organizations, the next larger scale of social organization. The properties that groups and formal organizations share are:

1. The unit is a plurality of persons considered jointly as a single entity, as contrasted with roles.[1]
2. This plurality of persons think of themselves as a unit. They identify with the unit and draw a sense of support from it. They therefore maintain at least a modicum of hostility to other groups/organizations or larger units of social organization.[2]
3. The unit has the capacity for joint action and engages in joint action.
4. The unit *qua* unit transcends the occasion of any single gathering of the members in an encounter.
5. Unlike encounters that are created instantly upon copresence, groups and organizations require at least weeks, perhaps, to achieve reasonable flower.
6. Because of the first five features, a more elaborate (but not unique) set of social processes and structures emerges. These include (*a*) a division of labor and leaders, (*b*) regulation of mem-

ber joining and leaving, *(c)* socialization to the entities' roles, and *(d)* internal control.

As here defined, groups differ from organizations in several ways.

1. Groups tend to have small populations, whereas organizations have large ones. As they occur in the real world, groups such as cliques, work crews, squads, and families tend to have on the order of three or four up to perhaps twenty members. Organizations can be small, but they also have the capacity for enormous populations, as with, for example, the United States government.

2. Groups tend to be informal in the sense of having no titled leader, membership list, written rules, explicit division of labor, and the like, as is the case with many families. They also tend to be informal in the sense of participants often developing diffuse, personal, and emotive bonds with (and knowledge of) one another.

3. Because they are small, groups come together easily and tend to assemble face-to-face with relative regularity. Even in groups within a formal organizational framework imposed from outside—as in all work groups in formal organizations—face-to-faceness promotes an informality that tends to counteract and to a degree supplant the formal framework. Contrastingly, the very size of many organizations makes full assembly cumbersome if not impossible, prompting use of formality to bring about joint action.

As used here, therefore, the label "group" is actually shorthand for the more accurate but too-long caption "small, informal group."

B. Elucidations

1. It is important to emphasize that groups (or organizations) are not simply several people acting in a similar fashion. The distinctive feature of both is *coordinated, differentiated, interdependent* action that makes possible a level of activity that cannot be achieved as individuals even if the individuals are acting identically. This becomes especially apparent when groups are themselves strategies. Coordinated, differentiated persons forming a group have a capacity for strategies much different from those available to encounters or roles *qua* strategies.

2. Strictly speaking, the smallest group probably has a population of three. As listed earlier, one distinctive feature of a group is member

belief in it as a transcending unit, as an entity whose existence is not dependent on any given member's personal participation. The group has a reality apart from each member's role relations to other members.[3] The degree to which there is such an independent psychic or social reality seems problematic for two-person groups. It may be, indeed, that two-person entities should be considered a level of social organization all their own, falling between roles and groups and called "relationships." However, for the practical purposes of this chapter, two-person entities will be considered groups.

3.   Units of social organization are entities that people act toward and in the context of (situations), *and* on the scale of (strategies). This difference was seen often in the chapters on encounters and roles, where each was treated alternately as an object of action (a situation) and scale of action (a strategy). In the same manner, we need now to distinguish groups as objects toward which people act (and as the context of their action) from groups as *acting units*—the scale of action.

II.   STARTING AND ENDING GROUPS

Because roles are embedded in social organizations, the beginnings and endings of personal involvements in groups and larger scale social organizations analytically overlap with beginnings and endings of involvements in roles. Much of this ground was therefore covered in the previous chapter. The focus there, however, was strategizing on the role (and encounter) scale of beginnings (entrances) and endings (exits). There are larger scale strategizings of startings and endings of involvements, of course, although these are seemingly little investigated at the group scale. They are better documented at the organizational scale and are discussed in the next chapter.

Strategies of people getting into groups, of groups inducing people to join their own or other groups, of groups and individuals avoiding, preventing, terminating, and removing members, are all analytically distinct from questions of starting (or preventing) and ending groups *per se*. The former cases take groups as given (as acting units and objects acted toward), whereas the latter are questions of taking groups themselves as problematic. Because, furthermore, group foundings are also frequently quasi-formal or formal organizational foundings, this class of question overlaps with organizational-scale situations and strategies and occupies us in the next chapter.

A. Starting Friendship. For now, we consider the formation of one special type of group, the friendship. Recasting in strategic terms the work of Gerald Suttles, we note that the American and similar society *situation* providing the context in which friendships must be forged is one in which:

1. The society is itself a composite of differentiated and mutually suspicious categorical divisions (by race, age, territory, sex, etc.), whose intentions are diverse, unknown, or hostile. Because of fear and uncertainty, relations across these categorical divisions have an artificial and fragile quality.
2. Schemes of public etiquette and propriety arise and are used as "codes" by means of which otherwise conflicting and suspicious persons can gingerly transact the business of living.
3. Basic uncertainty [from item 1] and the role playing of public propriety [from item 2] generate ambiguity over whether one is seeing the "true self" or merely the "public" self of other people.
4. Friendship as a tiny group is itself, in this context, a strategy whereby people feel they are seeing one another's "true selves." Friendship assures "...people of their mutual reality, dependability, or sincerity."[4]

If this is the situation, what are strategies people employ to foster friendship? Since friendship is centrally (but not exhaustively) a belief that one is viewing the spontaneous self of the other, how is such a perception achieved? How is the "sure coin of spontaneity" produced? A basic strategy is *violation of public propriety*, deviation from what is considered publicly correct. This takes two easy forms, individual and collective remission. *(a)* Individual remissions include such things as being vulgar, irreverent, outrageously drunk, refusing to be quiet, and larger, more enduring actions against others that candidate-friends *also* dislike. "Every friendship circle ...[has]...its inventory of stories about how its members have been 'horribly embarrassed' or expressed their feelings 'despite all.'"[5] *(b)* The social order offers ranges of occasions when people are collectively exempted from public propriety and encouraged to "let down" and "do" their "true self," as with cocktail parties, bar gatherings, smokers, orgies, and the like. Improprieties therein are taken to show "'beyond the facade' of contrivance."[6]

But it is not mere impropriety that is important; it must be impropriety *free of connivance* and voluntary. Thus involuntary exposure of impropriety such as occurs in total institutional situations like the military or mental hospitals and voluntary revelations among status unequals tainted by status strivings and exploitation are not strategically productive of friendship. Both violate "the central assumption friends must make...that they are presenting a self free of contrivance and ulterior motives."[7]

B. Constructing and Preventing Intimate Relations. Beyond and broader than friendship is "the intimate relation." As analyzed by Murray Davis, the *situation* of constructing an intimate relation has six aspects, six dimensions along which effort must be exercised. The would-be intimates must:

1. Achieve a *focus* of their "undirected yearning" upon one another.
2. Physically *intersect* with one another regularly.
3. Reveal their *feelings* to one another in intimate communication.
4. Provide each other with secret, discrediting information or *revelations*.
5. Give one another psychic and physical support and *helping*.
6. *Unite* the components of their selves in communion, to some degree.[8]

A complex array of tactics is brought to bear on all six of these dimensions of the situation. Here we simply indicate ways Davis suggests constructing intimates work to achieve the sixth aspect, a sense of communion or self-merging.

First, the unity of intimates is outwardly made real by means of keepsakes or *intimacy trophies,* physical objects they exchange.
    Second, they may undertake *joint ownership* of valuable objects.
    Third, intimates search for feelings, past experiences, and views they hold in common, discovery of which promotes "peak experiences" of communion.
    Fourth, they may strive to create a common social and natural environment that expands the range of experience about which they will ideally feel the same. One form of this is joint commitment to a common future.[9]

Communion has, of course, its complications and annihilating consequences for individuality and produces its own stresses for which there are also tactics.[10]

Strategies and tactics of how participants start groups provide only one-fourth of the starting story. There are, additionally, people not among the prospective group members who may take an interest in whether there is a group. Regardless of interested parties being prospective members or outsiders, the interest taken may be either *constructive* or *preventive*. There are thus four basic aspects of the question of group beginning, as illustrated in Figure 7.

Continuing our focus on intimacy, it is clear that outsiders to would-be groups often want to prevent the possibility of such groups forming in the first place (and have a keen interest in their disruption if started). Or, if they do not want to prevent intimacy groups *per se,* they want to prevent formation of the *wrong* intimacy groups. Such is the case with parents relative to their nubile young in all societies. As William Goode has argued, love—meaning "strong emotional attachment, a cathexis, between adolescents or adults of opposite sexes... with the components of sex desire and tenderness"[11]—is a potentially universal possibility between humans. Being a capricious, powerful, and rather random force, it is potentially disruptive of standing patterns of social class, ethnicity, and age. Love is, as they say, "blind" and "knows no bounds." It is also highly inefficient continually to have to destroy occurring relations. Wisdom counsels arrangements that forestall and prevent disruptive love groups in the first place. Such strategic arrangements assume many scales of social organization. Goode's analysis breaks the bounds of scale that bracket this treatise and is broadly "societal,"[12] but it is relevant nonetheless because it deals with the prevention of a type of group, which is a relevant unit.

1. Goode points out that child marriage is perhaps the simplest and historically most popular preventive strategy. People are taken off

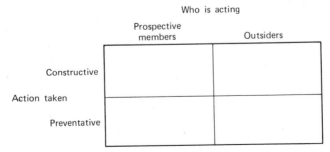

Figure 7. Aspects of group formation.

the "love market," as it were, long before they might even come on it.

2. Love may be allowed some rein, but defined as proper only with instances of certain, specific categories of people.

3. Some societies and social classes *isolate* the nubile from *all* possible love attachments, as with the harems of Islam.

4. Association is permitted but it is conducted under "close supervision by duennas or close relatives."[13]

5. Adolescents may be allowed to associate freely, as among the Americans, but parents influence the class of persons their nubile young encounter by neighborhood, school, and other structuring selections.

Goode only sketches out the broadest, most macroscopic strategies by means of which unwanted "love groups" are prevented. Such broad characterizations obviously have microscopic implementation—at the level of roles, encounters, and the like—especially in the case of the last-described strategy, the American pattern, which is additionally dependent on intricate face-to-face maneuvers aimed at channeling the nubile young.

In the same way that questions of entering groups overlap with questions of entering roles, questions of exiting and expeling from groups overlap with questions of exiting and expelling from roles. And all such questions considered as a class are distinct from questions of disrupting groups *per se*.

C. Terminating Intimacy. Continuing to confine our discussion to intimate groups, we may inquire into the situation of people desiring to terminate an intimate relation and how they go about doing it. Murray Davis' contributions are again signal. Once having been built, Davis asserts, the stability and vitality of intimate groups is problematic, a topic in the "doing" of groups to which we come in the next section (II.B.5). Reviving strategies often fail to function for three important classes of reasons that create the *situation* of one or both partners strategizing to dismantle their group: *(a)* a new intimate comes onto the scene for one of the partners, *(b)* spatial separation prevents revitalizing activities, *(c)* one or both partners change social and psychological characteristics over time. But although the group is in some sense spiritually dead, "the vitiated sociological skeleton of their relationship [tends]...to be difficult to dismantle."[14] Among the complex tangle of dismantling moves, four important ones are as follows:

1. The party who most wants to terminate forces the other actually to make the break.
2. A "have-it-out" (discussed in Section III.B.5) gets out of hand, leading to sudden overkill.
3. One or both experience "gestalt switch" such that the person whose features were once total good become totally bad.
4. Simple flight.[15]

III.   DOING GROUPS

Considered as a scale of action, established groups may be analyzed at two levels of specificity: strategic groups and group strategies. Paralleling the previous distinction between "strategic roles" and "role strategies,"[16] the "strategic group" perspective focuses on an entire instant group as a strategy in a containing situation. In contrast, the "group strategy" level of specificity elucidates the more micro activities by means of which the larger strategic group coping is accomplished. As indicated in the case of roles, the distinction is one of the analyst's distance from or closeness to the operation of the phenomenon. Any given study could (and perhaps should) provide both levels of analysis in the materials studied. In practice they do not. Hence the necessity to make this distinction.

A.   Strategic Groups: Groups for Managing Situations.   Strategic, small, informal groups range along a continuum from the public to the private, from openness to inspection by everyone to protection behind the walls of homes.

1.   Public Place Protection.   In reviewing encounter-scale strategies, public places were asserted to be a generic situation of socially unsupported, therefore threatening, exposure to strangers. Various encounter-scale body-management devices were considered in this light; namely, the sweet young thing, the nester, and the investigator.[17] The same situation is dealt with at several larger levels of social organization, among them the group-scale device of what Lyn Lofland calls "the traveling pack." To venture into public with several friends or acquaintances is to go forth with portable reassurance and social support. Members of traveling packs therefore feel free to act in ways utterly unlike the behavior of each when alone in public. Traveling packs may

> use public space with abandon, in such a way that, for example, a group of adolescents can choose to play running games in an air terminal. They feel free to indulge in backstage behavior, calling each other by name, yelling at one another across the expanse of the setting, using obscene language, and laughing loudly at private jokes. And they express proprietary attitudes. If their numbers are plentiful enough, they may even force others to depart, as when the overflow from a convention invades a city's nightspots.[18]

At even larger scales of such self-protection, Lofland discusses the "residents" of home territories and concentrated and dispersed urban villages.[19]

2. Strategic Cliques.   Between the surveillance of public places and the cloistering of homes fall the ambiguities of work organizations. The formality, intensity, and strife of work organizations, among other aspects, creates fertile ground for group-scale strategizing. Work organizations undergoing continual change in technology and organizations in which there is struggle for advancement and advantage provide a generic situation in which informal, protective, defensive, and offensive alliances grow. Studying several such work organizations, Melville Dalton reports a variety of strategic *clique* alliances that are built in and around the formal structure that harbors them.

> a. *Vertical Cliques* usually occur in a single department...between a top officer and some of his subordinates. They are vertical in the sense that they are up-and-down alliances between formal unequals.
>
> > (1) *Vertical Symbiotic Cliques.* The top officer is concerned to aid and protect his subordinates....The subordinates fully advise him of real or rumored threats to his position....There is a satisfying exchange of services.
> >
> > (2) *Vertical Parasitic Cliques.* The exchange of services between the lower and higher clique members is unequal. The lower ranked person or persons receive more than they give and may greatly damage the higher officer.

   b. Horizontal Cliques...cut across more than one department and embrace formal equals for the most part.

     (1) *Horizontal Defensive Cliques* are usually brought on by what its members regard as crises...[and] are strong for only the limited time necessary to defeat or adjust to a threat.

     (2) *Horizontal Aggressive Cliques* are a cross-departmental drive to effect changes rather than to resist them, to redefine responsibility, or even directly to shift it.

   c. Random Cliques are random in the sense that their members may come from any part of the personnel, managers, and managed, and they do not anticipate important consequences of their association.[20]

3. Showing Skill.   While working several summers as a bus driver for a large midwestern city, John Slosar was impressed that the structure of that role did not reward or even drastically punish very good or poor bus driving. Pay was almost totally determined by a seniority system and there was virtually no mobility upward in the transit service. The drivers, however, believed that driving requires a degree of skill—a condition not recognized or rewarded by the formal organization. In addition, the formal system of control allowed leeway in how driving was actually performed; to an extent, drivers were on their own. In this situation drivers had elaborated an informal, shared group-scale scheme by means of which they could exercise skill and put challenge into their work.

The strategy/scheme focused on demonstration of driving skill through minimizing the number of passengers carried, hence the amount of money collected, an item that drivers compared at the end of comparable runs. This reduction was accomplished by running ahead of schedule as much as possible, that is, as close as possible to the bus ahead of one on the same street, thus minimizing the amount of time in which people could collect for the next bus. It was, of course, against the rules to "run hot," but getting away with it was part of the skill (and apprehension entailed no or minor punishment). In thus involving the theft of time, Slosar labels this group-scale strategy/scheme of showing work skill "the society of bandits."[21]

4. Family Management of Stigma.   That most ubiquitous of relatively small, informal,, and *private* groups, the family, likewise strikes its poses. Classifications of types of families are virtually endless and their makers often forget that types are themselves strategies, as in the assertion that the "nuclear family" (one composed of only parents and their own children) is a strategic form in a mobility-oriented and rapidly changing industrial order. Among close-up, textured, and strategy-oriented studies, the work of Fred Davis on families in which there is a child crippled by polio is especially well done. The generic social situation of families in that topical circumstance is one of the child's problematic *(a) appearance* with regard to usual assumptions about people's physical attractiveness, wholeness, and symmetry of body parts; *(b) participation* in usual childhood activities; *(c) association* with peers.[22]

Since the stigma of polio was visible, the families could not employ the strategy of *passing*.[23] They used, instead, strategies of "normalization" or "disassociation."

> *a.* Normalization is the group-scale effort to make light of the handicap or to deny that it has any importance.
>
> *b.* Disassociation involves efforts to insulate the child and family as a whole from events and involvements that might force recognition of the handicap as a "difference." Disassociation frequently involves the following:
>
>> (1) Resentment and anger toward 'normals' accompanied by feelings of self-hatred deriving from the person's inability to live up to the prized normal standards.
>>
>> (2) Passive acceptance by the person of his exclusion from the world of 'normals' punctuated periodically by attempts to ingratiate himself or to prove himself a 'super nice guy'.
>>
>> (3) Retreat to a more or less privatized sphere of hopes and fantasies in which the harsh impress of the normal standard is tenuously kept at bay.
>>
>> (4) An attempt to recast and reformulate personal values, activities, and associations so as to avoid or remove the sting from the often negative, condescending, and depreciating attitudes of 'normals.'[24]

B. Group Strategies. Standing close to groups, we find them engaged in microscopic tactical adaptations and maneuvers.

1. Managing Demeanment. First considering work groups, true to the rather modest social backgrounds of social scientists and their consequent exposure to lower-level work settings, *negative* work situations have drawn their attention. Among college student jobs, Louis Zurcher and his associates became intrigued with the demeaning conflict experienced by undergraduate males who were also "hashers"— the lowest level of kitchen help—in sororities. They thought of themselves as "college men," hence as sophisticated, dominating, highly prestigious hail fellows well met, but these qualities were contradicted by the qualities of being hashers: menial workers, having low prestige, and obliged to be subservient. Ground in this "role conflict" Zurcher's associates (who were themselves hashers in several sororities) attended to how hashers interacted among themselves and directly with the sorority women they served. Their *shared* and *group-supported* words and deeds on the job made up a group-scale "defense pattern" against demeanment. It had six thematic micro practices.

   a. Rationalization (the job is only temporary).
   b. Denial (reluctance to identify with the job).
   c. Projection (the girls are "low born").
   d. Aggression (verbal and mitigated physical hostility toward the girls).
   e. Withdrawal (horseplay, general zaniness on the job, and threats to quit).
   f. Compensation (emphasis on discussions of sexual dominance).[25]

It is important to appreciate these are not "private" or individual or even "role" adaptations; they are expectations of the informal organization of the hasher work group. Thus

   a hasher who works too hard, who tries to please the girls, or who does not join in the horseplay is branded as a "brown noser," and suffers group ostracism. This seldom happens, though, since on the first day of his job as a hasher, the individual experiences role conflict and has need of some means for resolution of that conflict. He is [therefore] quite willing, in fact, eager, to accept the defense system that has become institutionalized in the informal work group. By enactment of these behaviors he not only implements functional defenses, but he gains the security of membership in the informal organization.[26]

2. Coping With Monotony. Among studies of industrial workers, Donald Roy's charmingly titled "Banana Time" stands as a champion report on group-scale coping (and is reprinted in Chapter 14). Roy was for two months a worker in a very small group of men who operated "clicking" machines, devices that stamp out leather or plastic parts. They worked six days a week, eleven to thirteen hours a day. The principal features of the situation were deadening monotony, consequent boredom, and "his twin brother, fatigue."[27]

At the individual self-encounter or role level, strategies focused on making a private "game of work." Thus the endless punching would be grouped into subgoals of doing a thousand "brown ones" before a thousand "white ones." The private game of work was pale, however, compared to the group-scale activities Roy analyzes into "times" and "themes."

> *a. Times* consisted of almost hourly group shared breaks and interruptions that served to punctuate the monotony. Roy enumerates a. variety of the times in the daily series: peach time (group sharing of a peach), banana time, window time, lunch time, pickup time (someone came for their recent output, occasioning talk), fish time, coke time, and so on.
>
> *b. Themes* consisted of the range of sometimes nonsense, sometimes serious *ad nauseam* talk in which operators engaged. There were a variety of kidding themes, sexual themes, themes about people's problems, and simple "chatter themes."[28]

Moving to more "private" groups, two situations faced by many families may be considered.

3. Crowding Management. Families in several societies live in what appear to Westerners to be "crowded" conditions. According to E. N. Anderson, for example, traditional Chinese households may be composed of several families who share a small number of rooms. In Penang, Malaysia, Anderson and his family shared with two other families an area in which twelve people occupied about 750 square feet of space. Elsewhere, he was one of fourteen people who shared some 600 square feet. He observed one household of twenty-two persons sharing 500 square feet! Despite such density, these households, among the traditional Chinese at least, seemed to be calm and orderly and enjoyed by their inhabitants. How is this accomplished? What are group-scale strategies that make it possible? Leaving aside values as strategies (e.g., large households are valued as ends in themselves; solitude is not valued), several practices function to achieve livable order.

a. Different rooms are defined as serving sharply different functions that are kept entirely separate.
b. Time management is loose and flexible, forestalling "jamming up" in the kitchen.
c. There is a strict hierarchy of what activity and what category of person supersedes another in the use of space: formal activities supersede informal ones; older people supersede younger ones, men supersede women, and so on.
d. Anyone can discipline anyone else's children.
e. Unrelated persons are expected not to become involved with one another; each family maintains a neutral and accommodating front.[29]

4. Off-Schedule Work. In a complex, industrial society many functions operate twenty-four hours a day. Some manufacturing processes, hospitals, railroads, and policing, for example, are "around the clock" enterprises. Other economic activities, such as janitorial work, are not around the clock but are still "off-schedule." To be employed in such organizations is often to work "off schedule" with the rest of the society. The two main forms of this are "swing shift" (typically from 4 P.M. to midnight) and "graveyard shift" (typically from midnight to 8 A.M.). Most of the social order, however, is organized around day-time work, as with schools, businesses, and leisure pursuits such as theatres and concerts. Off-schedule workers thus find themselves out of synchronization with their encompassing social order. Indeed, since most off-schedule workers have families, the family unit is thrown into a continuing situation of "schedule conflict," reports Claudette Cervinka who interviewed and observed a range of families on the swing shift. How, at the group-scale level, do families adapt to this situation? As analyzed by Cervinka, there are three main tactics:

First, most "usual," "on-schedule" activities are retained in the families' rounds but are reordered in the daily cycle. Swing shifters continue to sleep at night but "played" during the day, dined in the afternoon, lunched about 8 P.M., and tended to conceive the swing shift as a leisurely, "lazy" pace.

Second, the traditional division of family roles between husband as worker and wife as home and child manager seems even more pronounced in the swing shift working class family. Wives adjust and organize their days heavily to accommodate the husband's schedule of being home in the day (in order to be with him) and at work in the evening (when housework might be performed or childrens' social and school activities might be attended to).

Third, workers and their wives develop a virtual ideology that makes virtue of necessity and celebrates shift work as a way of life: the job atmosphere is less stressful, the couple is able to spend leisurely mornings together, the husband can more easily deal with organizations on conventional schedules, and the like.[30]

5. Reintegrating Intimates. Last, there are groups perhaps even more private than families; namely, the two-person "group" formed by intimates (who may or may not also be a family). Once established, an intimate relation (or any social organization for that matter) does not run along on its own internally generated, "natural" energy. Like biological organisms and physical machines, they require input. As Murray Davis phrases it: "Relationships require energy to operate and will waste away unless their energy supply is constantly renewed."[31] As an analytic stance, at least, we may assume that all intimate relations tend to "run down" and to "cool off." If this is a situation faced by all ongoing intimate relations, what are ways in which intimates go about reintegrating their group? Murray Davis has theorized that there are four basic lines along which this kind of work moves:

a. Cooling intimates often seek extreme environments, extremes either in being (1) "barren and hostile" or (2) "fertile and benign."[32] The former utilizes the well-known Simmelian proposition that conflict with external forces tends to unite the in-group. The latter strives for reintegration through exposure to natural and human-made settings of beauty and comfort as in walking on awe-inspiring beaches and arranging soft-lit and appealingly furnished rooms.

b. Intimates may of course speak directly of their relationship and its state, a process Davis calls "work-it-outs." It begins with a "State of the Union Address," which often consists of a summary of past performances, a listing of faults, and accusations of third-party involvements.

c. Work-it-outs may escalate into "have-it-outs" or arguments, which themselves have a highly expansive character because intimates are, by definition, related to each other wholistically. Since the ongoing relation is importantly equilibrated by acceptance of each other's behavior, either or both may now seek to test the limits of that acceptance. This testing can easily escalate into "overkill," however, and even though they can sometimes be successfully concluded, have-it-outs are "dangerous instruments by which to re-stitch a relationship that is coming apart at the seams...."[33]

d. Relationships may seek revitalization by means of several kinds of ceremonies. *Commemorative* ceremonies recall the origin of the relation (e.g., meeting, wedding) and various points of significance in the pair's history. Birthday and other individually commemorative ceremonies serve to indicate each treasuring the other. Less formal commemoratives may take the form of "remember whens" ("Remember when we...?"). In *piacular* ceremonies, which conclude work-it-outs and have-it-outs, each expiates guilt, forgives the other; they embrace, "kiss and make up," and the like. Daily, even hourly, *reassurance rituals* (e.g., "Gee! You're beautiful today!") signal to each the other's continued attachment.

Small, informal groups are both scales of action (strategies) and contexts or objects of actions (situations). Starting, ending, and "doing" groups are three prime aspects of their strategic analysis. Friendship and intimate relations were discussed relative to starting and ending groups. The "doing" of groups requires a distinction between groups *as* strategies and strategies *of* groups. Public place self-protection, strategic cliques, the showing of work skill and managing family stigma were discussed as instances of groups *as* strategies. Managing demeanment, monotony, crowding, off-schedule work, and sagging intimacy provide illustration of strategies *of* groups.

NOTES TO CHAPTER TEN

1. See Ch. 9, Section I.B., above.
2. I draw here from Erving Goffman, *Encounters* (Indianapolis: Bobbs-Merrill, 1961), pp. 7–14.
3. *Ibid.*, pp. 9–10.
4. Gerald D. Suttles, "Friendship as a Social Institution," in George McCall *et al.*, eds., *Social Relationships* (Chicago: Aldine, 1970), p. 132.

5. *Ibid.*, pp. 106–107.

6. *Ibid.*

7. *Ibid.*, p. 110.

8. Murray Davis, *Intimate Relations* (New York: Free Press, 1973), Chs. 2–6.

9. *Ibid.*, Ch. 6.

10. *Ibid.*

11. William J. Goode, "The Theoretical Importance of Love," *American Sociological Review,* **24:** 41 (February 1959).

12. See Ch. 4, Section III.

13. Goode, "Theoretical Importance of Love," *op. cit.,* p. 44.

14. Davis, *Intimate Relations, op. cit.,* p. 285.

15. *Ibid.*, Ch. 8.

16. Ch. 9, Section III.

17. Ch. 8, Section II.A, "Stranger Avoidance."

18. Lyn H. Lofland, *A World of Strangers* (New York: Basic Books, 1973), p. 139.

19. *Ibid.*, Ch. 7.

20. Melville Dalton, *Men Who Manage* (New York: Wiley, 1959), pp. 57–65. See also Tom Burns' discussion of cliques, cabals, and confidants in his essay "The Reference of Conduct in Small Groups," *Human Relations,* **8:** 467–486 (November 1955).

21. John A. Slosar, Jr., "Ogre, Bandit, and Operating Employee: The Problems and Adaptations of the Metropolitan Bus Driver," *Urban Life and Culture,* **1:** 339–362 (January 1973).

22. Fred Davis, *Illness, Interaction, and the Self,* (Belmont, Calif.: Wadsworth, 1971), pp. 108–115.

23. See Ch. 9, Section IV.C.1, above.

24. Fred Davis, *op. cit.,* pp. 115–130. On other family forms, for example, Carol Stack's formulation of "non-coresidential cooperative domestic networks" among some lower-class people is pointed in the right direction: *All Our Kin: Strategies for Survival in a Black Community* (New York: Harper & Row, 1974). Among other private groups, Louis Zurcher's "The Friendly Poker Game: A Study of an Ephemeral Role," *Social Forces,* **49:** 173–186 (December 1970) is an excellent study of what might be thought of as an "ephemermal group" rather than an ephemeral role.

25. Louis Zurcher, David Scnenschein, and Eric Metzner, "The Hasher: A Study of Role Conflict," *Social Forces,* **44:** 514 (June 1966).

26. *Ibid.*

27. Donald F. Roy, "Banana Time: Job Satisfaction and Informal Interaction," *Human Organization,* **18:** 160 (Winter 1959–1960), and reprinted in Ch. 14, below.

28. *Ibid.*, pp. 161–164. For description of what is in many ways an opposite type of work setting, a setting of extensive unpredictability, see the strategic analysis of Dorothy Nelkin, "Unpredictability and Life Style in a Migrant Labor Camp," *Social Problems,* **17:** 472–487 (Spring 1970). On group-scale strategies of dodging "prescribed being" in formal organizations, especially in total institutions, see Erving Goffman on "secondary adjustments" in his essay "The Underlife of a Public Institution," pp. 173–320 of his *Asylums* (Garden City, N.Y.: Doubleday-Anchor 1961).

29. E. N. Anderson, "Some Chinese Methods of Dealing with Crowding," *Urban Anthropology,* **1:** 141–150 (Fall 1972).

30. Claudette Cervinka, "Between Two Cycles: Tactics of Schedule Management on Swing Shift," manuscript, University of California, Davis, September 1974, summarized and quoted by permission of the author.

31. Murray Davis, *Intimate Relations, op. cit.,* p. 236.

32. *Ibid.,* p. 211.

33. *Ibid.,* p. 234.

CHAPTER ELEVEN

Organization-Scale Situations and Strategies

I. ORGANIZATIONS DEFINED

As indicated in the first section of Chapter 10, organizations have several basic and defining features that are the same as those of small, informal groups. Organizations also have their own distinctive attributes. For our purposes, these distinctive attributes are conscious goals and formal structure.

1.   Individual participants in the "smaller" scales of social organization have their own goals, desires, and the like, but the unit *qua* unit ofttimes lacks central, overt, stated, and guiding objectives toward which the unit is acknowledge to be directed. Organizations are different in that they always have such goals. Organizations are consciously created social instruments for the pursuit of goals, be these goals economic, political, educational, or military. Organizations have a distinctive *instrumental* character, at least at their outset.

2.   This conscious goal-pursuit is implemented by means of a *formal* structure of hierarchically arranged and differentiated positions—a formal division of labor. The organization is itself named, its internal positions are labeled, rules are written, and programs of activity are set forth. The participants of course relate to one another "personally," but the instrumentality and formality of the organization *per se* tends to constrain, channel, and control the degree to which relations become

wholistic, intimate, and diffuse, unlike many small, informal groups, which may indulge and even encourage opposite tendencies.

Conceived in terms of the four dimensions of time, space, population, and equipment, organizations have several *tendencies* that require noting even if they are not distinctive features.

(*a*) Formality, hierarchy, and delegation help make it possible for organizations to develop large, orderly populations. As is evident, large, formal organizations are distinctive to and dominate the modern world. They vie for sovereignty, indeed, with smaller settlements and even societies! Despite, however, their rather cancerous potential for growth, they all start somewhere and, by definition, they start small.

(*b*) Formality and sizable population are associated with relative longevity. Encounters, roles, and groups tend to have life spans far shorter than the lives of human beings, whereas many organizations (of the modern world at least) are coming to last far longer than human beings live.

(*c*) Sizeable populations and longevity increase the space over which organizations can operate. Some economic enterprises now act intensively over virtually the entire planet.

(*d*) Likewise, population and longevity, as these grow out of explicit goals and formality, increase the complexity and variety of material and equipment that organizations can acquire, process, and apply.

Thus our label "organization" is actually shorthand for the more accurate but too-long caption "large, formal organization."[1]

Qualitative materials on organizations in natural settings have focused on three fundamental classes of situations. First, *forming* an organization is problematic and needs to be strategized. Second, once formed, the organization *qua* organization must deal with its members. There are three primary types of *membering* situations: attracting and selecting new ones; socializing, converting, or committing them; and controlling them after they are reasonably committed. Third, as ongoing instrumental enterprises, organizations must strike postures toward their environments. *Posturing* strategies occur at three situational levels of breadth or narrowness: basic, structural, and tactical.

The review and analysis of major organizational situations presented in this chapter has a "skewed" character to which I must alert the reader. Because of my own interests in social movement organizations and the selective interests of people who do qualitative studies of organizations, the materials lean heavily toward voluntary associations of a collective behavior kind and toward educational institutions. There is relative neglect of business organizations. I see no special problem with this as long as the reader bears the selectivity in mind and appreciates that if a broader range of studies had been available, types of situations and strategies elucidated probably would have been different.

II. FORMING ORGANIZATIONS

Would-be formers of organizations find themselves in different types of situations that correspondingly structure the kind of organizing activity they should most auspiciously undertake.

1.   Their situations differ with respect to the degree they are or are not already members of *preexisting, amenable* social organizations. If they are, the strategy is that of "converting" an existing social organization into the proposed, new formal organization. This is itself strategized in two different situations, formal and informal. In the latter case, little, informal groups (in the sense described in the previous chapter) and clusters of them forming networks move from informality, friendship bonds, and lack of definite goals toward formality, secondary relations, and definite goals. Thus it is the action of Bob in the following passage that built "just buddies" into an organization that was an important instrument in accomplishing Bob's election to a city council.

> It...started with Bob talking with John last spring. John asked him if he'd ever thought of running for City Council. He had, a little. Then last June, I was at Bob's health food store; Bob and I were rapping about the 18-year-old vote and the Berkeley elections; I asked him if he's ever considered running, since he's the "natural young candidate" from being [university student body] president and stuff. He said yeah, he had. He'd talked to John and his good friend Valerie about it too. Then we were all at John and Lorie's place in the country, sitting around talking about it and it turned into a meeting, we wanted to do something...we decided to have another meeting. At this one there were about 12 to 15 people, mostly brought by John and Valerie from the ecology grad group; and Tom (a professor), John P. (local minister), and Chuck (student), they were brought by Bob.[2]

So, too, some religious organizations have been founded first on small groups of *kin*. Mormanism's founder, Joseph Smith, shifted his kin from kin to organizational disciples; the founder of Islam, Muhammed, did the same.[3] At the level of the family, at least, it is erroneous to assert that a prophet is without honor in his own country.[4]

The would-be organizer who is already a member of an amenable *formal* organization (which is itself likely to be harboring little groups) can strategize to convert that very organization, or large parts of it, into a new organization. This is particularly possible when the preexisting organization is nearing the end of a natural cycle of its existence, as when election campaign organizations have finished elections. The goal having been reached, the apparatus loses content and is ripe for re-forming. Thus the California-based Student Democratic Coalition arose from a student campaign organization constructed for the specif-ic and limited purpose of electing the governor in 1974. Accomplishing that, the broader-aimed organization arose from the old one, an orga-nization oriented to a wide variety of issues and to the presidential election than two years away.[5] On a larger scale, what became the Montgomery Improvement Association successfully organized a bus boycott in that city in 1955–1956 by (among other things) converting preexisting church organization into the new organization.[6] Co-opting existing organization as a vehicle on which the new organization at least *initially* rides is financially crucial. The old organization is quite literally a *vehicle:* it provides meeting places, telephones, printing facilities, and other mundane but indispensable necessities in addition to the more ethereal resources of structured relations in which people have experi-ence with one another and have built reputations and trust.[7]

If would-be organizers are *not* already members of an amenable social organization, the necessary strategy is rather obvious but funda-mental: seek out one or more amenable and preexisting informal groups or formal organizations. Thus in organizing poor people, the apparently effective policy promoted many years ago by the late Saul Alinsky, is to identify, "politicize," and thereby "organize" informal, natural groups and their leaders.[8] In the formation of a new wing of a millenarian religion, the carrier of that world view began the new organization by means of recruiting an entire friendship net.[9]

2.   The situations of would-be organization formers differ with re-spect to the degree to which the discontents and aspirations of prospec-tive members are *focused* or *unfocused*. Possible participants can be assumed to persist in their usual routines in the absence of events, happenings, episodes that draw their attention and convince them that new organization is needed (and that existing organization is inade-quate). In the absence of *focusing events,* aspirations and discontents are diffuse, amphorous, unfocused, and *unactionable*. The organizer's strat-

egy is therefore to act to organize in the context of a striking, nonroutine, symbolic event. Such events do not themselves simply happen: they are socially constructed and attention is called to them; thus the organizer's strategy is often that of being attuned to possible focusing events and being prepared to escalate occurrences into them. Professional social movement organizers sometimes even strive to create auspicious events that they can then escalate into focusing events, a process quite self-consciously advocated and practiced by Alinsky for the purpose of forming (and building) organization.[11]

III. ORGANIZATIONAL MEMBERING

Once in existence, an organization must manage its "self" and "others" in a way somewhat analogous to how self and others must be managed at the encounter and role scales of social organization. Three "self" aspects of the organization must be successfully tended for it to remain viable. First, members inevitably die or leave, and since an expanding membership is often a goal, strategies of *attraction, recruitment,* and *selection* are required. Second, once attracted, novices require indoctrination at the level of cognitive and motor skills and emotional and ideological commitment. They require, that is, converting or *socializing* to a greater or lesser degree. Third, even though socialized, the ongoing contingencies of social life create continuous problems of *controlling* members either as individuals or as internal groups and factions that become troublesome.

A. Attracting and Selecting. There are sizable bodies of materials on attracting prospective members to and selecting them for various kinds of organizations. Unfortunately for our purposes, these caches of materials are almost totally topical rather than generic in structure and descriptive rather than analytic in content. There is much valuable work to be done in this area.

B. Socializing. The situation with regard to socializing into organizations (and other scale units) is more promising. It has generated so much interest, indeed, that a few "consolidations" somewhat akin to the kind discussed in Chapter 7 have been attempted, even though the data available have not been fully auspicious. Immodestly, I report that I, assisted by Lyn H. Lofland, have attempted one. A large variety of studies were integrated around the need to determine what organizational-scale arrangements seem most strongly to facilitate a person taking an identity unto himself. Having internalized a conception of himself as a member of a specific unit of social organization, the person is then responsive to and acts in terms of the obligations it proffers. The range of important considerations seems to run along eleven lines, eleven strategic variations.

1. Unanimous Imputation. Internalization of an identity is faciliated when it is unanimously imputed to the "socializee." Stable self-conception and commitment are retarded to the degree that the "others" of the socializee's environment disagree on his being a proper member or a member at all.

2. Member and Nonmember Imputers. The new identity is made more "real" by being imputed not only by those who already wear it and share it but also by "outsiders" to it. Nonmember imputers of the new identity function dramatically to set the person off from the rest of the world.

3. Integrated Place Round. The "daily round" situations of the new member (and all of us for that matter) differ in the degree to which the people with whom the neophyte interacts also *interact among themselves.* Thus in a "segregated place round" the people with whom the socializee works, plays, and lives, for example, may all be unknown to one another. This inhibits the flow of information supporting any new organizational membership in that round, hence the intensity and unanimity of new identity imputation. An integrated place round, in contrast, informationally collapses the separate spheres of the socializee's life and fosters internalization.

4. New Identity Places. Organizations often have physical locales socially identified as being "theirs," and internalization of the new identity is facilitated insofar as this is the case, and to the degree that the socializee spends his days in or on the locales.

5. Disconfirming Identity Equipment Withdrawn. Memberships are concretized in and supported by physical objects socially defined as part of them: clothing, tools, furniture, vehicles, and writings, for example. Socialization is fostered by withdrawing all "identity equipment" that is not supportive of the new identity.

6. *Confirming Identity Equipment Supplied*. Correspondingly, assumption of the new identity is facilitated by supplying a rich range of equipment that signals, embodies, and supports the new identity.

7. *Personal Disorientation*. To maximize the impact of the foregoing organizational-scale arrangements, the socializee is best "arranged" in some rather than other ways. A firm sense of identity is supported and maintained by participation in a stable framework of social and cognitive referents that define events and provide devices for the management of everyday life. Possessed of such a working cognitive framework and management devices, persons experience themselves as *oriented*, as feeling manageable anxiety, fear, and consternation. The relative absence of a workable scheme for managing and defining events provokes the experience of *disorientation*—experiences of bewilderment, confusion, shock, astonishment, being at the bottom of the abyss, and so on. When disoriented, the person "actively seeks to establish [a cognitive frame of reference] through his own strivings by making use of significant and relevant information provided within the context of interaction."[12] Cognitive frames of reference provide personal identities. Therefore, to promote a person's receptivity to a new identity, it is facilitative to disorient his old identities, to bring him to a state of seeking for orientation, thereby making him more receptive to the new identity. Organizations sometimes accomplish this through the sheer process of forcibly removing the socializee from his old round of life, stripping him of his old identity equipment, and providing him with a new round of life.

8. *Positive and Negative Affective Bonds*. What humans accept as true, real, moral, and possible is intimately a function of the emotional ties they have to other humans. They tend to accept as true what is said by other people toward whom they have strong and positive emotive attachments and to disbelieve or doubt what is said by disliked or distrusted persons. Acceptance of a new identity is facilitated if the disoriented person is induced to form strong and positive affective bonds with his fellow members and to feel estranged from nonmembers.

9. *Cognitive Congruence*. Identity assumption is facilitated when the socializee's preexisting cognitive system is congruent with (or manipulated to seem congruent with) the one in which the new membership is embedded. "Congruence" refers to the similarities or differences in basic predicates about reality. Typically, incongruences revolve around disparities in attributing religious, psychological, or political meanings to events of ongoing life. When there is incongruence, organizations may strategize to shake the candidate loose from his old system (through disorientation) or to show how the new is "really," "basically" like the old, but better.

10. Comprehensive, Articulate Ideology. Cognitive systems bearing organizational identities differ in the degree to which they are comprehensive, articulate, and moralized. The ideologies of some identities seem to "speak about" a relatively narrow range of possible occurrences; they appear not to be clearly worked up into a system (and, ideally, written down) and to possess minimal and rudimentary moral justification of why the person should be a member. Other perspectives display the opposite features, especially psychiatric, political, and religious philosophies.

The socializee is likely to go through a period of trying-out and trying-on the proffered cognitive system of the new membership, testing it for capacity to define and manage events. Less comprehensive, articulate, and moralized perspectives provide less guidance, leaving gaps and posing difficulties. It is therefore facilitative if the supplied perspective is one that furnishes a powerful and clear complex of definitions and a morally supportive rhetoric.

11. Technical Knowledge and Skill. Last, assumption of a new identity is fostered under conditions of effective tutoring in whatever technical knowledge and skills may be required; many organizations are much more attentive to this dimension than to any of the others mentioned.[13]

It is important to point out that these eleven strategy variations are not simply eleven different factors that affect the forcefulness of assumption of a new, personal identity. Their force is derived from their *conjoint and cumulative* presence. The presence of all eleven in their strongest form over a prolonged period of time provides the greatest likelihood that the person will internalize the identity and therefore play it out. However it seems also to be the case that few persons are ever subjected simultaneously to the most facilitative arrangements of these eleven circumstances. They may go through strong versions of some but not others, or weak versions of them all. If more attenuated exposures are also empirically most common, there should be far fewer committed members of anything than there are persons who at one time or another simply become "involved with" membership. The common fact of attenuated exposure makes possible a vast amount of drifting in and out of memberships. Nonetheless, some persons receive the "full treatment" and form the core and stable populace of many organizations.

C.   Controlling.   The situation of controlling members is itself quite broad and requires internal partitioning for more fruitful analysis. Existing materials suggest at least three salient varieties of member control situations at the organizational scale: collective morale, member inadequacy, and factionalism.

1.   Collective Morale.   Organizations tend, by definition, to be highly task and goal oriented. They are collectivities engaged in the never-ending pursuit of a set of goals: the production or sale of N units of widgets, the raising of N dollars, the passage or blockage of N legislation, the making of N converts. All such never-ending pursuit of goals becomes tiresome. Regardless of whether the goals are regularly accomplished, the pursuit is itself a source of weariness, a source of what some psychologists label "response inhibition"—an increasing disposition not to act, the more the organism acts. The readiness of humans to harness themselves to organizational ends (or any ends) requires, therefore, *renewal* and procedures productive of it. The *periodicity* of much organizational functioning, the institutionalization of "coffee breaks," eating periods, the work day, the weekend, and the "vacation" are elements of one obvious strategy of renewal.

Additionally, organizations differ in the degree to which they have access to their members for purposes of renewal and general bolstering of morale, enthusiasm, and commitment. Members of some organizations are "full time" and assembled in one place, whereas others are part-time and geographically dispersed. Such is the case, for example, with an organization that sells plastic bowls and other articles by means of housewives staging "home parties." How, asked Dorothy Peven who analyzed that organization and situation, did the company boost the morale of their marginally committed, geographically dispersed, and minimally supervised labor force? Most broadly, the plastic bowl company strove to give its product a religious-revivalistic image. This took such forms as:

a. Frequent assemblies and rallies at which there was much singing, clapping, and pageantry that was similar to more conventional revival meetings.
b. Treating the product as a virtually sacred and special, almost mystical, object.[14]

Organizations vary, too, in the degree to which they in fact regularly achieve their self-set goals. Some are able to bask in the pride and the morale-boosting experience of regular goal achievement, but others must live with and manage a chronic gap between aim and actuality. This gap is often especially acute for conversionist-millenarian religions—religions committed to achieving a certain number of members before a given year, to ensure the meeting of a condition of ushering in the millennium. I studied one such religion in a period during which it cyclically experienced this agonizing problem of aiming for thousands of converts but acquiring only a handful. The four cycles of collective despair and high morale experienced over three years had the following features:

a. Some event occurring or plan devised that provided for them a collective sense of high morale and hope that many converts would soon be made.
b. Action would be organized around the event or plan, which,
c. Soon failed by their own estimation, leading to,
d. Low morale and despair over ever attaining their goal,
e. And the organization coming full circle back to a new event or plan.[15]

The strategic problem in this situation is to invent or devise plans that rebuild the organization's battered morale. At the scale of the organization *per se*,[16] the following morale-building strategies were observed:

a. The membership would decamp and migrate *en masse* to a new location, believed to be more favorable, for making converts. This has been a rather popular strategy of religions throughout history.
b. It would be announced that the organization's messiah, who was in a distant foreign country, was soon to arrive in America. Preparations for his coming had to be made. The exact time of his arrival would not be set.
c. The present and near future were defined as planning, organiz-

ing, and headquarters preparation time for a later time when, aided by things done now, conversion goals would be achieved.

  d. The membership would be geographically dispersed on missionary quests. Morale and a sense of expansion and potency were derived from new places and people, even if not from a larger membership.[17]

2. Member Inadequacy. For whatever reasons, organizations inevitably seem to have members they define as performing inadequately. At the organization-scale, such members must be coped with by restructuring the organization to contain and encyst the harm allegedly being done or by devising ways to expel them. Fortunately for most organizations, one supposes, the portion of members perceived as performing inadequately tends to be small. The task of encystment or expulsion therefore tends not to reach the organizational scale.[18] A few extraordinary organizations, however, have a high proportion of members whose performance is defined as inadequate. One such is the "open door" institution of postsecondary education, be it a state university or junior college. The situation of these organizations rises out of an ideology of an open class system and widespread aspiration to achieve a B.A.—aspirations that are contradicted by educator belief in maintaining standards. As described for other purposes in Chapter 6 and explained in full by Burton Clark in Chapter 15, these organizations employ two major strategies of "cooling out" what are defined as the unrealistically high educational aspirations of about a third of their students: the *hard,* quick flunk-out stance historically prominent among midwestern universities, and the *soft,* slow redirection stance devised by California junior ("community") colleges and now used nationwide. As also indicated in Chapter 6, the soft strategy has five main, topical phases and aspects: *(a)* intensive testing and recording, *(b)* counseling, *(c)* aspiration-assessment and redirection courses, *(d)* warning notices, and *(e)* drawn-out probation. More generically, this "soft" strategy involves the elements of *(a)* offering alternatives, *(b)* relying on gradual execution, *(c)* being extraordinarily objective, *(d)* employing agents of consolation, and *(e)* avoiding absolute standards.[19]

3. Factionalism. Organizations *qua* organizations are precarious achievements. First, since they tend to form and grow as conglomerates and mergers of preexisting social organizations, those prior allegiances and alliances tend to reassert themselves as adpative ties in times of stress. Previously established groups or organizations are easily tempted to "take a walk" back to their independence. Second, the course of organizational life is itself productive of new and emergent subgroupings who develop their own shared sense of themselves as entities and their own potentialities for exercising power or "splitting." When economic incentives or sheer coercive forces are not strongly employed as controlling devices (these two being the most common bases of organizational unity), "persuasion"-based strategies come to the fore.[20] Anthony Oberschall has suggested three main forms of such persuasion:

   a. The cultivation of a charismatic leader who focuses loyalty on himself, thereby transcending and superseding preexisting leadership loyalties of subcharismatic magnitude.
   b. The rapid elaboration of a new and distinctive subculture—"distinct dress, speech, life-style, heroes, history, and traditions..."—that supersedes and functions to obliterate previous practices.
   c. The construction of a member-supported and centralized organization that effectively absorbs and directs the preexisting leaders and the resources of members.[21]

IV. ORGANIZATIONAL POSTURING

A. Basic Posturing. Formal organizations *are* strategies. They are strategies of achieving goals, of dealing with situations. As such, we need to determine the most basic and fundamental ways in which these enterprises operate on their environments. How, at a constitutional level, do they go about "relating to" their environs in pursuit of their objectives and taking account of constraints posed by situations?

Standing furthest back and taking the longest and broadest view, following Ralph Turner and others,[22] organizations have only three primordial options: coercion, bargaining, and persuasion.

   1. *Coercion* is the basic posture of worsening by threat or deed the circumstances of other parties if they do not do what the organization wants. Episodic murder and assault or systematic programs

of terrorism are the strongest forms of coercion. Less strong forms invoke actual or threatened embarrassment and disgrace, as in blackmail and civil disobedience.

2. A *bargaining* posture offers to improve the situation of others if they assist the organization. There is an exchange of valued items—monetary or material—wherein the parties emerge in what both feel to be improved positions. This is decidedly different from coercion, which does not hold out any promise of improvement, only the possibility of not being worse off.

3. The posture of *persuasion* utilizes "strictly symbolic manipulation"[23] in operating on the environment. The organization does not employ either rewards (bargaining) or punishments (coercion). It is likely, nonetheless, verbally to call attention to rewards and punishments that will befall others if the words are not heeded. But the organization does not itself exercise such rewards and punishments.[24]

These are, of course, only pure types. Empirical organizations often employ "mixes" of all three.

B. Structural Posturings. Having elected one of the three primordial possibilities or some amalgam of them, organizations need to achieve a style of structural implementation, a pattern of internal form that bears on how the environment is manipulated.

Posturings at the structural level are usefully distinguished in terms of the degree to which they are *offensive* or *defensive*. Offensive structural posturings are predicated on positive visions of an environment actively to be altered. Action is proactive and aggressive in the sense of being self-initiated and guided by an internally generated program. Defensive structural posturings, in contrast, are predicated on pessimistic fears of an environment that must merely be responded to. Action is reactive and timid in the sense of being prodded by and developed as counter to external pressures.

1. Defensive. Organizations in situations where the social values they embody are precarious have a tendency to defensive structural posturings. As analyzed by Burton Clark, "precarious" means that the values are undefined, not fully legitimated, and not fully acceptable to the population environing the organization.[25] The adult education movement in California in the first half of the twentieth century is an instance of organizational embodiment of precarious values. Goals were vague, organization marginal, and enrollment pressures strict. Scrutinizing the emergent strategic structure of adult education, Clark asked: "How do...[organizations] attempt to implement their values when they are precarious, and what changes in meaning and acceptance are incurred[?]" Over the course of decades, adult education organizations have evolved a structure that renders them (a) increasingly able rapidly to decipher and respond to the shifting interests of local populations, and (b) increasingly able to employ a heterogeneous, shifting, part-time, and transient teaching force. By means of quick detection of changing interests and highly disposable teachers, such organizations survive.

Every structural posturing has its ideological overlay—its legitimizing rhetoric. In the case of adult education, the defensive evolution of the organizational pattern was accompanied by the *decline* of an ideology defending offerings on the grounds of intrinsic educational worth and professional competence and the *rise* of an ideology of pure service and meeting people's demands (called "needs").

Overall, the strategy is that of an organizational "neutrality" in which student demand dictates educational decisions.[26]

At the other extreme, organizations may find themselves forced to defensive structural posturing because their values are (or become) insufficiently precarious. Something of this sort appears to have befallen the Townsend Movement, a depression-spawned organization dedicated to securing pensions for older people. The group's general aims and issues were either achieved or eclipsed by social legislation and by World War II; the movement became a structure without a direction, and as depicted by Sheldon Messinger, it went through an "organizational transformation" of defensive, strategic decline in which:

a. Leaders no longer acted to promote the official program.
b. Emphasis was placed on selling various Townsend-approved health foods, toilet articles, publications, and the like.
c. Pure recreation emerged as the central activity.[27]

2. Offensive.   Of course nothing inherent in any organization's situation forces it into either a defensive or an offensive posture. Situations differ in their auspiciousness and therefore conduce or suggest directions, but actual directions are very much a matter of how the participants choose to feel about and define their situation. In the end, it is a matter of will.

As such, audacity and boldness of will vary Offensive-defensive is in reality "offensiveness-defensiveness"—a single continuum rather than two partitioned categories. Well-established, tradition-conscious organizations tend to move toward the offensive ends of things, but timidly. Thus we find that the various United States Presidents structurally posture their White House staff offensively but without special flair, despite variations from incumbent to incumbent. As depicted by Richard Johnson, recent Presidents have employed one or another of formal, competitive, or collegial posturings of structure. The formal posture has been most popular and was used by Truman, Eisenhower, Johnson, and Nixon. It is a tight pyramid that encourages orderly decisions through analysis (and "tends to distort information and...nourish scandals"). "Its antithesis is Franklin D. Roosevelt's 'competitive' style of pitting aides against each other; such a President receives more information but risks being caught up in office politics. Between the two extremes is John F. Kennedy's teamwork approach, a system that requires an intellectually keen staff and President."[28]

Such posturings are in sharp contrast to the darings of many social movement organizations who sometimes strike poses that are sociologically quite spectacular. What Philip Selznick has aptly labeled "the combat party" is one important instance of the most offensive of posturings. Features of combat parties specific to communist parties (which are primarily but not exclusively combat parties, and vice versa) include the following:

a. Remarkable persistence of the communist core membership despite great fluctuations and turnover.
b. Persistence of strategies and tactics of power aggrandizement despite significant shifts in political "line."[29]

The "distinctive competence" of the combat party is "to turn members of a voluntary association into disciplined and deployable political agents."[30] *Qua* organization, it embodies what Selznick calls "an operational code," a structural pattern of functioning with the following aspects:

a. The objective of...party organization is the creation of a highly manipulable skeleton organization of trained participants. This organization is sustained by continuous political combat and is linked to the mass movement as its members become leaders of wider groups in the community.

b. Adherents, giving only partial consent, are to be transformed into agents from whom total conformance can be demanded.

c. The party, through activity and indoctrination, absorbs and insulates the member, severing his ties to the outside world and maximizing his commitment to the movement.

d. To avoid the divisive and action-frustrating nature of democratic participation,...political contention within the party...[is] minimized. Power centers which challenge the official leadership are prohibited.

e. The keynotes of party organization are *mobilization* and *manipulation*. Everything must be subordinated to maximizing these values, for they define the combat character of the party.

f. The full potentialities of...ideology for morale building are to be exploited, but "dialectical" adaptations of doctrine to the requirements of the tactical situation are desirable....

g. The party is to be safeguarded against the twin inherent dangers of liquidation and isolation. Consequently there is constant emphasis on maintaining the integrity of the party organization and its access to the sources of power in society.

h. The party organization can be maintained only by a continuous struggle for power in every conceivable arena.

i. The party engages in conspiratorial activity regardless of fluctuations in the respectability of its immediate program and irrespective of the degree of political freedom in the arena. This is required by the aim of subordinating target groups to the party organization.

j. Public (legal) activity is always to be combined with conspiratorial (illegal) work, the latter supporting and advancing the former.[31]

Obviously there are a variety of postural structurings, especially among social movements, decidedly short of the long-haul tenacity and duplicity of combat parties. Naturalistic observers have only begun to discern and document them.[32]

C. Tactical Posturings. "Structural" postures provide capacities for and limitations on action. They point the organization in one or more directions by setting up certain general competencies and, correspondingly, vulnerabilities and lack of capacity for yet other directions and actions. To use the military metaphor, the level of basic and structural posturings define the plan of battle. Within and through that plan of battle, the battle itself must actually be fought. After commitment to a plan, maneuvering must occur within it. I refer to this micro and executional maneuvering as "tactical posturing."[33] As with structural postures, tactical postures tend in offensive versus defensive directions, the latter of which I will discuss first.

1. Tactics of Hyperconventionality. Organizations as well as persons in encounters and roles can feel a need to stand guard on the expressive implications of their actions. As in the "polite stranger" encounters discussed in Chapter 8 (Section III.A), organizations often strive to monitor their own behavior for incongruities with the "image" they are fostering. And they are of course likely to conduct such monitoring at the organizational-scale of action.

The felt need to stand guard on the expressive implications of actions is sometimes especially acute for organizations offering illegal and dangerous services to a "straight" and fearful clientele. Such was once the case for Mexican abortion clinics catering to North American women. As reported by Donald Ball, a clinic he observed was, objectively, not very hygienic or medically professional and safe, but it was carefully contrived at a superficial and interactional level to appear so. This appearance was contrived, additionally, as a guard against self-threatening implications to its women clients. A place defined as "medical" is likely to control clients better than one defined as a back alley shop.

Overall, the clinic's strategy was one of hyperconventionality in externals. Socially (but not technically), it was more elaborately "medical" than legitimate medical environments. The physical setting and decor were extremely modern and plush. The personnel were impressively uniformed and ostentatiously professional in manner. Medical equipment was conspicuously present (but not always used properly, or at all, because of its irrelevance to the clinic's operation).[34]

As was also seen at the level of role strategizing, then, acting units who are marginal sometimes feel the greatest need to act most conventional.[35]

2. Tactics of Dramaturgic Concealment. Going further, organizations (and individuals, even) sometimes seem to want to monitor their central actions to the point of virtual concealment from outsiders *and* from themselves! Such, at least, is the impression given by historical trends in the organization of state executions, operations in which a person officially is killed by the state in payment for crime. Over the course of some 250 years (ca. 1700–ca. 1950) the state executions of England, America, and many other countries have moved from what I have characterized as an "open" to a "concealed" dramaturgics. A concealed dramaturgics erects physical, social, and psychological barriers to perception, regulates the entrance and exit of participants and witnesses, controls publicity, and the like. An open dramaturgics allows and even promotes the opposite.

Taken in composite, modern state executions display the following dramaturgically concealing tactics that make up an overall strategy. These micro tactics contrast sharply with the open alternatives that are also mentioned.

a. The *confinement* prior to death allows few visitors, and these are regulated. A narrow range of activities is permitted. The condemned person is insulated from knowledge of preparations for his death. Historically, those condemned to die had many self-chosen visitors, engaged in a wide array of activities, and had knowledge of the preparations to kill them.

b. Modern executions are performed on socially inconspicuous days and *times* (early mornings or at night). Historical ones were in the early afternoon.

c. The *trip* from confinement to the death place is very short and fast; there are no events en route. (In the extreme, it has been as brief as eight steps and fifteen seconds.) Historic trips covered miles, required hours to complete, and included events en route.

d. Modern *places* of death are small, private, and enclosed. Historic ones were large, public, and outdoors.

e. Only a small, socially homogeneous and carefully selected set of witnesses are permitted at modern executions. Historically, thousands of heterogeneous persons attended executions.

f. Modern *executioners* are part-time, bland, trained, drilled, and virtually anonymous to the public. Historic ones were full-time, colorful, and public figures.

g. All these features of the modern execution induce the condemned person to keep actions and words to a minimum just before death. Historically, condemned individuals engaged in many more actions and words, especially "scaffold speeches."

h. Modern *death techniques* strive to be unfailing, fast acting, quiet, painless, nonmutilating, odorless, and concealed, provoking neither screams nor struggles. Historic ones were designed to be just the opposite in many of these regards.

i. There is a tendency to dispose of the *corpse* quickly and in a concealed fashion. Historically, the body was often put on public display.

j. Modern executions are permitted little *publicity;* historic ones were unrestricted in this respect.[36]

The state execution is likely not the only area in which there has been a movement from open to concealed dramaturgics. The primal scenes of birthing, fornicating, wedding, and dying (of humans and other animals) seem also to have shifted from relative openness to relative concealment, as have defecation and urination, and the management of their products. In addition, disease, hunger, and gross impairment and deformity of the body have been metaphorically and literally swept out of the streets and held behind walls. "Trends" of these kinds are not, of course, merely trends. Effort must be exerted to accomplish them. A proliferation of formal organizations geared to mount such defensive arrangements is required and have been developed.[37]

Offensive, tactical posturings and their situations may be conceived as varying broadly in terms of (a) the amount of change the posturing is striving to bring about and (b) the degree to which the striving organization is inside or outside the mainstream—the "establishment"—of its encompassing society. The amount of change sought may vary from an effort slightly to improve the organization's situation (as in cadging a slightly larger budget) to transforming the host society and running it. Degree of establishmentarianism may vary from being extremely central, unquestioned, and legitimate to the opposite.

The conventional wisdom asserts, probably correctly, that the less an organization is part of the establishment, the more change it is likely to seek, and vice versa. If these two variations are assumed to be inversely related and reasonably linear, they form a continuum along which we may range and review materials on offensive, tactical posturings. Existing studies do not cover the entire spectrum of possibilities along these continua, but they do point up some important possibilities.

3. Issue-Raising Tactics. Organizations seeking change sometimes must make their aims issues in the minds of relevant others who might support or effect that change. Issues do not simply exist. They must be created—they must be raised. As studied by Roger Cobb and Charles Elder, ways in which issues are phrased and conceived by promoting parties bear on the numbers of others who can be induced to take them seriously. Successful issue-raisers tend to use the following strategies:

    a. Define the issues in ambiguous rather than specific terms.
    b. Assert the issues to be of fundamental social significance.
    c. Claim the issues to be of long-term relevance.
    d. Frame the issues in a nontechnical manner.
    e. Claim that no precedents exist for dealing with the proposed issues; therefore attention is demanded.[38]

4. Tactics of Program Promotion.   Once raised by the tactics just enumerated and a wide variety of others in sore need of study, the program of change built out of the issues must be promoted. Two arenas of promotion need to be distinguished: *(a)* mustering and enlarging support with various constituency, target, and bystander groups,[39] *(b)* mustering and enlarging support in the specific context of change-enacting enclaves, namely, legislatures. Relative to the former, Cobb and Elder provide orienting suggestions of four such tactics:

    a. Arousal: information-oriented efforts to activate latent support.
    b. Provocation: abrasive action designed to provoke action when arousal strategies wane.
    c. Dissuasion: efforts to discourage opponents from acting.
    d. Demonstration of commitment: last-resort shows of strength.[40]

At the extremely concrete and detailed level, Gene Sharp has impressively catalogued virtually the entire spectrum of nonviolent "provocations," to use Cobb and Elder's term. Assembling tactics into five master classes, Sharp describes 198 specific forms (more topically than generically).

    a. Protest and Persuasion: Fifty-four forms grouped in part as formal statements, group presentations, symbolic public acts, drama and music, processions, honoring the dead.
    b. Social Noncooperation: Sixteen forms grouped in part as ostracism of persons and withdrawal from the social system.
    c. Economic Noncooperation: Forty-nine forms grouped as boycotts and strikes.

   d. Political Noncooperation: Thirty-eight forms grouped in part as rejection of authority and citizen noncooperation with government.

   e. Nonviolent Intervention: Forty-one forms grouped as psychological, social, economic, and political intervention.[41]

Relative to legislative enclaves, Eugene Bardach's *The Skill Factor in Politics* is suggestive of how tactical analysis might be developed in this area. Studying five mental health issues in the California State Legislature, Bardach attempts to derive generic situational features and corresponding generic tactics. The generic situation of political enterprise is conceived as having five main aspects or tasks.

   a. Mapping out the existing policy factions and alignments.
   b. Mobilizing effective allies.
   c. Gaining endorsement or neutrality from enough interests to impress relevant authorities.
   d. Stalling, inhibiting, or neutralizing opponents.
   e. Timing execution of moves properly in the moving contexts of opportunities and risks.[42]

Bardach delineates the situation much more carefully than strategies and tactics of dealing with the five major aspects of it. The fourth aspect is most articulately developed using notions of secrecy, touching base, and entrapment.[43] The raw empirical material otherwise reported, however, seem to be preeminently amenable to tactical analysis.

   One situation of political enterprise involves values to which everyone gives lip service but few people want to implement in behavior. Then, as analyzed by Leon Mayhew in the case of Massachusetts antidiscrimination legislation of 1946, the strategies and tactics of entrepreneurs in such a situation focus on *(a)* programs to reinforce and interpret lofty social values and *(b)* programs to force decision makers either to support the proposed legislation or to appear not to support the lofty values.[44] Stated as a more general principle, symbols implying that the opponent's position is not respectable are put forth and an immediate answer is demanded.[45]

5. Tactics of Political Campaigning. Moving into decidedly mainstream and public tacticizing, where relatively little change is sought, the dynamics of political campaigns and political struggle more generally invite enormously more detailed and systematic analysis than has yet been attempted. There is of course no end to the literature on "how to do" politics, especially election efforts. Relative to the latter, there are many guides to such matters as raising money, writing press releases, giving coffee hours, canvassing, holding rallies, and leafleting. Concrete and topical categories of that kind and corresponding treatment of them, however, rarely achieve generic and sociological dimensions.[46]

The topical and narrowly practical perspective on campaigning contrasts sharply with generic efforts such as those of Richard Merelman, who has sketched out highly promising directions in which case analyses can profitably move. Attuned to the developmental quality of political struggles—elections in particular—and adopting and adapting concepts from theories of dramatics, Merelman suggests eight "sensitizing," dramatic mechanisms of politics.

a. *Personification:* making issues concrete and visibly embodied in particular people and/or stereotypes.

b. *Identification:* persuading people to see their personal futures as dependent on the politician.

c. *Suspense:* building tension over the outcome of the struggle.

d. *Catharsis:* promising relief and bringing about at least seeming resolution to the suspense.

e. *Symbolism:* providing emotional satisfaction in a rich array of rituals and symbols.

f. *Climax:* providing series of turning points short of the larger catharsis.

g. *Peripety:* asserting decline in one's opponent and rise in one's own fortunes.

h. *Unmasking:* effecting a sudden change in evaluation of a person or object.[47]

As conceived by Merelman,

Politicians are more likely to fail the less successful the personification of opponents, the less able they are in applying their identification appeals, the less suspense they can build into their appeals, the less credible their promises of catharsis, and the fewer the symbols and rituals they are able to manipulate. They will also fail if unable to arrange climactic scenes for themselves, unmask opponents, or employ peripetal appeals.[48]

6. Tactics of Occupational Aggrandizement.   As mentioned in discussing role-scale strategies of "making out,"[49] the "vast churning of the modern world" gives rise to a variety of marginal and/or status-insecure and striving occupations. The role-scale strategies of two of these, the engineering technician and the art photographer, have been described. We come now to another striving occupation. Purchasing agent is an occupation on relatively equal terms with its neighboring occupations,[50] but those who practice it nonetheless feel anxious over relations with the various functional groups with which they must deal and over the degree of recognition they receive from higher management. George Strauss reports that the overall strategy of the occupation has been to seek *professionalism,* the main vehicle of which is an organization, the National Association of Purchasing Agents. Tactics of the occupation include the promotion of programs of professional education (e.g., college courses in "purchasing science"), efforts to develop state "certification" or licensing procedures, and promulgation of codes of ethics.

7. Establishment Tactics of Dissent Management.   Every arena of contending organizations has an "establishment," one or more organizations that are wealthier, more powerful, and more influential than others. Their decisions and actions inordinately guide, direct, stall, disrupt, or coerce the actions of others. They are therefore and properly the targets of the kinds of strategizing and tactizing described earlier in this chapter. Being powerful and being targets, they respond; they develop their own tactics of managing within the basic and strategic postures they have elected. One somewhat successful consolidating effort[52] and one case study point up features of more refined and grounded analyses of establishment tactics we can hope for in the future.

The modest consolidating effort is provided by Roger Cobb and Charles Elder who find it useful to distinguish between tactics directed toward dissenters as a group versus the issues they raise.

  a. Group-oriented tactics include efforts to:

   (1) Discredit the *membership* at large through negative characterizations such as "subversives," "chronically 'agin'," "psychopaths," "bums."

   (2) Discredit the *leaders* through embarrassing revelations, as with the McClellan Committee with regard to James Hoffa and General Motors with regard to Ralph Nader.

(3) Appeal over the heads of the leaders directly to members.

(4) Co-opt leaders by bringing them into prominent but controllable parts of the establishment, thereby cooling their ardor.[53]

b. Issue-oriented tactics include efforts to:

(1) Provide symbolic rewards and reassurances by ceremoniously, courteously, and seriously receiving and listening to grievances, but doing nothing else.

(2) Showcase or tokenize, by making highly visible but trivial changes in response to demands.

(3) Create new organizational units, such as new departments and study commissions to investigate and propose action and perhaps take some limited action.[54]

(4) Anticipate demands and initiate proposals in the hope that the credibility built will mean surrendering less than otherwise would be necessary.

(5) Co-opt the symbols of dissent and thereby debilitate and blunt them, as in the adoption by members of the establishment of elements of hippie and black language and dress.[55]

Establishments can also respond to the issues of dissent by claiming that there is "really" no disagreement on issues. The problem, rather, is alleged to be that the dissidents do not fully *understand* what the establishment is doing: if they understood, they would not dissent. Peter Hall and John Hewitt have argued that this was the strategy of the Nixon administration in dealing with the 1970 spring protests over conduct of the Indo-China war. The effort was to transform "substantive issues into technical problems of communication and understanding."[56] By focusing on "the forms and means of communication...the key issue of the Indo-China war" could be relegated "to a secondary position."[57] As Richard Nixon phrased it: "This is a time for communication rather than violence, and above all for mutal understanding."[58] "Try to understand what we are doing."[59] The tone of the tactic is "reassuring and concilatory" but "it also [serves] notice that ...further discord"[60] can be attributed to the defective understanding of the dissidents. An establishment can thus work itself into the position of saying: "We have responded sensibly and responsibly to crisis...we now expect...our critics [to be]...persuaded, if not that our actions are correct, then at least [of the necessity]...to confine protest to symbolic forms."[61] Having initially side-stepped joining the issues *per se,* the establishment may have set the stage for more intense protest, although the efficacy of the "communication tactic" should not be underestimated.

8. *Establishment Tactics of Resource Garnering.* Establishment organizations do more than contain the masses, of course. They offensively pursue advantage of other kinds, money being the most notable. Tactics of pursuing money are crucially a function of whether the organization operates in a traditional market and offers a product or service for a price versus riding on that confiscated money called taxes, for which pleas need to be made. The former is an entire field unto itself, albeit cast in technical, economic terms, with few sociological exceptions.[62] The latter concerns the revenue-greedy infighting of government agencies pushing to preserve what they have and to get more. Aaron Wildavsky's depiction of tactics such agencies use on the United States Congress provides a model that future studies might follow. Distinguishing between "ubiquitous" tactics—those "found everywhere and at all times in the budgetary system"—and "contingent" tactics—those dependent "on conditions of time, place, and circumstance"—Wildavsky discerns the following lines of action:

a. Ubiquitous tactics.

   (1) Cultivating clientele by finding, serving, expanding, and getting feedback from carefully activated segments.
   (2) Cultivating the confidence of other governmental organizations by "playing it straight," making personal friends, rehearsing for hearings, avoiding surprise, avoiding extreme claims that can be tested, and playing organizations against one another, among other devices.

b. Contingent tactics.

   (1) Defending against cuts in old programs by, among other strategems, cutting a popular program (which will always be restored) and declining to rank programs.
   (2) Inching ahead with existing programs by advantageous rounding of dollar requests, arguing the propriety of a set number of activities (whose price keeps increasing), and other measures.
   (3) Adding new programs by asking for a very small, initial

appropriation ("the wedge" or "the camel's nose"); defining the new program as temporary ("Is there anything more permanent than a temporary agency of government?"); claiming it to be an integral and necessary extension of what exists; asserting that it will reduce a "backlog;" saying that it will pay for itself, or that it meets a crisis; arguing that it strengthens national defense, and a host of other definitions.[63]

The eight situations of defensive and offensive tactical posturing just reviewed barely scratch the surface of the range and depth of the empirical world. My aim in detailing these treatments has been to display a type of focus and some suggestive concepts rather than to give an exhaustive account; materials for such an account do not yet exist in any event.[64]

Organizations are goal oriented and consciously coordinated collectivities. By dint of prospective and actual existence, they must strategize three main types of situations: initial formation, states of the membership, and the presenting environment. *(a)* A basic strategy of forming new organizations is to use preexisting informal or formal organizations as a generating vehicle. *(b)* Organizations require strategies of attracting and selecting members; socializing them to the organization itself; and controlling their morale, inadequacies, and factional conflicts. *(c)* Organizations strategize relations to their environment at three levels of specificity: basic, structural, and tactical. Basic postures can be coercive, bargaining, or persuasive. Structural postures tend in offensive or defensive directions. There are myriad tactical executions of basic and structural posturings. Tactics of hyperconventionality, dramaturgic concealment, occupational aggrandizement, and dissent management are among those discussed.

NOTES TO CHAPTER ELEVEN

1. Cf. Philip Selznick, "Foundations of the Theory of Organization," *American Sociological Review,* **13**:25–35 (February 1948).

2. Carol Dixon, "Dynamics of an Incipient Social Movement," paper presented at the Pacific Sociological Association Meetings, San Jose, Calif., March 1974, p. 23, quoted by permission of the author.

3. John Lofland, *Doomsday Cult* (Englewood Cliffs, N.J.: Prentice-Hall, 1966), pp. 60–62.

4. On difficulties in coalescing several different, informal groups, see "Gans on Granovetter's 'Strength of Weak Ties' " and "Granovetter Replies to Gans" *American Journal of Sociology*, **80:**524–531 (September 1974).

5. Steve Smith, "Strategies in Organizing," manuscript, University of California, Davis, March 1975.

6. Martin Luther King, Jr. *Stride Toward Freedom* (New York: Harper & Row, 1958) pp. 40–45; Anthony Oberschall, *Social Conflict and Social Movements* (Englewood Cliffs, N.J.: Prentice-Hall, 1973), pp. 126–7.

7. See further: Cesar Chavez, "La Causa and La Huelga," in Joan Levin Ecklein and Armand A. Lauffer, eds., *Community Organizers and Social Planners* (New York: Wiley, 1972), pp. 34–49; Maurice Jackson *et al.*, "The Failure of an Incipient Social Movement," *Pacific Sociological Review*, **3:**35–40 (Spring 1960); Jo Freeman "The Origins of the Women's Movement," *American Journal of Sociology*, **78:**792–811 (January 1973); Arthur Stinchcombe, "Social Structure and Organizations," in James March, ed., *Handbook of Organizations* (Skokie, Ill.: Rand McNally, 1965), pp. 142–143.

8. Saul Alinsky, *Rules for Radicals* (New York: Vintage Books, 1972).

9. Lofland, *Doomsday Cult, op. cit.*, Chs. 3–4.

10. Beyond this, would-be organizers of *social movements* may feel it necessary to create a wide range of conventional formal organizations (themselves built up out of informal groups), to have a base strong enough on which *then* to mount the originally desired activist social movement. Cesar Chavez ("La Cause," *op. cit.*,) reports this to have been his strategy. For further material on the problems of coalescing several organizations into a new organization, see Oberschall, *Social Conflict, op. cit.* pp. 143–4.

11. Alinsky, *op. cit.*

12. Robert Blake and J. Mouton, "Conformity, Resistance, and Conversion," in I. A. Berg and B. M. Bass, eds., *Conformity and Deviation* (New York: Harper & Row, 1961), p. 2.

13. Summarized and generalized from John Lofland, with the assistance of Lyn H. Lofland, *Deviance and Identity* (Englewood Cliffs, N.J.: Prentice-Hall, 1969), Parts II and III. For detailed discussion of ways in which these dimensions are concretely operationalized as in, for example, *initiation ceremonies,* see, among other works, John Wilson, *An Introduction of Social Movements* (New York: Basic Books, 1973), Ch. IX, "The Problem of Commitment," and Ralph Turner and Lewis Killian, *Collective Behavior,* 2nd ed. (Englewood Cliffs, N.J.: Prentice-Hall, 1972), Ch. 17, "Member Commitment and Control." In this context, the "total institution" as explicated by Erving Goffman may be seen as one prime and potent type of strategic organizational posturing for the socialization (and control) of members. See Erving Goffman, "The Characteristics of Total Institutions," in *Asylums* (Garden City, N.Y.: Doubleday-Anchor, 1961), Ch. 1.

14. Dorothy E. Peven, "The Use of Religious Revival Techniques to Indoctrinate Personnel: The Home-Party Sales Organizations," *Sociological Quarterly*, **9:**97–106 (Winter 1968).

15. J. Lofland, *Doomsday Cult, op. cit.*, Ch. 12.

16. There are, of course, many other devices employed at smaller scales of social organization, as explicated in previous chapters, specifically: Chapter 8, Section III.E on "Morally Questioned Conduct," and Chapter 8, Section V.A.3 on "Managing Rejection."

17. J. Lofland, *Doomsday Cult, op. cit.*, Ch. 12. On specific encounter-scale self- and other-management devices these persons employed to manage their morale, see *Ibid.*, pp. 244–5, which reports the three main themes of their balming conversational rhetoric. On morale and management in social movements more generally, the classic statement of Herbert Blumer, "Social Movements" in A. M. Lee, ed. *Principles of Sociology* (New York: Barnes & Noble, 1946), pp. 105–110 remains quite useful. See also Rosabeth Kanter, *Commitment and Community* (Cambridge, Mass.: Harvard University Press, 1972), Part II, J. Lofland, *op. cit.* Chs. 10 and 11, and Turner and Killian, *Collective Behavior, op. cit.*, Ch. 17.

18. See, thus, the account of "firing," Chapter 9, Section IV.A.6, above. For a suggestive description of group-scale expulsion processes that requires, however, a recoding for strategies, see Edwin Lemert's story of "Paranoia and the Dynamics of Exclusion," *Sociometry*, **25:**2–20 (March 1962).

19. Burton R. Clark, "The Cooling-out Function in Higher Education," *American Journal of Sociology*, **65:**569–676 (May 1960), reprinted in Chapter 15, this volume. On more serious, willful, and public deviance and strategies and tactics of coping with it, see Harold Garfinkel's (abstracted) statement on "Conditions of Successful Degradation Ceremonies," *American Journal of Sociology*, **61:**420–424 (March 1956).

20. Amitai Etzioni, *A Comparative Analysis of Complex Organizations* (New York: Free Press, 1961), Chs. 1–3.

21. Oberschall, *Social Conflict, op. cit.*, pp. 143–144.

22. Ralph Turner, "Determinants of Social Movement Strategies," in Tamotsu Shibutani, ed., *Human Nature and Collective Behavior* (Englewood Cliffs, N.J.: Prentice-Hall, 1970), pp. 146–64; Etzioni, *op. cit., Chs. 1–3*.

23. Turner, *op. cit.* p. 149.

24. *Ibid.*

25. Burton R. Clark, "Organizational Adaptation and Precarious Values: A Case Study," *American Sociological Review*, **21:**327–336 (June 1956).

26. The parallel with the situation and emerging strategy of higher education in America is all too obvious (and discomforting).

27. Sheldon Messinger, "Organizational Transformation: A Case Study of a Declining Social Movement," *American Sociological Review*, **20:**3–10 (February 1955).

28. *Newsweek*, January 6, 1975, on Richard Johnson, *Managing the White House: An Intimate Study of the Presidency* (New York: Harper & Row, 1974).

29. Philip Selznick, *The Organizational Weapon* (New York: Free Press, 1960), p. xii.

30. *Ibid.*, italics omitted.

31. *Ibid.*, pp. 72–73.

32. See, for example, Michael Useem, *Conscription, Protest, and Social Conflict: The Life and Death of a Draft Resistance Movement* (New York: Wiley, 1973), esp. pp. 153ff on "vanguard action...followed by cascading expansion of draft resistance."

33. This distinction was seen in the chapters on roles and groups in the contrasts between "strategic roles" and "strategic groups" (here called "basic" and "structural" posturing) on the one side, and "role strategies" and "group strategies" (here called "tactical posturings") on the other.

34. Donald W. Ball, "An Abortion Clinic Ethnography," *Social Problems*, **14:**294–301 (Winter 1967).

35. See Ch. 9, Section IV.C.1.

36. Summarized from John Lofland, "The Dramaturgics of State Executions," in Horace Bleackly and John Lofland, *State Executions Viewed Historically and Sociologically* (Montclair, N.J.: Patterson Smith, 1976).

37. For an account of how and why, see Lyn H. Lofland, *A World of Strangers: Order and Action in Urban Public Space* (New York: Basic Books, 1973), Part I. Along different but not carefully developed dimensions of tactical defensiveness, see, for example, Joseph D. Lohman's statement of five strategies of preventing a riot ["The Role of the Police Officer in Crowd Control," in Ralph Turner and Lewis Killian, *Collective Behavior,* 1st ed. (Englewood Cliffs, N.J.: Prentice-Hall, 1957), pp. 144–151] and Walter Wardwell's explication of how a stigmatized occupation—the chiropractic—mounts organizational-scale strategies of defense in "The Reduction of Strain in a Marginal Social Role," *American Journal of Sociology,* **61:**16–25 (July 1955).

38. Reformulated from Roger W. Cobb and Charles D. Elder, *Participation in American Politics: The Dynamics of Agenda-Building* (Boston: Allyn & Bacon, 1972), Ch. 6.

39. On the characteristics of these three classes of external groupings, see Turner, in Shibutani, ed., *Human Nature, op. cit.,* pp. 149–154.

40. Cobb and Elder, *op. cit.,* p. 9.

41. Gene Sharp, *The Politics of Nonviolent Action* (Boston: Porter Sargent, 1973), Part Two.

42. Eugene Bardach, *The Skill Factor in Politics: Repealing the Mental Commitment Laws in California* (Berkeley: University of California Press, 1972), Chs. 1–3, 9–11, esp. p. 183.

43. *Ibid.,* pp. 237–240.

44. Rephrased from page 80 of Leon Mayhew, *Law and Equal Opportunity: A Study of the Massachusetts Commission Against Discrimination* (Cambridge, Mass.: Harvard University Press, 1968).

45. Recast from conversation with Leon Mayhew.

46. See; for example, Chester Atkins with Barry Hock and Bob Martin, *Getting Elected: A Guide to Winning State and Local Office* (Boston: Houghton Mifflin, 1973) and Paul Van Riper, *Handbook of Practical Politics* (New York: Harper & Row, 1960). Two manuals containing some slight generic and sociological elements are Edward Swartzman, *Campaign Craftsmanship: A Professional's Guide to Campaigning for Elective Office* (New York: Universe Books, 1973) and Jerry Bruno and Jeff Greenfield, *The Advance Man* (New York: Bantam Books, 1972).

47. Richard M. Merelman, "The Dramaturgy of Politics," *The Sociological Quarterly,* **10:**216–241 (Spring 1969).

48. *Ibid.*, p. 227. Of course there are now public relations firms that specialize in managing matters of the kinds outlined by Merelman. Whitaker and Baxter of San Francisco has been one of the most sophisticated, seemingly, as reported by Stanley Kelley, Jr., *Professional Public Relations and Political Power* (Baltimore: Johns Hopkins Press, 1956), Ch. 2. Analysis of the house secrets of such organizations would doubtless teach us much.

49. Ch. 9, Section IV.C.5.

50. See Ch. 9, Section IV.B. "Role Strategies Among Equals."

51. George Strauss, "Work-Flow Frictions, Interfunctional Rivalry and Professionalism: A Case Study of Purchasing Agents," *Human Organization,* **23:**137–149 (Summer 1964).

52. On the nature of consolidating efforts, see Chapter 7.

53. The classic study of cooptation is by Philip Selznick, *TVA and the Grassroots: A Study in the Sociology of Formal Organization* (Berkeley: University of California Press, 1953).

54. Cf. Robert R. Alford, *Health Care Politics: Ideological and Interest Group Barriers to Reform* (Chicago: University of Chicago Press, 1975). Organizations under regular attack can be expected to develop specialized strategic roles for coping with it, as Tom Wolfe has brilliantly documented in *Radical Chic and Mau-Mauing the Flak Catchers* (New York: Bantam Books, 1971), pp. 117–184.

55. Cobb and Elder, *Participation, op. cit.,* Ch. 7. See also William Gamson, *Power and Discontent* (Homewood, Ill.: Dorsey, 1968), Ch. 6.

56. Peter M. Hall and John P. Hewitt, "The Quasi-Theory of Communication and the Management of Dissent," *Social Problems,* **18:**22 (Summer 1970).

57. *Ibid.*, p. 23.

58. Quoted *ibid.*

59. *Ibid.*, p. 20.

60. *Ibid.*, p. 25.

61. *Ibid.*, pp. 25–26.

62. One notable exception is Charles Perrow, *Organizational Analysis: A Sociological View* (Belmont, Calif.: Wadsworth, 1970).

63. Aaron Wildavsky, *The Politics of the Budgetary Process* (Boston: Little, Brown, 1964), Ch. 3.

64. For future reference, attention can be drawn to the "Trollope ploy" invented by Robert Kennedy [William Safire, *The New Language of Politics* (New York: Collier Books, 1972), p. 504] and to Richard Leighton, "OVERLORD Revisited: An Interpretation of American Strategy in the European War, 1942–44," *The American Historical Review,* **68:**919–937 (July 1963). Everywhere and anywhere, people as organizations are making decisions and need, indeed, to strategize that very process. The leading, lovingly empirical works are Charles Lindblom, "The Science of Muddling Through," *Public Administration Review,* **19:**79–88 (Spring 1959) and David Braybrooke and Charles Lindblom, *A Strategy of Decision: Policy Evaluation as a Social Process* (New York: Free Press, 1970), especially Parts I and II.

PART THREE

SELECTED QUALITATIVE STUDIES OF INTERACTION STRATEGIES

1.   A book arguing the indispensability of qualitative data would be remiss if it did not provide some! What has been argued abstractly must be exemplified concretely. This is a basic purpose of Part III. Four empirical studies are presented, one each at the encounter, role, group, and organizational scales of social organization. Each of them reasonably well exemplifies the four major criteria set forth in Chapters 2 through 5. In each case the researcher:

   a. Intensively immersed himself in a sector of social life and developed *intimate familiarity*.
   b. Was concerned to focus on, discern, and depict the *situation* faced by the participants being observed.
   c. Focused on interaction *strategies* and explicitly articulated their use by the participants.
   d. Abundantly documented the situations and strategies with qualitative data, thus ensuring that the concepts propounded are *disciplined abstractions*.

2.   The four studies presented are only a few of those that reasonably display these four features. A few others are listed at the end of each chapter, to highlight studies that illustrate the four principles most clearly. Many additional works have great value in other respects and have been described in Part II but are not as clear on the four dimensions I have stressed.

3. Moreover, the studies presented or mentioned in Part III should be gauged in relative as much as in absolute terms. To accomplish anything concretely, we must begin with and attend to inquiries as they actually exist, warts and all, rather than cling to ideal standards that no actual inquiry achieves. However important ideal standards may be as guides, progress is made by acting on the *relatively* most useful materials instead of not acting at all because no inquiry meets absolute standards of excellence.

CHAPTER TWELVE

Encounter-Scale Inquiries

Encounter-scale interaction devices are saliently distinguished by brevity and by individuality. They require but a short period of time to "play through"—typicaly, only a few minutes—and relatively little cooperation with others. These features, among others, set them off from role-scale devices (which are temporally much longer) and from group-scale devices (which are collectively elaborated and sustained). Coombs and Goldman's report of coping mechanisms among hospital staff in an intensive care unit illustrates several such brief and individual devices-—"escape into work" and "language alteration," in particular. ("Humor," however, has a group-sustained tendency much like the practices reported by Donald Roy in Chapter 14.)

Even though Coombs and Goldman might have drawn out the generic features of the situation more clearly, their report is otherwise quite generic, delineates strategies, presents their emergent abstractions in a disciplined manner, and builds on a foundation of intimate familiarity.

Reprinted from *Social Problems,* 20:342–355 (Winter 1973) with the permission of the authors and the Society for the Study of Social Problems. The authors gratefully acknowledge the critical insights of Patricia G. Lewis and Lois L. Starr. The assistance of Blake P. Boyle in the formative stages of the project is also appreciated. The research for this paper was partially supported by a grant from the National Institute of Mental Health (MH 19454-01). The interpretation and conclusions expressed are those of the authors and are not to be cpmstrued as official or as necessarily reflecting the policy of the California Department of Mental Hygiene.

I. A SITUATION OF DISTRESSED AROUSAL AND STRATEGIES OF EMOTIONAL DETACHMENT

Maintenance and Discontinuity of Coping Mechanisms in an Intensive Care Unit

Robert H. Coombs
and
Lawrence J. Goldman

In a crisis situation considerable emotionality is expected and tolerated; but there are those who must frequently confront emotional crises, yet maintain composure.[1] Those in the medical role, for example, are exposed to death, pain, and suffering, yet they are expected to respond with reason and restrained emotionality.

The training for such a role requires not only the learning of technical skills but the acquisition of an emotional capability to respond to people and situations which has come to be called "detached concern." In describing the social role which medical personnel expect of themselves in dealing with patients, Merton (1957:74) said, "The physician must be emotionally detached in his attitudes toward patients, keeping, 'his emotions on ice' and not becoming 'overly identified' with patients. But he must avoid becoming callous through excessive detachment, and should have compassionate concern for the patient." As an example, the nurse must be mother surrogate and healer with the wounded and critically ill (Schulman, 1958), yet maintain an acceptable emotional detachment. A nurse sobbing over a favorite patient is no nurse at all.

Although investigators have utilized the "detached concern" and similar concepts to describe how medical personnel function in their technical roles without becoming emotionally involved,[2] little attention has been given to the process by which such an attitude is maintained.

The present study focuses on the dynamics by which medical personnel remain emotionally objective while rendering compassionate care. The purpose is to investigate the various coping mechanisms used by such persons as they confront emotionally trying situations,[3] and to ascertain the circumstances where coping mechanisms fail and emotional involvement (over concern) or emotional aloofness (over detachment) prevail. The study setting was the Intensive Care Unit (I.C.U.) of a busy metropolitan hospital.

The Intensive Care Unit. The I.C.U. has a reputation among hospital personnel as an especially dramatic and tense setting, whose stresses prove physically and emotionally fatiguing for those who work there (Hackett *et al.,* 1968; Hammes, 1968; Koumans, 1965; Vreeland and Ellis, 1969). It is a busy, sometimes hectic environment, where the treatment procedures and nursing care keep the staff almost continually in motion. The controlling of physiologic processes necessitates constant watchfulness, and frequent crises require prompt and aggressive action. There is no room for hesitations due to insecurities about one's skill or knowledge.

Often the atmosphere is charged with tension. Patients are fearful; concerned family members haunt the corridors, waiting apprehensively for news; and physicians accompanying their patients from the operating room, anxious and fatigued, are not infrequently impatient and hypercritical.

Labelled "Death Valley" by some patients (Glaser and Strauss, 1968:41–42), the I.C.U. contains a constantly pulsing and humming assortment of technical equipment crowded together in a relatively small space with critically ill or postoperative patients. Some of these patients are unconscious, some disoriented; others demanding, uncooperative, or even paranoid; still others are dying—but rarely quietly (Koumans, 1965:163).

Tending successfully to the needs of these patients requires not only advanced knowledge and technical skills but an awareness of pertinent facts about each individual and an empathy with his fears and anxieties. But sustaining a proper balance between sympathy and objectivity is not easy in such a setting. The critically ill patient can be querulous and demanding; yet a nurse cannot afford to simply dismiss complaints, however suspicious she may be of their legitimacy. Each one must be investigated and evaluated. In order to avoid postoperative complications it may be necessary to employ one pain-inflicting measure after another—turning, deep breathing, the changing of dressing, etc. I.C.U. personnel must be firm in carrying out the required procedures in spite of patient pleas, yet still convey warmth and compassion (Vreeland and Ellis 1969:333).

The demanding nature of the work and specialized skills required prevent much staffing with relief personnel. Consequently, frequent changes in work schedules may be necessary in order to help patients through what may be their most life-threatening experience. These unanticipated changes result in long hours, fatigue, and frustration due to broken social engagements.

The Study Setting.   Located on the same floor as the Operating Room and the Anesthesiology Department, the unit contained 12 beds arranged around the perimeter of a central nursing desk and equipment cabinet. Six of the beds were housed in individual rooms; the other beds were separated from each other only by curtains.

The regular unit staff usually consisted of four to six nurses, one or two nurses' aids, one or two inhalation therapists, a ward clerk, and one or two attendants. Medical students worked on the unit as Nurse Technicians only during the summer months, when staff nurses were taking vacations. One of the registered nurses acted as charge nurse for the shift. She was generally responsible for seeing to it that the unit ran smoothly. For instance, she called physicians whose patients needed their attention and recorded special orders for individualized treatments.

Patients admitted to the unit came from all wards of the hospital, including the emergency room. The only criterion for admission was that, for one reason or another, the patients needed constant attention and immediate access to life-saving equipment. (The unit was well supplied with cardiac monitors, respirators, tracheal suctioning devices, and other emergency equipment.) The unit's beds were almost constantly in demand. As soon as one patient was moved to a different unit, another took his place.

Participant Observation.   An opportunity for a participant observational study in an I.C.U. presented itself when the second author obtained summer employment in an I.C.U. as a Nurse Technician. At the time he was also a Research Fellow under sponsorship of the senior author. Technically the I.C.U. position was a "moonlighting" operation; but it provided an opportunity to observe and to feel the attitudes and behaviors of nursing personnel confronted almost constantly with stressful experiences.[4]

Because the objective was to observe attitudes and behaviors in the most typical conditions, an effort was made to reduce contamination due to the researcher's presence by not revealing the research plan to the nursing staff. They were not informed until after the three months of data collection were completed.[5] Only the physician in charge of the unit was aware of the observer's dual role as clinician *and* researcher. Not only did he grant permission for the study, but was very helpful in seeing it carried through to a successful conclusion.

Because of the demanding nature of the clinical work, the observer was completely caught up as a participant. As an integral part of the clinical effort, the observer felt and reacted as did the regular I.C.U. staff; thus impressions were recorded from the perspective of internal reaction as well as visual observation. It was not until the observer was away from the unit that observations were recorded and interpretations generated.[6]

Because the observer, a second year medical student, had had little actual clinical experience, it was particularly interesting to record the adjustment of his own inner feelings to the stresses encountered.[7] During his early exposure to the I.C.U., one of the nurses warned the observer, "You've got to be 'toughened up' to survive around here." The wisdom of her counsel was made abundantly clear in the following months. At first, the observer spent restless nights dreaming about such things as "washing my hands after dealing with a patient with a very contagious and drug-resistant proteus infection," and "irrigating nasogastric tubes after having a patient whose tubes had to be irrigated every two hours." During the first week of exposure he recorded, "I've had a problem sleeping at night; I tend to dream about the more depressing cases I see." After four weeks of work in the unit, however, the bad dreams and restless nights ceased.

> I still worry about my patients while on duty, but I have been able to dissociate from the situation during my sleep periods. I cannot pinpoint when this change occurred, but I believe it was a gradual acclimation to the situation rather than an abrupt one.

An apparent lack of emotional response on the part of some hospital personnel to death made a deep impression on the observer during the early stages of the study.

> I met an inhalation therapist today in the cafeteria. In a matter of fact tone he said, "Remember Mr. J.? He died last night." He seemed to have totally removed himself from the emotions which grip people when confronted with death.

Several weeks experience on the unit, however, led the observer to quite a different conclusion about the apparent coldness of the staff. It became increasingly clear that emotional dissociation was an acquired technique for coping with stress. After two months exposure on the unit, he concluded that "This is not coldness on the part of the therapist, but rather his way of cushioning himself against the many depressing incidents which occur regularly on the unit." He explained:

A certain amount of emotional distance must be incorporated into an I.C.U. staff member's outlook. If one were to become emotionally involved with each patient, it would seriously hinder the professional effectiveness of that person. At times it seemed that some staff members were really "cold" in their attitudes toward patients; but with time it because quite obvious that this detachment doesn't come naturally, it must be perfected. It takes a definite effort to effectively develop this attitude.

In spite of the necessity for emotional detachment, veteran members of the I.C.U. staff placed a high priority upon concern for patient welfare and were critical of those who seemed callous in this regard.

Many times the nurses feel that Dr. S. is quite cold and almost inhumane in his attitude toward patients in the unit. This typically occurs when a decision is made affecting the treatment of terminal patients. One nurse told me she felt like telling the doctor off because he seemed so unconcerned. What was actually bothering her was his readiness to accept the fact that the patient was beyond hope.

Coping Mechanisms.   In order to maintain the necessary emotional detachment while caring for critically ill and dying patients, I.C.U. personnel developed several psychosocial techniques, the most apparent of which were humor, escape into work, language alteration, and rationalization.

Humor.   One of the most common techniques used to "manage" emotional stress was humor.[8] A good deal of joking and kidding went on almost every night mostly consisting of good-natured ribbing among the staff members about such things as their home towns and hospitals at which they trained. "Small things are called attention to in order to make fun of them. Examples are the hairstyle of one of the aides and the fact that one of the girls tied the back of her lab coat in a knot and was unable to get out."

All members of the staff took part in this effort to keep the atmosphere as light as possible, though it appeared that the experienced personnel were more aware of the need for "clowning" than the new nurses and paramedics. When a staff member became too serious, others attempted to involve him in the light-hearted banter. "Tonight one of the aides complained to me that I was being too quiet and was not kidding around enough. Actually I had just been too busy with my patients."

Sometimes patients were also drawn into the joking. After listening to the groaning of a semiconscious patient for a long period of time, one of the attendants said to a neighboring patient, "If you start hollering we can start a chorus." They both laughed, and then the latter patient began to joke about the matter also.

Lightheartedness in the midst of such painful human drama would seem inappropriate to most observers, but this joking did not appear to interfere with the staff's ability to do a good job. If anything, it contributed to the quality of performance, since it reduced the emotional strain created by the constant stream of critically ill patients. In fact, if some such release were not available, the emotional pressure would probably result in a deterioration of performance. On one occasion, a nursing supervisor who came into the unit was disturbed to hear so much laughter. One of the nurses explained, "You couldn't work in this place without laughing or you would go crazy."

Escape into Work.   Another basic method for handling stress was naturally supplied by the busy I.C.U. environment itself.[9] It was easy to bury one's emotions in the work of the unit; especially on a busy night, one could get lost in work and not even notice the patients.

A patient, seriously injured in an automobile accident, had a cardiac arrest and was transferred to the I.C.U. after being revived. His loud moaning and babbling continued throughout the night. But, as the observer noted, "most of the staff just carried on with their duties as *though they did not even hear him.*" The observer's impression was that his absorption in work constituted an escape from a distressing situation. "Most of them were so busy they did not have time to think or hear the moaning." The observer's own experience served to confirm his belief that keeping busy afforded some distraction from emotional stress. "I noticed that the only time I was bothered by the moaning was when I sat down for a while."

The observer found after a few particularly hectic weeks on the unit that the emotional protection provided by this device was only partial. Although the major problem at these times was "getting the entire job done and not forgetting anything that must be done during the shift," one still had "time to observe the depressing aspects of each case." The chief benefit of this coping mechanism seemed to be that "one does not have time to sit around and ponder."

Escape into work, an obvious coping mechanism on extremely busy nights, was favored by some of the personnel even when the work load decreased. Younger nurses, those who had only been out of school for one or two years, seemed to rely almost exclusively on "constant work activity" because they were too serious about their responsibility to use other mechanisms such as humor. "Some of these nurses never sit still from the time they enter the unit until they get off at the end of the shift." The rest of the staff appeared to reserve constant activity for those occasions when it was the most appropriate and natural choice. As the observer noted, escape into work could supplant other coping mechanisms by sheer necessity:

> There was much less obvious kidding around as on past nights. It is possible that we were all too busy to joke since we had a full house tonight, or was it that we were so busy and wrapped up in our work that we did not need something to take our minds off some of the depressing cases up there?

Language Alteration.   The frequent use of technical language in referring to death suggested that language operated as another type of coping mechanism.[10] While I.C.U. personnel might prefer the terms "arrest" or "cardiac arrest" to "heart attack" because the latter was a layman's term—misleading, uninformative, imprecise, or simply unscientific, they might also have found it less stressful in the circumstances to use "trade" terms. It was interesting to note, however, that the staff members were more likely to use the term "heart attack" when referring to patients who were *recovering* from one. Perhaps technical terms insulated and isolated the deaths by classifying them as medical events which occurred in professional life rather than in personal life—and thus permitted easier and freer discussion of them.

Indirect speech was also used to soften references to stressful events. For example, "the situation" or "the incident" was often used to refer to death. During such stressful times speech tended to become vague, oblique, and allusive. Presumably this vagueness reduced the anxiety which might be created by too bald or too frequent a reference to death.

Euphemisms could also be used in the same way as indirect speech— —to conceal the event or fact in question. I.C.U. personnel spoke of patients who were "not going to make it" and who were "on a hopeless decline," "Critically ill," while not a euphemism, functioned as one when it was desirable to avoid referring to a patient as "dying."

Latin derivative terms also appeared to reduce stress and made discussion of difficult subjects easier. "To perish" or "to expire" are identical in meaning with "to die," but neither term has the immediacy or emotional force of the Anglo-Saxon. For the I.C.U. personnel there was a difference between suffering the emotional shock of watching a patient die and suffering "the emotional shock of watching a patient expire." So although Latinate terms functioned differently than the euphemism, the *effect* created was the same—a softening, a concealing of the fact. As George Orwell (1954:173) stated, "inflated style is itself a kind of euphemism. A mass of Latin words falls upon the facts like soft snow, blurring the outlines and covering up all the details."

Euphemisms and technical language also could serve to reduce stress by concealing facts from others. There were certain situations in which facts about a patient and his condition had to be communicated in the presence either of the patient (during teaching rounds for instance) or of his family. It was often undesirable to expose the patient or his family to anything which would upset them, as the consequences for the staff of such disclosures would have been disastrous. In order to minimize stress, medical personnel conversed in a language which was foreign to the patient. One staff member might alert another to possible psychiatric problems by using the code term "superintentional lesion" (psychosis). He could also point out certain symptoms of "mitotic figure disease" (cancer). In both cases, the speaker employed language as a coping mechanism.

Rationalization.   Discussions with staff about their methods of coping with emotional stress revealed that death was often rationalized, regarded as a welcome relief from the suffering caused by the patient's illness. A typical comment at the time of death was "he's better off that way." This attitude, taken in advance of death, allowed the staff to fortify themselves against the emotional repercussions of a likely death.[11]

At the death of a small child, several of the staff were noticeably upset. Others, however, seemed to go about their business in a normal manner. "Most had already accepted the fact that the child just didn't have a chance and had already prepared themselves for the event."

One result of this pre-death rationalization was that nurses and technicians were prone to spend a greater amount of time caring for patients who appeared to have a fair chance for surviving than with patients in a "hopeless decline." This tendency was reinforced by the hectic pace of activity on the unit. "This is not to say that the 'hopeless patient' does not receive adequate care; but the greatest effort is given where it is most likely to have the greatest effect."

Discontinuity of Coping Mechanisms. In certain circumstances the vital balance between concern and detachment was altered and the usual coping mechanisms became ineffective. Some patients elicited so much concern that an emotional detachment was not maintained.

Young Versus Old Patients. The patient's age seemed to be the most important factor affecting the vital balance between detachment and concern. As noted by Glaser (1966) and by Glaser and Strauss (1964), much social and emotional significance is attributed to youthful patients. These emotional overtones were visible among the I.C.U. staff whenever a child was introduced into the unit. At one point during the admission procedures for a child, there were nine medical staff people in the room with the patient. (Normally there would be about 12 people on the unit on any given night, with four of them handling a regular admission.) No doubt, the seriousness of the child's condition accounted for some of the additional personnel; but various members of the staff looked in on the child throughout the night to inquire about her condition. In another case, the "drawing power" of children was demonstrated by the fact that nurses actually volunteered to care for the child. "One nurse told me that she was disappointed because she was not assigned to the child. She said that the following day she would ask to be assigned." Nurses who had not been assigned would use their free time to visit his room and "make sure everything was going right."

The nurses on the I.C.U. seemed to go out of their way to mother young children. In one case, a nurse spent much of her time consoling and cuddling the three-year old assigned to her (far more time than she spent in caring for her other patient, a woman in her 60s suffering a heart attack). In another case, where two nurses were frequent

visitors at a seven-year-old's bedside, "one came in just to play games
with him. Watching her with Billy was like watching a mother with her
child." On occasion, the involvement became so great that it affected
the nurse's performance. "One of the nurses in charge of giving medi-
cines asked another nurse to give the child his intramuscular shot, as
she did not want to cause him any more pain."

Other personal characteristics such as race, sex, socioeconomic status,
or physical attractiveness did not prevent the staff members from
identifying with youthful patients. "It appears that in the minds of the
nurses, children are not perceived as being black or white, rich or poor,
male or female; they are just children."

This tendency to identify was apparent even when the child's physical appearance or condition was actually replusive:

> The baby's attractive powers could not be attributed to physical
> features, as its appearance was quite grotesque due to the burned
> and charred skin from the fire, the large gashes made by the fan
> blades when the fan exploded, and the surgical incisions down both
> arms and legs....

Another child had a foul-smelling wound; a third child was "far from
attractive" because of a cleft palate and lip. In each of these cases, the
child received an unusual amount of personal attention in spite of
these drawbacks.

In some cases the coping mechanisms normally enlisted to face death
and resultant stress seemed to fail completely when the patient was a
child.[12] An I.C.U. nurse responsible for the care of a severely burned
child became distraught when the child died. Although it was a fore-
gone conclusion that the child would not survive, the nurse indicated
that she considered herself personally responsible for the death. Her
grief could be seen in her expression and behavior; and it was all the
more obvious since she was usually quite a jovial and garrulous person.
A short while after the death occurred, she asked if she could take a
break, and then left the unit for 15 minutes.

> The major effect of the death seemed to "wear off" in about two
> hours. At that time she appeared to have gotten over the emotional
> shock and was now back to her old self. It was as though her defense
> mechanisms had been torn down by the death, and it had taken two
> hours to rebuild the walls which protected her enough to return to
> work.

The contrast between reactions to the young and the old was readily apparent.[13] This polarity of reaction was found in the observer's comment about "toughening up" to pain and suffering:

As much as a person tried to guard himself against shock and depression, it seems that things still get to him. Accepting death and disease in the elderly is one thing, but it is a totally different situation seeing infants who have had open-heart surgery, or an eighteen-year-old all broken up from a car accident. I cannot speak for the others, but I cannot see myself ever getting "toughened up" enough to pass over these situations. I don't believe anyone ever gets *that* tough.

Usually there was no emotional response among I.C.U. staff members when an elderly person died; with these patients, death appeared to be taken in stride as part of their job. With the death of an elderly gentleman, those who were directly involved "seemed to go about their task in a very mechanical way showing no emotional involvement." Those who were not directly involved with the old man "went about their chores as if nothing had happened; and little mention was made of the incident the rest of the night. It was treated as though it were 'all in a day's work.'"

Cooperative Versus Uncooperative Patients. Another type of patient who inspired involvement and concern was the one with a pleasant personality and a willingness to cooperate with the staff.[14] In analyzing his own reactions to patients early in the I.C.U. experience, the observer noted:

I tend to give a greater amount of care to patients whom I feel more comfortable with. I tend to make an extra effort to cater to needs of patients who "hit me" the right way. It is not that I don't make an effort to care for each of my patients, but I seem to put a little extra into catering to the needs of the patients with whom I can relate well.

Further experience made it clear that he and other I.C.U. staff preferred cooperative patients. "Next to being a child, I believe the most attractive asset a patient can have is his or her willingness to cooperate with the staff." Evaluating the solicitous attitude of the personnel toward a 14-year-old surgery patient, the observer decided that the boy's exceptionally cooperative attitude was a major factor in the staff's willingness to "put themselves out" a little more than usual. "It was as though the more he attempted not to be a burden to the staff, the more they were concerned about his care."

The importance of patient cooperation in promoting concern was seen especially in the I.C.U. environment. Upon admission, patients could often be "difficult"—disoriented, bewildered, fearful, agitated, or hysterical. Sometimes it was necessary to subdue a patient with straps or drugs simply to administer treatment to him. However, as treatment progressed and the patient's initial anxiety subsided, a more normal and pleasant personality might emerge, and the patient was then prepared to cooperate with the staff. But those members of the staff who were exposed to him when he was first admitted often had a more distant, less positive response than those who came into contact with him at a later date. For example, a patient with a bullet in his brain was received in the I.C.U. On admission he was combative and verbally uncooperative, but as he began to recover he revealed an affable personality. Those who were exposed to him when he was admitted were not as empathetic or concerned about his condition as those whose contact with him was limited to a later period when he was defined as more cooperative. The response that would ordinarily have been evoked by his affability had been neutralized by the initial impression of him as an uncooperative patient.

Another case illustrates the importance of cooperation in maintaining staff involvement once it had been established. The patient—a young, good-looking male with a pleasant personality—was quite cooperative throughout most of his stay in the unit. Although a tracheotomy tube prevented him from speaking, staff nurses still looked in frequently to ask how he was or simply to say hello. "As the weeks went by and more of the staff became exposed to the patient's affable personality, more people became actively aware of his needs, and staff members at all levels stopped in periodically to see how he was progressing and ask if there was anything he needed." This concern and responsiveness was not a fixed and unchanging feature of the staff's attitude toward him. When the patient's demands became excessive according to the staff's criteria, and the patient's response to a concerned question was a demand for care, then "changes in staff attitude became evident." Gains in concern made by pleasantness and initial cooperation were lost to detachment by staff-defined "lack of cooperation."

If the undemanding, cooperative patient aroused staff sympathy and stimulated them to make an extra effort on his behalf, the demanding, uncooperative patient had the opposite effect (Martin:1957).

Mr. M. had a paralytic disease which totally paralyzed all the muscles below the neck, preventing him from breathing. For this reason he had to be hooked up to a respirator and kept in the I.C.U. until he recovered enough to breathe on his own. After being on the unit for a short time, he began to demand more attention from the staff than they felt his condition justified:

> Although his psychological condition might have necessitated the extra attention he wanted, his physical condition was stable, which meant he was way down on the "attention list" of the staff. They did not have time to stop in and cater to his every demand, as they were busy with other more critically ill people. It got to the point where personnel would walk the long way across the room to avoid being summoned by the patient. Many times they would act as though they didn't hear him and continue about their business. On several occasions staff members would tell the patient that they were busy with other patients and would get around to him as soon as they had a free moment. After a few weeks of this some of the staff became visibly antagonistic toward the patient.

Conclusion.   Since Merton's abbreviated description, several investigators have elaborated upon the social role expected of medical personnel in maintaining a balance between emotional detachment and compassionate concern for patients; but relatively little research has been done concerning the dynamics by which such a difficult relationship is maintained. The present study was designed to investigate the typical coping mechanisms utilized by medical personnel in "keeping their emotions on ice" while dealing with emotionally trying circumstances. Since the observer had had almost no prior clinical experience, it was possible to note the adjustment of his own feelings when confronting such emotionally stressful scenes for the first time.

The Intensive Care Unit might appropriately be labeled The Hospital Stress Center and its staff The Trauma Squad. Remaining psychologically intact in such a setting requires considerable expertise on the part of everyone—patients as well as staff. Some patients develop what I.C.U. personnel refer to as "I.C.U. psychosis" or "I.C.U.-itis", i.e., they become progressively disoriented, irritable, and mistrusting. Nurses on the unit attribute this not only to the severity of their medical problems but also to the environment itself (i.e., constant activity, lights burning round the clock, and irregular beeping of cardiac monitors, as well as mystery pertaining to the death of neighboring patients). This explains why one seasoned physician is reported to have said, "I don't want to be brought to the I.C.U. no matter how sick I am."

Those who work in the I.C.U. must learn to acquire the mechanisms which help them function effectively to serve the interests of those patients whose lives, in many cases, literally lie in their hands. And in order to perform this vital function, they must, paradoxically, resist the demands those cases make on their own feelings. But in spite of this "defensive insensitivity," they do remain susceptible to the pathos of the dramas occurring around them. The experience does not destroy their capacity to feel, it simply alerts them to the necessity of managing feelings both in their own interest and that of the patients.

Notes

1. Everett C. Hughes (1951) coined the item "routinized emergency" to refer to those situations in which practitioners must deal in a routine manner with what others regard as emergencies.

2. Fox (1959), like Merton *et al.* (1957), used the idea of "a dynamic balance" between attitudes of detachment and concern. Similarly, Mumford and Skipper (1967) suggested the professional ideal as a balance between detachment and sentiment. Bloom (1963) borrowed the term "affective-neutrality" from Parsons (1951). Each of these different designations applies to the same general idea that medical professionals are expected to be detached enough to be objective in applying technical skills and at the same time concerned enough to give compassionate care to the sick (Johnson and Martin, 1958).

3. Coping mechanisms have been defined by Coehlo *et al.* (1963) as being psychosocial mechanisms which help maintain self-management of feelings in stressful situations. Haan (1965) differentiated between coping mechanisms and defense mechanisms, another method of handling stress, by saying that the former are flexible, purposive, reality oriented, and differentiated; while the latter are rigid, compelling, reality distorting, and undifferentiated. As such, coping mechanisms are more socially desirable than defense mechanisms (Alker, 1968).

4. This formed an ideal situation for the active type of participant observation described by Schwartz and Schwartz (1955). The observer had the opportunity to increase his identification with the observed, thereby becoming aware of the subleties of various forms of interactions. Zelditch (1962) conceded that in the case of "unverbalized norms," participant observation has a valid claim which cannot be adequately fulfilled by quantitative methods.

5. It was agreed that, after the three months of data collection, the nursing staff would be fully informed of the note-taking and at that time their approval would be solicited before proceeding with publication. When informed, the typical response

was one of laughter followed by comments like, "I wondered why you asked so many questions." For discussions of "disguised observation" in participant observation studies see Erikson (1970) and Roth (1970).

6. Gold (1958) described the advantages of complete participation as the opportunity to interact naturally with the observed and at the same time to become aware of "role-pretense." Potential problems were self-consciousness about the new role and "going-native" by incorporating the role. The demanding nature of the work, however, required the observed to lose himself in the assigned tasks. "Cooling off" periods, as Gold suggests, were utilized by recording observations away from the observation site.

7. Originally this was the senior author's principal objective. At the time, he was principal investigator of a five year longitudinal study entitled, "Marital and Socialization Stresses in Medical Training" (Coombs and Vincent, 1971).

8. Reviewing the usage of humor and laughter in a classic article, Flugel (1954:732) concluded that laughter freed the individual from an "immense burden of anxiety, confusion, cruelty, and suffering." According to Freud (1950:220), humor operates in terms of psychic economy and offers ego comfort through its meaning, "Look here! This is all that this seemingly dangerous world amounts to. Child's play—the very thing to jest about!" Coleman (1964) pointed out that humor, a socially acceptable outlet for tension, utilizes the body energy in constructive activities which reduce tension. In a medical setting, Fox (1959) also found that humor was a means of tension release. Similarly in a study of hospital patients, Coser (1959) reported that humor offered a "safety valve" of tension release for the individual and also had the advantage of social economy by allowing participants to reinterpret experiences, reassure, communicate, and give solidarity by transforming individual experiences into collective experiences.

9. Escape into work has been found to be a relatively standard technique for overcoming anxiety and avoiding painful involvement in stressful experiences. For example, Chodoff et al. (1964) suggested this as a consciously determined adaptation among parents of children with malignant disease. Menzies (1960) found this adaptation technique among nurses. Skipper (1965) reported that, while escape into work kept patients at a distance, barriers to communication with patients were imposed by the impression that medical staffs were "busy and overworked."

10. Bloom (1953) and Menzies (1960) have pointed out that medical jargon allows medical students to relate to patients as diseases or as diagnostic categories—e.g., "The gall bladder in room 421." Language can be used to focus attention on symptoms and to isolate doctors and nurses from the patient as a person (Baziak and Dentan, 1960).

11. Glaser and Strauss (1964) reported that certain "loss rationales" justified death, making it more tolerable. Examples of such justifications were, "It was a blessing he passed on, he was in such great pain"; or "You wouldn't ask him to suffer any longer would you?" In another article, Glaser and Strauss (1968) suggested that acceptance of death in advance tended to define the individual as socially dead.

12. In a study of emergency care, Sudnow (1967) noted that nurses had been known to break into tears at a child's death. He said, "In such cases, particularly, 'dying' and 'death' temporarily ceased to have their firmly grounded, organizationally routinized meanings, activities and consequences."

13. This contrast has been explored by Glaser (1966) and by Glass and Strauss (1964, 1968) in their studies of dying patients. Aged patients, they maintain, represented a low social loss to medical personnel. That is, aged people were consistently seen as having had a full past, little or no contributing present, and no future worth (Glaser, 1966); thus dying was accepted in stride. A study of patients who were dead on arrival at the hospital emergency room found that the aged were more quickly and more cursorily pronounced dead than the young (Sudnow, 1967). This study found that the death of the elderly represented an anticipated death. It was treated with little notice and accepted as routine. This observation coincides with Glaser's (1966) contention that geriatric patients were treated by nursing staff as socially dead while biologically alive.

14. Glaser and Strauss (1966) mentioned "personality" as one of the characteristics upon which the social value of a patient is calculated. Applying the same criteria, Glaser (1966) found that personality was one of the mitigating factors in enhancing the status of aged patients. Attractive personality qualities (cheerful, friendly, non-demanding) resulted in better care for the patient.

References

Alker, Henry A. 1968. "Coping, Defense and Socially Desirable Responses," *Psychological Reports*, **22**:985–988.

Baziak, Anna Teresa, and Robert Knox Dentan. 1960. "The Language of the Hospital and its Effects on the Patient." ETC: A Review of General Semantics, **17** (September):261–268

Bloom, Samuel W. 1963 . *The Doctor and His Patient.* New York: Russell Sage Foundation).

Chodoff, Paul, Stanford B. Friedman, and David A. Hamburg. 1964. "Stress, Defenses and Coping Behavior: Observations in Parents of Children with Malignant Disease," *American Journal of Pyschiatry,* **120** (February):743–749.

Coelho, George V., David A. Hamburg, and Elizabeth B. Murphey. 1963. "Coping Strategies in a New Learning Environment: A study of American College Freshmen," *Archives of General Psychiatry,* **9**:433–443.

Coleman, James C. 1964. *Abnormal Psychology and Modern Life.* (Glenview, Ill: Scott Foresman).

Coombs, Robert H., and Clark E. Vincent, (eds.). 1971. *Psychosocial Aspects of Medical Training.* (Springfield, Ill: Charles C. Thomas).

Coser, Rose Laub. 1959. "Some Social Functions of Laughter: A Study of Humor in a Hospital setting," *Human Relations,* **12**:171–182.

Erikson, Kai T. 1970. "A Comment on Disguised Observation in Sociology," in William J. Filstead, (ed.), *Qualitative Methodology: Firsthand Involvement with the Social World.* (Chicago: Markham), pp. 252–260.

Flugel, J. C. 1954. "Humor and Laughter," in Gardner Lindzey, (ed.), *Handbook of Social Psychology.* (Reading, Mass.: Addison-Wesley), pp. 709–733.

Fox, Renée C. 1959. *Experiment Perilous.* (Glencoe, Ill.: The Free Press).

Freud, Sigmund. 1950. "Humor," in James Strachey, (ed.), *Collected Papers,* (London: Hogarth Press.), pp. 215–221.

Glaser, Barney A. 1966. "The Social Loss of Aged Dying Patients," *The Gerontologist,* **6**:(June)-70–80.

Glaser, B. G., and A. L. Strauss. 1964. "The Social Loss of Dying Patients," *American Journal of Nursing*, **64** (June)-119-121.

Glaser,, B., and A. L. Strauss. 1968. *Time for Dying*. (Chicago: Aldine).

Gold, Raymond L. 1958. "Roles in Sociological Field Observations," *Social Forces*, **36**:217-223.

Haan, Norma. 1965. "Coping and Defense Mechanisms Related to Personality Inventories," *Journal of Consulting Psychology*, **29**:(March) 373-378.

Hackett, T. P., N. H. Cassem, and H. A. Wishnie, 1968. "The Coronary-Care Unit: An Appraisal of its Psychological Hazards," *New England Journal of Medicine*, **279** (December): 1365-1370.

Hammes, H. J. 1968. "Reflection on 'Intensive Care,'" *American Journal of Nursing*, **68** (February)-330-340.

Hughes, Everett C. 1951. "Work and Self," in John H. Rohrer and Muzafer Sherif, (eds.), *Social Psychology at the Crossroads* (New York: Harper & Row), pp. 313-323.

Johnson, Miriam M., and Harry W. Martin. 1958. "A Sociological Analysis of the Nurse Role." *American Journal of Nursing*, **58** (March): 373-377.

Koumans, A. J. R. 1965. "Psychiatric Consultation in an Intensive Care Unit," *Journal of the American Medical Association*, **194** (November): 163-167.

Martin, William. 1957. "Preferences for Types of Patients," in Robert K. Merton, George G. Reader, and Patricia L. Kendall, (eds.), *The Student Physician: Introductory Studies in the Sociology of Medical Education* (Cambridge, Mass.: Harvard University Press), pp. 189-206.

Menzies, Isabel. 1960. "A Case-Study in the Functioning of Social Systems as a Defense Against Anxiety: A Report on a Study of the Nursing Service of a General Hospital," *Human Relations* **13** (May):95-121.

Merton, Robert K. 1957. "Some Preliminaries to a Sociology of Medical Education," in Robert K. Merton, George G. Reader, and Patricia L. Kendall, (eds), *The Student Physician: Introductory Studies in the Sociology of Medical Education* (Cambridge, Mass.: Harvard University Press), pp. 3-79.

Mumford, Emily and James K. Skipper, Jr. 1967. *Sociology in Hospital Care* (New York: Harper & Row).

Orwell, George. 1954. *A Collection of Essays* (Garden City, N.Y.: Doubleday).

Parsons, Talcott. 1951. *The Social System*. (Glencoe, Ill: Free Press).

Roth, Julius A. 1970. "Comments on 'Secret Observations,' " in William J. Filstead, (ed.), *Qualitative Methodology: Firsthand involvement with the Social World* (Chicago: Markham), pp. 278-280.

Schulman, Sam. 1958. "Basic Functional Roles in Nursing: Mother Surrogate and Healer," in E. Gartley Jaco (ed.), *Patients, Physicians and Illness*. (Glenco Ill: Free Press), pp. 528-537.

Schwartz, Morris S. and Charlotte Green Schwartz. 1955. "Problems in Participant Observation," *American Journal of Sociology* **60**:343-354.

Skipper, James K., Jr. 1965. "Communication and the Hospitalizd Patient," in James K. Skipper, Jr., and Robert C. Leonard, (eds), *Social Interaction and Patient Care*. (Philadelphia: Lippincott), pp. 61-68.

Sudnow, David. 1967. "Dead on Arrival," *Trans Action*, **5** (November): 36-43.

Vreeland, R. and G. L. Ellis. 1960. "Stress of the Nurse in an Intensive Care Unit," *Journal of the American Medical Association*, **208** (April): 332-334.

Zelditch, Morris, Jr. 1962. "Some Methodological Problems of Field Studies." *American Journal of Sociology,* **67**:566–576.

II. SELECTED STUDIES OF ENCOUNTER–SCALE INTERACTION STRATEGIES.

The notation following each entry indicates the section of Chapter 8 in which it is capsulized.

Bernstein, Stan, "Getting It Done: Notes on Student Fritters," *Urban Life and Culture* **1**:275–292 (October 1972). (V.A.2)

Bigus, Odis, "The Milkman and His Customer: A Cultivated Relationship," *Urban Life and Culture,* **1**:131–165 (July 1972). (III.C)

Bittner, Egon, "Police Discretion in Emergency Apprehension of Mentally Ill Persons," *Social Problems,* **14**:278–292 (Winter 1967). (III.B)

Dixon, Carol, "Guided Options as a Pattern of Control in a Headstart Program," *Urban Life and Culture,* **1**:203–216 (July 1972). (III.B)

Gmelch, George. "Baseball Magic," *Trans-Action,* June 1971, pp. 39-41, 54. (V.B)

Henderson, Margaret R., "Acquiring Privacy in Public," *Urban Life and Culture,* **4**:446–455 (January 1975).

Henslin, James M., "Guilt and Guilt Neutralization: Response and Adjustment to Suicide," in Jack D. Douglas, ed., *Deviance and Respectability* (New York: Basic Books, 1970), pp. 192–228. (V.A.5)

Lee, Alfred McClung, and Elizabeth Bryant Lee, eds., *The Fine Art of Propaganda* (New York: Harcourt Brace, Jovanovich, 1939). (III.D)

Lofland, Lyn, *A World of Strangers* (New York: Basic Books, 1973), Chs. 6 and 7. (II.A)

Pearlin, L. and Morris Rosenberg, "Propaganda Techniques in Institutional Advertising," *Public Opinion Quarterly,* **16**:5–26 (Spring 1952). (III.D)

Walum, Laurel Richardson, "The Changing Door Ceremony: Notes on the Operation of Sex Roles in Everyday Life," *Urban Life and Culture,* **2**:506–515 (January 1974). (III.A)

CHAPTER THIRTEEN

Role-Scale Inquiries

Ironically, scholars favoring the qualitative strategy approach have done more work at the role than at the other scales of social organization, but their analyses have been less detailed and textured than at the other levels. I tried in Chapter 9 to call attention to the relative abstractness and generality of much role-scale analysis by means of the distinction between "strategic roles" and "role strategies." A strategic role analysis simply asserts the existence of some type of role (and its salient, defining features), whereas a role strategy analysis attempts to elucidate the more detailed mechanisms of performing a role. Roger Straus' treatment of the seeker role, presented here, well illustrates the role strategy level of interaction devices. The notions of "creative bumbling" and "creative exploitation" and their phases and components are transencounter patterns of behavior that link through time and "composite" into the strategic roles of "seeker" and "redhot." (The transencounter nature of these devices makes them, that is, role rather than merely encounter devices of interaction.)

Straus' report also serves concretely to show forms that activist accounts of "conversion" might take. His effort is an important reorientation of the passivist-dominated literature on identity-change and socialization and begins, to use his image, to turn "socialization on its head." Although the work necessarily exhibits the typical problems of first-of-a-kind efforts, the problems ought not be allowed to obscure the new pathways of analysis to which the author points.

I. A SITUATION OF DESIRED SELF–CHANGE AND STRATEGIES OF SELF–TRANSCENDENCE

Changing Oneself:
Seekers and the
Creative Transformation
of Life Experience

Roger Straus

Sociologists of identity change tend to employ an image of humans as essentially passive creations of their circumstances. "Passivism" especially dominates studies of religious movements, commonly pigeonholing them as pseudo-solutions to real socioeconomic problems (e.g., Wilson, 1961; Smelser, 1963). Luther Gerlach and Virginia Hine's work (1970) is a notable exception—but even they treat personal quests for transcendence (reconstruction of the process of experiencing a world so as to transform everyday life) as products of group strategies to recruit susceptible individuals and literally convert them into followers and believers.

"Passivist" imagery and the style of research it implies is, at best, misleading. The present study seeks to counter passivist assumptions by starting from the individual human acting creatively within a natural life setting in order to construct a satisfying life. From this base I will elucidate an alternative way of looking at life-changing careers that supplements traditional analyses while capturing, in its native complexity, the practical situation of actual individuals comprising any transformative movement.

When "normal" resources and strategies cease to maintain an individual's sense that his life is tolerable, he may act to change it. If he develops a career around the pursuit of transformation, he is a *seeker*. Various forms of seeking are documented in several studies such as Lofland (1966) and Klapp (1969), but I will here focus only on the form associated with *transcendentally oriented trips* (collective quests for transcendence, as defined above, usually with reference to an Ultimate Reality).

Life-change is accomplished through a sequence of behaviors or strategies by means of which (a) transformative means are discovered and then *(b)* instrumentally exploited. The first phase is characterized by seemingly passive and chance strategies of *creative bumbling*: the individual seizes on potential opportunities for discovering a way of transforming his life within his sociocultural and circumstantial environment. As he acts, his self-conception as a "seeker" develops and he builds up an array of seeking tactics. Upon locating a promising means of life-change, he proceeds *creatively to exploit* its potentials by developing a further array of tactics analyzed by other social scientists as responses to group strategies but conceived here as intentional, utilitarian moves toward his goal of changing himself and his life.

This model of creative bumbling and exploitation has been developed from material gathered in a series of 15 two-hour "guided conversations" with people selected because they were locally available during the period of fieldwork and were involved with "trips" I knew enough about to categorize as transcendental. These included evangelical and charismatic Christian groups, Nichiren Soshu (Sokka Gakkai), Divine Life (Guru Maharaj Ji), Transcendental Meditation, Kundalini Yoga (Yogi Bhajan), Eckankar, and Scientology. The materials cover more than these, actually, since each interviewee related several distinct sequences of finding, checking out, entering, and leaving a variety of trips. In this way, the materials encompass activities of different seekers under different circumstances and at different times encountering, checking out, and entering or rejecting the same trip. Interviewees were mostly college seniors around 22 years old, from middle-class backgrounds, white, and of both sexes. A few had either more or less formal education or ranged up to age 32—but their "stories" were essentially identical. The interview material is supplemented with observations I have gathered over a decade's involvement with various groups, trips' internal literature, and social scientific reports.

A. The Strategy of Creative Bumbling. Every seeker's basic problem is to find some means of changing himself and/or his life. In contemporary America, practicable means have increasingly become "owned and operated" by various trips. This condition structures the options available to a seeker. Seekers use *creative bumbling,* the strategic employment of situations as they occur or are made to occur in order to discover means of transformation and trips within which they might be institutionalized. I use "bumbling" to convey the image of seeker and sought colliding like particles in Brownian motion. Working with a similar metaphor of "groping," Klapp (1969) echoes Sorokin's earlier conclusion, derived from study of published biographical materials, that critical events in life-changing "were neither planned nor deliberately arranged. They just occurred" (1967, p. 169). Indeed, my own interviewees on first being queried explained these turning points passively:

> It just happened. You must realize that for most of my life I was semiconscious. A friend mentioned this group. I cruised into it. Saw it on TV. Ran across a book. A poster. I looked over the list of classes and went, "Far out...." That's how I operate. It seems I kinda fall into things.

Not accepting such statements as final, I repeatedly probed for details, "So what did *you do,* exactly?" After reiterating the same segment of their careers over and again, they got down to blow-by-blow detail. Such information revealed more active tactics, supplanting the initial explanations, which were typically couched in general, passive, or ideological terms.[1]

1. Development of Seeking. Tactics and self-conception revealed patterned development. The sense that "I am a seeker (after transcendence)" only arises after the person has repeatedly acted and interacted as a seeker over some period of time. A novice's self-conception rarely involves more than a vague sense of wanting change. Dissatisfaction usually focuses on specific, practical life problems ranging from difficulties with the opposite sex to a feeling "there must be more to life than this." Specification of problem and goal alike emerges in the process of seeking and undergoes continuous redefinition as the seeker interacts with new trips, persons, and ideas.

People begin as *closet seekers* covertly investigating change through objectified representations of trips (i.e., books, tracts, articles, recordings, TV shows, etc.). Interviewees related television programs such as Billy Graham Crusades, Richard Hittleman's Yoga, even "Kung Fu" to have been pivotal in "turning them on" to trips or even seeking itself. TV and radio, however, offer scant instruction in actually going about self-transformation. Rather, they serve to direct novices to books or organizations offering such instruction. Yet other closet seekers began with printed rather than electronic media and went on from there. *Autobiography of a Yogi* (Yogananda, 1946), *Dianetics; the Modern Science of Mental Health* (Hubbard, 1950), and, of course, the Bible were fre-

quently reported critical in the development and focusing of interviewees' careers.

Even printed "self-help" guides to life-changing seem to offer only
enough information to interest readers in a trip, lead them to feel they
"really want" the sort of change that trip offers, and help them concep-
tualize their situation and possible resolutions in a specific way. Experiments with books do not usually lead to a satisfactory sense of transformation, but the actions of experimentation constitute the first definitive
motions toward a seeking career for many. Started doing something
about their lives, novices often "graduate" into *covert seekers,* now
prodding friends and acquaintances for new ideas, suggestions, information.[2]

> A pot-smoking, beer-drinking buddy of mine said there was a group
> of people gonna have a meeting. You know, what the fuck do you do
> when you're a grad student and you don't have a lot of homework?
> It was something to do and it sounded out of the ordinary and so we
> went to see what was going on. That's how we got into the Gurdjieff
> thing.

*   *   *

> It was very easy to get into the...movement. I talked over with my
> friends what sort of things you can do to effect change. We decided
> one thing was to propel yourself into a different circle, to join
> something. So I went down and signed up for a consciousness-rais-
> ing group.

Through repeated actions "to see what's going on" or simply discussing ideas about transformation, the seeker becomes willing to interact
as a seeker and identify himself as a seeker (if only as a seeker after
practical goals or solutions). As an *overt seeker* he intentionally proceeds
to develop his array of tactics for tapping what remain essentially
happenstance situations and encounters:

> Old friends turned up unexpectedly and turned me on to acid/
> Christ/Transcendental Meditation....Our neighbor's brother hap-
> pened to be one of Swami Satchidananda's disciples....I met this guy
> in a bookstore who said he was into something called "Eck...."

The strategic promotion and exploitation of chance is the essence of creative bumbling. The overt seeker develops creative tactics to *(a)* maximize the probability of trip encounters while *(b)* discovering the potentials they represent. But so long as he is searching, he is constrained to play the odds.

2. Searching Tactics. The overt seeker's intentional activity in creative bumbling, then, is primarily aimed at discovery. His tactics characteristically seek to create a sense of intimacy and comraderie that prompt others to reveal whatever information they might possess. Seekers exploit deeply ingrained societal understandings about "friendliness." Tactics range from promiscuously smiling at strangers and saying "Hello" to systematic devices for meeting people and finding out what they know. Ploys are usually so subtle as to appear "casual" and "spontaneous":

> I was a drummer at an "in" club and after sets I would just sit down and talk with someone, get them to talk about themselves. I'd ask where they were from, what their name is, what they do. That usually took care of it. They'd start talking away a mile a minute about themselves and the things they were into. In this way I'd learn about new ways to do things or things I should check into.

*   *   *

> I had two strategies. I became the "donut girl," making runs for people to the town bakery. Also I decided I was going to meet some guys so I'd go to a dorm with my physics book and see somebody interesting leave his room. I'd ask if I could study in their room for a while. That made me a chick who they knew, so I could talk with them and get to know them.

*   *   *

> I'd just walk up to people and start rapping. You can tell what sort of jokes they'd consider funny. Like all the "in" jokes about dope and dopers—"so and so's ripped" and all that. By becoming the life of the party I got to know people and the people they knew and we'd naturally talk about stuff just hanging around.

Experienced seekers often develop sophisticated information extraction tactics that continue throughout their careers:

> I read what's put under my nose. I ask people what I can, until they say they can't tell me any more, and then I ask who knows more and I ask *them.* One handy technique is drop a key word in the middle of a sentence, watch for a reaction and follow it up. If they try to dodge, get them to talk about its opposite. You can talk to damn near anybody about damn near anything if you ask questions in a somewhat naive way. I just store each bit of data and the picture starts to fill in as I enter more and more dots....

Other tactics are often employed to increase the probability of exploitable encounters and circumstances. These can involve changing one's social and physical spheres of interaction by moving to new locations, changing cliques or hangouts, or even the nature of one's work and recreational activities:

> I go to places where interesting people would be. One of them is the women's centers. That is my strategy—to become friends, looking for people who share my values. Another is to pursue things I want to do because *I* want to do them, fun things. When you're feeling good about yourself you meet the people you want to meet, never when you're desperate.

In contemporary America there is, of course, a great deal of routine personal mobility associated with status passage, such as going off to college. Individuals are often thrust willynilly into new environments, but the mature seeker typically locates himself within new situations intentionally so as to facilitate discovery of life-changing means.

3. Recognition. Search tactics maximize the probability of situations within which a seeker will perceive a prospective life-changing means—i.e., achieve "recognition." The discovery process also sensitizes a seeker to the possibility and probable nature of a recognition event and of what might be recognizable as a "find." Recognition is a complex "gating process" of selective perception within the interaction of seeker, trip, trip agents, and a situation—it cannot be taken for granted (Bruner *et al.,* 1956). Favorable conditions include seeming correspondence between what an agent or trip "gives off" and a seeker's prior standards, apparent practicality, and desirableness of promised changes, etc. Most possible agents are rejected without thought, the remainder recognized matter-of-factly with such statements as "why not?"

As in other phases, before reflection seekers tend to look back on recognition as something that "just happened." Orrin Klapp reports an exemplary autobiographical account of this kind:

> I had just about given up hope [after years of church-hopping] when a woman came to my door with a *Watchtower* magazine....Oh, it just had the ring of truth. I can't really explain it, but I felt it right away. All of a sudden it was there. I knew I had found what I was looking for. Klapp, (1969, pp. 41–42.)

One must probe deeper, however, asking exactly what did this woman do when the Jehovah's Witness came to her door? She obviously didn't slam the door in that person's face mumbling, "Go to hell." My data suggest, for instance, that one recognition tactic is to advertise seekerhood whenever possible so as to attract the attention of *trip agents*—people already involved in a trip and willing "to spread the word." Agents will then act to attract the seeker's attention to themselves, revealing "inside" information about the trip, its promises, and techniques of entry. In this jiu-jitsu the seeker works to get defined as someone to be solicited:

> What I do is either appear to be less than I am in the sense that I make myself appear vulnerable in a manner which is obvious to them that they can exercise control over me, or be overconfident, or show some other obvious weakness or failing such that it seems obvious that the other person is superior to or can have control over me.

Other cases reveal a wide variety of ways a person might "give off" a desire for or need of help, ranging from asking conspicuous agents outright, "What can your trip do for me?", playing up a female sex role of vulnerability, to writing short stories implicitly crying for help. In all cases the most competent proselytizer remains dependent upon the actions of the prospect that, wittingly or not, redefine him from "object" to "prospect."

B. Strategies of Creative Exploitation. Upon recognition, seekers shift gears, cease bumbling, and initiate the *creative exploitation* of prospective means of change. The process of seeking displays a logic that centers on developing the most economical means of achieving transformation in one's life. The seeker is predisposed against "making a decision" to enter a trip. Decisions require programmatic information gathering, evaluation of opportunity costs, deliberate subordination to a group that might, after all, be trying to take advantage of you. The seeker's logic is a study in decision-avoidance, in the exploitation of social, cultural, and psychological mechanisms for "painless rebirth." In effect, the seeker now proceeds to exploit the would-be exploiters constituting any trip.

He first *checks out* the trip he's uncovered, often by attending its public meetings "to get his feet wet." If, after this, the trip still seems to be for him, the seeker proceeds to *engineer* his transformation using those means presented by that specific trip. The output phase of engineering, its realization, is to *immerse* oneself within the day-to-day, taken-for-granted world of trip members.

1. Checking Out. Recognition generally triggers an open-ended process of testing the trip and its means of change by observing group members in their natural habitats, official and private. Testing— "checking out"—consists mainly of asking questions and comparing answers with one's sense of how things should be, testing the substantive means of transformation for efficacy, and seeing how the trip and its people feel to one as a gestalt—"feeling out the vibes." Quite wary of "being taken," seekers initiate "checking out" as an extension of recognition:

> A Scientologist picked me up hitchhiking and started rapping this insane rap about past lives on other planets. I was digging it because it was cosmic, something out of the ordinary—but something about the guy put me off. He came on too strong, without real love. I decided whatever Scientology was it was not for me.

In his discussion of conversion Matza (1969) makes much of "changing one's mind," conceiving the process in literal, existentialist terms. However, as the seeker understands himself to be *testing* the activity or trip he can "fail" it anytime—complicated only by such investments as he has had to make in it along the line (Becker, 1964). Contemporary seekers are far more ingenious than social scientific and lay writers imagine them (or their forebears) to be, operating with a step-by-step *experimental* rationality. This becomes evident as the seeker proceeds to check out a trip through its meetings or other formal scenes. He consistently rationalizes his behavior as checking it out. Often as not the seeker is disappointed:

> My ride mentioned this Zen retreat and I went there. Everyone was real quiet and I said, "Peace, that's what I want." They asked me to dig something up so I grabbed a shovel and began digging a hole, then I remembered this lid I had in my pocket. Figuring it was something I'd have to shine on if I was going to grow, I threw the grass into the hole and buried it. That night I was rapping with one of the guys there and he told me about the dynamite meditation sessions he'd had on hash. My heart fell. I thought about digging up my grass but decided it was useless. Well, I stayed two more days and it kept turning into a bummer so I gave up, packed my knapsack, and split.

Klapp cites a case of successful checking out (1969, p. 157):

> One night by mere accident I tuned my radio in on a broadcast by the Self Realization Fellowship. It was not convincing to me, but it did serve to arouse my interest. I attended a few meetings of the Yoga Church. But they antagonized me. I was still interested, however, and then came the...moment...which instantly changed my life. I came face to face with the Master himself. When he looked into my eyes all my...doubts fell away.

Most significantly the characteristic sense of "looking into it," "giving it a try" is often carried over throughout the seeker's career within any one trip. This experimental rationale serves to make each new inward step accountable while avoiding definitive decisions. A beturbaned Kundalini Yoga instructor remarked at the end of our interview:

> I'm interested how long I'll stay with Yogi Bhajan. I always told myself if it gets too weird I can always quit, walk away—and I still keep that idea in my mind.

---

2. *Engineering Transformation.* Checking out leads into "trying it out" and trying it out is essentially *doing* it. There need be no decision or even desire to "get converted" or "become a -------," merely an awareness that the obvious next step is to see if the means of transformation will work for you. This passage can be seen as the bridge into *engineering*. The seeker ceases acting the disinterested onlooker and begins to get his hands dirty with the mechanics of changing himself. This process has three main substages.

(a) Association. With the onset of engineering, a seeker must engage the organized group within which a means of transformation is institutionalized. He must cope with group efforts to exact from him an immediate and unqualified commitment either in exchange for the right to use its technology or—in Christian conversion rituals—as an integral part of that technology. Seekers typically develop tactics of *association* to circumvent what has been described as the "process of commitment" (Lofland, 1966; Gerlach and Hine, 1970; Harrison, 1974). These play upon friendliness once again: the seeker enters social networks of trip members and/or institutionalizes himself within the local group as a kind of fixture. Association serves to make him virtually invisible to the group by reason of familiarity while he assimilates through daily social intercourse the trip's proprietary world of language, ways of seeing, and of living. He is in effect "casing the joint" to ascertain the best way to exploit whatever that trip has to offer him. The crux of association is to prove yourself "one of us" to trip members, slipping into their friendship networks. The seeker acts to achieve this:

> You can set up how you come across to others so they invite you to parties and stuff. You go around with a blank look on your face and look a little lost but very interested and you laugh at their jokes. When you've become their very good friend, they can initiate you into new states of consciousness 'cause that's the kind of thing friends do.

Other tactics include tagging along after trip members, employing relevant sexual wiles, presenting oneself as smart, as a celebrity or friend of celebrities, etc. Often a seeker will quietly withdraw from formal group functions to concentrate on fraternizing with group members at their hangouts or parties.

A prime association tactic is establishing oneself as a hanger-on, a role known in every trip. Time is spent socializing and looking like group members but participating marginally (if at all) in the activities the trip is "all about":

> You have these guys hanging around every Scientology center who never do anything more than the Introductory Course. They date Scientologists, screw Scientologists, go to parties with Scientologists, look, act and talk like Scientologists, but never *do* any Scientology. A few years later and you see them coming on course, getting processing, joining staff. Most of us get our training and processing and then join to help others get what we've gotten, but these guys usually sign a staff contract first, so they get services half-price. They take years to get all their training and processing but somehow these are the guys who get the fast promotions, free course awards, and so on, while the rest of us are working our asses off.

Hangers-on generally graduate into active participants but they tend to become the opportunists and hustlers within the trip rather than idealists. At the same time they tend to be more stable, less easily disgruntled by the actualities of group life—perhaps because they have most conscientiously investigated how to integrate actual living as a trip member with their life-changing quest.[3] O'Dea (1970) reports similarly that Puerto Rican immigrants would attend Pentecostal meetings for months before acting to join the congregation. He mentions that they explained their shift from audience to participant as coming to feel at home within the community of believers. Harrison (1974) also notes that friendship preceded formal entrance, while Lofland earlier (1960) postulates affinitive ties as critically predisposing "conversion."

(b) Formal Entrance. Traditional and "passivist" analyses of transformation focus upon the phenomenon called "conversion." Studies of social movements, especially, emphasize formal entrance rituals governing status passage into full membership, and these are then equated with conversion (Cantril, 1941; Klapp, 1969; Gerlach and Hine, 1970; Harrison, 1974). Such a conceptualization represents an after-the-fact labeling of the seeker's passage into a new affiliation. It does not

attempt to capture the process by which a creative individual actively
engages with ongoing social enterprises. While the seeker generally
finds himself constrained to undergo formal entrance rituals in order
to gain access to the trip's means of transformation, he need not *like*
what he has to do—even in the classic case of Christian public confession where the transformative lever *is* the ritual act:

> At Calvary Chapel they tell you what you have to do to get to the
> peace and understanding of the Lord is surrender your individuality
> and become part of what's going on there. They make it really safe
> for you to do this, the place is so beautiful and loving. You have to
> stand up during the altar call and say a sinner's prayer and that's
> with all the people. I didn't want to do a thing just because everyone
> else was doing it, but the only way I could get around that was
> pretend to do their thing but do something else in my head, so I
> stood up and went forward with the others.

Even this sort of ritual requires, ultimately, the seeker to do the
work—and remains vulnerable to what the group would define as
"misuse." For this reason Christian groups typically demand new converts to prove their conversion within the context of "intensive interaction" such as described by Lofland (1966) and Harrison (1974).

Non-Christian trips establish some kind of initiation ceremony, if
only a series of classes, within which the candidate is taught or given
access to the trip's means of transformation:

> You pay $35 and go to two lectures. Then you go in on a Saturday
> and sit in a room. The instructor does something in Hindi, sings a
> verse to Maharishi, and offers him fruit and rice. It was all very
> mystical and intriguing to me. Then he whispers to you your mantra
> and you kind of repeat it over and over until you have it memorized.

*   *   *

> I walked into the Scientology center, asked the receptionist who
> could tell me what I had to do to go Clear and become an auditor
> [Scientology practitioner]. She kept trying to send me to the public
> lecture, but I finally got to see a Registrar who went over the

Routing and Gradation Chart with me and told me what I had to do. I filled out the official contracts, plunked down my money, and got an appointment to begin processing that very afternoon.

In every case—Christian, mystical, or whatever—the objectified group institutions for the socialization of recruits prove viable only because of their creative exploitation by seekers personally strategizing to realize their life-changing potential.[4]

   (c) *Transforming Oneself.* Throughout the engineering phase, the seeker acts to learn the technology offered by the trip and change his life with it. Transformative technologies consist of an *objectified agency of change* (meditation, yoga *asanas,* chanting, singing, encounter groups, Scientology auditing, drugs, etc.) and the techniques for its use—*knowhow.* Sociologists have, however, characteristically focused on a different aspect of transformative means: the ways groups organize and act to promote the specific changes labeled "conversion." Therefore, attention has been directed to the social milieu (Dohrmann, 1958; Lofland, 1966; Turner and Killian, 1972). Unfortunately our thinking has been dominated by the American experience with evangelical Christianity whose apocalyptic, quantum-leap rhetoric of "rebirth" and subordination of technique within communal practices like congregational worship and prayer meetings has been too promiscuously generalized. In extreme form this leads to denial of significance to objective technical elements, as in Matza's (1969) discussion of marijuana use as an example of the mentalistic process he calls "affiliation." Christian groups do approximate the communal pattern even though all my Christian interviewees reported the centrality to *individuals* of specifically *technological* practices such as "maintaining a strong prayer life." Eckankar, in contrast, mandates no communal life. One can take its "discourses" by mail and practice the technology on one's own. Most trips have, however, institutionalized *both* social and technical elements to some degree, utilizing the first (as the social science literature suggests) to control recruit behavior and the second to produce the experience of transformation.

3. Realizing Life Change. While it is behavioristic chauvinism to maintain that transformation *only* resides in its manifestations within a social world, it is expedient to proceed as if this were so. We find the new transformee acting first to verify the fact of being changed, as in this case of a Christian convert who has passed through a rebirth experience:

> I knelt at the altar and let it all go, saying "Take me, Lord, everything I am or have is Yours—just let it be tonight." A feeling came over me like something being lifted off me and I was flooded with this ecstatic joy as I kneeled there praising and thanking God. I got up and began marching around the deserted chapel, praising Him out loud. Eventually I kneeled once more and this beautiful peace came over me—I was numb from my head to my toes.
>
> I left the Newman Center like that still, and I went back to my dorm and lay down. I immediately called up my friend C. and told him what had occurred and he said, "You just proved it to me because you're confessing it. Just lay down and enjoy it and we'll see you at church tomorrow."

This is an excellent example of how, even where the Christian quantum-leap experience occurs in complete privacy, the seeker feels constrained to place it within the shared communal world by "confessing his faith before men":

> This initial testifying objectifies a subjective experience and "fixes" it as a reality, both for the convert and for his group. Without this step in the commitment process, much of the transforming effect of the commitment event would be lost (Gerlach and Hine, 1970, p. 136).

The pattern holds for many non-Christian cases so long as there remains a definitive commitment event. Other trips institutionalize testifying in diverse forms. Scientology officially requires one to attest to completion of each stage in the stepwise transforming process of "auditing" and immediately thereafter write a "success story" about one's "gains."

However, even the Scientologist demonstrates that a single seeker may, at various points in his career, employ an impressive range of verification tactics ranging from testifying to introspective assessment of changedness:

> Often I didn't realize anything had happened until the auditor put down his pencil and said, "That's it." Then I'd probe around in

myself to see what had changed. Other times I felt *something*, a sort of tingly electrical sensation or a feeling of mass shifting around in my mind, even before that point. Sometimes I just felt relief at completing the level as I attested, was checked out by the Examiner and so on, until I was escorted to the public lobby and announced, "F... J..., a new Grade Four Release!" When everyone stood and applauded, I'd blush and feel this rush and feel good [that] everybody felt I was groovy then. It was different every time.

The point is that the seeker himself attempts to verify his transformation. It is not only a sort of inspection by the group. Nor is it surprising, then, that the most prized verification in every trip is unsolicited reinforcement from disinterested outsiders:

> ....People began giving me feedback, "Oh, you're looking so much better." They would come up to me and be interested in me and attracted to *me*!

For this new Nichiren Soshu chanter (practitioner) these events "just happened" and so proved conclusively that she had undergone a positive transformation. However, the earlier part of her statement also illustrates how seekers will prompt such "unsolicited" verification by *acting changed:*

> I started getting my habits together, eating and getting to sleep on time. I began dressing better—I was no longer paranoid about being looked at, so why not? I'd chant for things like being able to be sociable at parties, and people began giving me feedback....

(a)   The Redhot Phase.   The central theme of realizing transformation is that the seeker, through action within the shared human world, immerses self, consciousness, and life within the taken-for-granted reality of transcendence. The central tactic of immersion is: the way to *be* changed is *act* changed. A new transformee is in the position of any novice—every practical detail of living the transformed life requires explicit attention. To get on with operating as a life-changed being, he must master the myriad day-to-day details of his new life and relegate them to unnoticed routine. He achieves this by initially taking the role of a *redhot,* acting the ideal-typical trip member to a point of exaggera-

tion. Actively exploiting "commitment," he discovers what those details are and then builds them into taken-for-granted routine. This process places his subjective "psychological" transformation within the world of other people.

The redhot phase is characterized by tactics of *proving* in which seekers *(a)* act the idealized group member, *(b)* identify themselves as transformed by symbolic behaviors or props that promote instant recognizability as a trip adherent, while *(c)* disidentifying them from their former life:

> When I first received the Lord I cut my hair and beard and carried round this big black Bible like I saw my friends do, figuring then everyone would know I was a Christian. The last thing I wanted was an old buddy to come along and get me stoned—I couldn't have handled that.

*   *   *

> For a while we did the whole heavy scene passing out leaflets, going around actually confronting people, telling them about Maharaj Ji. For one thing it really gets you high just doing it, and it puts you more in tune with the Source if you're always talking about It.

*   *   *

> Yogi Bhajan says it's a good thing to wear all white, so a lot of people who haven't been into the trip very long but would like to be start wearing white clothing, beads hanging off their arms and necks, turbans on their heads, with very peaceful expressions on their faces—it's very far out.

These examples, of course, illustrate the group-oriented "process of commitment" so often described by sociologists (Kanter, 1968; Gerlach and Hine, 1970; Harrison, 1974). They *also* show, however, that when probed more deeply, this process cannot be analyzed without reference to creative exploitation. These individuals are *using* institutional provisions of a trip toward what they conceived of as their own life-changing ends. In fact, settled trip members often express uneasiness with the exaggerated behavior of redhot newcomers (Strauss, 1959). "Mature" Christian transformees, for example, often advise the newly "Spirit-filled" believer that he will settle down in a year or so (Sherrill, 1964). Such guidance can be institutionalized, as in Eckankar:

> At first you sit up and meditate all day, start being a redhot—the period of overreaction I was telling you about—but they teach you right off, you have this thing called responsibility and you can't zip out there all the time. You gotta earn your freedom, make the best of things while you're here on this plane. When I read back over the discourses I realized I must have misunderstood the first time through...

(b)   Transition to Maintenance.   By "redhot" exploitation of commitment, the seeker prepares to settle within the world of his trip "for the duration." Mastering the practical art of living a transformed life, he can proceed to the continuing business of creating a satisfying life experience within that new context:

> My relationship with God no longer depends on externals. At first I was real defensive. I felt a legalistic burden to share Christ with everyone I met. I devoted every evening to Christian activities—I'm trying to cut down somewhat now. Fellowship remains an important tool for spiritual growth, but I've come to a place where someone doesn't have to lay it all out for me. I still fast and pray when I feel a need and worship at a church where people worship in the Spirit. Last year I felt a call to quit graduate school so I can devote my attention to helping others in the Lord. I still do most of the things I've done all along but now I'm more aware of God in my heart—it all kind of comes naturally to me now.

The shaping role of group processes in this transition has been well documented in studies of social movements. Additionally, I find a critical factor in navigating (or precipitating, depending on your view) the transition to maintenance is to begin acting as a trip agent rather than seeker. Beginning in the redhot phase, this emerges as a volitional and/or group-sponsored tactic of focusing one's intentional activity upon an appropriate agent role:

> After I'd been chanting for a while E. insisted on giving me this girl to take care of. She told me, "K., I want you to teach this girl to

practice Buddhism." That's when things really started to happen in my life, when I committed myself in this fashion.

* * *

I quit my job to go on staff after I'd received my lower levels of auditing, but what made it easy for me to settle in Scientology was that I managed to become a staff auditor myself. That was everyone's goal, but somehow I pulled it off. Not only was I experiencing changes but then I could do it to others and have them experience the same reality through me.... Later, when I tried to do the same kind of thing as a Christian, it just never worked out and I was never really able to get into the trip.

Successful transition into steady-stating within a transcendental life-world for any length of time invariably exhibits this pattern of "activism." There is no evidence for the oft-encountered presumption that some "Them"—some differentiated, con-artist elite—preys upon gullible or malintegrated "followers." There are only seekers at different stages in their life-changing career trajectories who, engaged in a joint enterprise, generate the group.

C. Discussion. Transcendental forms of questing are a subset of a ubiquitous phenomenon in contemporary American society: the quest to change one's life. Such transformative quests can take any number of forms centering around any combination of the cultural, practical, political, or economic aspects of modern life. In all cases, the technology, the means by which personal or collective transformation is brought about, takes on a central significance. It specifies the substantive visualization of a goal or end, conditions the form and organization of collectivities engaged in the quest, and ultimately *allows* transformation by the technical manipulation of social and/or experiential reality.

Seeking, moreover, is not itself tangential to modern life. Contemporary sociocultural actuality increasingly requires every individual to become a seeker of some kind and to some degree—or else devise a no less creative means of avoiding the need for transformation:

You go down to the bar Friday night, get crocked, go back to the dorms, smoke a pack of cigarettes, maybe do a couple of numbers and go back to bed...study during the week, you know, then blow it all out Saturday night.

The contemporary conceptualization of "youth" as an emergent, groping stage of life (Erikson, 1968; Kenniston, 1968) is, moreover, consistent with the portrait of seekers that emerges here.

Placed in a larger context, the seekers of earlier studies and times (e.g., Cantril, 1941; Catton, 1957; Dohrmann, 1958; Lofland, 1966) seem generally malintegrated, socioculturally marginal "losers" who began seeking after personal crisis or failure *as adults*. Seekers of the contemporary scene are quite different. They are younger, less patently malintegrated, better educated, and—if not the spectacular "successes" within their cohort, as "normal society" measures such things—certainly not its dregs. Whether or not the suspended adolescence concept of "youth" describes anything in actuality, it seems that for the contemporary cohort of young adults seeking is no longer a marginal, stigmatized behavior and cannot be naively compared to similar behaviors of their predecessors.

Be these matters as they may, this paper's intent is essentially methodological. It has sought to illustrate the kind of analysis that must be undertaken if we are to pay more than lip service to the conceptualization of the creative actor. It is far from revolutionary to see humankind in this light. Marx saw that:

> The fact is, therefore, that definite individuals who are productively active in a definite way enter into these definite political and social relations....The social structure and the State are continually evolving out of the life-processes of definite individuals (1970, p. 46).

In striving to establish social analysis upon a historical rather than idealistic base, Marx sought to prove that "circumstances make men just as much as men make circumstances" (1970, p. 59). Discussing Mead's social psychology, Blumer makes a similar statement: "A society is seen as people meeting the varieties of situations that are thrust upon them by their conditions of life...by working out joint actions" (1966, p. 542). Both statements recognize a complex interaction between active individuals and their constraining environments but, with rare exceptions, social scientists have routinely chosen to concentrate upon the compelling forces of circumstance and the actions of others. It becomes necessary to drive home the point that "people make circumstances just as much as circumstances make people"—and then to follow up that point in doing research. As a social process, "socialization" must be stood on its head. The interesting and appropriate question becomes not how do groups metabolize human beings, but how do individuals generate, operate, and use their groups in the continuous creation of their lives?

Notes

1. Indeed, conventional self-editing of biography so downplays the individual's own role in his life that many seekers exclaimed, "You know, I never looked at it in this way before." Moreover, this sort of interview blurs the distinction between data gathering and psychotherapy. While it is extremely gratifying for interviewer and interviewee alike to feel that their interaction has contributed to the subject's personal growth (as suggested by the quoted statement), this raises any number of procedural and ethical questions.

2. Covert seeking underlies the importance noted by Lofland and expanded by Gerlach and Hine (1970) of "friendship networks" in the recruitment patterns of transformative groups. Sexual attraction can be especially potent in both development and exploitation of that affectual closeness central to creative bumbling tactics, as has also been pointed out by Lofland (1966). See, further, my discussion of associational tactics in the engineering of transformation in Section B.2 of this paper.

3. Tactics of checking out and association are based on very similar objectives to those of sociologists engaged in fieldwork. For this reason, sociological manuals on participant observation and similar methods provide excellent catalogs of associational strategems (e.g., Lofland, 1971; Schatzman and Strauss, 1973). Also see Lofland's appendix, "How the Data Were Collected" (1966, pp. 269–275) for a discussion of problems and tactics used in "casing" a trip.

4. Interviewees also reported career sequences virtually identical to those involved in clearly transcendental trips but having to do, rather, with nervous breakdowns, encounter groups, psychedelics, direct sales organizations, the Montessori education movement, and even marriage. The similarities suggest that the phenomena under discussion here are generic rather than limited to "religious" seekership. For example, the exploitation of formal rituals is not limited to the sort of cases focused on in this paper: "I got tricked into dating this guy whom I thought was a jerk. He was, but I discovered him to be a nice jerk. I ended up deciding to marry him because he'd provide for me a safe environment, support me financially, and protect me from hassles. The way things were going it was all too much for me to cope with. What I did was I got pregnant by semiwittingly eschewing contraceptives—and so we got married when I was three weeks overdue."

References

Becker, H. S. 1964. "Personal Change in Adult Life," *Sociometry* **27** (March): 40–53.

Blumer, H. 1966. "Sociological Implications of the Thought of George Herbert Mead," *American Journal of Sociology,* **71** (March): 535–544.

Bruner, J. S., J. Goodnow, and G. Austin. 1956. *A Study of Thinking.* (New York: Wiley).

Cantril, H. 1941. *The Psychology of Social Movements* (New York: Wiley).

Catton, W. R., Jr. 1957. "What Kind of People Does a Cult Attract?" *American Sociological Review* **22** (October): 561–566.

Dohrmann, H. T. 1958. *California Cult* (Boston: Beacon).

Erikson, E. 1968. *Identity, Youth, and Crisis* (New York: Norton).

Gerlach, L. P., and Virginia H. Hine. 1970. *People, Power, Change: Movements of Social Transformation* (Indianapolis: Bobbs-Merrill).

Harrison, M. J. 1974. "Preparation for Life in the Spirit," *Urban Life* **2** (January): 387–413.

Hubbard, L. R. 1950. *Dianetics: The Modern Science of Mental Health* (Los Angeles: American Saint Hill Organization).

Kanter, R. 1968. "Commitment and Social Organization," *American Sociological Review* **33** (August): 499–517.

Keniston, K. 1968. *Young Radicals: Notes on Committed Youth* (New York: Harcourt, Brace, Jovanovich).

Klapp, O. E. 1969. *The Collective Search for Identity* (New York: Holt, Rinehart & Winston).

Lofland, J. 1966. *Doomsday Cult* (Englewood Cliffs, N.J.: Prentice-Hall).

Lofland, J. 1971. *Analyzing Social Settings* (Belmont, Calif.: Wadsworth).

Marx, K. and F. Engels. 1970. *The German Ideology* C. J. Arthur, ed. (New York: International).

Matza, D. 1969. *Becoming Deviant* (Englewood Cliffs, N.J.: Prentice-Hall).

O'Dea, T. H. 1970.. *Sociology and the Study of Religion* (New York: Basic Books).

Schatzman, L. and A. Strauss. 1973. *Field Research: Strategies for a Natural Sociology* (Englewood Cliffs, N.J.: Prentice-Hall).

Sherrill, J. 1964. *They Speak with Other Tongues.* (New York: Pyramid).

Smelser, N. J. 1963. *Theory of Collective Behavior* (New York: Free Press).

Sorokin, P. A. 1967. *The Ways and Power of Love* (Chicago: Henry Regnery).

Strauss, A. 1959. *Mirrors and Masks: the Search for Identity* (San Francisco: Sociology Press).

Turner, R. and L. Killian. 1972. *Collective Behavior* (Englewood Cliffs, N.J.: Prentice-Hall).

Wilson, B. R. 1961. *Sects and Society* (Berkeley: University of California Press).

Yogananda, P. 1946. *Autobiography of a Yogi* (Los Angeles: Self Realization Fellowship).

II SELECTED STUDIES OF ROLE-SCALE INTERACTION STRATEGIES

The notation following each entry indicates the section of Chapter 9 in which it is capsulized.

Bittner, Egon, "The Police on Skid Row: A Study of Peace Keeping," *American Sociological Review* **32**:669–715 (October 1967). (IV.A.3)

Boyd, James, "The Ritual of Wiggle: From Ruin to Reelection," *The Washington Monthly*, **2**(7):28–43 (September 1970). (IV.A.5)

Christopherson, Richard W., 'Making Art with Machines: Photography's Institutional Inadequacies," *Urban Life and Culture* **3**:3–34 (April 1974); "From Folk Art to Fine Art: A Transformation in the Meaning of Photographic Work," *Urban Life and Culture* **3**:123–157 (July 1974). (IV.C.5)

Davis, Fred, "Deviance Disavowal: The Management of Strained Interaction by the Visibly Handicapped," in his *Illness, Interaction and the Self* (Belmont, Calif.: Wadsworth, 1972), pp. 130–149. (IV.C.3)

Hamburg, David, Beatrix Hamburg, and Sydney DeGoza, "Adaptive Problems and Mechanisms in Severely Burned Patients," *Psychiatry* **16**:1–20 (February 1953). (VI.A)

Kaplan, Howard B., Ina Boyd, and Samuel Bloom, "Patient Culture and the Evaluation of Self," *Psychiatry* **27**:116–126 (May 1964). (VI.A)

Larsen, Kenneth, "Foundation Managers, Candidates and Grantees: A Study of Classification and Control," *Urban Life and Culture,* **3**:396–441 (January 1975). (IV.A.4)

Mechanic, David, *Students Under Stress* (New York: Free Press, 1962), Ch. 7.

Schwartz, Charlotte Green, "Strategies and Tactics of Mothers of Mentally Retarded Children for Dealing with the Medical Care System," in Norman Bernstein, ed., *Diminished People: Problems and Care of the Mentally Retarded* (Boston: Little, Brown, 1970), pp. 73–105. (IV.C.2)

Seeman, Melvin, "The Intellectual and the Language of Minorities," *American Journal of Sociology,* **64**:25–35 (July 1958). (IV.C.1)

Simmons, J. L., "On Maintaining Deviant Belief Systems," *Social Problems,* **11**:250–256 (Winter 1964). (VI.B)

Strauss, George, "Tactics of Lateral Relationship: The Purchasing Agent," *Administrative Science Quarterly,* **7**:161–186 (September 1962). (IV.B)

Turner, Ralph, "The Navy Disbursing Officer as a Bureaucrat," *American Sociological Review,* **12**:342–348 (June 1947). (II.A)

CHAPTER FOURTEEN

Group-Scale Inquiries

Group-scale strategies of interaction are the cooperative and joint elaborations of a limited number of persons who are collectively subject to a situation. Donald Roy's depiction of "times" and "themes" in a work group well illustrates this cooperative and joint character and how such strategies are sharply to be distinguished from individual behavior such as "the game of work," the self-management device he also discusses.

Roy's study is itself one of the classic, even poetic, achievements of fieldwork in modern social science. The situation is clearly delineated, scales of strategy are shown, and both are masterfully intertwined with empirical materials gained through intimate familiarity.

I. A SITUATION OF MONOTONY AND STRATEGIES OF VARIETY

"Banana Time"
Job Satisfaction
and Informal
Interaction

Donald F. Roy

Reprinted from *Human Organization*, **18:** 158–168 (Winter 1959–1960) with the permission of the author and the Society for Applied Anthropology.

This paper undertakes description and exploratory analysis of the social interaction which took place within a small work group of factory machine operatives during a two-month period of praticipant observation. The factual and ideational materials which it presents lie at an intersection of two lines of research interest and should, in their dual bearing, contribute to both. Since the operatives were engaged in work which involved the repetition of very simple operations over an extra-long workday, six days a week, they were faced with the problem of dealing with a formidable "beast of monotony." Revelation of how the group utilized its resources to combat the "beast" should merit the attention of those who are seeking solution to the practical problem of job satisfaction, or employee morale. It should also provide insights for those who are trying to penetrate the mysteries of the small group.

Convergence of these two lines of interest is, of course, no new thing. Among the host of writers and researchers who have suggested connections between "group" and "joy in work" are Walker and Guest, observers of social interaction on the automobile assembly line.[1] They quote assembly-line workers as saying, "We have a lot of fun and talk all the time,"[2] and, "If it weren't for the talking and fooling, you'd go nuts."[3]

My account of how one group of machine operators kept from "going nuts" in a situation of monotonous work activity attempts to lay bare the tissues of interaction which made up the content of their adjustment. The talking, fun, and fooling which provided solution to the elemental problem of "psychological survival" will be described according to their embodiment in intragroup relations. In addition, an unusual opportunity for close observation of behavior involved in the maintenance of group equilibrium was afforded by the fortuitous introduction of a "natural experiment." My unwitting injection of explosive materials into the stream of interaction resulted in sudden, but temporary, loss of group interaction.

My fellow operatives and I spent our long days of simple, repetitive work in relative isolation from other employees of the factory. Our line of machines was sealed off from other work areas of the plant by the four walls of the clicking room. The one door of this room was usually closed. Even when it was kept open, during periods of hot weather, the consequences were not social; it opened on an uninhabited storage room of the shipping department. Not even the sounds of work activity going on elsewhere in the factory carried to this isolated work place. There were occasional contacts with "outside" employees, usually on matters connected with the work; but, with the exception of the daily calls of one fellow who came to pick up finished materials for the next step in processing, such visits were sporadic and infrequent.

Moreover, face-to-face contacts with members of the managerial hierarchy were few and far between. No one bearing the title of foreman ever came around. The only company official who showed himself more than once during the two month observation period was the plant superintendent. Evidently overloaded with supervisory duties and production problems which kept him busy elsewhere, he managed to pay his respects every week or two. His visits were in the nature of short, businesslike, but friendly exchanges. Otherwise he confined his observable communications with the group to occasional utilization of a public address system. During the two-month period, the company president and the chief chemist paid one friendly call apiece. One man, who may or may not have been of managerial status, was seen on various occasions lurking about in a manner which excited suspicion. Although no observable consequences accrued from the peculiar visitations of this silent fellow, it was assumed that he was some sort of efficiency expert, and he was referred to as "The Snooper."

As far as our work group was concerned, this was truly a situation of laissez-faire management. There was no interference from staff experts, no hounding by time-study engineers or personnel men hot on the scent of efficiency or good human relations. Nor were there any signs of industrial democracy in the form of safety, recreational, or production committees. There was an international union, and there was a highly publicized union-management cooperation program; but actual interactional processes of cooperation were carried on somewhere beyond my range of observation and without participation of members of my work group. Furthermore, these union-management get-togethers had no determinable connection with the problem of "toughing out" a twelve-hour day at monotonous work.

Our work group was thus not only abandoned to its own resources for creating job satisfaction, but left without that basic reservoir of ill-will toward management which can sometimes be counted on to stimulate the development of interesting activities to occupy hand and brain. Lacking was the challenge of intergroup conflict, that perennial source of creative experience to fill the otherwise empty hours of meaningless work routine.[4]

The clicking machines were housed in a room approximately thirty by twenty-four feet. They were four in number, set in a row, and so arranged along one wall that the busy operator could, merely by raising his head from his work, freshen his reveries with a glance through one of three large barred windows. To the rear of one of the end machines sat a long cutting table; here the operators cut up rolls of plastic materials into small sheets manageable for further processing at the clickers. Behind the machine at the opposite end of the line sat another table which was intermittently the work station of a female employee who performed sundry scissors operations of a more intricate nature on raincoat parts. Boxed in on all sides by shelves and stocks of materials, this latter locus of work appeared a cell within a cell.

The clickers were of the genus punching machines; of mechanical construction similar to that of the better-known punch presses, their leading features were hammer and block. The hammer, or punching head, was approximately eight inches by twelve inches at its flat striking surface. The descent upon the block was initially forced by the operator, who exerted pressure on a handle attached to the side of the hammer head. A few inches of travel downward established electrical connection for a sharp, power-driven blow. The hammer also traveled, by manual guidance, in a horizontal plane to and from, and in an arc around, the central column of the machine. Thus the operator, up to the point of establishing electrical connections for the sudden and irrevocable downward thrust, had flexibility in maneuvering his instrument over the larger surface of the block. The latter, approximately twenty-four inches wide, eighteen inches deep, and ten inches thick, was made, like a butcher's block, of inlaid hardwood; it was set in the machine at a convenient waist height. On it the operator placed his materials, one sheet at a time if leather, stacks of sheets if plastic, to be cut with steel dies of assorted sizes and shapes. The particular die in use would be moved, by hand, from spot to spot over the materials each time a cut was made; less frequently, materials would be shifted on the block as the operator saw need for such adjustment.

Introduction to the new job, with its relatively simple machine skills and work routines, was accomplished with what proved to be, in my experience, an all-time minimum of job training. The clicking machine assigned to me was situated at one end of the row. Here the superintendent and one of the operators gave a few brief demonstrations, accompanied by bits of advice which included a warning to keep hands clear of the descending hammer. After a short practice period, at the end of which the superintendent expressed satisfaction with progress and potentialities, I was left to develop my learning curve with no other supervision than that afforded by members of the work group. Further advice and assistance did come, from time to time, from my fellow operatives, sometimes upon request, sometimes unsolicited.

The Work Group.   Absorbed at first in three related goals of improving my clicking skill, increasing my rate of output, and keeping my left hand unclicked, I paid little attention to my fellow operatives save to observe that they were friendly, middle-aged, foreign-born, full of advice, and very talkative. Their names, according to the way they addressed each other, were George, Ike, and Sammy.[5] George, a stocky fellow in his late fifties, operated the machine at the opposite end of the line; he, I later discovered, had emigrated in early youth from a country in Southeastern Europe. Ike, stationed at George's left, was tall, slender, in his early fifties, and Jewish; he had come from Eastern Europe in his youth. Sammy, number three man in the line, and my neighbor, was heavy set, in his late fifties, and Jewish; he had escaped from a country in Eastern Europe just before Hitler's legions had moved in. All three men had been downwardly mobile as to occupation in recent years. George and Sammy had been proprietors of small businesses; the former had been "wiped out" when his uninsured establishment burned down; the latter had been entrepreneuring on a small scale before he left all behind him to flee the Germans. According to his account, Ike had left a highly skilled trade which he had practiced for years in Chicago.

I discovered also that the clicker line represented a ranking system in descending order from George to myself. George not only had top seniority for the group, but functioned as a sort of leadman. His superior status was marked in the fact that he received five cents more per hour than the other clickermen, put in the longest workday, made daily contact outside the workroom, with the superintendent on work matters which concerned the entire line, and communicated to the rest of us the directives which he received. The narrow margin of superordination was seen in the fact that directives were always relayed in the superintendent's name; they were on the order of, "You'd better let that go now, and get on the green. Joe says they're running low on the fifth floor," or, "Joe says he wants two boxes of the 3-die today." The narrow margin was also seen in the fact that the superintendent would communicate directly with his operatives over the public address system; and, on occasion, Ike or Sammy would leave the workroom to confer with him for decisions or advice in regard to work orders.

Ike was next to George in seniority, then Sammy. I was, of course, low man on the totem pole. Other indices to status differentiation lay in informal interaction, to be described later.

With one exception, job status tended to be matched by length of workday. George worked a thirteen-hour day, from 7 A.M. to 8:30 P.M. Ike worked eleven hours, from 7 A.M. to 6:30 P.M.; occasionally he worked until 7 or 7:30 for an eleven and a half- or a twelve-hour day. Sammy put in a nine-hour day, from 8 A.M. to 5:30 P.M. My twelve hours spanned from 8 A.M. to 8:30 P.M. We had a half hour for lunch, from 12 to 12:30.

The female who worked at the secluded table behind George's machine put in a regular plant-wide eight-hour shift from 8 to 4:30. Two women held this job during the period of my employment; Mable was succeeded by Baby. Both were Negroes, and in their late twenties.

A fifth clicker operator, an Arabian *emigré* called Boo, worked a night shift by himself. He usually arrived about 7 P.M. to take over Ike's machine.

The Work. It was evident to me, before my first workday drew to a weary close, that my clicking career was going to be a grim process of fighting the clock, the particular timepiece in this situation being an old-fashioned alarm clock which ticked away on a shelf near George's machine. I had struggled through many dreary rounds with the minutes and hours during the various phases of my industrial experience, but never had I been confronted with such a dismal combination of working conditions as the extra-long workday, the infinitesimal cerebral excitation, and the extreme limitation of physical movement. The contrast with a recent stint in the California oil fields was striking. This was no eight-hour day of racing hither and yon over desert and foot-hills with a rollicking crew of "roustabouts" on a variety of repair missions at oil wells, pipe lines, and storage tanks. Here there were no afternoon dallyings to search the sands for horned toads, tarantulas, and rattlesnakes, or to climb old wooden derricks for raven's nests, with an eye out, of course, for the telltale streak of dust in the distance which gave ample warning of the approach of the boss. This was standing all day in one spot beside three old codgers in a dingy room looking out through barred windows at the bare walls of a brick warehouse, leg movements largely restricted to the shifting of body weight from one foot to the other, hand and arm movements confined, for the most part, to a simple repetitive sequence of place the die,—punch the clicker,—place the die,—punch the clicker, and intellectual activity reduced to computing the hours to quitting time. It is true that from time to time a fresh stack of sheets would have to be substituted for the clicked-out old one; but the stack would have been prepared by someone else, and the exchange would be only a minute or two in the making. Now and then a box of finished work would have to be moved back out of the way, and an empty box brought up; but the moving back and the bringing up involved only a step or two. And there was the half hour for lunch, and occasional trips to the lavatory or the drinking fountain to break up the day into digestible parts. But after each momentary respite, hammer and die were moving again: click,—move die—click,—move die.

Before the end of the first day, Monotony was joined by his twin brother, Fatigue. I got tired. My legs ached, and my feet hurt. Early in the afternoon I discovered a tall stool and moved it up to my machine to "take the load off my feet." But the superintendent dropped in to see how I was "doing" and promptly informed me that "we don't sit down on this job." My reverie toyed with the idea of quitting the job and looking for other work.

The next day was the same: the monotony of the work, the tired legs and sore feet, and thoughts of quitting.

The Game of Work.   In discussing the factory operative's struggle to "cling to the remnants of joy in work," Henri de Man makes the general observations that "it is psychologicallly impossible to deprive any kind of work of all its positive emotional elements," that the worker will find *some* meaning in any activity assigned to him, a "certain scope, for initiative which can satisfy after a fashion the instinct for play and the creative impulse," that "even in the Taylor system there is found luxury of self-determination."[6] De Man cites the case of one worker who wrapped 13,000 incandescent bulbs a day; she found her outlet for creative impulse, her self-determination, her meaning in work by varying her wrapping movements a little from time to time.[7]

So did I search for *some* meaning in my continuous mincing of plastic sheets into small ovals, fingers, and trapezoids. The richness of possibility for creative expression previously discovered in my experience with the "Taylor system"[8] did not reveal itself here. There was no piecework, so no piecework game. There was no conflict with management, so no war game. But, like the light bulb wrapper, I did find a "certain scope for initiative," and out of this slight freedom to vary activity, I developed a game of work.

The game developed was quite simple, so elementary, in fact, that its playing was reminiscent of rainy-day preoccupations in childhood, when attention could be centered by the hour on colored bits of things of assorted sizes and shapes. But this adult activity was not mere pottering and piddling; what it lacked in the earlier imaginative content, it made up for in clean-cut structure. Fundamentally involved were (a) variation in color of the materials cut, (b) variation in shapes of the dies used, and (c) a process called "scraping the block." The basic procedure which ordered the particular combination of components employed could be stated in the form: "As soon as I do so many of these. I'll get to do those." If, for example, production scheduled for the day featured small, rectangular strips in three colors, the game might go: "As soon as I finish a thousand of the green ones, I'll click some brown ones." And, with success in attaining the objective of working with brown materials, a new goal of "I'll get to do the white ones" might be set. Or the new goal might involve switching dies.

Scraping the block made the game more interesting by adding to the number of possible variations in its playing; and, what was perhaps more important, provided the only substantial reward, save for going to the lavatory or getting a drink of water, on days when work with one die and one color of material was scheduled. As a physical operation, scraping the block was fairly simple; it involved application of a coarse file to the upper surface of the block to remove roughness and unevenness resulting from the wear and tear of die penetration. But, as part of the intellectual and emotional content of the game of work, it could be in itself a source of variation in activity. The upper left-hand corner of the block could be chewed up in the clicking of 1000 white trapezoid pieces, then scraped. Next, the upper right-hand corner, and so on until the entire block had been worked over. Then, on the next round of scraping by quadrants, there was the possibility of a change of color or die to green trapezoid or white oval pieces.

Thus the game of work might be described as a continuous sequence of short-range production goals with achievement rewards in the form of activity change. The superiority of this relatively complex and self-determined system over the technically simple and outside-controlled job satisfaction injections experienced by Milner at the beginner's table in a shop of the feather industry should be immediately apparent:

> Twice a day our work was completely changed to break the monotony. First Jennie would give us feathers of a brilliant green, then bright orange or a light blue or black. The "ohs" and "ahs" that came from the girls at each change was proof enough that this was an effective way of breaking the monotony of the tedious work.[9]

But a hasty conclusion that I was having lots of fun playing my clicking game should be avoided. These games were not as interesting in the experiencing as they might seem to be from the telling. Emotional tone of the activity was low, and intellectual currents weak. Such rewards as scraping the block or "getting to do the blue ones" were not very exciting, and the stretches of repetitive movement involved in achieving them were long enough to permit lapses into obsessive reverie. Henri de Man speaks of "clinging to the remnants of joy in work," and this situation represented just that. How tenacious the clinging was, how long I could have "stuck it out" with my remnants, was never determined. Before the first week was out this adjustment to the work situation was complicated by other developments. The game of work continued, but in a different context. Its influence became decidedly subordinated to, if not completely overshadowed by, another source of job satisfaction.

Informal Social Activity of the Work Group: Times and Themes.   The change came about when I began to take serious note of the social activity going on around me; my attentiveness to this activity came with growing involvement in it. What I heard at first, before I started to listen, was a stream of disconnected bits of communication which did not make much sense. Foreign accents were strong and referents were not joined to coherent contexts of meaning. It was just "jabbering." What I saw at first, before I began to observe, was occasional flurries of horseplay so simple and unvarying in pattern and so childish in quality that they made no strong bid for attention. For example, Ike would regularly switch off the power at Sammy's machine whenever Sammy made a trip to the lavatory or the drinking fountain. Correlatively, Sammy invariably fell victim to the plot by making an attempt to operate his clicking hammer after returning to the shop. And, as the simple pattern went, this blind stumbling into the trap was always followed by indignation and reproach from Sammy, smirking satisfaction from Ike, and mild paternal scolding from George. My interest in this procedure was at first confined to wondering when Ike would weary of his tedious joke or when Sammy would learn to check his power switch before trying the hammer.

But, as I began to pay closer attention, as I began to develop familiarity with the communication system, the disconnected became connected, the nonsense made sense, the obscure became clear, and the silly actually funny. And, as the content of the interaction took on more and more meaning, the interaction began to reveal structure. There were "times" and "themes," and roles to serve their enaction. The interaction had subtleties, and I began to savor and appreciate them. I started to record what hitherto had seemed unimportant.

Times. This emerging awareness of structure and meaning included recognition that the long day's grind was broken by interruptions of a kind other than the formally instituted or idiosyncratically developed disjunctions in work routine previously described. These additional interruptions appeared in daily repetition in an ordered series of informal interactions. They were, in part, but only in part and in very rough comparison, similar to those common fractures of the production process known as the coffee break, the coke break, and the cigarette break. Their distinction lay in frequency of occurrence and in brevity. As phases of the daily series, they occurred almost hourly, and so short were they in duration that they disrupted work activity only slightly. Their significance lay not so much in their function as rest pauses, although it cannot be denied that physical refreshment was involved. Nor did their chief importance lie in the accentuation of progress points in the passage of time, although they could perform that function far more strikingly than the hour hand on the dull face of George's alarm clock. If the daily series of interruptions be likened to a clock, then the comparison might best be made with a special kind of cuckoo clock, one with a cuckoo which can provide variation in its announcements and can create such an interest in them that the intervening minutes become filled with intellectual content. The major significance of the interactional interruptions lay in such a carryover of interest. The physical interplay which momentarily halted work activitiy would initiate verbal exchanges and thought processes to occupy group members until the next interruption. The group interactions thus not only marked off the time; they gave it content and hurried it along.

Most of the breaks in the daily series were designated as "times" in the parlance of the clicker operators, and they featured the consumption of food or drink of one sort or another. There was coffee time, peach time, banana time, fish time, coke time, and, of course, lunch time. Other interruptions, which formed part of the series but were not verbally recognized as times, were window time, pickup time, and the staggered quitting times of Sammy and Ike. These latter unnamed times did not involve the partaking of refreshments.

My attention was first drawn to this times business during my first week of employment when I was encouraged to join in the sharing of two peaches. It was Sammy who provided the peaches; he drew them from his lunch box after making the announcement, "Peach time!" On this first occasion I refused the proffered fruit, but thereafter regularly consumed my half peach. Sammy continued to provide the peaches and to make the "Peach time!" announcement, although there were days when Ike would remind him that it was peach time, urging him to hurry up with the mid morning snack. Ike invariably complained about the quality of the fruit, and his complaints fed the fires of continued banter between peach donor and critical recipient. I did find the fruit a bit on the scrubby side but felt, before I achieved insight into the function of peach time, that Ike was showing poor manners by looking a gift horse in the mouth. I wondered why Sammy continued to share his peaches with such an ingrate.

Banana time followed peach time by approximately an hour. Sammy again provided the refreshments, namely, one banana. There was, however, no four-way sharing of Sammy's banana. Ike would gulp it down by himself after surreptitiously extracting it from Sammy's lunch box, kept on a shelf behind Sammy's work station. Each morning, after making the snatch, Ike would call out, "Banana time!" and proceed to down his prize while Sammy made futile protests and denunciations. George would join in with mild remonstrances, sometimes scolding Sammy for making so much fuss. The banana was one which Sammy brought for his own consumption at lunch time; he never did get to eat his banana, but kept bringing one for his lunch. At first this daily theft startled and amazed me. Then I grew to look forward to the daily seizure and the verbal interaction which followed.

Window time came next. It followed banana time as a regular consequence of Ike's castigation by the indignant Sammy. After "taking" repeated references to himself as a person badly lacking in morality and character, Ike would "finally" retaliate by opening the window which faced Sammy's machine, to let the "cold air" blow in on Sammy. The slandering which would, in its echolalic repetition, wear down Ike's patience and forbearance usually took the form of the invidious comparison: "George is a good daddy! Ike is a bad man! A very bad man!" Opening the window would take a little time to accomplish and would involve a great deal of verbal interplay between Ike and Sammy, both before and after the event. Ike would threaten, make feints toward the window, then finally open it. Sammy would protest, argue, and make claims that the air blowing in on him would give him a cold; he would eventually have to leave his machine to close the window. Sometimes the weather was slightly chilly, and the draft from the window unpleasant; but cool or hot, windy or still, window time arrived each day. (I assume that it was originally a cold season development.) George's part in this interplay, in spite of the "good daddy" laudations, was to encourage Ike in his window work. He would stress the tonic values of fresh air and chide Sammy for his unappreciativeness.

Following window time came lunch time, a formally designated half-hour for the midday repast and rest break. At this time, informal interaction would feature exchanges between Ike and George. The former would start eating his lunch a few minutes before noon, and the latter, in his role as straw boss, would censure him for malobservance of the rules. Ike's off-beat luncheon usually involved a previous tampering with George's alarm clock. Ike would set the clock ahead a few minutes in order to maintain his eating schedule without detection, and George would discover these small daylight saving changes.

The first "time" interruption of the day I did not share. It occurred soon after I arrived on the job, at eight o'clock. George and Ike would share a small pot of coffee brewed on George's hot plate.

Pickup time, fish time, and coke time came in the afternoon. I name it pickup time to represent the official visit of the man who made daily calls to cart away boxes of clicked materials. The arrival of the pickup man, a Negro, was always a noisy one, like the arrival of a daily passenger train in an isolated small town. Interaction attained a quick peak of intensity to crowd into a few minutes all communications, necessary and otherwise. Exchanges invariably included loud depreciations by the pickup man of the amount of work accomplished in the clicking department during the preceding twenty-four hours. Such scoffing would be on the order of "Is that all you've got done? What do you boys do all day?" These devaluations would be countered with allusions to the "soft job" enjoyed by the pickup man. During the course of the exchange news items would be dropped, some of serious import, such as reports of accomplished or impending layoffs in the various plants of the company, or of gains or losses in orders for company products. Most of the news items, however, involved bits of information on plant employees told in a light vein. Information relayed by the clicker operators was usually told about each other, mainly in the form of summaries of the most recent kidding sequences. Some of this material was repetitive, carried over from day to day. Sammy would be the butt of most of this newscasting, although he would make occasional counterreports on Ike and George. An invariable part of the interactional content of pickup time was Ike's introduction of the pickup man to George. "Meet Mr. Papeatis!" Ike would say in mock solemnity and dignity. Each day the pickup man "met" Mr. Papeatis, to the obvious irritation of the latter. Another pickup time invariably would bring Baby (or Mable) into the interaction. George would always issue the loud warning to the pickup man: "Now I want you to stay away from Baby! She's Henry's girl!" Henry was a burly Negro with a booming bass voice who made infrequent trips to the clicking room with lift-truck loads of materials. He was reputedly quite a ladies' man among the colored population of the factory. George's warning to "Stay away from Baby!" was issued to every Negro who entered the shop. Baby's only part in this was to laugh at the horseplay.

About midafternoon came fish time. George and Ike would stop work for a few minutes to consume some sort of pickled fish which Ike provided. Neither Sammy nor I partook of this nourishment, nor were we invited. For this omission I was grateful; the fish, brought in a newspaper and with head and tail intact, produced a reverse effect on my appetite. George and Ike seemed to share a great liking for fish. Each Friday night, as a regular ritual, they would enjoy a fish dinner together at a nearby restaurant. One these nights Ike would work until 8:30 and leave the plant with George.

Coke time came late in the afternoon, and was an occasion for total participation. The four of us took turns in buying the drinks and in making the trip for them to a fourth floor vending machine. Through George's manipulation of the situation, it eventually became my daily chore to go after the cokes; the straw boss had noted that I made a much faster trip to the fourth floor and back than Sammy or Ike.

Sammy left the plant at 5:30, and Ike ordinarily retired from the scene an hour and a half later. These quitting times were not marked by any distinctive interaction save the one regular exchange between Sammy and George over the former's "early washup." Sammy's tendency was to crowd his washing up toward five o'clock, and it was George's concern to keep it from further creeping advance. After Ike's departure came Boo's arrival. Boo's was a striking personality productive of a change in topics of conversation to fill in the last hour of the long workday.

Themes. To put flesh, so to speak, on this interactional frame of "times," my work group had developed various "themes" of verbal interplay which had become standardized in their repetition. These topics of conversation ranged in quality from an extreme of nonsensical chatter to another extreme of serious discourse. Unlike the times, these themes flowed one into the other in no particular sequence of predictability. Serious conversation could suddenly melt into horseplay, and vice versa. In the middle of a serious discussion on the high cost of living, Ike might drop a weight behind the easily startled Sammy, or hit him over the head with a dusty paper sack. Interaction would immediately drop to a low comedy exchange of slaps, threats, guffaws, and disapprobations which would invariably include a ten-minute echolalia of "Ike is a bad man, a very bad man! George is a good daddy, a very fine man!" Or, on the other hand, a stream of such invidious comparisons as followed a surreptitious switching-off of Sammy's machine by the playful Ike might merge suddenly into a discussion of the pros and cons of saving for one's funeral.

"Kidding themes" were usually started by George or Ike, and Sammy was usually the butt of the joke. Sometimes Ike would have to "take it," seldom George. One favorite kidding theme involved Sammy's alleged receipt of $100 a month from his son. The points stressed were that Sammy did not have to work long hours, or did not have to work at all, because he had a son to support him. George would always point out that he sent money to his daughter; she did not send money to him. Sammy received occasional calls from his wife, and his claim that these calls were requests to shop for groceries on the way home were greeted with feigned disbelief. Sammy was ribbed for being closely watched, bossed, and henpecked by his wife, and the expression "Are you man or mouse?" became an echolalic utterance, used both in and out of the original context.

Ike, who shared his machine and the work scheduled for it with Boo, the night operator, came in for constant invidious comparison on the subject of output. The socially isolated Boo, who chose work rather than sleep on his lonely night shift, kept up a high level of performance, and George never tired of pointing this out to Ike. It so happened that Boo, an Arabian Moslem from Palestine [sic], had no use for Jews in general; and Ike, who was Jewish, had no use for Boo in particular. Whenever George would extol Boo's previous night's production, Ike would try to turn the conversation into a general discussion on the need for educating the Arabs. George, never permitting the development of serious discussion on this topic, would repeat a smirking warning, "You watch out for Boo! He's got a long knife!"

The "poom poom" theme was one that caused no sting. It would come up several times a day to be enjoyed as unbarbed fun by the three older clicker operators. Ike was usually the one to raise the question, "How many times you go poom poom last night?" The person questioned usually replied with claims of being "too old for poom poom." If this theme did develop a goat, it was I. When it was pointed out that I was a younger man, this provided further grist for the poom poom mill. I soon grew weary of this poom poom business, so dear to the hearts of the three old satyrs, and, knowing where the conversation would inevitably lead, winced whenever Ike brought up the subject.

I grew almost as sick of a kidding theme which developed from some personal information contributed during a serious conversation on property ownership and high taxes. I dropped a few remarks about about two acres of land which I owned in one of the western states, and from then on I had to listen to questions, advice, and general nonsensical comment in regard to "Danelly's farm."[10] This "farm" soon became stocked with horses, cows, pigs, chickens, ducks, and the various and sundry domesticated beasts so tunefully listed in "Old McDonald Had a Farm." George was a persistent offender with this theme. Where the others seemed to be mainly interested in statistics on livestock, crops, etc., George's teasing centered on a generous offering to help with the household chores while I worked in the fields. He would drone on, *ad nauseam,* "when I come to visit you, you will never have to worry about the housework, Danelly. I'll stay around the house when you go out to dig the potatoes and milk the cows, I'll stay in and peel potatoes and help your wife do the dishes." Danelly always found it difficult to change the subject on George, once the latter started to bear down on the farm theme.

Another kidding theme which developed out of serious discussion could be labeled "helping Danelly find a cheaper apartment." It became known to the group that Danelly had a pending housing problem, that he would need new quarters for his family when the permanent resident of his temporary summer dwelling returned from a vacation. This information engendered at first a great deal of sympathetic concern and, of course, advice on apartment hunting. Development into a kidding theme was immediately related to previous exchanges between Ike and George on the quality of their respective dwelling areas. Ike lived in "Lawndale," and George dwelt in the "Woodlawn" area. The new pattern featured the reading aloud of bogus "apartment for rent" ads in newspapers which were brought into the shop. Studying his paper at lunchtime, George would call out, "Here's an apartment for you, Danelly! Five rooms, stove heat, $20 a month, Lawndale Avenue!" Later, Ike would read from his paper, "Here's one! Six rooms, stove heat, dirt floor. $18.50 a month! At 55th and Woodlawn." Bantering would then go on in regard to the quality of housing or population in the two areas. The search for an apartment for Danelly was not successful.

Serious themes included the relating of major misfortunes suffered in the past by group members. George referred again and again to the loss, by fire, of his business establishment. Ike's chief complaints centered around a chronically ill wife who had undergone various operations and periods of hospital care. Ike spoke with discouragement of the expenses attendant upon hiring a housekeeper for himself and his children; he referred with disappointment and disgust to a teen-age son, an inept lad who "couldn't even fix his own lunch. He couldn't even make himself a sandwich!" Sammy's reminiscences centered on the loss of a flourishing business when he had to flee Europe ahead of Nazi invasion.

But all serious topics were not tales of woe. One favorite serious theme which was optimistic in tone could be called either "Danelly's future" or "getting Danelly a better job." It was known that I had been attending "college," the magic door to opportunity, although my specific course of study remained somewhat obscure. Suggestions poured forth on good lines of work to get into, and these suggestions were backed with accounts of friends, and friends of friends, who had made good via the academic route. My answer to the expected question, "Why are you working here?" always stressed the "lots of overtime" feature, and this explanation seemed to suffice for short-range goals.

There was one theme of especially solemn import, the "professor theme." This theme might also be termed "George's daughter's marriage theme"; for the recent marriage of George's only child was inextricably bound up with George's connection with higher learning. The daughter had married the son of a professor who instructed in one of the local colleges. This professor theme was not in the strictest sense a conversation piece; when the subject came up, George did all the talking. The two Jewish operatives remained silent as they listened with deep respect, if not actual awe, to George's accounts of the Big Wedding which, including the wedding pictures, entailed an expense of $1000. It was monologue, but there was listening, there was communication, the sacred communication of a temple, when George told of going for Sunday afternoon walks on the Midway with the professor, or of joining the professor for a Sunday dinner. Whenever he spoke of the professor, his daughter, the wedding, or even of the new son-in-law, who remained for the most part in the background, a sort of incidental like the wedding cake, George was complete master of the interaction. His manner, in speaking to the rank-and-file of clicker operators, was indeed that of master deigning to notice his underlings. I came to the conclusion that it was the professor connection, not the straw-boss-ship or the extra nickel an hour, which provided the fount of George's superior status in the group.

If the professor theme may be regarded as the cream of verbal interaction, the "chatter themes" should be classed as the dregs. The chatter themes were hardly themes at all; perhaps they should be labeled "verbal states," or "oral autisms." Some were of doubtful status as communication; they were like the howl or cry of an animal responding to its own physiological state. They were exclamations, ejaculations, snatches of song or doggerel, talkings-to-oneself, mutterings. Their classification as themes would rest on their repetitive character. They were echolalic utterances, repeated over and over. An already mentioned example would be Sammy's repetition of "George is a good daddy, a very fine man! Ike is a bad man, a very bad man!" Also, Sammy's repetition of "Don't bother me! Can't you see I'm busy? I'm a very busy man!" for ten minutes after Ike had dropped a weight behind him would fit the classification. Ike would shout "Mamariba!" at intervals between repetition of bits of verse, such as:

Mama on the bed,
Papa on the floor,
Baby in the crib
Says giver some more!

Sometimes the three operators would pick up one of these simple chatterings in a sort of chorus. "Are you man or mouse? I ask you, are you man or mouse?" was a favorite of this type.

So initial discouragement with the meagerness of social interaction I now recognized as due to lack of observation. The interaction was there, in constant flow. It captured attention and held interest to make the long day pass. The twelve hours of "click,—move die,—click,—move die" became as easy to endure as eight hours of varied activity in the oil fields or eight hours of playing the piecework game in a machine shop. The "beast of boredom" was gentled to the harmlessness of a kitten.

Black Friday: Disintegration of the Group.   But all this was before "Black Friday." Events of that dark day shattered the edifice of interaction, its framework of times and mosaic of themes, and reduced the work situation to a state of social atomization and machine-tending drudgery. The explosive element was introduced deliberately, but without prevision of its consequences.

On Black Friday, Sammy was not present; he was on vacation. There was no peach time that morning, of course, and no banana time. But George and Ike held their coffee time, as usual, and a steady flow of themes was filling the morning quite adequately. It seemed like a normal day in the making, at least one which was going to meet the somewhat reduced expectations created by Sammy's absence.

Suddenly I was possessed of an inspiration for modification of the professor theme. When the idea struck, I was working at Sammy's machine, clicking out leather parts for billfolds. It was not difficult to get the attention of close neighbor Ike to suggest *sotto voce,* "Why don't you tell him you saw the professor teaching in a barber college on Madison Street?...Make it near Halsted Street."

Ike thought this one over for a few minutes, and caught the vision of its possibilities. After an interval of steady application to his clicking, he informed the unsuspecting George of his near West Side discovery; he had seen the professor busy at his instructing in a barber college in the lower reaches of Hobohemia.

George reacted to this announcement with stony silence. The burden of questioning Ike for further details on his discovery fell upon me. Ike had not elaborated his story very much before we realized that the show was not going over. George kept getting redder in the face, and

more tight-lipped; he slammed into his clicking with increased vigor. I
made one last weak attempt to keep the play on the road by remarking
that barber colleges paid pretty well. George turned to hiss at me,
"You'll have to go to Kankakee with Ike!" I dropped the subject. Ike
whispered to me, "George is sore!"

George was indeed sore. He didn't say another word the rest of the
morning. There was no conversation at lunchtime, nor was there any
after lunch. A pall of silence had fallen over the clicker room. Fish time
fell a casualty. George did not touch the coke I brought for him. A very
long, very dreary afternoon dragged on. Finally, after Ike left for
home, George broke the silence to reveal his feelings to me:

> Ike acts like a five-year-old, not a man! He doesn't even have the
> respect of the niggers. But he's got to act like a man around here!
> He's always fooling around! I'm going to stop that! I'm going to
> show him his place!...Jews will ruin you, if you let them. I don't care
> if he sings, but the first time he mentions my name, I'm going to
> shut him up! It's always "Meet Mr. Papeatis! George is a good
> daddy!" And all that. He's paid to work! If he doesn't work, I'm
> going to tell Joe! [The superintendent.]

Then came a succession of dismal workdays devoid of times and
barren of themes. Ike did not sing, nor did he recite bawdy verse. The
shop songbird was caught in the grip of icy winter. What meager
communication there was took a sequence of patterns which proved
interesting only in retrospect.

For three days, George would not speak to Ike. Ike made several
weak attempts to break the wall of silence which George had put
between them, but George did not respond; it was as if he did not hear.
George would speak to me, on infrequent occasions, and so would Ike.
They did not speak to each other.

On the third day George advised me of his new communication
policy, designed for dealing with Ike, and for Sammy, too, when the
latter returned to work. Interaction was now on a "strictly business"
basis, with emphasis to be placed on raising the level of shop output.
The effect of this new policy on production remained indeterminate.
Before the fourth day had ended, George got carried away by his
narrowed interests to the point of making sarcastic remarks about the
poor work performances of the absent Sammy. Although addressed to
me, these caustic depreciations were obviously for the benefit of Ike.
Later in the day Ike spoke to me, for George's benefit, of Sammy's

outstanding ability to turn out billfold parts. For the next four days, the prevailing silence of the shop was occasionally broken by either harsh criticism or fulsome praise of Sammy's outstanding workmanship. I did not risk replying to either impeachment or panegyric for fear of involvement in further situational deteriorations.

Twelve-hour days were creeping again at snail's pace. The strictly business communications were of no help, and the sporadic bursts of distaste or enthusiasm for Sammy's clicking ability helped very little. With the return of boredom, came a return of fatigue. My legs tired as the afternoons dragged on, and I became engaged in conscious efforts to rest one by shifting my weight to the other. I would pause in my work to stare through the barred windows at the grimy brick wall across the alley; and, turning my head. I would notice that Ike was staring at the wall too. George would do very little work after Ike left the shop at night. He would sit in a chair and complain of weariness and sore feet.

In desperation, I fell back on my game of work, my blues and greens and whites, my ovals and trapezoids, and my scraping the block. I came to surpass Boo, the energetic night worker, in volume of output. George referred to me as a "day Boo" (day-shift Boo) and suggested that I "keep" Sammy's machine. I managed to avoid this promotion, and consequent estrangement with Sammy, by pleading attachment to my own machine.

When Sammy returned to work, discovery of the cleavage between George and Ike left him stunned. "They were the best of friends!" he said to me in bewilderment.

George now offered Sammy direct, savage criticisms of his work. For several days the good-natured Sammy endured these verbal aggressions without losing his temper; but when George shouted at him "You work like a preacher!" Sammy became very angry, indeed. I had a few anxious moments when I thought that the two old friends were going to come to blows.

Then, thirteen days after Black Friday, came an abrupt change in the pattern of interaction. George and Ike spoke to each other again, in friendly conversation:

I noticed Ike talking to George after lunch. The two had newspapers of fish at George's cabinet. Ike was excited; he said, "I'll pull up a chair!" The two ate for ten minutes....It seems that they went up to the 22nd Street Exchange together during lunch period to cash pay checks.

That afternoon Ike and Sammy started to play again, and Ike burst once more into song. Old themes reappeared as suddenly as the desert flowers in spring. At first, George managed to maintain some show of the dignity of superordination. When Ike started to sing snatches of "You Are My Sunshine," George suggested that he get "more production." Then Ike backed up George in pressuring Sammy for more production. Sammy turned this exhortation into low comedy by calling Ike a "slave driver" and by shouting over and over again, "Don't bother me! I'm a busy man!" On one occasion, as if almost overcome with joy and excitement, Sammy cried out, "Don't bother me! I'll tell Rothman! [the company president] I'll tell the union! Don't mention my name! I hate you!"

I knew that George was definitely back into the spirit of the thing when he called to Sammy, "Are you man or mouse?" He kept up the "man or mouse" chatter for some time.

George was for a time reluctant to accept fruit when it was offered to him, and he did not make a final capitulation to coke until five days after renewal of the fun and fooling. Strictly speaking, there never was a return to banana time, peach time, or window time. However, the sharing and snitching of fruit did go on once more, and the window in front of Sammy's machine played a more prominent part than ever in the renaissance of horseplay in the clicker room. In fact, the "rush to the window" became an integral part of increasingly complex themes and repeated sequences of interaction. This window rushing became especially bound up with new developments which featured what may be termed the "anal gesture."[11] Introduced by Ike, and given backing by an enthusiastic, very playful George, the anal gesture became a key component of fun and fooling during the remaining weeks of my stay in the shop:

> Ike broke wind, and put his head in his hand on the block as Sammy grabbed a rod and made a mock rush to open the window. He beat Ike on the head, and George threw some water on him, playfully. In came the Negro head of the Leather Department; he remarked jokingly that we should take out the machines and make a playroom out of the shop.

Of course, George's demand for greater production was metamorphized into horseplay. His shout of "Production please!" became a chatter theme to accompany the varied antics of Ike and Sammy.

The professor theme was dropped completely. George never again mentioned his Sunday walks on the Midway with the professor.

Conclusions. Speculative assessment of the possible significance of my observations on informal interaction in the clicking room may be set forth in a series of general statements.

Practical Application. First, in regard to possible practical application to problems of industrial management, these observations seem to support the generally accepted notion that one key source of job satisfaction lies in the informal interaction shared by members of a work group. In the clicking-room situation the spontaneous development of a patterned combination of horseplay, serious conversation, and frequent sharing of food and drink reduced the monotony of simple, repetitive operations to the point where a regular schedule of long work days became livable. This kind of group interplay may be termed "consumatory" in the sense indicated by Dewey, when he makes a basic distinction between "instrumental" and "consumatory" communication.[12] The enjoyment of communication "for its own sake" as "mere sociabilities," as "free, aimless social intercourse," brings job satisfaction, at least job endurance, to work situations largely bereft of creative experience.

In regard to another managerial concern, employee productivity, any appraisal of the influence of group interaction upon clicking-room output could be no more than roughly impressionistic. I obtained no evidence to warrant a claim that banana time, or any of its accompaniments in consumatory interaction, boosted production. To the contrary, my diary recordings express an occasional perplexity in the form of "How does this company manage to stay in business?" However, I did not obtain sufficient evidence to indicate that, under the prevailing conditions of laissez-faire management, the output of our group would have been more impressive if the playful cavorting of three middle-aged gentlemen about the barred windows had never been. As far as achievement of managerial goals is concerned, the most that could be suggested is that leavening the deadly boredom of individualized work routines with a concurrent flow of group festivities had a negative effect on turnover. I left the group, with sad reluctance, under the pressure of strong urgings to accept a research fellowship which would involve no factory toil. My fellow clickers stayed with their machines to carry on their labors in the spirit of banana time.

Theoretical Considerations.   Secondly, possible contribution to ongoing sociological inquiry into the behavior of small groups, in general, and factory work groups, in particular, may lie in one or more of the following ideational products of my clicking-room experience:

1.   In their day-long confinement together in a small room spatially and socially isolated from other work areas of the factory, the Clicking Department employees found themselves ecologically situated for development of a "natural" group. Such a development did take place; from worker intercommunications did emerge the full-blown sociocultural system of consumatory interactions which I came to share, observe, and record in the process of my socialization.

2.   These interactions had a content which could be abstracted from the total existential flow of observable doings and sayings for labeling and objective consideration. That is, they represented a distinctive subculture, with its recurring patterns of reciprocal influencings which I have described as times and themes.

3.   From these interactions may also be abstracted a social structure of statuses and roles. This structure may be discerned in the carrying out of the various informal activities which provide the content of the subculture of the group. The times and themes were performed with a system of roles which formed a sort of pecking hierarchy. Horseplay had its initiators and its victims, its amplifiers and its chorus; kidding had its attackers and attacked, its least attacked and its most attacked, its ready acceptors of attack and its strong resistors to attack. The fun went on with the participation of all, but within the controlling frame of status, a matter of who can say or do what to whom and get away with it.

4.   In both cultural content and the social structure of clicker group interaction could be seen the permeation of influences which flowed from the various multiple group memberships of the participants. Past and present "other-group" experiences or anticipated "outside" social connections provided significant materials for the building of themes and for the establishment and maintenance of status and role relationships. The impact of reference group affiliations on clicking-room interaction was notably revealed in the sacred, status-conferring expression of the professor theme. This impact was brought into very sharp focus in developments which followed my attempt to degrade the topic, and correlatively, to demote George.

5.   Stability of the clicking-room social system was never threatened by immediate outside pressures. Ours was not an instrumental group,

subject to disintegration in a losing struggle against environmental obstacles or oppositions. It was not striving for corporate goals; nor was it faced with the enmity of other groups. It was strictly a consumatory group, devoted to the maintenance of patterns of self-entertainment. Under existing conditions, disruption of unity could come only from within.

Potentials for breakdown were endemic in the interpersonal interactions involved in conducting the group's activities. Patterns of fun and fooling had developed within a matrix of frustration. Tensions born of long hours of relatively meaningless work were released in the mock aggressions of horseplay. In the recurrent attack, defense, and counterattack there continually lurked the possibility that words or gestures harmless in conscious intent might cross the subtle boundary of accepted, playful aggression to be perceived as real assault. While such an occurrence might incur displeasure no more lasting than necessary for the quick clarification or creation of kidding norms, it might also spark a charge of hostility sufficient to disorganize the group.

A contributory potential for breakdown from within lay in the dissimilar "other group" experiences of the operators. These other-group affiliations and identifications could provide differences in tastes and sensitivities, including appreciation of humor, differences which could make maintenance of consensus in regard to kidding norms a hazardous process of trial-and-error adjustments.

6. The risk involved in this trial-and-error determination of consensus on fun and fooling in a touchy situation of frustration—mock aggression—was made evident when I attempted to introduce alterations in the professor theme. The group disintegrated, *instanter.* That is, there was an abrupt cessation of the interactions which constituted our groupness. Although both George and I were solidly linked in other-group affiliations with the higher learning, there was not enough agreement in our attitudes toward university professors to prevent the interactional development which shattered our factory play group. George perceived my offered alterations as a real attack, and he responded with strong hostility directed against Ike, the perceived assailant, and Sammy, a fellow traveler.

My innovations, if accepted, would have lowered the tone of the sacred professor theme, if not to "Stay Away From Baby" ribaldry, then at least to the verbal slapstick level of "finding Danelly an apartment." Such a downgrading of George's reference group would, in turn, have downgraded George. His status in the shop group hinged largely upon his claimed relations with the professor.

7. Integration of our group was fully restored after a series of changes in the patterning and quality of clicking-room interaction. It might be said that reintegration took place *in* these changes, that the series was a progressive one of step-by-step improvement in relations, that reequilibration was in process during the three weeks that passed between initial communication collapse and complete return to "normal" interaction.

The cycle of loss and recovery of equilibrium may be crudely charted according to the following sequence of phases: *(a)* the stony silence of "not speaking"; *(b)* the confining of communication to formal matters connected with work routines; *(c)* the return of informal give-and-take in the form of harshly sarcastic kidding, mainly on the subject of work performance, addressed to a neutral go-between for the "benefit" of the object of aggression; *(d)* highly emotional direct attack, and counterattack, in the form of criticism and defense of work performance; *(e)* a sudden rapprochement expressed in serious, dignified, but friendly conversation; *(f)* return to informal interaction in the form of mutually enjoyed mock aggression; *(g)* return to informal interaction in the form of regular patterns of sharing food and drink.

The group had disintegrated when George withdrew from participation; and, since the rest of us were at all times ready for rapprochement, reintegration was dependent upon his "return." Therefore, each change of phase in interaction on the road to recovery could be said to represent an increment of return on George's part. Or, conversely, each phase could represent an increment of reacceptance of punished deviants. Perhaps more generally applicable to description of a variety of reunion situations would be conceptualization of the phase changes as increments of reassociation without an atomistic differentiation of the "movements" of individuals.

8. To point out that George played a key role in this particular case of reequilibration is not to suggest that the homeostatic controls of a social system may be located in a type of role or in a patterning or role relationships. Such controls could be but partially described in terms of human interaction; they would be functional to the total configuration of conditions within the field of influence. The automatic controls of a mechanical system operate as such only under certain achieved and controlled conditions. The human body recovers from disease when conditions for such homeostasis are "right." The clicking-room group regained equilibrium under certain undetermined conditions. One of a

number of other possible outcomes could have developed had conditions not been favorable for recovery.

For purposes of illustration, and from reflection on the case, I would consider the following as possibly necessary conditions for reintegration of our group: *(a)* Continued monotony of work operations; *(b)* Continued lack of a comparatively adequate substitute for the fun and fooling release from work tensions; *(c)* Inability of the operatives to escape from the work situation or from each other, within the work situation. George could not fire Ike or Sammy to remove them from his presence, and it would have been difficult for the three middle-aged men to find other jobs if they were to quit the shop. Shop space was small, and the machines close together. Like a submarine crew, they had to "live together"; *(d)* Lack of conflicting definitions of the situation after Ike's perception of George's reaction to the "barber college" attack. George's anger and his punishment of the offenders was perceived as justified; *(e)* Lack of introduction of new issues or causes which might have carried justification for new attacks and counterattacks, thus leading interaction into a spiral of conflict and crystallization of conflict norms. For instance, had George reported his offenders to the superintendent for their poor work performance; had he, in his anger, committed some offense which would have led to reporting of a grievance to local union officials; had he made his anti-Semitic remarks in the presence of Ike or Sammy, or had I relayed these remarks to them; had I tried to "take over" Sammy's machine, as George had urged; then the interaction outcome might have been permanent disintegration of the group.

9.   Whether or not the particular patterning of interactional change previously noted is somehow typical of a "reequilibration process" is not a major question here. My purpose in discriminating the seven changes is primarily to suggest that reequilibration, when it does occur, may be described in observable phases and that the emergence of each succeeding phase should be dependent upon the configuration of conditions of the preceding one. Alternative eventual outcomes may change in their probabilities, as the phases succeed each other, just as prognosis for recovery in sickness may change as the disease changes.

10.   Finally, discrimination of phase changes in social process may have practical as well as scientific value. Trained and skillful administrators might follow the practice in medicine of introducing aids to reequilibration when diagnosis shows that they are needed.

Notes

1. Charles R. Walker and Robert H. Guest, *The Man on the Assembly Line* (Cambridge, Mass.: Harvard University Press, 1952).

2. *Ibid.,* p. 77.

3. *Ibid.,* p. 68.

4. Donald F. Roy, "Work Satisfaction and Social Reward in Quota Achievement: An Analysis of Piecework Incentive," *American Sociological Review,* **18:** 507–514 (October 1953).

5. All names used are fictitious.

6. Henri de Man, *The Psychology of Socialism* (New York: Holt, Rinehart & Winston, 1927), pp. 80–81.

7. *Ibid.,* p. 81.

8. Roy, *op. cit.*

9. Lucille Milner, *Education of An American Liberal* (New York: Horizon Press, 1954), p. 97.

10. This spelling is the closest I can come to the appellation given me in George's broken English and adopted by other members of the group.

11. I have been puzzled to note widespread appreciation of this gesture in the "consumatory" communication of the working men of this nation. For the present I leave it to clinical psychologists to account for the nature and pervasiveness of this social bond and confine myself to joining offended readers in the hope that some-day our industrial workers will achieve such a level of refinement in thought and action that their behavior will be no more distressing to us than that of the college students who fill our our questionnaires or form groups for laboratory experimentation.

12. John Dewey, *Experience and Nature* (Chicago: Open Court Publishing, 1925), pp. 202–206.

II. SELECTED STUDIES OF GROUP–SCALE INTERACTION STRATEGIES

The notation following each entry indicates the section of Chapter 10 in which it is capsulized.

Dalton, Melville, "Power Struggles in the Line," in *Men Who Manage* (New York: Wiley, 1959), pp. 52–71. (III.A.2)

Davis, Fred, "The Family of the Polio Child: Some Problems of Identity," in his *Illness, Interaction and the Self* (Belmont, Calif.: Wadsworth, 1972), pp. 108–115. (III.A.4)

Slosar, John A., Jr., "Ogre, Bandit, and Operating Employee: The Problems and Adaptations of the Metropolitan Bus Driver," *Urban Life and Culture* **1:** 339–362 (January 1973). (III.A.3)

Zurcher, Louis A., David Scnenschein, and Eric L. Metzner, "The Hasher: A Study of Role Conflict, *Social Forces* **44:** 505–514 (June 1966). (III.B.1)

CHAPTER FIFTEEN

Organization-Scale Inquiries

A strategic and naturalistic imagery of organizations has been propounded and promoted most articulately by sociologist Philip Selznick and his students. An important portion of the materials reviewed in Chapter 11 were, indeed, inspired by Selznick. Burton Clark's study of community colleges, reprinted here, well exemplifies the Selznickian genre and the ideal-typical features of inquiry elaborated in Part I.

I. THE SITUATION OF ENDS–MEANS DISJUNCTURE AND STRATEGIES OF THE REORIENTING PROCESS

The "Cooling Out" Function in Higher Education

Burton R. Clark

Reprinted from *The American Journal of Sociology*, **65:** 569–576 (May 1960) by permission of the author and the University of Chicago Press. [Copyright 1960 by the University of Chicago Press] Revised and extended version of paper read at the 54th Annual Meeting of the American Sociological Association, Chicago, September 3–5, 1959. The author is indebted to Erving Goffman and Martin A. Trow for criticism and to Sheldon Messinger for extended conceptual and editorial comment.

A major problem of democratic society is inconsistency between encouragement to achieve and the realities of limited opportunity. Democracy asks individuals to act as if social mobility were universally possible; status is to be won by individual effort, and rewards are to accrue to those who try. But democratic societies also need selective training institutions, and hierarchical work organizations permit increasingly fewer persons to succeed at ascending levels. Situations of opportunity are also situations of denial and failure. Thus democratic societies need not only to motivate achievement but also to mollify those denied it in order to sustain motivation in the face of disappointment and to deflect resentment. In the modern mass democracy, with its large-scale organization, elaborated ideologies of equal access and participation, and minimal commitment to social origin as a basis for status, the task become critical.

The problem of blocked opportunity has been approached sociologically through means-ends analysis. Merton and others have called attention to the phenomenon of dissociation between culturally instilled goals and institutionally provided means of realization; discrepancy between ends and means is seen as a basic social source of individual frustration and recalcitrance.[1] We shall here extend means-ends analysis in another direction, to the responses of organized groups to means-ends disparities, in particular focusing attention on ameliorative processes that lessen the strains of dissociation. We shall do so by analyzing the most prevalent type of dissociation between aspirations and avenues in American education, specifying the structure and processes that reduce the stress of structural disparity and individual denial. Certain components of American higher education perform what may be called the cooling-out function,[2] and it is to these that attention will be drawn.

The Ends-Means Disjuncture. In American higher education the aspirations of the multitude are encouraged by "open-door" admission to public-supported colleges. The means of moving upward in status and of maintaining high status now include some years in college, and a college education is a prerequisite of the better positions in business and the professions. The trend is toward an ever tighter connection between higher education and higher occupations, as increased specialization and professionalization insure that more persons will need more preparation. The high school graduate seeing college as essential to success, will seek to enter some college, regardless of his record in high school.

A second and allied source of public interest in unlimited entry into college is the ideology of equal opportunity.[3] Strictly interpreted, equality of opportunity means selection according to ability, without regard to extraneous considerations. Popularly interpreted, however, equal opportunity in obtaining a college education is widely taken to mean unlimited access to some form of college: in California, for example, state educational authorities maintain that high school graduates who cannot qualify for the state university or state college should still have the "opportunity of attending a publicly supported institution of higher education," this being "an essential part of the state's goal of guaranteeing equal educational opportunities to all its citizens."[4] To deny access to college is then to deny equal opportunity. Higher education should make a seat available without judgment on past performance.

Many other features of current American life encourage college-going. School officials are reluctant to establish early critical hurdles for the young, as is done in Europe. With little enforced screening in the precollege years, vocational choice and educational selection are postponed to the college years or later. In addition, the United States, a wealthy country, is readily supporting a large complex of colleges, and its expanding economy requires more specialists. Recently, a national concern that manpower be fully utilized has encouraged the extending of college training to more and different kinds of students. Going to college is also in some segments of society the thing to do; as a last resort, it is more attractive than the army or a job. Thus ethical and practical urges together encourage the high school graduate to believe that college is both a necessity and a right; similarly, parents and elected officials incline toward legislation and admission practices that insure entry for large numbers; and educational authorities find the need and justification for easy admission.

Even where pressures have been decisive in widening admission policy, however, the system of higher education has continued to be shaped partly by other interests. The practices of public colleges are influenced by the academic personnel, the organizational requirements of colleges, and external pressures other than those behind the open door. Standards of performance and graduation are maintained. A commitment to standards is encouraged by a set of values in which the status of a college, as defined by academicians and a large body of educated laymen, is closely linked to the perceived quality of faculty,

student body, and curriculum. The raising of standards is supported by
the faculty's desire to work with promising students and to enjoy
membership in an enterprise of reputed quality—college authorities
find low standards and poor students a handicap in competing with
other colleges for such resources as able faculty as well as for academic
status. The wish is widespread that college education be of the highest
quality for the preparation of leaders in public affairs, business, and
the professions. In brief, the institutional means of the students' progress toward college graduation and subsequent goals are shaped in
large part by a commitment to quality embodied in college staffs,
traditions, and images.

The conflict between open-door admission and performance of high
quality often means a wide discrepancy between the hopes of entering
students and the means of their realization. Students who pursue ends
for which a college education is required but who have little academic
ability gain admission into colleges only to encounter standards of
performance they cannot meet. As a result, while some students of low
promise are successful, for large numbers failure is inevitable and
structured. The denial is delayed, taking place within the college instead
of at the edge of the system. It requires that many colleges handle the
student who intends to complete college and has been allowed to
become involved but whose destiny is to fail.

Responses To Disjuncture. What is done with the student whose
destiny will normally be early termination? One answer is unequivocal
dismissal. This "hard" response is found in the state university that
bows to pressure for broad admission but then protects standards by
heavy drop-out. In the first year it weeds out many of the incompetent,
who may number a third or more of the entering class.[5] The response
of the college is hard in that failure is clearly defined as such. Failure is
public; the student often returns home. This abrupt change in status
and in access to the means of achievement may occur simultaneously in
a large college or university for hundreds, and sometimes thousands,
of students after the first semester and at the end of the freshman year.
The delayed denial is often viewed on the outside as heartless, a
slaughter of the innocents.[6] This excites public pressure and anxiety,
and apparently the practice cannot be extended indefinitely as the
demand for admission to college increases.

A second answer is to sidetrack unpromising students rather than
have them fail. This is the "soft" response: never to dismiss a student
but to provide him with an alternative. One form of it in some state

universities is the detour to an extension division or a general college, which has the advantage of appearing not very different from the main road. Sometimes "easy" fields of study, such as education, business administration, and social science, are used as alternatives to dismissal.[7] The major form of the soft response is not found in the four-year college or university, however, but in the college that specializes in handling students who will soon be leaving—typically, the two-year public junior college.

In most states where the two-year college is a part of higher education, the students likely to be caught in the means-ends disjuncture are assigned to it in large numbers. In California, where there are over sixty public two-year colleges in a diversified system that includes the state university and numerous four-year state colleges, the junior college is unselective in admissions and by law, custom, and self-conception accepts all who wish to enter.[8] It is tuition-free, local, and under local control. Most of its entering students want to try for the baccalaureate degree, transferring to a "senior" college after one or two years. About two-thirds of the students in the junior colleges of the state are in programs that permit transferring; but, of these, only about one-third actually transfer to a four-year college.[9] The remainder, or two out of three of the professed transfer students, are "latent terminal students": their announced intention and program of study entails four years of college, but in reality their work terminates in the junior college. Constituting about half of all the students in the California junior colleges, and somewhere between one-third and one-half of junior college students nationally,[10] these students cannot be ignored by the colleges. Understanding their careers is important to understanding modern higher education.

The Reorienting Process.   This type of student in the junior college is handled by being moved out of a transfer major to a one- or two-year program of vocational, business, or semiprofessional training. This calls for the relinquishing of his original intention and he is induced to accept a substitute that has lower status in both the college and society in general.

In one junior college[11] the initial move in a cooling-out process is preentrance testing: low scores on achievement tests lead poorly qualified students into remedial classes. Assignment to remedial work casts doubt and slows the student's movement into bona fide transfer courses. The remedial courses are, in effect, a subcollege. The student's achievement scores are made part of a counseling folder that will become increasingly significant to him. An objective record of ability and performance begins to accumulate.

A second step is a counseling interview before the beginning of the first semester, and before all subsequent semesters for returning students. "At this interview the counselor assists the student to choose the proper courses in the light of his objective, his test scores, the high school record, and test records from his previous schools."[12] Assistance in choosing "the proper courses" is gentle at first. Of the common case of the student who wants to be an engineer but who is not a promising candidate, a counselor said: "I never openly countermand his choice, but edge him toward a terminal program by gradually laying out the facts of life." Counselors may become more severe later when grades provide a talking point and when the student knows that he is in trouble. In the earlier counseling the desire of the student has much weight; the counselor limits himself to giving advice and stating the probability of success. The advice is entered in the counseling record that shadows the student.

A third and major step in reorienting the latent terminal student is a special course entitled "Orientation to College," mandatory for entering students. All sections of it are taught by teacher-counselors who comprise the counseling staff, and one of its purposes is "to assist students in evaluating their own abilities, interests, and aptitudes; in assaying their vocational choices in light of this evaluation; and in making educational plans to implement their choices." A major section of it takes up vocational planning; vocational tests are given at a time when opportunities and requirements in various fields of work are discussed. The tests include the "Lee Thorpe Interest Inventory" ("given to all students for motivating a self-appraisal of vocational choice") and the "Strong Interest Inventory" ("for all who are undecided about choice or who show disparity between accomplishment and vocational choice"). Mechanical and clerical aptitude tests are taken by all. The aptitudes are directly related to the college's terminal programs, with special tests, such as a pre-engineering ability test, being given according to need. Then an "occupational paper is required of all students for their chosen occupation"; in it the student writes on the required training and education and makes a "self-appraisal of fitness."

Tests and papers are then used in class discussion and counseling interviews, in which the students themselves arrange and work with a counselor's folder and a student test profile and, in so doing, are repeatedly confronted by the accumulating evidence—the test scores, course grades, recommendations of teachers and counselors. This procedure is intended to heighten self-awareness of capacity in relation to choice and hence to strike particularly at the latent terminal student. The teacher-counselors are urged constantly to "be alert to the problem of unrealistic vocational goals" and to "help students to accept their limitations and strive for success in other worthwhile objectives that are within their grasp." The orientation class was considered a good place "to talk tough," to explain in an *impersonal* way the facts of life for the overambitious student. Talking tough to a whole group is part of a soft treatment of the individual.

Following the vocational counseling, the orientation course turns to "building an educational program," to study of the requirements for graduation of the college in transfer and terminal curriculum, and to planning of a four-semester program. The students also become acquainted with the requirements of the colleges to which they hope to transfer, here contemplating additional hurdles such as the entrance examinations of other colleges. Again, the hard facts of the road ahead are brought to bear on self-appraisal.

If he wishes, the latent terminal student may ignore the counselor's advice and the test scores. While in the counseling class, he is also in other courses, and he can wait to see what happens. Adverse counseling advice and poor test scores may not shut off his hope of completing college; when this is the case, the deterrent will be encountered in the regular classes. Here the student is divested of expectations, lingering from high school, that he will automatically pass and, hopefully, automatically be transferred. Then, receiving low grades, he is thrown back into the counseling orbit, a fourth step in his reorientation and a move justified by his actual accomplishment. The following indicates the nature of the referral system:

> *Need for Improvement Notices* are issued by instructors to students who are doing unsatisfactory work. The carbon copy of the notice is given to the counselor who will be available for conference with the student. The responsibility lies with the student to see his counselor. However, experience shows that some counselees are unable to be sufficiently self-directive to seek aid. The counselor should, in such cases, send for the student, using the Request for Conference blank. If the student fails to respond to the Request for Conference slip,

this may become a disciplinary matter and should be referred to the deans.

After a conference has been held, the Need for Improvement notices are filed in the student's folder. *This may be important* in case of complaint concerning the fairness of a final grade.[13]

This directs the student to more advice and self-assessment, as soon and as often as he has classroom difficulty. The carbon-copy routine makes it certain that, if he does not seek advice, advice will seek him. The paper work and bureaucratic procedure have the purpose of recording referral and advice in black and white, where they may later be appealed to impersonally. As put in an unpublished report of the college, the overaspiring student and the one who seems to be in the wrong program require "skillful and delicate handling. An accumulation of pertinent factual information may serve to fortify the objectivity of the student-counselor relationship." While the counselor advises delicately and patiently, but persistently, the student is confronted with the record with increasing frequency.

A fifth step, one necessary for many in the throes of discouragement, is probation: "Students [whose] grade point averages fall below 2.0 [C] in any semester will, upon recommendation by the Scholarship Committee, be placed on probationary standing." A second failure places the student on second probation, and a third may mean that he will be advised to withdraw from the college altogether. The procedure is not designed to rid the college of a large number of students, for they may continue on probation for three consecutive semesters; its purpose is not to provide a status halfway out of the college but to "assist the student to seek an objective (major field) at a level on which he can succeed."[14] An important effect of probation is its slow killing-off of the lingering hopes of the most stubborn latent terminal students. A "transfer student" must have a C average to receive the Associate in Arts (a two-year degree) offered by the junior college, but no minimum average is set for terminal students. More important, four-year colleges require a C average or higher for the transfer student. Thus probationary status is the final blow to hopes of transferring and, indeed, even to graduating from the junior college under a transfer-student label. The point is reached where the student must permit himself to be reclassified or else drop out. In this college, 30 percent of the students enrolled at the end of the spring semester,

1955–56, who returned the following fall were on probation; three out of four of these were transfer students in name.[15]

This sequence of procedures is a specific process of cooling out;[16] its effect, at the best, is to let down hopes gently and unexplosively. Through it students who are failing or barely passing find their occupational and academic future being redefined. Along the way, teacher-counselors urge the latent terminal student to give up his plan of transferring and stand ready to console him in accepting a terminal curriculum. The drawn-out denial when it is effective is in place of a personal, hard "No"; instead, the student is brought to realize, finally, that it is best to ease himself out of the competition to transfer.

Cooling Out Features.   In the cooling-out process in the junior college are several features which are likely to be found in other settings where failure or denial is the effect of a structured discrepancy between ends and means, the responsible operatives or "coolers" cannot leave the scene or hide their identities, and the disappointment is threatening in some way to those responsible for it. At work and in training institutions this is common. The features are:

1. Alternative Achievement.   Substitute avenues may be made to appear not too different from what is given up, particularly as to status. The person destined to be denied or who fails is invited to interpret the second effort as more appropriate to his particular talent and is made to see that it will be the less frustrating. Here one does not fail but rectifies a mistake. The substitute status reflects less unfavorably on personal capacity than does being dismissed and forced to leave the scene. The terminal student in the junior college may appear not very different from the transfer student—an "engineering aide," for example, instead of an "engineer"—and to be proceeding to something with a status of its own. Failure in college can be treated as if it did not happen; so, too, can poor performance in industry.[17]

2. Gradual disengagement.   By a gradual series of steps, movement to a goal may be stalled, self-assessment encouraged, and evidence produced of performance. This leads toward the available alternatives at little cost. It also keeps the person in a counseling milieu in which advice is furnished, whether actively sought or not. Compared with the original hopes, however, it is a deteriorating situation. If the individual does not give up peacefully, he will be in trouble.

3. Objective denial.   Reorientation is, finally, confrontation by the facts. A record of poor performance helps to detach the organization and its agents from the emotional aspects of the cooling-out work. In a sense, the overaspiring student in the junior college confronts himself, as he lives with the accumulating evidence, instead of the organization. The college offers opportunity; it is the record that forces denial. Record-keeping and other bureaucratic procedures appeal to universal criteria and reduce the influence of personal ties, and the personnel are thereby protected. Modern personnel record-keeping, in general, has the function of documenting denial.

4. Agents of consolation.   Counselors are available who are patient with the overambitious and who work to change their intentions. They believe in the value of the alternative careers, though of lower social status, and are practiced in consoling. In college and in other settings counseling is to reduce aspiration as well as to define and to help fulfil it. The teacher-counselor in the "soft" junior college is in contrast to the scholar in the "hard" college who simply gives a low grade to the failing student.

5. Avoidance of Standards.   A cooling-out process avoids appealing to standards that are ambiguous to begin with. While a "hard" attitude toward failure generally allows a single set of criteria, a "soft" treatment assumes that many kinds of ability are valuable, each in its place. Proper classification and placement are then paramount, while standards become relative.

Importance of Concealment.   For an organization and its agents one dilemma of a cooling-out role is that it must be kept reasonably away from public scrutiny and not clearly perceived or understood by prospective clientele. Should it become obvious, the organization's ability to perform it would be impaired. If high school seniors and their families were to define the junior college as a place which diverts college-bound students, a probable consequence would be a turning-away from the junior college and increased pressure for admission to the four-year colleges and universities that are otherwise protected to some degree. This would, of course, render superfluous the part now played by the junior college in the division of labor among colleges.

The cooling-out function of the junior college is kept hidden, for one thing, as other functions are highlighted. The junior college stresses

"the transfer function," "the terminal function," etc., not that of transforming transfer into terminal students; indeed, it is widely identified
as principally a transfer station. The other side of cooling out is the
successful performance in junior college of students who did poorly in
high school or who have overcome socioeconomic handicaps, for they
are drawn into higher education rather than taken out of it. Advocates
of the junior college point to this salvaging of talented manpower,
otherwise lost to the community and nation. It is indeed a function of
the open door to let talent be uncovered.

Then, too, cooling out itself is reinterpreted so as to appeal widely.
The junior college may be viewed as a place where all high school
graduates have the opportunity to explore possible careers and find the
type of education appropriate to their individual ability; in short, as a
place where everyone is admitted and everyone succeeds. As described
by the former president of the University of California:

> A prime virtue of the junior college, I think is that most of its
> students succeed in what they set out to accomplish, and cross the
> finish line before they grow weary of the race. After two years in a
> course that they have chosen, they can go out prepared for activities
> that satisfy them, instead of being branded as failures. Thus the
> broadest possible opportunity may be provided for the largest num-
> ber to make an honest try at further education with some possibility
> of success and with no route to a desired goal completely barred to
> them.[18]

The students themselves help to keep this function concealed by
wishful unawareness. Those who cannot enter other colleges but still
hope to complete four years will be motivated at first not to admit the
cooling-out process to consciousness. Once exposed to it, they again will
be led not to acknowledge it, and so they are saved insult to their
self-image.

≺≺≺≺≺≺≺≺

In summary, the cooling-out process in higher education is one
whereby systematic discrepancy between aspiration and avenue is covered over and stress for the individual and the system is minimized.
The provision of readily available alternative achievements in itself is

an important device for alleviating the stress consequent on failure and so preventing anomic and deviant behavior. The general result of cooling-out processes is that society can continue to encourage maximum effort without major disturbance from unfulfilled promises and expectations.

Notes

1. "Aberrant behavior may be regarded sociologically as a symptom of dissociation between culturally prescribed aspirations and socially structured avenues for realizing these aspirations" (Robert K. Merton, "Social Structure and Anomie," in *Social Theory and Social Structure* [rev. ed.; Glencoe, Ill.: Free Press, 1957], p. 134). See also Herbert H. Hyman, "The Value Systems of Different Classes: A Social Psychological Contribution to the Analysis of Stratification," in Reinhard Bendix and Seymour M. Lipset, eds., *Class, Status and Power: A Reader in Social Stratification* (Glencoe, Ill.: Free Press, 1953), pp. 426–42; and the papers by Robert Dubin. Richard A. Cloward, Robert K. Merton, and Dorothy L. Meier, and Wendell Bell, in *American Sociological Review*, **24** (April 1959).

2. I am indebted to Erving Goffman's original statement of the cooling-out conception. See his "Cooling the Mark Out: Some Aspects of Adaptation to Failure," *Psychiatry*, **15**: 451–463 (November 1952), Sheldon Messinger called the relevance of this concept to my attention.

3. Seymour Martin Lipset and Reinhard Bendix, *Social Mobility in Industrial Society* (Berkeley: University of California Press, 1959), pp. 78–101.

4. *A Study of the Need for Additional Centers of Public Higher Education in California* (Sacramento: California State Department of Education, 1957), p. 128. For somewhat similar interpretations by educators and laymen nationally, see Francis J. Brown, ed., *Approaching Equality of Opportunity in Higher Education* (Washington, D.C.: American Council on Education, 1955), and the President's Committee on Education Beyond the High School, *Second Report to the President* (Washington, D.C.: Government Printing Office, 1957).

5. One national report showed that one out of eight entering students (12.5 percent) in publicly controlled colleges does not remain beyond the first term or semester; one out of three (31 percent) is out by the end of the first year; and about one out of two (46.6 percent) leaves within the first two years. In state universities alone, about one out of four withdraws in the first year and 40 percent in two years (Robert E. Iffert, *Retention and Withdrawal of College Students* [Washington, D.C.: Department of Health, Education, and Welfare, 1958], pp. 15–20). Students withdraw for many reasons, but scholastic aptitude is related to their staying power: "A sizeable number of students of medium ability enter college, but...few if any of them remain longer than two years" (*A Restudy of the Needs of California in Higher Education* [Sacramento: California State Department of Education, 1955], p. 120).

6. Robert L. Kelly, *The American Colleges and the Social Order* (New York: Macmillian., 1940), pp. 220–21.

7. One study has noted that on many campuses the business school serves "as a dumping ground for students who cannot make the grade in engineering or some

branch of the liberal arts," this being a consequence of lower promotion standards than are found in most other branches of the university (Frank C. Pierson, *The Education of American Businessmen* [New York: McGraw-Hill, 1959], p. 63). Pierson also summarizes data on intelligence of students by field of study which indicate that education, business, and social science rank near the bottom in quality of students (*ibid.,* pp. 65–72).

8. Burton R. Clark, *The Open Door College: A Case Study* (New York: McGraw-Hill 1960), pp. 44–45.

9. *Ibid.,* p. 116.

10. Leland L. Medsker, *The Junior College: Progress and Prospect* (New York: McGraw-Hill, 1960), Ch. IV.

11. San Jose City College, San Jose, Calif. For the larger study see Clark, *op. cit.*

12. San Jose Junior College, Handbook for Counselors, 1957–58, p. 2. Statements in quotation marks in the next few paragraphs are cited from this.

13. *Ibid.,* p. 20.

14. Statement taken from unpublished material.

15. San Jose Junior College, "Digest of Analysis of the Records of 468 Students Placed on Probation for the Fall Semester, 1956," September 3, 1956.

16. Goffman's original statement of the concept of cooling-out referred to how the disappointing of expectations is handled by the disappointed person and especially by those responsible for the disappointment. Although his main illustration was the confidence game where facts and potential achievement are deliberately misrepresented to the "mark" (the victim) by operators of the game, Goffman also applied the concept to failure in which those responsible act in good faith (*op. cit.,* passim). "Cooling out" is a widely useful idea when used to refer to a function that may vary in deliberateness.

17. Goffman, *op. cit.,* p. 457; cf. Perrin Stryker, "How To fire an Executive," *Fortune,* **50:** 116–117, 178–192 (October 1954).

18. Robert Gordon Sproul, "Many Millions More," *Educational Record,* **39:** 102 (April 1958).

II. SELECTED STUDIES OF ORGANIZATION–SCALE INTERACTION STRATEGIES

The notation following each entry indicates the section of Chapter 11 in which it is capsulized.

Ball, Donald W., "An Abortion Clinic Ethnography," *Social Problems,* **14:** 294–301 (Winter 1967). (IV.C.1)

Clark, Burton R., "Organizational Adaptation and Precarious Values: A Case Study, "*American Sociological Review,* **21:** 327–336 (June 1956). (IV.B.1)

Messinger, Sheldon, "Organizational Transformation: A Case Study of a Declining Social Movement," *American Sociological Review,* **20:** 3–10 (February 1956). (IV.B.1)

Peven, Dorothy E., "The Use of Religious Revival Techniques to Indoctrinate Personnel: The Home-Party Sales Organizations," *Sociological Quarterly,* **9:** 97–106 (Winter 1968). (III.C.1)

Strauss, George, "Work-Flow Frictions, Interfunctional Rivalry and Professionalism: A Case Study of Purchasing Agents, "*Human Organization* **23:**137–149 (Summer 1964). (I.V.C.6)

Wildavsky, Aaron,*The Politics of the Budgetary Process* (Boston: Little, Brown, 1964). (IV.C.8)

CHAPTER SIXTEEN

Concluding Remarks

Several important points bear restatement at the conclusion of our journey, and other points emerging in the course of it need to be discussed. Together, these topics relate to procedures and foci on the one side and moral preferences on the other.

I. PROCEDURES AND FOCI

A. The Task Restated: Inchoate to Choate. Immersed in living, acting, and dealing with proximate and practical immediate contingencies, humans experience and cope with the flow of their lives more than they articulately analyze, reflect, and coherently understand it. Experiences and involvements are partially coherent and understandable, to be sure. But to a significant degree, experiences and involvements display an *inchoate* quality, a phenomenological quality of disorder, incoherence, unorganization, and vagueness. Emotions are frequently half-articulated; perceptions are dim, distant, and half-conscious. The meaning of an experience is frequently just beyond grasping and is not grasped because the flowing stream of experiences forces attention ever forward to deal with constantly new, half-grasped experiences that are felt more than defined. Gut emotions, in particular, remain vague feelings, be these pleasant gnawings, churnings, ill-defined anxieties, or little leaps of the heart.

It is this large element of inchoateness in human experience and emotional life that creates a demand for—an interest in—persons who would order the inchoate and make it *choate*. The social foundations of social science endeavor, specifically, are inchoate, deep, brute emotions and flowing, disordered experiences (as well as being, of course, the foundations of more literary enterprises). *It is a prime task of social science to render choate the inchoate emotions and experiences of humans.* It has been stated beautifully by machine shop participant-observer Donald Roy, who initially viewed the social life around him as a "stream of disconnected bits of communication which did not make much sense."[1] But upon paying close social science attention, "the disconnected became connected, the nonsense made sense, the obscure became clear, and the silly actually funny...as the content of the interaction took on more and more meaning, the interaction began to reveal structure."[2]

Such an obvious directive has some implications that are not so obvious. One, the social scientist must *begin* by examining experience itself. The social scientist begins by discovering what it is that people are feeling, feeling deeply, doing, and involving themselves in. Actual life as lived must be the starting point of social science inquiry, not lab settings, pencil marks on questionnaires, "theories," or other substitutes for life-as-lived in the terms known to the participants. Two, the inchoate becomes choate not simply through observing and recording it, but rather through *articulating and analyzing and propounding concepts that crystallize experience.* Three, since a central objective is to help people achieve a more orderly understanding of their unorderly experience (thereby gain more control over it—the ability to make more informed decisions about their experiences and involvements), analysis for the sake of analytic structure must be avoided. Rather, analysis must always be constrained by the discipline of embedment in the experiences and involvements being analyzed. Concepts and analysis are tools in the task of rendering the inchoate choate. Tools divorced from the setting of their proper use become mere museum curiosities or collectors' trivia. Concepts as tools are kept sharp through use in the workshop of the experiences to which they are addressed.

We might think, then, of the "social sciences" as the "experiential sciences," as disciplines whose role it is to articulate, to clarify, to render intelligible the incoherent, the confused, the only felt. This book has been addressed to *one* prime manner in which we may go about the task of making the inchoate choate.

B. Contrasting Concepts. The concepts of "situation" and "strategy" providing the focus of this treatise are but one special way of drawing an utterly familiar distinction. In one sense it is merely the distinction otherwise stated as stimulus and response, question and answer, problem and solution, function and structure. But in another sense, it is not. As should be clear, the emphasis is on ranges of options, on qualitatively documented courses of action, on juggling, on diversity; that is, an emphasis on the *creative, probing* aspects of humans. The terms "situation" and "strategy" strike me as at least slightly superior in their connotative capacity to evoke such aspects and to keep them topmost in the analyst's mind when dealing with the stuff of social interaction.

C. Topics of Inquiry. The range of substantive topics dealt with in this volume, determined by studies available in the literature, may, indeed, reveal evidence of debilitated and impoverished imagination among social scientists doing qualitative strategy work. The message should be clear: it is one's personal and creative task to study what seems to one important. One is utterly unbound by the topical and generic preoccupations of the past. Social science and sociology in general and the particular kind promoted here are points of view, ways of looking at and ordering reality as much or more than specific contents. Along positive lines I thus note the dearth of attention to more enjoyable aspects of social life and their qualitative strategy analysis. What are strategies of topics such as parties, festivals, friendships, love affairs, artistic creation, transcending experiences? Sociologists too often concentrate on trips that are basically "down." Let us also have a host of uppers.

D. Procedure and the Gift. I have tried in the foregoing to make it easier to see the strategic structure of social life. I have tried to do this at the level of doing studies (Part I) and at the level of showing what has been and what could be accomplished (Parts II and III). Despite all this, I retain a degree of pessimism about how much help has been given. For there remains a huge residual category of variation in the success with which people actually perform such studies. I can only label this residual "having the gift"—possessing the spontaneous ability to "see" strategies, to abstract patterns in interaction, to label and typify them, and to order ranges of empirical materials. For those having the gift, these basic acts are hardly acts of will, effort, or struggle. They simply happen. One implication is that the reader should not fret if this book makes no sense, shows him or her nothing, and does not help make new things visible. Just forget it. This simply indicates the lack of the peculiar twist of perception that casts social life into strategic light. If, on the other hand, the reader likes what is presented here and finds it helpful in ordering experience, he has the gift and should exercise it: it is an important and somewhat rare talent.

II. MORAL PREFERENCES

A. The National Context. This work is informed by, grows out of, and codifies a part of what is known among sociologists as "symbolic interactionism." Born of such early twentieth—century American philosophers as John Dewey and George Herbert Mead, midwifed by sociologists such as Robert Park, Herbert Blumer, and Everett Hughes, and reared by two generations of intellectual heirs,[3] interactionism emphasizes the constructed, emergent, and open-ended nature of experience, persons, and social life. It is distinctively and peculiarly the sociology of Americans, who themselves have been a constructed, emergent, open-ended people—imbued, congruently, with *optimism*. Americans have significantly made themselves in the course of their doing. In a real and structural sense, the gut, basic sociology of early twentieth-century American society was necessarily such a freewheeling, flowing sociology. Forces in the opposite direction are, however, strong and growing—in American society more generally and in sociology in particular. It is my hope, though, that interactionist sociology was not only appropriate to and congruent with an earlier America. Instead, I hope that it can be again the distinctively American sociology, that the society it reflects will regain its constructed, emergent, and open-ended—and optimistic—character. The fortunes of interactionist sociology may, in a sense, be a barometer of larger activist or passivist trends.

B. The Qualitative Strategy Perspective as a Humanistic Perspective. Paradoxically, by emphasizing the active, *manipulative* aspects of social life, the qualitative strategy perspective is sometimes accused of being cynical and antihumanistic. Younger, more innocent, trusting, and naively hopeful students are especially prone to being put off by what they feel is an overemphasis on the "hard-eyed," "mean," and deceitful aspects of life. As one commentator has represented the tendencies of such feelings, a strategy perspective "appears to divest us of our sanctity by suggesting that we are all incorrigible 'con artists'..."[4] Humanity is reduced to an act or performance. Moreover, surveying the inquiries and essays capsulized in Part II, two coping devices appear with unnerving, transsituational regularity. One, people often deal with situations by *avoiding* them. Two, if they confront them actively, the confrontation often involves *distortion* and/or *denial* of what we as outsiders see as the actual facts of the situation.

In such ways, then, qualitative strategy analysis seems to be less than humanistic. Who can love a social science in which the central players are distorting and avoiding phonies? Let us not, however, confuse the whole of the strategy perspective with only a few of its parts. Distorting and avoiding phonies are there, to be sure, but it has more parts than these, and even these need themselves to be properly understood. Let me first indicate some milder ways in which works of the qualitative strategy genre embody a positive, humanistic impulse.

(*a*) Deception and phoniness *in fact* run deep in our mobile, achievement-oriented social order. Deception is the warp and woof of our interpersonal behavior, given the necessity to promote ourselves and our goods, and our likelihood of failure.[5] It is humanistic, I suggest, to face up to that social fact. Moreover, to point up deception and phoniness is not necessarily to indicate approval. Indeed, works highlighting these traits are characterized by a consistent and more or less overt condemnation of them.

(*b*) The logical structure of the qualitative strategy perspective emphasizes ways in which people *qua* people are *similar* rather than different. The stress is upon *forms of action* rather than on personal or structural variations in humans that account for their action. People may strategize differently, but they are fundamentally the same in that they are all strategizers. This is the burden of Erving Goffman's remark that "behind many masks and many characters, each performer tends to wear a single look, a naked unsocialized look, a look of concentration, a look of one who is privately engaged in a difficult treacherous task."[6] This picture of what we all look like may not be pretty, one can assert, but it is at least a picture of what *we all* look like. The focus is our *common humanity*. That is in decided contrast to the bulk of current social science, which strives to show how "we all" are actually many different "alls" differentiated along class, sex, race, personality, and other lines.

(c)   Social interaction in a mobile, competitive, stranger-encountering society of distorting and avoiding phonies has a *precarious* quality. As Goffman has expressed it: "Conjoint involvement appears to be a fragile thing, with standard points of weakness and decay, a precarious unsteady state that is likely at any time to lead the individual into some form of alienation."[7] Social interaction carries a heavy load of concealed discomfort. The qualitative strategy perspective performs the important humanistic task of socializing—of making public—these privately felt fears and anxieties. It tells people that the interactional agonies of their life conditions (their encounter, role, group, organization, or other situations) are not their personal peculiarities but are common circumstances.

Second, there are several much stronger humanistic aspects of the qualitative strategy perspective. *(a)* It is profoundly humanistic to insist that people act upon the world, not that the world merely acts on them. It is profoundly humanistic to go beyond simply espousing this philosophical doctrine and to execute lines of empirical inquiry that embody such a view, as has been accomplished by the dozens of people whose work is recounted in this book. Cynicism, delusion, and avoidance may emerge, but these are qualities of a gauging, perceiving, choosing, and adaptive creature rather than the puppetry of a doll controlled by social forces. The resultant human may not be totally noble, but he *is* alive. *(b)* Articulation of the range of things that people do in situations promotes the possibility of choice. The articulation of choice is an important precondition of the possibility of personal freedom. To be free is, in part, to know of alternatives for conduct. To the degree that qualitative strategy analysis provides pictures of options, to that degree it promotes the humanism of freedom. Moreover, there is a humanism in the higher order fact that people might *with self-awareness* choose those very strategies we are so wont to condemn; namely, avoidance and delusion. *(c)* The discomfort of the naive and trusting who confront a world of deluded and avoiding phonies is in part a discomfort over being thrust from a personal and interactional Garden of Eden in which oneself and others are thought to be cognitively correct and forthright authentics. That discomfort is humanistically appropriate. It is a properly debilitating wedge between one's self and one's actions. It weakens naive commitment to one's own performances; it helps one not to be unthinkingly taken in by one's own show. Then one is not overly impressed by the interactional shows put on by other people. This is a morally healthy *distance* and cynicism for it facilitates compassion and forgiveness toward oneself and others by tempering and bracketing sentiments. It fosters a recognition of our frailties in common, our shared dramaturgic plight. *(d)* Last and most prosaically, the qualitative strategy perspective is humanistic because it seeks to provide practical quides to action. It strives to shortcut the process of blundering by making analyzed options available in advance of or in the midst of situations with which people actually must deal. Perhaps that is the most humanistic aspect of all.

NOTES TO CHAPTER SIXTEEN

1. Donald F. Roy," 'Banana Time': Job Satisfaction and Informal Interaction," *Human Organization* **18**:161 (Winter 1959–60). Roy's study is reprinted in Chapter 14 of this volume.
2. *Ibid.*
3. On symbolic interactionism, see Jerome G. Manis and Bernard N. Meltzer, eds., *Symbolic Interaction*, 2 ed. (Boston: Allyn & Bacon, 1972).
4. R. P. Cuzzort, *Humanity and Modern Sociological Thought* (New York: Holt, Rinehart & Winston, 1969), p. 175.
5. I draw here and below from my "Morals Are the Message: The Work of Erving Goffman," *Psychiatry and Social Science Review,* **4** (9):17–19, (July 1970).
6. Erving Goffman, *The Presentation of Self in Everyday Life* (Garden City, N.Y.: Doubleday-Anchor, 1959), p. 235.
7. Erving Goffman, *Interaction Ritual* (Garden City, N.Y.: Doubleday-Anchor, 1967), p. 117.

Index